THE CAMBRIDGE COMPANION TO MEDIEVAL ENGLISH LITERATURE 1100–1500

The medieval period was one of extraordinary literary achievement sustained over centuries of great change, anchored by the Norman invasion and its aftermath, the re-emergence of English as the nation's leading literary language in the fourteenth century and the advent of print in the fifteenth. This Companion spans four full centuries to survey this most formative and turbulent era in the history of literature in English. Exploring the period's key authors – Chaucer, Langland, the Gawain-poet, Mergery Kempe, among many – and genres – plays, romances, poems and epics – the book offers an overview of the riches of medieval writing. The essays map out the flourishing field of medieval literary studies and point toward new directions and approaches. Designed to be accessible to students, the book also features a chronology and guide to further reading.

LARRY SCANLON is Associate Professor of English at Rutgers University.

A complete list of books in the series is at the back of this book.

THE CAMBRIDGE COMPANION TO
MEDIEVAL ENGLISH LITERATURE 1100–1500

Edited by

LARRY SCANLON

CAMBRIDGE
UNIVERSITY PRESS

University Printing House, Cambridge CB2 8BS, United Kingdom

Cambridge University Press is part of the University of Cambridge.

It furthers the University's mission by disseminating knowledge in the pursuit of education, learning and research at the highest international levels of excellence.

www.cambridge.org
Information on this title: www.cambridge.org/9780521602587

First published 2009

A catalogue record for this publication is available from the British Library

Library of Congress Cataloguing in Publication data
The Cambridge companion to medieval English literature,
1100–1500 / [edited by] Larry Scanlon.
p. cm.
Includes bibliographical references and index.
ISBN 978-0-521-84167-2 (hardback) – ISBN 978-0-521-60258-7 (pbk.)
1. English literature–Middle English, 1100–1500–History and criticism. 2. Civilization, Medieval, in literature. I. Scanlon, Larry. II. Title.
PR255.C34 2009
820′.9′001–dc22
2009015144

ISBN 978-0-521-84167-2 Hardback
ISBN 978-0-521-60258-7 Paperback

CONTENTS

ABBREVIATIONS

CHMEL	David Wallace, ed., *The Cambridge History of Medieval English Literature* (Cambridge University Press, 1999)
EETS; EETS os; EETS ES; EETS SS	Early English Text Society; Early English Text Society, original series; Early English Text Society extra series; Early English Text Society, supplementary series
Idea of the Vernacular	Jocelyn Wogan-Browne, Nicholas Watson, Andrew Taylor, and Ruth Evans, eds. *The Idea of the Vernacular: An Anthology of Middle English Literary Theory, 1280–1520* (University Park: Pennsylvania State University Press, 1999)
JEGP	*Journal of English and Germanic Philology*
JMEMS	*Journal of Medieval and Early Modern Studies*
NML	*New Medieval Literatures*
Piers Plowman	William Langland, *The Vision of Piers Plowman*, ed. A.V.C. Schmidt, second edn (London: Everyman, 1995)
Riverside	Geoffrey Chaucer, *The Riverside Chaucer*, ed. Larry Benson *et al.* (Boston: Houghton-Mifflin, 1987)
SAC	*Studies in the Age of Chaucer*
SP	*Studies in Philology*
YES	*Yearbook of English Studies*
YLS	*Yearbook of Langland Studies*

CONTRIBUTORS

SARAH BECKWITH is Marcello Lotti Professor of English and Professor of Religion and Professor of Religious Studies and Theater Studies at Duke University.

ARDIS BUTTERFIELD is Reader in English at the University College of London.

CHRISTINE CHISM is Associate Professor of English at Rutgers, the State University of New Jersey.

RITA COPELAND is Edmund J. and Louise W. Kahn Endowed Term Professor in the Humanities, Professor of Classical Studies and English, and Chair of the Program in Comparative Literature and Literary Theory at the University of Pennsylvania.

RICHARD FIRTH GREEN is Humanities Distinguished Professor of English at Ohio State University.

RALPH HANNA is Professor of Paleography at the University of Oxford and Tutorial Fellow in English at Keble College, Oxford.

ETHAN KNAPP is Associate Professor of English at Ohio State University.

REBECCA KRUG is Associate Professor of English at the University of Minnesota.

STEVEN F. KRUGER is Professor of English and Medieval Studies at Queens College and the Graduate Center, the City University of New York.

SALLY MAPSTONE is Tutor in Medieval English Literature, Joanna Morse Memorial Fellow, and Reader in Older Scottish Literature at St. Hilda's College, Oxford University.

RICHARD NEWHAUSER is Professor of English at Arizona State University.

LARRY SCANLON is Associate Professor of English at Rutgers, the State University of New Jersey.

WENDY SCASE is Geoffrey Shepherd Professor of Medieval English Literature at the University of Birmingham.

JAMES SIMPSON is Douglas P. and Katherine B. Loker Professor of English at Harvard University.

LYNN STALEY is Harrington and Shirley Drake Professor in the Humanities at Colgate University.

SARAH STANBURY is Associate Professor of English at the College of the Holy Cross.

DAVID WALLACE is Judith Rodin Professor of English at the University of Pennsylvania.

DIANE WATT is Professor of English at the University of Aberystwyth.

CHRONOLOGY

1066	Normans invade England after the death of Edward the Confessor. William the Conqueror becomes monarch. He installs his retainers as tenants-in-chief throughout the realm, essentially creating a new nobility in one fell swoop.
1086	Appearance of the *Domesday Book*, a comprehensive survey of the people, and property holdings of the entire realm commissioned by William in the last year of his realm. The *Anglo-Saxon Chronicle* comments bitterly, "not one yard of land, not ... one ox, not one cow, not one pig was left out."[1] The Domesday survey demonstrates an interest in centralization and bureaucratic organization that will become the hallmark of English monarchy for most of the later Middle Ages, a structural feature that stays relatively constant in spite of the many dynastic disruptions.
1100	Generally accepted by historical linguists as the dividing line between Old and Middle English.
1100	Henry I, youngest legitimate son of William, accedes to the throne, after the death of his brother William Rufus in a hunting accident. A capable administrator, he is succeeded by Stephen in 1135, the son of his older sister Adela, who soon becomes embroiled in a civil struggle with Henry's daughter Matilda.
1121–55	*Peterborough Chronicle*; begun as a version of the *Anglo-Saxon Chronicle*, it includes entries for the years 1122–31. Entries for later years are added in 1155, in prose showing many features of early Middle English grammar already well established.

1137	Geoffrey of Monmouth, *Historia regum Britanniae (History of British Kings).*
1154	Henry II, grandson of Henry I, accedes to the throne with the death of Stephen. During the course of his forty-five-year reign he greatly strengthens the power of the monarchy, often at the expense of the barons. He institutes, or regularizes, a system of writs that becomes the basis of a distinctive English common law. He conquers Ireland. His court attracts a number of important writers, including Geoffrey of Monmouth, Walter Map, and Marie de France.
1170	Archbishop Thomas à Becket murdered in Canterbury Cathedral during dispute with Henry over relations between bishops and royal authority.
1170	Death of Saint Godric, reputed to be author of earliest surviving lyrics in Middle English.
c. 1170	Marie de France, *Lais.*
c. 1180	Marie de France, *Fables.*
1189–1250	Laȝamon, *Brut.*
1190–1200	*The Owl and the Nightingale.*
1200–1225	*Ancrene Riwle*; the "Wooing Group"; the "Katherine Group".
1214	Fourth Lateran Council (so-called because it is held in the Lateran palace) makes confession an annual obligation of all believers.
1215	Magna Carta ("The Great Charter") signed by King John and his barons. Often looked to as the founding text of English liberty, its more immediate intent is to put some restraint on the growth of royal power at the expense of the aristocracy.
1216	Henry III succeeds his father at the age of nine. He reigns even longer than his grandfather, fifty-six years. In spite of several crises the power of the monarchy continues to grow.
c. 1225	*King Horn.*
c. 1250	"Sumer is icumen in."
1250–1300	*Arthour and Merlin.*

1272	Edward I becomes king in possibly the smoothest succession in all of the English Middle Ages. Accomplishments include the conquest of Wales, and the subjection of Scotland. Through the *quo warranto* hearings – designed to make lesser lords demonstrate "by what warrant" they exercised justice – he consolidates all legal jurisdictions under the ultimate authority of the Crown.
1275–1300	*South England Legendary. Debate between the Body and the Soul.*
1280–1300	*Havelok the Dane.*
1281	John Pecham, Archbishop of Canterbury, *Ignorancia sacerdotum* (also known as the "syllabus").
1300	Richard Rolle born.
c. 1300	*Cursor Mundi. Amis and Amiloun. Bevis of Hampton. Guy of Warwick. Kyng Alisaunder. Lay le Freine. Richard Coer de Lion. Sir Orfeo.*
1300–25	*Sir Degaré.*
1300–50	*Sir Launfal. Sir Cleges.*
1303	Robert Mannyng, *Handlyng Synne.*
1307	Edward II succeeds his father. The victim of long pent-up grievances among the barony, military difficulties on the Scots border, and his own incompetence, he is deposed and executed two decades later when his queen Isabella and son turn against him.
1320–30	*The Simonie.*
1325–50	*Lybeaus Desconus.*
1330	Edward III becomes king. In 1340 he claims the French throne, initiating the Hundred Years War. During his forty-seven-year reign, Parliament, originally an extension of the King's Council, emerges as an independent institution, in part because of the recurring need to raise taxes to fund the war.
c. 1330	John Gower and William Langland born.
1330–40	Auchinleck manuscript (Edinburgh, National Library of Scotland, MS Advocates' 19.2.1).
1340	Dan Michel of Northgate, *Ayenbite of Inwyt.*

c. 1340	Geoffrey Chaucer born. Harley manuscript (London, British Library, MS Harley 2253).
c. 1342	Julian of Norwich born.
1349	Richard Rolle, *Form of Living*. Rolle dies this same year.
c. 1350	*Joseph of Arimathie. Octavian. Sir Eglamour of Artois.*
1350–61	*William of Palerne.*
1350–70	*Gamelyn.*
1350–75	*Speculum Vitae.*
1350–1400	*Ipomadon. Robert of Cisyle.*
c. 1352	*Winner and Waster.*
1357	*Lay Folks' Catechism.*
1359	Chaucer captured while serving in Hundred Years War; ransomed the next year.
1360	John Mandeville, *Mandeville's Travels.*
c. 1360	Alliterative *Morte Arthure.*
1360–70	Chaucer, *Romaunt of the Rose.*
1360–78	Chaucer travels to Italy and France on diplomatic missions.
1365–70	A version of *Piers Plowman.*
c. 1365–75	Cambridge, Magdalene College, MS Pepys 2498.
c. 1368	Thomas Hoccleve born.
c. 1370	Chaucer, *Book of the Duchess.*
1370–80	Gower moves to the Priory of St. Mary Overeys, Southwark.
c. 1371	John Lydgate born; enters the Benedictine abbey at Bury St. Edmund's as a boy.
1373	Julian, *Showings*, short text.
c. 1373	Margery Kempe born.
1374	Edward III appoints Chaucer Controller of Custom, a post he holds until 1386.
1374–78	Gower, *Mirour de l'Omme; Cinkante Balades.*
1375–1400	*The Awntyrs off Arthure. Cloud of Unknowing. Poems of the Gawain*-manuscript (British Library MS Cotton.Nero.x): *Pearl*, *Patience*, *Cleanness*, *Sir Gawain and the Green Knight.*

1376	York plays performed.
1376–79	B version of *Piers Plowman.*
1377	Richard II succeeds to the throne at the age of twelve. His reign is marked by recurrent constitution struggles with baronial factions, and ends with his deposition.
1378	Chaucer grants Gower power of attorney.
c. 1380	Chaucer, *House of Fame. Sir Firumbras.* Early version of the Wycliffite Bible begun. Later version will be completed in late 1390s.
after 1380	*Death and Life.*
1380–90	*The Pore Caitif.*
1380–1400	Richard Lavynham, *A Litil Tretys on the Seven Deadly Sins.*
1381	English Rising. also called the Peasant's Revolt, although the rebels are not exclusively peasants. The rebellion begins in Essex and Kent, touched off by attempts to collect a poll tax. The rebels march on London, invade the Tower, burn John of Gaunt's Savoy Palace, behead the Archbishop of Canterbury, and extract from Richard II a promise to end lordship and abolish serfdom. Once they disband, Richard disavows his promise, captures the leaders, executes them and has their heads displayed on stakes on the city wall. In spite of its failure most social historians now view the Rising as a longer term catalyst for the decline of serfdom, which becomes largely obsolete by 1430.
1381–85	Gower, *Vox clamantis*, revised version. Original version predates the 1381 Rising. Gower revises the poem again in the 1390s. Chaucer, *Troilus and Criseyde*; *Boece.*
1381–90	C version of *Piers Plowman.*
1382	The Blackfriars' Council finds heretical and erroneous propositions in the writings of John Wyclif.
c. 1382	Chaucer, *Parliament of Fowls.*
1384	Wyclif dies.
1385	Chaucer appointed Justice of the Peace in Kent.
c. 1385	Chaucer, *Legend of Good Women.* John Clanvowe, *Cuckoo and the Nightingale.* Thomas Usk, *Testament of Love.*

1386	Chaucer elected to Parliament.
c. 1386–1400	Chaucer, *Canterbury Tales.*
1387–91	Hoccleve enters the office of the Privy Seal.
1389	Richard II appoints Chaucer Clerk of the King's Works.
c. 1390	Langland dies. John Mirk, *Festial. Parlement of the Thre Ages.*
1390–93	Gower, *Confessio Amantis.*
1390–1400	Vernon manuscript (Oxford, Bodleian Library MS Poet. Eng. 1). *The Siege of Jerusalem.*
1391	Chaucer, *Treatise on the Astrolabe.* Chaucer becomes deputy forester of the royal forest of North Petherton.
1393–1415	*The Crowned King. Mum and the Sothsegger. Pierce the Ploughman's Crede. Richard the Redeless.*
c. 1393	Julian, *Showings*, long text.
1394	Processional route for York plays established. *Twelve Conclusions of the Lollards* nailed to Westminster Hall.
1396	Death of Walter Hilton, author of *Scale of Perfection.*
1398	Gower marries.
c. 1398	Gower, *Traitié pour Essampler les Amantz Marietz.*
1399	Henry Bolingbroke leads a successful rebellion against Richard II. He takes the throne as Henry IV. Thomas Arundel, Archbishop of Canterbury is the intellectual architect of the complex succession and relations between Church and Crown grow much closer than in previous reigns.
1400	Chaucer dies.
c. 1400	Gower, *Cronica Tripertita. Book for a Simple and Devout Woman. Emaré. The Erle of Toulous. Laud Troy Book.* stanzaic *Le Morte Arthur. Sir Gowther. The Sowdane of Babylon, The Siege of Melayne.*
after 1400	Prose *Alexander.*
1400–25	*Castle of Perseverance.*
1401	The statute *De heretico comburendo* declares heresy a capital offense.
1402	Hoccleve, *Letter of Cupid.*
1403	Richard Wyche's letter.

c. 1406	Hoccleve, *La Male Regle.*
c. 1406–08	Lydgate at Gloucester College at Oxford.
1407–09	Archbishop Arundel's *Constitutions.*
c. 1407	*Testimony of William Thorpe.*
1408	Gower dies.
1409–14	*The Lanterne of Liȝt.*
c. 1409	Nicholas Love, *The Mirror of the Blessed Life of Jesus Christ.*
1410–12	Hoccleve, *Regiment of Princes.*
1412	Henry V takes the throne upon his father's death. In 1415 he gains a great victory over the French at Agincourt. He dies seven years later of dysentery during another campaign in France.
1412–20	Lydgate, *Troy Book.*
1413–22	Lydgate, *Life of Our Lady*; *A Defence of Holy Church.*
1415	Hoccleve, *Letter to Oldcastle.*
1419–21	Hoccleve, the *Series.*
1421–22	Lydgate, *Siege of Thebes.*
c. 1422	Earliest record of Chester plays.
1423	Lydgate appointed prior at Hadfield Regis, an office he holds until 1429–30; returns to Bury St. Edmund's in 1434.
1425–50	Compilation of the N-Town plays.
after 1425	*Destruction of Troy.*
1426	d. Hoccleve. Lydgate, *Title and Pedigree of Henry VI*; *Pilgrimage of the Life of Man.*
c. 1426	Lydgate, *Danse Machabré.*
1427	Lydgate, *Mumming at London*; *Mumming at Hertford.*
1428	Lydgate, *Mumming at Eltham.*
1429	Nine months old when his father died, Henry VI now crowned as king at the age of eight. Though he enjoys some success in his twenties, social unrest, the ruinous cost of the war and England's defeat, and finally his own physical and mental infirmities all take their toll, leading to the Wars of the Roses and eventually his deposition.

	Lydgate, *Mumming for Mercers of London*; *Mumming for the Goldsmiths of London.*
c. 1429	Julian of Norwich dies.
1430–60	*The Court of Sapience.*
1431–38	Lydgate, *The Fall of Princes.*
1432	Lygate, *King Henry VI's Triumphal Entry into London.*
1434–36	Lydgate, *Life of Saints Edmund and Fremund.*
1436–38	*The Book of Margery Kempe.*
c. 1440	Robert Henryson born. Margery Kempe dies.
1443–47	Osbert Bokenham, *Legendys of Hooly Wummen.*
1446–49	Lydgate, translation of *Secretum secretorum.*
1449	Lydgate dies.
1450	Jack Cade's Rebellion.
c. 1450	*The Floure and the Leafe. Wars of Alexander.*
1450–61	Wars of the Roses.
1450–1500	Towneley Cycle.
1461	Edward, Earl of March, eldest son of Richard Duke of York, crowned Edward IV. He descends from Edward III through Lionel, Duke of Clarence, Edward's second son. In 1469 he is forced into exile as Henry VI is restored to the throne. Edward regains the throne two years later.
c. 1461	*Croxton Play of the Sacrament.*
1465–70	*Mankind. Wisdom.*
1465–1500	*Assembly of Ladies. Lancelot of the Laik. Rauf Coilyear.*
c. 1470	Sir Thomas Malory, *Morte Darthur*; Caxton's edition appears in 1485.
1470–95	Henryson, *Orpheus and Eurydice*; *Fables*; and the *Testament of Cresseid.*
1471	Malory dies.
1476	William Caxton establishes his press in Westminster; his first edition appears in the next year.
1478	Caxton's edition of Chaucer's *Canterbury Tales.*

1483	In April Edward V, aged twelve, becomes king on his father's death. His uncle, Richard, Duke of York, persuades Parliament to declare Edward IV's marriage invalid and Edward V illegitimate. In June, Edward and his younger brother are murdered. In July Richard is crowned Richard III.
	Caxton, *The Golden Legend.*
1485	Caxton's edition of Malory's *Morte Darthur.* Richard's forces defeated by Henry Tudor at Bosworth field. Henry becomes Henry VII. This event is traditionally taken to mark the end of the Middle Ages in England.
1490	Caxton, *Eneydos.*
c. 1506	Henryson dies.
1510–25	Earliest print fragment of *Everyman.*

1 *The Anglo-Saxon Chronicles*, ed. and tr. Michael Swanton (London: Phoenix Press, 2000), 216.

Introduction

About 1300, somewhere in the north of England, on the eve of what would prove to be one of the most remarkable centuries in all of Anglophone literary tradition, a cleric, most likely a monk, sat down to write a history of the world from Creation to Judgment Day. It would consist mainly of biblical paraphrase. He called it the *Cursor Mundi*, literally "the runner of the world": "For almast it overrrennes all."[1] This work comes down to us in nine manuscripts, not an inconsiderable number, especially as they show a wide geographical distribution. But it is almost unknown except among scholars of Middle English literature, and even among them, it is not especially well read. At first glance, it seems to confirm the worst stereotypes about medieval literary culture. Clearly derivative, ostensibly little more than a very long exercise in plot summary, it would seem to offer little in the way of poetic originality, and not much of poetic value of any sort. The manuscripts suggest that the work found an audience, perhaps even a sizable one. Yet that would seem only to make the poem even more foreign – a religious work for a religious age. The literary values we might identify in such a work seem notable only for their stark differences from our own.

However, in point of fact, the *Cursor Mundi* is quite a lively, sophisticated, and poetically accomplished work. An obvious aspect of its sophistication occurs in its introduction, where the author meditates on precisely those issues that seem to mark its difference: its religiosity, its relation to previous tradition and its notion of its prospective readership. He treats all of them as specifically poetic problems. The first two lines declare, "Man yhernes rimes for to here / And romances red on maneres sere" (1–2: Man yearns to hear rhymes / And romances read in various manners). The couplet initially seems to treat "rimes" and "romances" as identical, an impression reinforced by the next twenty lines, which catalog many of the period's most popular romances, such as the tales of Alexander, the Arthurian cycle, Charlemagne, and Tristan and Isolde. But the *Cursor* author invokes this canon because he wants to redirect the desire for rhymes toward more religious subjects. The initial, unobtrusive distinction between rhymes and romance enables him to claim religious narrative is equally worthy of verse on poetic grounds, and superior on spiritual ones. He will offer the figure of the Virgin Mary as the specific site where his poem meets and transcends the value of romance. There is no mistaking this desire for transcendence. But in the very comparison, however fleeting, he seeks between the Virgin and the fallible ladies of romance, he still maintains the poetic as the standard of reference.

This commitment to the poetic becomes even more productive as he moves on to his next topic: his choice of language. He acknowledges his debt to French sources but he also makes the acknowledgment an occasion for a certain proto-nationalist defiance. For the sake of "hali kirkes state," he explains, he translates his book into English, "For luue of englijs lede, / Englis lede of meri ingeland / For þe comen to vnþerstand" (231, 234–36). Most "rimes" are written in French (the lingering effect of the Norman invasion two and a half centuries earlier, among other things). French rhymes are wrought for "Frankis man"; what is there for those who know only English? "Of England the nacion, / Es Inglis men þar in commune": the English nation is a community of English speakers. The most useful language – the one which "most may spede" – will necessarily be the most spoken (241–43). The English tongue is seldom used in France for any reason. It is thus hardly an outrage if we grant each nation its own language. This author writes for unlearned English speakers, especially those at spiritual risk, so that they may learn to amend their lives.

There is no mistaking the ferocity of the *Cursor*'s devotion to English – a ferocity all the more noteworthy given that its author must necessarily have been trilingual, and that his institutional position might have inclined him to prefer either Latin or French. But even more noteworthy is the appeal to the ideal of the English common reader – monolingual and unlearned, in need of spiritual instruction, yet unjustly neglected – as the sturdy bearer of England's national linguistic identity. These common English speakers signify by virtue of their participation in an otherwise undifferentiated mass. This sort of commonality makes them a public. Modern literary scholarship tends to treat the ideal of the common reader as a distinctively modern invention – not unreasonably, as the actual phrase *the common reader* was coined by Samuel Johnson. Yet this passage from the *Cursor Mundi* reaffirms one of Medieval Studies' favorite secrets: most of what modernity takes to be uniquely its own actually has much older roots. Without actually using the term *common reader* the *Cursor* author nevertheless adumbrates an ideal of commonality that anticipates Johnson's both in the projection of a reading public at once broad and unifiable and in the search of moral improvement through reading.

The fourteenth century would indeed see an expansion of the English reading public, as we can infer from the increased production of texts in English, especially after 1350. As the *Cursor* author claims, at the beginning of the fourteenth century French, or Anglo-Norman, dominated vernacular written production, a lingering effect of the Norman invasion, and a continuing effect of the international prestige of French culture. By century's end English had largely shunted Anglo-Norman aside. Like the *Cursor* author, many writers explicitly called attention to their choice of English, characteristically affirming a similar ideal of commonality and national linguistic solidarity. The ideal of the commons would also emerge as a central locus of political and ideological contestation. During the fourteenth century Parliament evolved from an extension of the King's Council into a distinct institution. The House of Commons played an increasingly pivotal role in this process, especially after 1350. These "commons" were still relatively elite, burgesses and lesser nobility, some of whom had acquired additional power in their local shires as agents of an expanding royal legal authority. There was resistance to this restrictive sense of the commons, most notably from the rebels of 1381, whose watchword was "with King Richard and the true commons!" As Paul Strohm has convincingly argued, with this slogan the rebels styled themselves as "an enlarged and regenerated commons," as opposed to "that group of usurping and self-aggrandizing middlemen who ironically claimed the very title of commons, those rural landowners and urban entrepreneurs who were constituted as the commons of Parliament."[2] The 1380s also saw the emergence of Lollardy, medieval Britain's only heresy. With its distrust of the clergy and its advocacy of biblical translation, Lollardy also imagined a common reader, albeit of a very specific doctrinal stripe, which Lollard writers frequently associated with such phrases as "þe pepel of Englond," "we English men," "þe comoun pepel," and the claim that "Englische is comoun langage to oure puple."[3] Somewhat ironically, in spite of the wide doctrinal differences, more orthodox writers, like the *Cursor* author himself, anticipated in less radical fashion this desire to bring spiritual instruction directly to the common English reader, as much of the increased vernacular production in English in the fourteenth century consisted of religious works.

These ideals of commonality are not identical to their later counterparts, nor is the crucial point to relocate the beginning of modernity. Nevertheless, continuities such as this one, and modernity's anxious relation to them, insure that the problem of the literary in the later Middle Ages will never be a merely antiquarian one. In addition to its own intrinsic interest, medieval literary culture has an enduring value to modernity for the differences in the way it approaches similar problems. To be sure, not every Middle English work articulates the ideal of the common reader. But most are as sophisticated and self-conscious as the *Cursor Mundi* in their own way. The *Cursor Mundi* forces us to think differently about the common reader; it should also encourage us to think differently about poetic originality and the relation between past and present. The poem presages a century when a common national identity and religious faith would be as much a matter of conflict as a source of unity. It announces a common written tradition emerging largely out of translation. Indeed, translation would become a keynote of most of the writing in English to follow, including that of figures like Langland and Chaucer, whom posterity would judge the most important and original. Even if we were to view translation as purely a derivative exercise – and the Middle Ages definitely did not – it would not do to view Middle English as simply a descendant of Anglo-Norman. Anglo-Saxon England possessed by far the most active and sophisticated vernacular literary culture of the time in all of Western Europe. The Conquest did not immediately destroy all of it and some residue remained to influence later vernacular writing both Anglo-Norman and Middle English, although how much and in what way are questions we may never be able fully to answer. Thus, the fourteenth century hardly qualifies as a moment of origin in any simple sense. Perhaps the best way to view it is as the most obvious irruption in a much longer continuum, one that stretches back before the Norman Conquest in 1066 and forward to the end of the fifteenth century. The definitive emergence of Middle English tradition in the fourteenth century would be followed by an even broader and more voluminous outpouring in the fifteenth, such that one might well argue that it was the fifteenth century that cemented the literary authority of English once and for all.

This Companion offers a concise overview of literature in Middle English from 1100 to 1500. Treatment of this period by modern scholarship has been somewhat anomalous and uneven. One cause of the neglect is almost as old as the period itself. The Renaissance in England coincided roughly with the Reformation, fortifying Renaissance literature's anxious relation to its immediate predecessors in the later Middle Ages with a strong devotional edge. Sixteenth-century English writers assured themselves of their own value in part by jettisoning large portions of the medieval past. They salvaged only a few figures. Sidney's famous remark from his *Apology for Poesy* is typical:

> Chaucer, undoubtedly, did excellently in his *Troilus and Cressida*; of whom, truly, I know not whether to marvel more, either that he in that misty time could see so clearly, or that we in this clear age walk so stumblingly after him.[4]

The effects of this great act of historical repression – the Middle Ages becomes "that misty time" so Sidney can understand his own present as "this clear age" – linger even now. They haunted the nineteenth century, even though medieval literature in the form that we now have it is largely the product of nineteenth-century philology, which systematically set about to recover the whole of the medieval past. Moreover, when literary studies as a fully-fledged academic discipline emerged just after the First World War, in spite of its debt to philology, it defined its fundamental interest in the problem of literary form as antithetical to philology's more historical and linguistic interests. In the United States in particular, this hostility to philology extended to the medieval literature which had been one of philology's central objects.

Accordingly, Middle English literary scholarship has long been caught between competing methodological imperatives, and for most of the last century the split worked mainly to the field's disadvantage. That began to change around 1980 as the result of the confluence of quite different scholarly trends. In spite of its lowered prestige in the field of literary studies as a whole philological work had continued apace. Although most major works had already been edited in the nineteenth century, some more than once, a large amount of material remained unedited, and many existing editions grew outdated. In addition, as all of academia grew more specialized related fields such as codicology and palaeography, which had been mainly seen as ancillary to the task of editing, became forms of inquiry in their own right. With a majority of texts in dependable modern editions a more certain and complete picture of the period's literary culture has emerged, not just of the texts themselves, but also of the circumstances of their production, the patterns of their dissemination, and their possible readership. At the same time, challenges to the reigning formalist paradigms from feminism, new historicism, deconstruction, and related theoretical approaches opened up substantially new avenues of interpretive inquiry. Important new departures in the critical tradition of established major figures such as Chaucer, Langland, and the *Pearl*-poet coincided with much more sustained attention to neglected figures such as Gower, Hoccleve, Lydgate, and others, treated as minor in spite of their undeniable prominence in the period. For the first time, scholars also devoted sustained attention to the two most important woman writers of the period, Julian of Norwich and Margery Kempe. The work of Anne Hudson, her students, and others has produced a revival of interest in John Wyclif and the Lollards that in its breadth far surpasses previous activity in the field regarding that topic. If claims for the centrality of the Lollards have sometimes been overstated, there is little doubt that this new work has encouraged a more general reexamination of the relation between religion and literature in the period. There have been analogous developments in the study of drama, the lyric, romance – in short, in almost every genre and tradition the period has to offer.

Thus, this is a particularly propitious moment for offering this Companion. The volume has tried to present as diverse a picture of the field of Middle English studies as possible within the constraints of length. It has also tried to balance current states of knowledge with what seem to be the most promising directions for new research. Here the editor has tended to err on the side of what seemed established wisdom, although what seems simply settled truth to one observer can simultaneously seem trendy speculation to another and hopelessly outmoded to a third. The volume is divided into two parts. The first, entitled "Contexts, genres, and traditions," has two aims. First, it aims to give the reader new to Middle English studies a map of what one might call the discursive economy of later Middle English literature, even if that phrase seems a bit too systematic for a reality produced mainly by historical accretion. The second aim is more pragmatic and specific to this volume. That is simply to provide a transparent means of covering as completely as possible those portions of the field left out of the second part of the volume, "Authors." Part I begins with two very general introductions to the conditions of literary production in the period, the first concentrating on linguistic issues, the next on social formation and readership. Then follows something of a catch-all chapter on religious writing, concentrating on hagiography, *pastoralia*, and devotional and contemplative works. That chapter is followed by four chapters on literary modes or genres, broadly construed: "Romance," "Dialogue, debate, and dream vision," "Drama," and "Lyric." Part I closes with a chapter on "Lollard writings."

Conceptually, Part II should be self-explanatory. The category of the author remains the most fundamental and durable of modern literary study, in spite of its limitations, some of which contributors to this volume astutely note. Here is a point where the editor's preference for the established can be quite clearly seen, not merely in the retention of the author as a category, but in the choice of particular authors, and even in the emphasis on the fourteenth and fifteenth centuries, which is most obvious here, but can also be detected elsewhere. I have tried to offer a framework that accurately represents the historical interests of the field, leaving it to the contributors to explore in each case the complications introduced by more recent research. That I believe they have all done brilliantly. In any case, the field's interest in the fourteenth and fifteenth centuries has its roots in characteristics of its object of study that are empirically verifiable in both philological and literary terms. It is hard to deny, as a brute philological fact, the profusion of writing in English after 1300 and the marked increase after 1350. From a more literary standpoint, it is equally hard to deny that the period before 1350 offers little of the array of major individual authors which we can find in the period afterward. Invidious or unfashionable as it may seem to say, there is simply no figure from the earlier period who comes close to matching Langland, Chaucer, Gower, or Lydgate, for subsequent influence, nor any that match these or any of the other authors treated in the second part of this Companion for their contemporary significance. The closest one can come would probably be Geoffrey of Monmouth, or Marie de France, and then the field of inquiry would have to be expanded to include Latin and Anglo-Norman.

That is precisely what some scholars have argued the field needs to do. The point is a fair one. Later medieval England possessed a multilingual culture: trilingual at its centre, with a variety of Celtic languages at its margins. Middle English studies has generally paid less attention to writings in these other languages. That is now beginning to change, especially in regard to Anglo-Latin and Anglo-Norman. Reexaminations of the role these languages played in British culture constitute one of the field's newest trends. They have certainly left their trace on this volume, most notably perhaps in Wendy Scase's account of the relation between the language of Middle English and its literature, Ardis Butterfield's account of the lyric, and Ralph Hanna's treatment of Langland, but in many of the other essays as well. If the pattern of the last twenty years is any guide, this further attempt to expand the intellectual and social frame of reference for literary culture in medieval Britain will grow in influence. At the same time, it seems unlikely that, whatever intrinsic interest these inquiries have on their own – and that may well be considerable – their impact on the study of Middle English texts will ever be more than supplemental. Later medieval England, in spite of its trilingual culture, was not a trilingual society. Its trilingual character was the effect mainly of levels of learning, not of three distinct and competing political communities. Some of the more passionate advocates of Anglo-Norman have suggested Middle English scholarship's concentration on English writing is a hangover from the nationalist ideals embedded in nineteenth-century philology. While there is no denying the nationalism of the nineteenth century, whatever effect those ideals had was one of emphasis rather than invention. The literary preference for English began in later medieval England itself. Moreover, as the example from the *Cursor Mundi* clearly shows, the culture clearly understood that preference as an expression of inclusion and popularization. Paradoxically, that may well provide the best way to understand this nascent emergence of the dominance of English: a testament to the "yearning for rime" and the desire of each community for its own language.

NOTES

1 *Cursor Mundi*, ed. Richard Morris, EETS os 57 (1874) p. 22, line 268. All subsequent quotations are from this edition. Line numbers will be given in the text.

2 Paul Strohm, *Hochon's Arrow: The Social Imagination of Fourteenth Century Texts*; with an appendix by A. J. Prescott (Princeton University Press, 1992), pp. 41–42.

3 Jill C. Havens, "'As Englishe is comoun langage to our puple': The Lollards and Their Imagined 'English' Community," in *Imagining a Medieval English Nation*, ed. Kathy Lavezzo (Minneapolis and London: University of Minnesota Press, 2004), pp. 96–128.

4 Sir Philip Sidney, *An Apology for Poetry*, ed. Geoffrey Shepherd (London: Thomas Nelson, 1965), p. 133.

PART I

Contexts, genres, and traditions

I

WENDY SCASE

Re-inventing the vernacular: Middle English language and its literature

"So gret diversite": characteristics of Middle English

And for ther is so gret diversite
In Englissh and in writyng of oure tonge,
So prey I God that non myswrite the,
Ne the mysmeter for defaute of tonge;
And red wherso thow be, or elles songe,
That thow be understonde, God I biseche!

(*Troilus and Criseyde*, V. 1793–98)[1]

A language of great diversity: so Chaucer, at the close of *Troilus and Criseyde*, sums up the characteristics of English. They are characteristics that might lead to miscopying, misreading of the meter, and misunderstanding of his great epic. Clearly, the nature of the medium was of central concern and anxiety to Chaucer. But quite what he meant by "gret diversite" is not nearly so obvious to the modern reader of Chaucer and other texts of the period. Modern editions of medieval English literary texts often filter out original language features and introduce modern conventions, giving readers more easily accessible texts but reducing their exposure to the language. Modernized editions and translations limit even more their readers' access to medieval English.

Chaucer describes both the language, and writing the language down, as diverse. Two of the most important kinds of diversity (or variation) are change across time, and regional variation. "Middle English" denotes the language *c.* 1100–*c.* 1500 in all its variety, as distinct from "Old English" (or "Anglo-Saxon"), the language used before the Norman Conquest of 1066. Within that large category, linguists distinguish two broad historical varieties: early Middle English, and late Middle English, and five broad regional varieties: northern, east Midlands, west Midlands, southeastern, and southwestern. When it comes to written English, the regional and historical vectors of change intersect. During the early Middle English period no regional variety has any preeminence over the others; during the late

Middle English period the English used in the Midlands is adopted as the foundation for a supra-regional variety which is the ancestor of modern standard written English. It is important to realize that these are broad categories of convenience; real language follows no precise geographical or regional boundaries. Real medieval texts are even less cooperative. It is actually very difficult to map most Middle English texts as they are found in the manuscripts onto the frameworks given in the grammars and histories of the language. Like editions and readers, the grammars and the histories too may filter out the messiness, complexity, and challenge of real texts.

In the first section of this chapter I shall illustrate what diversity means in practice, analyzing some examples of early writing and discussing the limitations of the evidence. In the second section I shall outline the cultural circumstances that shaped the texts, finishing with a reading of a short poem to illustrate the cultural relations of English, and their complexities. In the third section I shall survey some attempts to refine and improve English during the period. Finally, I shall very briefly outline the history of scholarship on the subject and indicate possible future directions.

The following two crucifixion lyrics provide examples of the wide regional variation found in English writings of this period. They also show the diversity in representing English in writing, and illustrate the ways in which real texts elude systematic dialectal categorization:

a. Cambridge, Trinity College, MS 323, f. 83v
Wose seþe on rode ih*esu*s is lefmon
sori stod him bi wepinde sent marie & sent Ion
is hewid him al abutun wid þornis ip*ri*kit
is faire hondin & is waire wed wid naylis ystickit
ys rug wid yerdis suonke*n* ys syde wid sp*er* yvundit
al for su*n*ne of mon sore he may wepin & bitt*r*e
teris letin mon þad of luue con

[Whosoever sees on the cross, Jesus his dear one (Saint Mary and Saint John stood by him weeping sorrowfully), his head pricked with thorns all round, his fair hands and feet stuck through with nails, his back scourged with rods, his side probed with a spear, all for the sins of man – he may sorrowfully weep, and let fall bitter tears, that man that is able to love.]

b. London, British Library, Royal MS 12 E, f. 194v
Qua*n*ne hic se on rode ih*e*su mi le*m*man An be siden him
stonden marie an
Iohan And his rig isuongen and his side istungen for þe luue
of man Wel ou hic to wepen and sinnes forleten yif hic of luue
kan yif hic of luue kan yif hic of luue kan

[When I see on the cross, Jesus my dear one, and beside him stand Mary and John, and his back scourged, and his side pierced, for the love of man, well ought I to weep, and give up sins, if I am able to love, if I am able to love, if I am able to love.]

The scribes represent the sound [hw] using *w* and *qu*: (a) "wose" (line 1); (b) "quanne" (line 1); *qu* is typical of northern texts. Words which had a rounded sound spelt *y* in Old English (pronounced like the vowel in French *tu*) are spelt differently: (a) "rug" (line 5), "sunne" (line 6), (b) "rig" (line 2), "sinnes" (line 3). The *u* spelling in (a) is characteristic of west Midlands texts. Also characteristic of the west Midlands are the -on spellings in (a) "lefmon" (line 1), "mon" (lines 6 and 7), "con" (line 7), where (b) has "lemman" (line 1), "man" (line 3), "kan" (line 4). Other points of variance include the spelling of the unstressed vowel in the infinitive ending: (a) "wepin" (line 6), (b) "wepen" (line 3); the spelling of the unstressed vowel in the plural ending: (a) "naylis" (line 4), "yerdis" (line 5), (b) "sinnes" (line 3); and the spelling of the pronoun *his* in a low stress position: (a) drops the aspirate in "is" (lines 1, 3, 5), and "ys" (line 6), but (b) keeps the Old English spelling with initial *h*, "his" (line 2). These differences between the two texts suggest that they were written in different dialect areas, (a) having several characteristics that suggest localization in the west Midlands, a localization supported by the present participle ending in "wepinde" (line 2) which is characteristic of the southwest Midlands (northern texts have -ande, eastern texts -inde). But (a) does not fit exactly into a dialect, for there are internal inconsistencies. "Waire wed" (a, line 4) is characteristic of southwestern texts, suggesting a voiced initial sound in "fair feet." But earlier in the line we have "faire," suggesting that the scribe is not systematically representing the sounds of speech in his dialect. Possibly we have layers of different dialects; certainly the scribe does not have a consistent system for writing.

These texts were written down in the earlier part of our period. The manuscript of (a) is thirteenth century, that of (b) early fourteenth century. They give us some hint of the broad variations in the spoken language that continued throughout the period. Other kinds of evidence are rare. In the later fourteenth century John Trevisa describes the language of northerners ("especially at York") as "scharp, slyttyng, and frotyng and vnschape."[2] The Londoner Chaucer, Trevisa's close contemporary, famously attempts to imitate northern English in the *Reeve's Tale*. The students John and Aleyn are incomers in the East Anglian town of Cambridge, having been born "fer in the north." Chaucer marks their speech with features distinctive of northern English:

"By God, right by the hopur wil I stande,"
Quod John, "and se howgates the corn gas in.
Yet saugh I nevere, by my fader kyn,
How that the hopur wagges til and fra."
Aleyn answerde, "John, and wiltow swa?
Thanne wil I be bynethe, by my croun,
And se how that the mele falles doun
Into the trough; that sal be my disport.
For John, y-faith, I may be of youre sort;
I is as ille a millere as ar ye." (I 4036–45)

John and Aleyn use distinctively northern vocabulary. "til and fra" (line 4039) echoes the "til ok fra" of the Scandinavian settlers in the north. "gas" (line 4037, "goes"), "fra" (line 4039, "fro"), and "swa" (line 4040, "so") have an unrounded sound where southern English would have a rounded vowel. "gas" has the modern -s ending for the third person present tense singular, where southern English preferred "goth" (the miller's wife cries "youre hors goth to the fen" (4080)). Aleyn says "ar ye" (line 4045), using *are*, the familiar modern part of the verb *to be*, where southern English would have *ben*. There is exaggeration too: "I is" (line 4045) is simply an invention. It is a moot point whether Chaucer is laughing at the northerners, or the northerners are laughing at the Miller, or both.

Of course, variation of sound, grammar, and vocabulary must have characterized Old English, and diversity in spoken English continues, obviously, to this day. What characterizes Middle English above all is diversity in writing the language. In periods before and after the Middle English period conventions for writing English were more standardized, concealing variation in the spoken language, and changes over time. Surviving pre-Conquest English texts were copied by scribes trained to write in a fairly uniform way. From the turn of the fifteenth century we have the beginnings of supra-regional standard written Englishes. In the Middle English period, by contrast, scribes were not trained to write English according to any set of conventions, or agreement about what was "correct." This state of affairs explains the inconsistencies in writing within and between the two poems we looked at in this section. The reasons for it, and its implications for English literature, will be explored in the next section.

Middle English in multilingual Britain

The way that English was written down – and whether and when it was written down at all – are matters intimately connected with the writing in the period of two other languages of literature: Latin and French. After the

Norman Conquest, the status of English changed. English continued to be the mother tongue of the majority of the population – although it was not, of course, the only vernacular language used in Britain. But the status of English as a language for literature was compromised and pre-Conquest traditions of literary production disrupted. They did not cease altogether. Old English texts continued to be copied in a number of centers in the twelfth century, and in some cases Anglo-Saxon traditions of prose composition were kept up. A copy of the *Anglo-Saxon Chronicle* was made at Peterborough abbey *c.* 1121, and a number of additions were made up to the mid-twelfth century. But by the first half of the thirteenth century a Worcester scribe (known as the "Tremulous Hand" because of his distinctively shaky handwriting) glossed texts written in Old English, providing Latin and Middle English equivalents for Old English words – showing that for this scribe at least, written Old English was no longer a living tradition.

As for new composition, just as people continued to use English for everyday purposes, so they must have continued to sing and to tell stories in English. But there was, it seems, no significant tradition of writing such texts down; the few scraps that we have survive by chance. For example, toward the end of the twelfth century, Gerald of Wales wrote in his *Gemma Ecclesiastica* that a Worcestershire priest mistakenly began his sermon with a love song, from which Gerald quoted: "swete lamman dhin are" ("sweet darling, your mercy"), while another love lyric dated *c.* 1200 is jotted in the margin of a Worcester manuscript.[3]

Whereas homilies, histories, saints' lives, and pastoral works had been written in English prose before the Conquest (as well as in Latin), now Latin became once again the chief medium for learned and religious composition. For some time after the Conquest, many authors were immigrants and settlers from the continent. Some never even learned to speak English, and none had any reason to write it even if they could have done so. They brought with them the traditions of composition of the monasteries of northern France. For example, Anselm (*c.* 1033–1109), Archbishop of Canterbury, the son of a Lombard, and educated at the abbey of Bec, in Normandy, came to Canterbury in 1070. He composed works of theology and philosophy, as well as poems, prayers, meditations, and religious poems. Links with the continent flourished particularly during the reign of Henry II (r. 1154–89), whose empire comprised a large swathe of Britain and continental Europe. From this period date the great Anglo-Latin writers of the twelfth-century Renaissance, such as John of Salisbury, Peter of Blois, Gerald of Wales, and Walter Map, all of them Latinists whose European outlook was cultivated by education on the continent.

Throughout the period Latin remained the preeminent medium for works of learning of all kinds. A few examples of later works include: all of the works of the theologian John Wyclif (d. 1382), John Gower's apocalyptic vision *Vox clamantis* (before 1386), Thomas Walsingham's *Chronica majora* (*c.* 1422), Thomas Gascoigne's memoir *Dictionarium theologicum* (*c.* 1457) and from the very end of the period, Thomas More's *Utopia* (1516), by which time the influences of continental Latin were powerful once again. The vast majority of books that survive from the period contain Latin texts – many of them consist exclusively of Latin texts. As well as being the preeminent medium for learned literature in England, Latin was an important medium for administrative texts and documents. Latin is the language of many charters, wills, court records, and ecclesiastical records, and also of many official letters.

For most of the period with which we are dealing, French was the main alternative to Latin as a language of literature and administration. Even before the Conquest there were of course contacts between England and Normandy. When the Normans replaced the English ruling class with their own men, French replaced English as the regular spoken language of the powerful in England. Anglo-Norman (as linguists term the French used by the settlers in England) was spoken in the court, and often in schools and monasteries, and provided a medium for secular or lay literature. The Normans brought with them traditions of poetry which they soon naturalized and developed. The continental French epic the *Chanson de Roland* was copied in England in the mid-twelfth century. At about the same time Wace wrote the *Roman de Brut* (an Anglo-Norman verse version of Geoffrey of Monmouth's Latin *Historia regum Britanniae*), and the *Jeu d'Adam*, an Anglo-Norman Genesis play, was composed. From a little later in the century date Anglo-Norman versions of the Tristan legend, by Thomas d'Angleterre and Béroul, Anglo-Norman narratives of the Horn romance, fables by Marie de France, and saints' lives by the nun Clemence of Barking. From about 1200 through to the fifteenth century and beyond, French was the language of petitions, letters, legal records, and accounts. It continued to be used as a medium for literary composition in England too. Late examples include John Gower's *Mirour de l'Omme* (*c.* 1377) and some of the poems of Charles d'Orléans, who was captive in England 1415–40.

Competence in Latin and French was restricted by economic and social status, and by gender, meaning that access to literature was closely associated with social and economic privilege. Those destined for careers in the Church would usually be taught some Latin at school. Because medieval society recruited talent into the Church from lower as well as higher social groups, Latinity was not entirely restricted by social class. But it was restricted by gender. Because they could not enter the Church or receive a formal education, women could only learn Latin informally (perhaps from their mother or chaplain), if they could learn it at all. An ability to read the prayers in a primer must have been the summit of aspiration for most women.

Anglo-Norman gradually acquired features that distinguished it from French spoken on the continent. In related developments, it became associated with social anxiety and aspiration, becoming a language that was taught rather than being acquired as a mother tongue. Those aspiring to circulate in polite society, or to careers in administration or law, would learn some French. Some received basic French tuition as part of the business studies curriculum at university. Others must have been taught "on the job" of clerking or accountancy or estate management. Still others must have been taught by chaplains or other members of gentry and noble households.

One of the earliest surviving secular lyrics, the early thirteenth-century Cuckoo Song "Svmer is icumen in," illustrates some aspects of the cultural and literary relationships between English, French, and Latin, including their rich complexity:

> Svmer is icumen in +Lhude sing cuccu Groweþ sed and bloweþ med and springþ þe wde nu Sing cuccu Awe bleteþ after lomb lhouþ after calue cu Bulluc sterteþ bucke uerteþ
>
> Murie sing cuccu Cuccu cuccu Wel singes þu cuccu ne swik þu nauer nu
>
> *Pes* {Sing cuccu nu Sing cuccu
> {Sing cuccu Sing cuccu nu[4]
>
> [Summer has arrived – sing loudly, cuckoo! The seed grows and the meadow blooms, and the wood springs into leaf now. The ewe bleats after her lamb, the cow lows after her calf. The bullock leaps, the buck farts, sing merrily, cuckoo! Cuckoo, cuckoo, you sing well cuckoo! Never cease now! *Background song*: Sing cuckoo now, sing cuckoo, sing cuckoo, sing cuckoo now.]

The song is set to music, and marked up with instructions in Latin for singing as a *rota* (round song). The singers must stagger their entries. When the first singer reaches "Lhude" the second begins at "Svmer" and so on, so the song is an endless cycle. At the same time two other singers cycle the *pes*, so the call of the cuckoo repeats endlessly as a background, illustrating what the other singers sing: "you sing well, cuckoo, never cease now."

Old English offers nothing to parallel this Middle English love lyric; it refers to the French love lyric. French literature offered models for the spring song or *reverdie*, in which spring and its natural music – birdsong – provide an occasion to sing about the pains of human love. In the English song, birdsong is associated with the sufferings of love, but the focus is less on the tragic lover than on the comic deceived husband, since the French word *cuccu* is the origin of *cuckold* (ME *cokewold*). The endless repetition of "cuccu" in the *pes*, and the command ("never cease"), suggest that the deception of husbands is as predictable and recurrent as the cycle of the seasons. The song is no love-lorn lover's plaint, but an energetic warning.

The Cuckoo Song is closely associated with liturgical Latin, its music and singers, as demonstrated by its manuscript context. The proximity of the lyric with the words and music of the Latin liturgy is also shown in another way. Under the English words are alternative Latin words to be sung to the same musical notes. The Christian is exhorted to pay heed to how the "heavenly husbandman" (God) has sacrificed his son. The sobriety of the Latin and the exuberance of the English stand in creative moral tension.

The Cuckoo Song refers to two other spring "songs": the bleating of the ewe after her lamb, and the lowing of the cow after her calf. Like the lyric, these animal sounds are instances of the "mother tongue." Bleating and lowing are among the many thrustings and emissions of spring described in the poem – farting, starting, growing, blooming, and birthing – suggesting a continuum between the vernacular song and the reproductive forces of the natural world. The Cuckoo Song takes its energy from the creative tensions among several varieties of "song": English, French, Latin, bird, animal. It at once invents, celebrates, and ironizes the sounds of English song.

Re-inventing English

The two crucifixion lyrics and the Cuckoo Song illustrate two key aspects of Middle English: its diversity of written expression, and its lack of prestige as a medium for literature. It was against this background that all Middle English texts were produced. In this section I propose to focus on some of the writers and texts which attempt to improve the language, to overcome the problems of linguistic diversity and poverty. I shall distinguish two broad categories of experiment: texts and authors which aim to enrich the language, and projects which aim to systematize and regularize it.

George Ashby (*c.* 1390–1475), Lancastrian court poet, praised Chaucer, Gower, and Lydgate for their improvement of the English language:

> Maisters Gower, Chaucer and Lydgate,
> Primier poetes of this nacion,
> Embelysshing oure Englisshe tendure algate,
> Firste finders to our consolacioun
> Off fresshe, douce Englisshe and formacioun
> Of newe balades not used before,
> By whome we all may have lernyng and lore.[5]

According to Ashby, his three distinguished predecessors "embellished" English, finding (inventing) "fresh, sweet English," and making new "balades" (stanza forms) "not used before." Chaucer and his successors looked to the verse of the continental French and Italian courts as models and sources for enriching the versification of English. Leading continental poets demonstrated their virtuosity by writing in a range of demanding forms. The *balade* had three stanzas and often an "envoy" (examples include Chaucer's poems *Truth* and *Lak of Stedfastnesse*). Each stanza had a fixed form, with a fixed number of syllables in each line and a standard rhyme scheme. The seven-line stanza ("rime royal") has decasyllabic lines and a rhyme scheme ababbcc, as illustrated by Chaucer's *Parliament of Fowls*:

> The lyf so short, the craft so long to lerne,
> Th'assay so hard, so sharp the conquerynge,
> The dredful joye alwey that slit so yerne:
> Al this mene I by Love, that my felynge
> Astonyeth with his wonderful werkynge
> So sore, iwis, that whan I on hym thynke
> Nat wot I wel wher that I flete or synke. (1–7)

A variant was the eight-line stanza that rhymed ababbccb, used by Chaucer in *The Complaint of Venus*. It is thought that Chaucer exploited a flexibility over whether the unstressed final -e was pronounced or silent to meet the demands of syllabic versification. Rhyme was a key feature of continental verse forms, with particularly taxing schemes permitting poets to display their virtuosity. The virelay as used by Machaut required a refrain with only two rhyme sounds, and stanzas with only one additional rhyme; ideally all of the rhymes should be sonorous (for example "Dame le doulz souvenir" is restricted to the rhymes -ir, -our, -er).[6] In *The Complaint of Venus*, Chaucer laments the lack of rhymes in English:

> Syth rym in Englissh hath such skarsete,
> To folowe word by word the curiosite
> Of Graunson, flour of hem that make in Fraunce. (80–83)

Experiments in versification were associated with an increase in the importance of words of French or Latin origin, leading to the "aureate," polysyllabic, Latinate diction of poets such as Lydgate. For example, a lyric rhyme scheme might use *attendaunce / varyaunce / repentaunce / affyaunce*.

Other poets in the period wrote alliterative verse. Critics often see alliterative poetry as using obsolescent poetic vocabulary and meter associated with Old English traditions. But here I shall present it as another response to the "improvement" agenda. Enrichment of versification and vocabulary was sought and displayed by alliterative poets. The alliterative line does not have a fixed syllable count, but rather a pattern of stressed and unstressed syllables that falls into two halves. In a normative line, the first half-line must have at least two stressed, alliterating syllables, the first stressed syllable of the second half-line must also alliterate, whilst the final stressed syllable does not alliterate:

In the **mon**ethe of **Ma**ye // when **mirth**es bene **fele**[7]

Here the alliteration falls on the syllables printed in bold. The alliterative line required a wide vocabulary rich with synonyms to permit alliteration on a range of sounds. Poets displayed their virtuosity by deploying funds of specialized vocabulary. For example, describing a feast, *Winner and Waster* includes a long list of game birds and their culinary treatment:

Barnakes and buturs and many bylled snyppes,
Larkes and lyngwhittes lapped in sogoure,
Wodcokkes and wodwales full wellande hote,
Teeles and titmoyses to take what hym lykes[8]

Specialized vocabularies deployed in *Sir Gawain and the Green Knight* include those of hunting, armor, weaponry, courtly costume, and topography, while *Pearl* draws on the language of lapidary, which dealt with the names, meanings, and properties of precious stones. As well as drawing on the vocabularies of the skills and knowledges of the courtly life, alliterative poets also draw on the language of *clergie*: the vocabularies and linguistic habits used by scholars and Churchmen. The model for this practice was *Piers Plowman*:

Nede anoon righte nymeth hym under maynprise.
And if hym list for to lape, the lawe of kynde wolde
That he dronke at ech dych, er he [deide for thurst].
So Nede, at gret nede, may nymen as for his owene,
Withouten conseil of Conscience or Cardynale Vertues –
So that he sewe and save *Spiritus Temperancie.*[9]

This passage from *Piers Plowman* uses the language of common law ("maynprise") alongside that of moral theology ("conscience"), legal theory ("lawe of kynde"), and political theory ("conseil").

We know that *Piers Plowman* achieved distribution across the different regions of England. Yet there is evidence to suggest that there are elements of regionality in the production and distribution of alliterative poetry. Chaucer's Parson disclaims any skill in alliterative meter because of his southern origins:

But trusteth wel, I am a Southren man;
I kan nat geeste "rum, ram, ruf," by lettre (X. 42–43)

This implies that alliterative verse was associated with the northern and western provinces, an association borne out by the dialect of some alliterative poems. Some variation in the acceptability of alliterative meter is suggested by comparisons of the Winchester manuscript of Malory's *Morte Darthur* with Caxton's print of it. Malory drew in part on the alliterative *Morte Arthure*, retaining traces of its distinctive alliterative vocabulary in his text. But Caxton's edition eliminates these traces, which suggests that, although acceptable to Malory, they seemed to Caxton too archaic, or dialectal, to please his market.

Caxton's project was to reach as wide an audience as possible. He needed an English that would transcend regional differences because of the commercial pressures of printing. His is one of the projects of linguistic improvement which imagines and attempts to reach a supra-local or regional audience. Analysis has suggested that his model for a "standard" English may have been the writing of the offices of the royal government, or Chancery. Until the early fifteenth century, most government documents and records were written in Latin or Anglo-Norman. But from the 1420s government offices began to use English for many documents. Texts produced by Chancery clerks show attempts to regularize spelling and grammar. For example, whereas *con* and *kan* are variants in our crucifixion lyrics, *can* is the usual form in Chancery documents. Where the lyrics vary in spelling the unstressed vowel in noun plurals -is and -es, Chancery documents prefer -es. In Chancery documents, the northern *qu* spelling for [hw] is extremely rare; *wh* is the preferred spelling.[10] This regularization can be attributed to the setting and transmission of standard practices by senior Chancery clerks. These circumstances also provided for the spread of this standard more broadly. Administrative documents achieved wide distribution, providing authoritative models for subjects to imitate. It has been argued that this was the turning-point in the development of a system of writing that developed with a degree of independence from the spoken language.

Chancery documents also provided a model for composition in English. Previously, there had been no models for letter writing in English, because the arts of letter writing were practiced in Latin and French. Writers imitated the letters exemplified in French and Latin formularies, following prescribed formulae and structural divisions. Chancery documents provided examples of texts that reproduced these forms in English, and the fact that they emanated from the royal government offices gave them authority. Analyses of letters of the fifteenth century (for example, the Paston Letters, the correspondence of a prominent landowning family in Norfolk) prove that Chancery forms impacted far beyond the royal writing offices on household scribes and clerks and their noble and gentry employers.

We have evidence of various attempts to refine and regularize English in connection with religious agendas. Famous early examples include *Ancrene Wisse* and the "Katherine Group," devotional texts in prose of the early thirteenth century, and the *Ormulum*, a homiletic text in verse written perhaps a decade or two earlier. The prose texts provide instructional and meditative reading for women recluses. The *Ormulum* provides paraphrases and interpretations of gospel stories, probably in support of preaching and teaching to laypeople. Both exhibit an attempt to regularize the way English is written, but both base their system on their own local spoken variety: the east Midlands in the case of the verse, the west Midlands in the case of the prose. Neither imagines a supra-regional audience or achieved one (though in different forms *Ancrene Wisse* eventually became quite widely disseminated).

Lollard writings attempt to regularize in the interests of a massive supra-regional religious agenda. A cluster of literary projects – at least two translations of the Bible (1382–95), aids to bible study, sets of sermons, and satirical and polemical tracts – was carried out by followers of the heretic John Wyclif. The Lollards developed an English prose which could communicate across dialectal boundaries; Wycliffite English is based on the dialect of the south and central Midlands, the variety which came to underpin standard English. They also developed distinctively Lollard meanings for words. For example, *prelate*, normally a neutral word meaning "senior ecclesiastic," is a pejorative term in Lollard writings. Lollards made it possible for the first time for people who knew only English to access theology and the Bible. On the "improvement" question, they insisted that English was a perfectly adequate medium in which to discuss theological and philosophical subjects usually confined to Latin. They claimed that arguments about the superiority of Latin over English really served the interests of corrupt clergy who wanted to avoid being challenged by laypeople.

Along with these projects of refinement and regularization goes the development of a language in which to formulate and debate questions raised by such projects. The Lollards contributed to the development of a vocabulary and conceptual frameworks for discussing the vernacular when they debated issues of language superiority. Theoretical vocabularies also developed in relation to discussion of translation, images, education, and devotional reading. The terms of Middle English literary and linguistic theory are numerous, provisional, and improvisatory. They emanate from various, sometimes unrelated or conflicted, frames of reference.[11] They thus have not a little in common with the vocabularies of contemporary critical and linguistic theory.

Changing agendas in Middle English studies

When formal study of Middle English began in the nineteenth century, scholars worked to deduce the sounds and grammar of English in order to describe its dialects, and to map linguistic change. They also examined the impact of other languages, particularly on vocabulary, charting and analyzing the uses of loans from Old Norse, French, and Latin. When study moved from the disciplinary aegis of "comparative philology" to that of a new discipline of "English," the new agenda brought with it new conceptual problems: where does the story of "English" begin, and what is the earliest "English Literature"? These problems lie behind a question which crops up in various guises and contexts (often in the study of early Middle English prose, and of alliterative poetry): to what extent can we trace "continuity" all the way through from Old English to Chaucer and beyond? With modern critiques of the discipline of "English," and the breaking down of boundaries with cultural history and the study of the other languages of medieval Britain, new perspectives are emerging. Interest has waned in narratives of how English rose from humble medieval origins to positions of imperial power and global reach. The time is ripe for creative reinvention of language study in the analysis of medieval literature and culture.

NOTES

1 Geoffrey Chaucer, *Troilus and Criseyde*, in *Riverside*, p. 584. All Chaucer references are to this edition. Line numbers and titles will be given in the text.

2 Kenneth Sisam, ed., *Fourteenth Century Verse and Prose* (Oxford: Clarendon Press, 1921), p. 150.

3 Carleton Brown, ed., *English Lyrics of the XIIIth Century* (Oxford: Clarendon Press, 1932), pp. xi–xii.

4 London, British Library, MS Harley 978, f. 11v.

5 *Idea of the Vernacular*, p. 59.

6 James I. Wimsatt, *Chaucer and His French Contemporaries: Natural Music in the Fourteenth Century* (University of Toronto Press, 1991), pp. 27–28.

7 *The Parlement of the Thre Ages*, in *Alliterative Poetry of the Later Middle Ages: An Anthology*, ed. Thorlac Turville-Petre (London: Routledge, 1989), p. 70, line 1.

8 *Winner and Waster*, in *Alliterative Poetry*, p. 58, lines 349–53.

9 *Piers Plowman*, pp. 346–47, 20.17–22.

10 John H. Fisher, Malcolm Richardson, and Jane L. Fisher, eds., *An Anthology of Chancery English* (Knoxville: University of Tennessee Press, 1984), pp. 27, 31, 35.

11 See a glossary of such terms in *Idea of the Vernacular*, pp. 393–446.

2

RICHARD FIRTH GREEN

Textual production and textual communities

Some years ago, when I was teaching in eastern Canada, I attended a lecture, liberally illustrated with slides, given by a local sculptor on his recent visit to Japan. Unsurprisingly, in view of his vocation, he tended to dwell on monumental and architectural subjects rather than landscapes or human figures and for the best part of an hour we were invited to reflect upon the elegant simplicity of Japanese stone-carving and woodworking. At the end of the talk a slide of weathered wooden shingles silhouetted against a slate-gray sky appeared on the screen; it seemed to us a natural complement to the roof trusses and door jambs of the Shinto shrine we had just been contemplating, and we duly gazed at it with reverential awe. Just before the lecturer snapped the lights back on, he informed us that we were looking at the side of a cattle barn on Nova Scotia's Tantramar Marshes, not ten miles away from where we were sitting. All of us, I believe, experienced the same shock to our unreflective compartmentalization of the exotic and the familiar. It was, of course, a cheap trick, but it provided a vivid illustration of how readily we see what we expect to see, of how easily our eyes can be conditioned, or trained, or fooled into seeing only one aspect of a polysemous image.

In many ways it is the same with reading. One reader reads *Bleak House* because it's a good story, another because she enjoys the eccentric characters, a third because he is inspired by its social criticism – are all three, then, reading the same text? The answer of course must depend on how one defines "text," but from the point of view of the reader-response theorist they would appear to be reading three closely related but nonetheless distinguishable *Bleak Houses*. What is of most interest to the reader-response theorist, however, is less the potentially limitless variety of such atomistic readings, but the common ground shared by larger groups of readers – what such readers will generally look to find in Dickens's novel (their so-called "horizon of expectation"). To oversimplify, there is no final way to adjudicate between a group of law-students that insists that *Bleak House* is about the reform of the Victorian legal system and a group of medical students that sees it as a novel about outbreaks of smallpox in insanitary slums, but at least the basis of their disagreement can be identified and explained (though this may be far from obvious to the groups themselves): each group constitutes, in a phrase introduced by Stanley Fish, a different "interpretive community."[1]

Three years after Fish popularized the term "interpretive community" (in 1980), Brian Stock, in *The Implications of Literacy*, coined the phrase "textual community." While these two terms are far from synonymous, they have much in common, so it is somewhat surprising to find that neither Fish nor his medievalist fellow-traveler Hans Robert Jauss appears in Stock's bibliography. However, where Fish's interpretive communities concern themselves with the text as an *object* of interpretation, for Stock textuality is itself a *kind* of interpretation, the source of hermeneutic activity, as it were. In the medieval world, where every book was laboriously copied by hand, textuality in the modern sense could never be taken for granted. When literacy was a rare commodity, Stock argues, to think textually was to think in ways not shared by the great mass of the population, and this in turn was to have consequences for the ways communities of readers and writers thought about and defined themselves. Such textuality made for highly self-conscious and self-fashioning communities (whereas a commonality of interpretive assumptions of the kind Fish is concerned with will generally define its community after the fact). Or, to put it in Marshall McLuhan's terms, whereas for Fish the message completely dominates its medium (there is *no* text in the class – to answer Fish's own provocative question), stock sees the two as inextricably entwined: "the degree to which society recognizes written principles of operation," writes Stock, affects not only communal relationships, but also "the way people conceptualize such relations."[2] His particular area of interest was heretical communities in the early Middle Ages, but Stock does suggest that his insights might usefully be applied to other medieval groups, "orthodox religious orders such as Cluny, for instance, or the communal guilds of Italy and the Low Countries" (p. 89). Since "heretics in particular provided a cutting edge for literacy" (p. 90), Stock claims that their study offered him particular advantages, a point fully borne out by transferring his paradigm from the Latin heresies of eleventh- and twelfth-century Europe to the major vernacular heresy of late fourteenth- and fifteenth-century England – Lollardy. In many ways the clearest example of a textual community, in Stock's sense, that the English Middle Ages has to offer is that of the Lollard "conventicle."[3]

The Oxford theologian and reformer, John Wyclif (*c.* 1330–84), following the lead of one of Stock's earlier heretics, Berengar of Tours, anticipated the later Protestants by arguing that the bread and the wine of the Eucharist were not the actual body and blood of Christ but merely commemorative symbols of them. Self-evidently such an insight is only available to someone who thinks textually, someone capable, in Stock's terms, of distinguishing "between the *sacramentum* and the *res sacramenti*, that is, between figure and truth, the visible and the invisible."[4] It is not surprising then to find that Wyclif's followers made something of a fetish of literacy,[5] that they transcribed and circulated the English Bible and other theological writings, and that, more significantly, they formed groups to read and discuss them. Thus, in 1430, on trial for heresy before William Alnwick, Bishop of Norwich, a repentant Lollard wrote:

> I, Thomas Moon, ... have be right homely and privy with many heretics, knowing them for heretics, and them I have received and harbored in mine house, and them I have concealed, comforted, supported, maintained, and favored with all my power – which heretics' names be these [fifteen names follow] and many others – which oft times have kept, held, and continued schools of heresy in privy chambers of mine, in the which schools I have heard, conceived, learned and reported the errors and heresies which be written and contained in these indentures: [a list follows].[6]

There can be little doubt that public reading took place in these schools: one witness deposes that she was invited to the house of Margery Baxter (an associate of Thomas Moon and his wife) by night "and there she heard [Margery's] husband read them the *Lex Christi*, and this *Lex* was contained in a book which her husband was accustomed to read to Margery at night, and she said that her husband was the best teacher of Christianity [*doctor Christianitatis*]" (pp. 47–48). Ralph Hanna vividly conveys not only the communal nature of such an activity but the way it is woven into the very fabric of Lollard discourse: "book use thus represented one extension of a trusted domestic community. And in fact the powerful evocations of household values – the conjugal chamber, the hospitable hearth, the communion of the dinner table, cooperative labor – are inextricably bound with the contents of those books that constituted heterodox belief."[7] When Moon pledged that in future he would report to the proper authorities "any persons making privy conventicles or assemblies, or holding of any diverse or singular opinions from the common doctrine of the church" (p. 180), it is quite clear that both "textual" and "interpretive" communities were in question: in other words, Moon, his family, and his friends defined themselves in relation to a set of texts – they thought textually, as it were – but they had also evolved a distinctive way of interpreting them.

Brian Stock was able to examine a number of the texts associated with his heretical interpretive communities from the early Middle Ages, but the Norwich heresy trials furnish us with the names of only two books, and unfortunately one of these (*Dives and Pauper*) is not conspicuously heretical while the other (Margery Baxter's book of the *Lex Christi*) can no longer be identified. Many Lollard tracts and commentaries do survive, however, and it is not difficult to imagine the kind of reading matter that was copied, circulated, and discussed by Thomas Moon's family and friends. The most significant feature of many of these texts is that they were written in the vernacular. In fact by 1409 the authorities had become so threatened by this kind of activity that the Archbishop of Canterbury officially proscribed all but the most innocuously pastoral kinds of religious writing in the vernacular,[8] and it was presumably for this reason that even the relatively inoffensive *Dives and Pauper* fell under suspicion in the ecclesiastical court in Norwich. Evidently, functional literacy was now so widely disseminated throughout society that complex theological concepts which in the twelfth century had been restricted to the Latin clerisy were now being freely debated by intelligent laypeople in their native tongue.

Of course, as in the earlier period, textual communities might be formed which were entirely orthodox, and the same fifteenth-century East Anglia that harbored Thomas Moon's conventicle, witnessed a circle of pious laywomen devoted to reading the lives of female saints. In this case, however, instead of working from an identifiable community to a hypothetical collection of texts, we must begin with the texts themselves, and then hypothesize the community that formed around them. Osbern Bokenham, an Augustinian friar from the convent of Stoke by Clare in Suffolk, tells us that on the evening January 5, 1445, he was entertained by Lady Isabel Bourchier, the countess of Eu (the sister of the duke of York), "while this lady's four young sons were engaged in revels and dancing," and that,

> wyth me to talke
> It lykyd my lady of hyr ientylnesse
> Of dyuers legendys, wych my rudnesse
> From latyn had turnyd in-to our language,
> Of hooly wummen, now in my last age. (5036–40)[9]

[It pleased my lady, out of her goodness, to talk to me about various lives of holy women which I had crudely translated from Latin into English in my declining years.]

When Countess Isabel learns that Bokenham is in the middle of translating a life of Saint Elizabeth, "whose life affords a mirror of absolute perfection to all wives," for Lady Elizabeth de Vere, countess of Oxford, she asks him if he will translate a life of Mary Magdalene for her. Possibly Isabel later told her cousin Katherine Howard about Bokenham's poetic talents since Howard apparently commissioned him to write her a life of Saint Katherine; on the other hand, Howard could also have heard about him from Katherine Denston of Melford in Suffolk, since Bokenham says that he wrote it for the "spiritual consolation and comfort" (ll. 6365–66) of both of them, and Denston had been mentioned earlier at the end of his life of Saint Anne (l. 2093). A fifth lady, Agnes Flegge, who is mentioned by Bokenham in his life of Saint Agnes, was probably also known to Countess Isabel, since Agnes's husband was an associate of her brother-in-law. Furthermore, Katherine Howard, Katherine Denston, and Agnes Flegge all lived within a sixteen-mile radius of Bokenham's convent of Stoke by Clare, and the two countesses, Isabel and Elizabeth, also had strong East Anglian connections. A sixth lady, Isabel Hunt, for whom Bokenham wrote a life of Saint Dorothy, is a more shadowy figure but presumably also belonged to the same circle. Moreover, Osbern Bokenham is not the only East Anglian writer to have written an English saint's life for a female patron. He was preceded in this by John Lydgate, a monk of the Benedictine Abbey of Bury St. Edmunds, who had written a life of Saint Margaret for Anne Mortimer, Lady March, while around the same time, his fellow Augustinian, John Capgrave, prior of Bishop's Lynn, was writing a life of Saint Augustine at the request of an anonymous "noble creatur, a gentill woman." A. S. G. Edwards even argues for the existence of a number of linked centers in East Anglia catering to such lay readers of vernacular religious works.[10] While we have no concrete external evidence for the same kind of textual community as the one that formed around the Lollards Thomas Moon and his wife, we do have the surviving saints' legends themselves, and from them it has been plausibly inferred that, "with their meditations on the saint's virtues and their lengthy passages of prayer and exposition [they] assume an audience that will 'abyde thervpon' [linger over them] and treat reading as a form of 'preysynge and preyynge to god'."[11] If this is the case, this group of East Anglian ladies appears to have constituted another late medieval textual community, and doubtless an interpretive one as well.

From what has been said, we can derive a set of minimum requirements for establishing the existence of a medieval textual community: we need (1) a set of texts which share many of the same features, (2) an identifiable group of early readers of these texts who can be shown to have known one another, and (3) evidence, either internal or external, that their self-consciously literate habits of thought led such readers to evolve a distinctive way of using and interpreting these texts. Given the nature of medieval records and the conditions under which they have been preserved, we will rarely be able to satisfy all three requirements to our complete satisfaction and will often be forced to fill in the gaps with inference and conjecture.

In Thomas Moon's Lollard conventicle and in Osbern Bokenham's circle of pious ladies I have presented two of the clearest examples of a medieval English textual community known to me, but neither appears very substantial compared with a well-documented modern literary movement, such as the Bloomsbury Group. There is much about both that must remain unknown and unknowable. There are two other, still less substantial, medieval communities for which a similar claim might possibly be made: one that formed around Sir Thomas Berkeley (1352–1417) in Gloucestershire,[12] and the other around John Shirley (*c.*1366–1456) in London.[13] There is in fact a connection between the two men, since for much of his life Shirley was in the service of Richard Beauchamp, earl of Warwick, and Warwick was married to Thomas Berkeley's daughter Elizabeth.

The reputation of many medieval patrons depends on little more than the fact that they are known to have owned books or had books dedicated to them (which leaves moot the important question of whether they actually read these books), but with Thomas Berkeley, there is rather more to go on. From 1379 to *c.* 1402 Berkeley employed as his chaplain a Cornishman called John Trevisa, and during that time commissioned him to translate three substantial Latin works into English: a universal chronicle – Ranulf Higden's *Polychronicon*; an encyclopedia – Bartholomew the Englishman's *De proprietatibus rerum*; and a book of statecraft – the *De regimine principum*. A fourth work, Vegetius's *De re militari* (a book of Roman military science) was translated for Berkeley after Trevisa's death by a man who may have been called John Walton, or possibly William Clifton.[14] All four works have a distinctly utilitarian cast to them, the kind of books that a hard-working local magnate might feel he could usefully consult to help him deal with the contingencies of daily life. If this were all there were to it, we would hardly be justified in attributing a distinctive textual consciousness to him, but there survives a dialogue between a cleric and a lord (evidently a mouthpiece for Berkeley's own views) written by Trevisa, which points to a rather more ideologically driven program. In Ralph Hanna's words, "in Trevisa's 'Dialogue', the clerical hope of retaining textual power, of keeping Ranulph Higden's history the exclusive property of a Latinate community, is routed by the Lord's insistence upon the rights of secular readership ... The Lord speaks for a broader public denied textual access by arbitrary linguistic barriers" (p. 895).

With so much that is translation, and so little original composition, it is difficult to go much further than this; it is also very difficult to sketch in an actual textual community surrounding Lord Berkeley. Ralph Hanna has argued for a Berkeley circle that included a long-time associate called Sir John Greyndour, possible sponsor of the translation of a religious work called the *Memoriale Credentium*, a young retainer called Robert Shottesbrooke, who was later to translate a devotional text called *Aventure and Grace*, and finally Berkeley's daughter Elizabeth, the countess of Warwick, who commissioned a translation of Boethius's *De consolatione philosophiae* from John Walton of Oseney. These three books seem so different in subject matter from the majority of Thomas Berkeley's surviving commissions (though he *is* known to have owned a work by the English mystic, Richard Rolle, and John Trevisa *did* translate the apocryphal *Gospel of Nichodemus* for him) that to regard this Berkeley "circle" as a textual community in the fullest sense might seem to be stretching things.

With John Shirley the situation is rather different. We have good evidence that he was at the center of a large community of readers, but it is very difficult to identify them with any precision or say much about the way they approached their reading. A considerable number of manuscripts can be associated with Shirley in one way or another: six were copied by him in whole or in part; a further seven show signs of having been owned by him or having passed through his hands; and eight more were apparently copied from Shirley originals.[15] While Shirley did on occasion translate texts from both Latin and French, his chief contribution was as an anthologist of works in both verse and prose, chiefly of a courtly or instructional nature; Geoffrey Chaucer and John Lydgate are both well represented in his anthologies. Shirley often adds brief notes identifying authors or giving the circumstances of composition, but he rarely includes any kind of interpretive information. Two lengthy versified lists of contents make it clear that some at least of his manuscripts were intended for public circulation; in one he requests his reader, "That ye send this book again / Home to Shirley," and in the other, "but send this book to me again, / Shirley I mean." A similar plea is made in a rhymed "bookplate" that appears in two of his manuscripts, but as Margaret Connolly has written, "it gives no indication whatsoever as to the nature, status, or identity of these [borrowers]."[16] Shirley was a public figure and many names can be associated with him, but only one can be shown to have had direct literary relations with him: a squire called Richard Sellyng, a fellow retainer in Warwick's household, sent him a poem which ends with the plea,

  to amende where it is amisse;
And also for pleasaunce and for disporte,
And for olde acqueintance, & newe resorte
That is fallen to us boþe now by grace,
Þat we may mete daylye in on place
And assemble to speke of thynges trewe,
Off fern yeeris alsoo oure talis renuwe.[17]

[To correct its errors, and also for pleasure and amusement, and for the sake of our old friendship, thankfully recently renewed, so that we can now get together every day and speak about actual events and reminisce about old times.]

This is a touching little insight into the familiar relationship of two old retainers who had served together in the same household, but as the basis for program of literary interpretation, let alone as evidence for a well-established textual community it is clearly less than adequate.

As the example of John Shirley suggests, medieval anthologies offer a particularly fertile field for speculation about implied textual communities for it is natural for us to wonder what principles underlie the selection of anthologized items and for whose benefit the selections were made. In most cases, however, it is unlikely that these questions can ever be answered with complete satisfaction. Three fourteenth-century anthologies, in particular, have generated a great deal of speculation of this kind: the Auchinleck manuscript (National Library of Scotland, MS Advocates 19.2.1), a collection (probably made in London in the 1330s) particularly famous for its romances; the so-called Harley manuscript (British Library, MS Harley 2253), a rich collection of courtly, religious, and satirical verse, written in English, Latin, and French in Herefordshire in the 1340s; and the Vernon manuscript (Bodley, MS Eng. poet. a. 1), a vast collection of religious poetry (including the A-text of *Piers Plowman*, the version generally considered the earliest) written in the west of England in the last decade of the fourteenth century. It has been claimed that Geoffrey Chaucer knew the Auchinleck manuscript (since it contains versions of many of the romances he parodies in *Sir Thopas*), but other than the obvious inference that it would have looked rather old-fashioned to royal courtiers in the late fourteenth century, it is difficult to say much more about the attitudes of its early readers; there is general agreement that it is of London provenance, but whether is was written for aristocrats or professionals, or even for a predominantly male or female audience, remains uncertain. We are on safer grounds with the Harley manuscript since Carter Revard has devoted a lifetime to searching out legal documents copied in the hand of its scribe and to building up a picture of the circle of gentry families around Ludlow in Shropshire with whom he did business;[18] even so, when it comes to describing their literary tastes and their reading habits, we must fall back on the internal evidence of the manuscript itself and, as so often, on the patently circular argument that this is the kind of thing they appreciated because this is the kind of thing that was available to them. There is some evidence that the Vernon manuscript (which has a sister volume, the Simeon manuscript, now in the British Library) was copied in a religious house, such as Bordesley Abbey in Worcestershire; its great size suggests that it was intended for public reading but what precisely this implies in terms of a textual community is far less easy to establish. Indeed it remains unclear whether it, too, was intended for a primarily male or female audience.[19] In one sense, of course, every medieval monastery, where the reading, copying, and studying of religious texts was a routine activity, constituted an *ipso facto* textual community (and a strong case could be made for one particular fifteenth-century foundation, that of the nuns of Syon Abbey, forming an important interpretive community as well), but whether the house where the Vernon and Simeon manuscripts were copied was distinctive in its literary tastes, or how precisely it approached the reading and interpretation of these vernacular texts, is now impossible to know for certain.

Not only are these anthologists and most of the works they anthologized anonymous, but much of their material seems to have been designed for recitation or even (in the case of the lyric verse) for singing, so that reconstructing an original textual community for them raises serious theoretical as well as practical objections. Can, for instance, the audience for an oral performance, even where the work is being read from the page rather than recited from memory, be properly categorized as textual? The question is equally relevant for an anonymous romance like *Sir Gawain and the Green Knight*, even though it was evidently composed by a highly literate and exceptionally skilled poet. In the case of an identifiable author whose life-history is well known to us, such as Geoffrey Chaucer, the problems are rather different. There is a famous near-contemporary picture that purports to show Chaucer reading his *Troilus and Criseyde* to a group of elegant courtiers (it is the frontispiece to a *Troilus* manuscript in Corpus Christi College, Cambridge), but the value of such an image as a guide to his actual audience is clearly limited.[20] Certainly we should not look to those who may have heard Chaucer reading his poems aloud for his primary literary community, but rather to the far smaller circle of his close associates. Paul Strohm has narrowed down Chaucer's known acquaintances to a core group of "several knights in royal and civil service whom Chaucer knew in the 1370s and 1380s, including William Beauchamp, Lewis Clifford, Philip la Vache, John Clanvowe, William Nevill, and Richard Stury; London acquaintances of the 1380s, including Ralph Strode and (with certain qualifications) John Gower; and newcomers of the 1390s, including Henry Scogan and Peter Bukton."[21] Notable for their exclusion from this list of intimates are the writers Thomas Usk and Thomas Hoccleve, the first as a probable parvenu and the second as being too young. Strohm makes quite clear the criteria for those included on his list: (1) their "involvement with the affairs of Richard II," (2) their occupation of "social positions like Chaucer's own," and (3) their manifestation of "some degree of literary predisposition, either as owners of books, as addressees in contexts that suggest their capacity for appreciation, or as writers in their own right" (pp. 42–44). Despite a great deal of evidence for shared literary sensibilities within this group (most of its members are either addressed by Chaucer in his works, or are themselves the authors of "chaucerian" poems), Strohm is clearly right to categorize this as a "circle" rather than a "textual community." No doubt they shared a similar interpretive horizon, but their assumption of a shared textual consciousness appears to have been too ingrained ever to be a dominant factor in their self-fashioning.

When Paul Strohm excluded Thomas Usk and Thomas Hoccleve from Chaucer's circle, he did not even consider William Langland as a candidate, but more recently there has been a movement, associated primarily with Katherine Kerby-Fulton and Steven Justice, to construct a rival (bureaucratic) circle (or coterie) linking Langland with Chaucer and including not only Thomas Hoccleve and Thomas Usk, but a number of "civil servants and legal clerks, many of whom participated in book production themselves."[22] One of the key features of their argument is the fact that one of the scribes (the so-called Scribe D) who copied early manuscripts of Gower and Chaucer (working in one case with Thomas Hoccleve), also copied an important manuscript of *Piers Plowman*, and strong reinforcement for their position has recently been provided by Linne Mooney's claim that a professional scribe called Adam Pinkhurst (who may well be the Adam Scriveyn to whom Chaucer addressed a celebrated short poem) also copied a manuscript of *Piers Plowman* (and also worked with Hoccleve).[23] Though there is a danger in all this of confusing what Ralph Hanna has called "transmissional" and "authorial" communities, we can hardly doubt that these discoveries have added enormously to our knowledge of Chaucer, Langland (and Gower), and the conditions under which they worked.[24]

However, whether we see Chaucer as participating in a courtly coterie (with Strohm) or a bureaucratic one (with Kerby-Fulton) is finally less important than the recognition that neither of these could ever have constituted a full textual community in Stock's sense. For a group of heretics in Norfolk, a circle of pious ladies in Suffolk, or even a magnate's household in Gloucestershire, thinking textually may still have been a novel and exciting experience, but it was clearly second nature to men like Chaucer and Langland. Indeed there is evidence that some writers at this period were striving to free themselves from the tyranny of a textual identity: in their different ways, what Kerby-Fulton calls Langland's "bibliographic ego," and what Ethan Knapp sees as the "mutually constitutive" language of bureaucracy and autobiography in Hoccleve, are both symptomatic of an awareness that their textual roles might sometimes be more stifling than liberating.[25] Even Chaucer's much-discussed ironic persona might be read as an elegant response to this dilemma. Paradoxically, then, the more that manuscript studies prove the world of Chaucer, Langland, Gower, and Hoccleve to have been thoroughly textual (in other words, the closer we see these writers bound together by the routine mechanics of textuality), the less meaningful it becomes to talk of their circles as "textual communities." In late fourteenth-century Westminster we are surely moving toward something more like Fish's "interpretive communities" where, heuristically at least, we might conceive of someone asking Richard II, "is there a text in this court?"

NOTES

1 Stanley Fish, *Is There a Text in this Class? The Authority of Interpretive Communities* (Cambridge, MA: Harvard University Press, 1980), esp. pp. 303–71.
2 Brian Stock, *The Implications of Literacy: Written Language and Models of Interpretation in the Eleventh and Twelfth Centuries* (Princeton University Press, 1983), p. 88.
3 Anne Hudson, *The Premature Reformation: Wycliffite Texts and Lollard History* (Oxford: Clarendon Press, 1988), pp. 174–200.
4 Stock, *Implications of Literacy*, p. 91.
5 Margaret Aston, *Lollards and Reformers: Images and Literacy in Late Medieval Religion* (London: The Hambledon Press, 1984), pp. 193–217.
6 *Heresy Trials in the Diocese of Norwich, 1428–31*, ed. Norman P. Tanner, Camden Society, 4th ser., vol. 20 (London: Royal Historical Society, 1977), pp. 178–79 (spelling modernized).
7 "Some Norfolk Women and Their Books, *c.* 1390–1440," in *The Cultural Patronage of Medieval Women*, ed. June Hall McCash (Athens: University of Georgia Press, 1996), p. 291.
8 Nicholas Watson, "Censorship and Cultural Change in Late-Medieval England: Vernacular Theology, the Oxford Translation Debate, and Arundel's Constitutions of 1409," *Speculum* 70 (1995), 822–64.
9 Osbern Bokenham, *Legendys of Hooly Wummen*, ed. Mary S. Serjeantson, EETS, OS 206 (London: Oxford University Press, 1938), p. 138. Subsequent citations are to this edition.
10 A. S. G. Edwards, "The Transmission and Audience of Osbern Bokenham's *Legendys of Hooly Wummen*," in *Late-Medieval Religious Texts and their Transmission: Essays in Honour of A. I. Doyle*, ed. A. J. Minnis (Woodbridge: D. S. Brewer, 1994), pp. 163–65.
11 Karen A. Winstead, *Virgin Martyrs: Legends of Sainthood in Late Medieval England* (Ithaca, NY: Cornell University Press, 1997), p. 129.
12 Ralph Hanna III, "Sir Thomas Berkeley and His Patronage," *Speculum* 64 (1989), 878–916.

13 Margaret Connolly, *John Shirley: Book Production and the Noble Household in Fifteenth-Century England* (Aldershot: Ashgate, 1998).
14 Hanna, "Sir Thomas Berkeley," 900–01.
15 See the article on John Shirley in the *ODNB* by Jeremy Griffiths.
16 Connolly, *John Shirley*, pp. 193, 208 (ll. 97–98) and 210 (ll. 81–82) (spelling modernized).
17 Ibid., 190 (modern punctuation and word-division added).
18 Carter Revard, "Scribe and Provenance," in *Studies in the Harley Manuscript: the Scribes, Contents, and Social Contexts of British Library MS Harley 2253*, ed. Susanna Fein (Kalamazoo: Medieval Institute Publications, 2000), 21–109.
19 See N. F. Blake, "Vernon Manuscript: Contents and Organization," in *Studies in the Vernon Manuscript*, ed. Derek Pearsall (Cambridge: D. S. Brewer, 1990), p. 58.
20 Derek Pearsall, "The 'Troilus' Frontispiece and Chaucer's Audience," *YES* 7 (1977), 68–74.
21 Paul Strohm, *Social Chaucer* (Cambridge, MA: Harvard University Press, 1989), p. 41.
22 Kathryn Kerby-Fulton and Steven Justice, "Langlandian Reading Circles and the Civil Service in London and Dublin, 1380–1427," *NML* 1 (1997), 70.
23 A. I. Doyle and M. B. Parkes, "The Production of Copies of the *Canterbury Tales* and the *Confessio Amantis* in the Early Fifteenth Century," in *Medieval Scribes, Manuscripts & Libraries: Essays Presented to N. R. Ker*, ed. M. B. Parkes and Andrew G. Watson (London: Scolar Press, 1978), pp. 163–210; Linne Mooney, "Chaucer's Scribe," *Speculum* 81 (2006), 97–138.
24 Ralph Hanna, "Reconsidering the Auchinleck Manuscript," in *New Directions in Later Medieval Manuscript Studies: Essays from the 1998 Harvard Conference*, ed. Derek Pearsall (Rochester, NY: York Medieval Press, 2000), p. 102.
25 Kathryn Kerby-Fulton, "Langland and the Bibliographic Ego," in *Written Work: Langland, Labor, and Authorship*, eds. Steven Justice and Kathryn Kerby-Fulton (Philadelphia: University of Pennsylvania Press, 1997), pp. 67–143; Ethan Knapp, "Bureaucratic Identity and the Construction of Self in Hoccleve's *Formulary* and *La male regle*," *Speculum* 74 (1999), 357–76.

3

RICHARD NEWHAUSER

Religious writing: hagiography, *pastoralia*, devotional and contemplative works

The bulk of extant Middle English literature is made up of a wide variety of religious works. This chapter will deal with three prominent categories: hagiography, or the narrative presentation of the lives of saints and the holy family; contemplative and devotional writings, or mystical and meditative presentations of the desire for not just salvation, but perfection; and *pastoralia*, or edification in matters of doctrine by sermons, catechetical texts, and other pastoral writings. It should be stressed that these headings represent differences of emphasis and not unbridgeable distinctions, for catechetical purposes may be fulfilled by a saint's life and catechetical manuals may offer a reader the aesthetic pleasure provided by narrative. In fact, no literary form can be limited to only one function alone, and no function can be fulfilled exclusively by one type of literature.[1] Moreover, prominent and broad as these categories are, they do not include, for example, descriptions of ritual practice (religious, but intended as workaday guides, especially to the administration of the sacraments), or books on monastic organization (religious, but often meant to be more practical than inspirational), as well as philosophical works like Middle English translations from Cicero (inspirational and ethical, but not strictly speaking religious). Middle English works of religious inspiration were produced in an environment that tended to favor their preservation in manuscripts, unlike more ephemeral texts such as drama or some lyric poetry. Nevertheless, there is no doubting their preponderance among all vernacular works produced in the Middle English period or their cultural importance.

Taken as a whole, there are many more works of religious inspiration preserved in Middle English than are represented in any other category of literary production in English in the high and late Middle Ages. Individually, as well, these works were often transmitted in many more manuscripts than most other Middle English texts. Such is the case, first of all, with Scripture itself, for there are over 250 extant manuscripts of the Wycliffite translation of the Bible. *The Pricke of Conscience*, a poetic meditation on the wretchedness of the world and the popular understanding of the four last things (death, judgment of the soul, the pains of hell, and the joys of heaven), is preserved in the largest number of manuscripts (more than 120) of any work written originally in Middle English. Because *The Pricke of Conscience* was also transmitted throughout all of England and is preserved in every dialect of the language, it has a genuine claim to be known as the most popular English work of the Middle Ages. Other texts of religious inspiration enjoyed wide circulation, as well: the popular collection of English saints' lives, *The South English Legendary* (*SEL*), composed in the last quarter of the thirteenth century and the earliest poem to achieve a national audience in England, has been transmitted in more than sixty manuscripts, for example; Nicholas Love's early fifteenth-century *The Mirror of the Blessed Life of Jesus Christ*, a translation and adaptation of an early Franciscan work in Latin that circulated widely in England, is also extant in more than sixty manuscripts; and *Speculum Vitae*, a catechetical poem of the third quarter of the fourteenth century derived from the *Somme le roi*, is preserved in forty codices.[2] Furthermore, the transmission of some works of religious inspiration in English, Latin, and French versions testifies to the wide variety of readers – socially, politically, and geographically – who were among the audience for the texts. The *Ancrene Riwle*, part practical, part contemplative guide composed for three lay anchoresses in the first quarter of the thirteenth century, is extant in all three of these languages. It is characteristic of works of religious inspiration in England that even large pastoral manuals circulating in the British Isles in French (*Somme le roi*, [lit. "Compendium for the King"] *Manuel des péchés* ["Manual of Sins"], and *Miroir du monde* ["Mirror of the World"] and Latin (especially the *Summa de vitiis et virtutibus* by the Dominican William Peraldus [lit. "Compendium of Vices and Virtues"] attracted English derivatives and translations, often with a self-conscious recognition of the needs of a local reading public: Dan Michel of Northgate, who completed the *Ayenbite of Inwyt*, a close translation of the *Somme le roi*, in Canterbury in 1340, noted that he had composed this work in the local dialect for the moral edification of mothers and fathers in Kent.[3]

The authorship of most of the works of religious inspiration is not known, but there is more involved in this phenomenon than the general state of anonymity of the majority of medieval works. It is clear that the preponderance of these Middle English texts was written by clerics or men in religious orders, and that their anonymity is the literary reflex of an attitude of pious humility that the authors of the texts meant to embody and share with their audiences. This outlook is well represented in the prologue of

The Pore Caitif, a popular late fourteenth-century compendium of biblical, devotional, mystical, and catechetical material assembled probably by a clerical author for lay instruction: "This tretyse," the text begins, was "compiled of a pore caityf and nedy of gostly help of al cristen peple ..." (this treatise [was] compiled by a poor wretch who is in need of spiritual help from all Christians).[4] Beyond this, however, many of the religious texts produced in England are programmatically anonymous, which is to say that they represent the subsuming of the individual voice of the author in a "corporate" system of ecclesiastically regulated discourse. Concrete details within the authors' time-bound framework were, of course, an essential element of these works, but in this literature the historically limited details from medieval England did not aim for topicality – they served the purposes of the author in supporting a position in a moral universe viewed as eternal. By the early fifteenth century, moreover, there were also more urgent political reasons for remaining anonymous. Lollards (heretical followers of the Oxford theologian John Wycliffe), wished to avoid the repercussions of their beliefs, while orthodox writers whose texts might be appropriated by Lollards, wished to avoid the accusation of heretical sympathies. In these cases, remaining nameless was not only an allegiance to the ideology of humility; it was also a political expediency.

The audience of the works of religious inspiration changed over the course of the high and late Middle Ages in a clear direction, from clergy or religious – whether members of an order or not – to include the secular laity, as well. This is not to say, however, that all of the initial readership of Middle English religious texts was male, for a number of important early thirteenth-century works from the West Midlands were designed for female readers: *Ancrene Riwle* and texts closely related to it in dialect, time of composition, and probable place of origin in the "Wooing Group" (a series of prayers in rhythmic prose, including such pieces as *On Lofsong of Ure Lefdi* [A Love-Song for Our Lady], *Þe Oreisun of Seinte Marie* [The Prayer of Saint Mary], and *Þe Wohunge of Ure Lauerd* [The Wooing of Our Lord]) were composed for female religious. The *Ancrene Wisse* also continued to exert an influence on ascetic ideals throughout the Middle Ages, traveling across borders of gender affiliation and geographical location in ways that constantly transformed what had been intended originally as a text for recluses. The canons of the Fourth Lateran Council (1215–16) which led to an increased emphasis on pastoral instruction, with the initial goal being a better-educated clergy itself, also resulted eventually in the growth of educational tools in English designed to facilitate the clergy's tutelage of the laity (and even – within limits – a father's schooling of his children) in catechetical matters, in particular within the framework of preaching and confession, but in a variety of other contexts as well. In all of this, the clergy continued to exert an influence in the production, transmission, and content of books of instruction destined for the laity. The authors of many of these works consciously note that they have composed their texts for the unlearned, and this is especially true for the late fourteenth and early fifteenth centuries, when instruction in the elements of orthodox belief was also a way to counteract the influence of Lollardy. In the *Memoriale credencium* (lit. "Reminder to the Faithful"), for example, composed in Gloucestershire in the first half of the fifteenth century, the author observes that "this tretys is y made to ensaumple of þe commune puple þat can nouȝt vnderstonde latyn ne frensh and for cristen men þat leueþ in god shuld haue þyngus þat here beþ y wrytt ofte yn mynde" (this treatise has been composed as an example for the common people who cannot understand Latin or French and so that Christians who believe in God may often keep in mind the things written here).[5]

By the fifteenth century, the laity gained access to much of the same kind of contemplative and devotional material that had earlier typified works intended for the recluses of the thirteenth century: in Winchester College MS 33, for example, a mid-fifteenth-century miscellany produced perhaps in Winchester itself, one finds along with other kinds of texts also contemplative material like *The Abbey of the Holy Ghost* and *The Charter of the Abbey of the Holy Ghost*, which had both been included in the late fourteenth-century summation of vernacular spirituality contained within the Vernon manuscript (Oxford, Bodleian Library MS Eng. poet. a.1), as well as selections from *SEL*.[6] This lay appropriation of the texts of religious inspiration also came to supersede direct clerical control and to make hagiographical, contemplative and devotional, and catechetical texts a matter of lay promulgation and organization, perhaps from a corpus of texts that could be combined to match the predilections of individual readers. In a few cases it also resulted, in privileged and mercantile circles in fifteenth-century London, in a method to fund, collect, and circulate vernacular spiritual texts in volumes which described themselves as "common-profit books." These volumes, which provided pious texts for reading in the lay household, were paid for by the estates of well-to-do merchants and were explicitly intended to circulate among many readers and to pass in ownership from one person to the next, both men and women, as long as the book was in existence. They, and other volumes like them of the mid- to late-fifteenth century, testify to the ways in which powerful merchants in London justified their position in spiritual terms as an urban elite.

Hagiography

From its inception in the early Middle Ages, the writing of saints' lives had served the purpose of exciting the minds of Christian readers to imaginative association with the paradigmatic deeds of holy men and women. Because the essential paradigm for these sacred biographies was provided by Jesus' triumphant victory over torture and death, the narrative structure of saints' lives was comedic, not tragic: no matter how severe the martyrdom and how horrifying the pains suffered by the saints, their lives provided testimony of the ultimate rise in fortunes conveyed by sanctification. Saints' lives played a crucial role in the literary culture of medieval England by making this ideology apprehensible in the dramatized deeds of men and women. At the same time, they provided an outlet for narrative innovation, catechetical teaching, and social critique. The Middle English vocabulary used to describe this genre was based on the equivalent Latin terminology, but designations like "legende" (Lat. *legenda*) and "lyf" (Lat. *vita*) were often applied in a less technical way. Nevertheless, when Chaucer's Miller announces that he will requite the Knight's use of pagan antiquity by telling "a legende and a lyf / Bothe of a carpenter and of his wyf," the audience would have anticipated, and appreciated the irony of not receiving, a hagiographical treatment of the holy family, a subject that had grown in importance in Middle English literature by the end of the fourteenth century.[7]

A passage in the early thirteenth-century *Seinte Marherete þe Meiden ant Martyr*, along with the lives of Saint Katherine and Saint Julianna part of the "Katherine Group" closely associated with the *Ancrene Riwle* and like it localized in the West Midlands, gives a view of the way in which the efficacy of a saint's life could be imagined. In her final prayers, Saint Margaret beseeches her audience that "hwa-so-eauer boc writ of mi liflade, oðer biȝet hit iwriten, oðer halt hit ant haueð oftest an honde, oðer hwa-so hit eauer redeð, oðer þene redere liðeliche lustnið, weldent of heouene, wurðe ham alle sone hare sunnen forȝeuene" (whoever writes a book about my life, or acquires it once it is written, or holds it very often in hand, or whoever reads it, or gladly listens to someone reading it, oh ruler of heaven, forgive them quickly for their sins).[8] The lives in the Katherine Group are prose texts, and they are indicative of both the continuity of composition in English from the Anglo-Saxon period through the Norman Conquest and the tenuous position of English as a literary language under the dominance of writing in French and Latin in the early Middle English period. As variations on the hagiographical narrative of the virgin martyr, the three saints' lives also reinforce the view that the protagonists were designed to appeal especially to those living a life of holy virginity, though it has also been speculated that these lives had a general lay audience as well: in each life, a young Christian virgin, who is also a member of the nobility, rebuffs the efforts of a pagan ruler to convince her to turn her back on her religion. After enduring imprisonment and torture, and inspiring many conversions to Christianity, the young woman is beheaded and reaps the reward of life in heaven. As such, the three saints are endowed with a good deal of agency, something which one will only see increase in later saints' lives of virgin martyrs.

Produced in the last quarter of the thirteenth century, *SEL* was copied and expanded for almost two centuries and versions of it are represented in all regions of England. Its earliest form, found in Oxford, Bodleian Library MS Laud misc. 108, demonstrates that the structure of *SEL* is based on the moveable feasts connected with the life of Jesus, such as Advent and Easter (the *temporale* cycle of the liturgical calendar) and on the fixed days for the feasts of saints (the *sanctorale* cycle). Two manuscripts from the early fourteenth century (London, British Library MS Harley 2277, and Cambridge, Corpus Christi College MS 145) contain a version that adds the lives of Judas and Pilate at the end of the text and is organized according to the calendar of the secular year. The most inclusive version of the text is found in Oxford, Bodleian Library MS Bodley 779, from the fifteenth century, which adds twenty-seven legends to the collection, fourteen of which are unique to this text in Middle English literature. Both of the earlier versions were compiled in the area of Gloucestershire and Worcestershire, though it is unclear whether the text originated in a religious house there, and doubtful whether *SEL* was limited to consumption by religious: it has much about it that would have appealed to the laity as well, including the lives of saints of national importance (Wulfstan, Cuthbert, Oswald, Edmund Rich, Augustine of Canterbury). In a way that demonstrates some of the connections between the saint's life genre and that of medieval romance, the prologue, in fact, emphasizes the qualities of the lives as action narratives as much as texts of religious edification:

> Men wilneþ muche to hure telle . of bataille of kynge
> And of kniȝtes þat hardy were . þat muchedel is lesynge
> Wo so wilneþ muche to hure . tales of suche þinge
> Hardi batailles he may hure . here þat nis no lesinge
> Of apostles & martirs . þat hardy kniȝtes were
> Þat studeuast were in bataille . & ne fleide noȝt for fere ...[9]

[People desire very much to hear someone tell about the battle of a king and of knights who were brave, though it is generally a matter of falsehood. Whoever desires very much to hear stories of such matters, he can hear about bold battles here that contain no falsehood: of apostles and martyrs who were brave knights, who were steadfast in battle and did not flee for fear ...]

O. S. Pickering has argued that early forms of the collection functioned as both instruction and entertainment through oral delivery to a less-educated audience, but other scholars have noted that the oral formulas may be merely conventions of composition, as they frequently are in the genre of romance, and not indications of the method of delivery.[10]

An indication of the importance of the genre of saints' lives is the degree to which writers of other literary genres felt called on to compose their own hagiographic texts, as well. Geoffrey Chaucer, for example, included two legends in *The Canterbury Tales*: the *Second Nun's Tale* and the *Prioress's Tale* (though the romance of Custance in the *Man of Law's Tale* has many points of contact with saints' lives, too). The first of these, often called the finest saint's life in Middle English, is a virgin martyr narrative of Saint Cecilia, whose alleged martyrdom at Rome was first related in an account of the late fifth to mid-sixth century. In writing the narrative and its prologue, Chaucer drew on Dante's *Paradiso*, Jacobus de Voragine's *Legenda aurea*, and a liturgical abridgement of the Latin *Passion of St. Cecilia* used in the Vatican and by the Franciscans.[11] In Chaucer's work, as well as in the "Katherine Group,", the implications of the protagonist's agency go far beyond the story itself, for Cecilia acts as a preacher, instructing Tiburce in theological matters such as the Trinity (VIII.337–41) and salvation history (VIII.342–47), and she skillfully debates philosophical matters with Almachius, proving his wisdom to be foolishness and his sight blindness (VIII.421–511). The legend demonstrates a relation between women as preachers and teachers in the late Middle Ages and the importance of lay devotion and education. In this, the tale reveals an engagement with contemporary issues that belies its setting in late-antique Rome. Cecilia's transformation of her marriage to Valerian into a chaste arrangement (VIII.141–61) is part of her confrontation with, and victory over, secular authority – and Chaucer is considered to have composed the tale precisely in a period (*c.* 1373–86) in which challenges to secular authority had resulted in the open rebellion of 1381. As opposed to the purity and simplicity of the church of Cecilia and Urban, however, Chaucer's fractured and schism-riven church could only look to its origins as a lost ideal.

Contemporary interests can be registered again in the *Prioress's Tale*, a representative of the genre of miracles of the Virgin in which the child protagonist is treated as a saint. The narrative is set in a metropolis in Asia in which Jews cut the throat of a young Christian who is devoted to Mary as he walks through a ghetto. They then throw him into a latrine.

Miraculously, the child does not stop singing an antiphon to the Virgin until a seed is removed from his tongue that Mary had placed there. The Prioress specifically calls the child a "martir" (VII.680) when she narrates his entombment, and then she connects this geographically distant story to her own society by gratuitously referencing the story of Hugh of Lincoln, whose "martydom" at the hands of Jews took place in 1255:

O yonge Hugh of Lyncoln, slayn also
With cursed Jewes, as it is notable,
For it is but a litel while ago,
Praye eek for us ... (VII.684–87)

[Oh, young Hugh of Lincoln, slain also by cursed Jews, as is well known, for it happened only a short while ago, pray for us also ...]

As Lee Patterson has argued, the typological ahistoricism which sees an event occurring 150 years ago as having happened in the recent past is fitting for a cloistered narrator who has sworn to withdraw from the historical life, but it and the emotional anti-Semitism of the tale and its constant invocations of the Virgin also amount to a short-circuit of the "inwardness and penitential self-examination" of contemplative and devotional writers in Middle English.[12] As such, the Prioress demonstrates indirectly yet another form of critique of contemporary practices within the Church.

Though we do not know a great deal about the early reception of *SEL* and other early Middle English collections of saints' lives, some later legendaries and individual lives of saints have been transmitted with more extensive indications of their initial audiences. John Lydgate increased the variety of presentations of saints' lives normally included in English legendaries, composing many very brief invocations to saints as well as more complete narratives of their lives, and he often dedicated his works explicitly to guilds or other institutions, both lay and religious. He undertook the rhetorically ornate *Life of Saints Edmund and Fremund* at the request of William Curteys, abbot of his own Benedictine house in Bury St. Edmunds, to commemorate Henry VI's celebration of Christmas at the monastery in 1433. One of the manuscripts of the text (London, British Library MS Harley 2278) contains an illumination of the poet presenting his poem to the King. Lydgate's *Legend of St. George* was undertaken at the request of the guild of armorers in London "for þonour of þeyre broþerhoode and þeyre feest of Saint George" (in honor of their guild and their feast of Saint George).[13] The prologue emphasizes the same connection with knighthood seen already in *SEL*, but Lydgate stresses the decorousness of Saint George's connection with the Order of the Garter rather than the romance adventures of knightly battles (ll. 5–14, p. 145). Lydgate's major hagiographical work is his *Life of Our Lady*, extant in nearly fifty manuscript copies and in early printed editions as well. Like Thomas Hoccleve's many poems for the Virgin, Lydgate's major work testifies to the growing importance of the life of the holy family for late-medieval spirituality, though his work is more a series of hymns to Mary than a sustained narrative of her life, a text which may have been meant for oral delivery to members of a monastic community, but was able to be adapted to the needs of a courtly audience and their meditative listening as well.

The production of saints' lives was at times markedly gendered in the later Middle Ages, as women came to play a much larger role in the composition and consumption of literary texts. Osbern Bokenham (b. *c.* 1392), for example, composed in a variety of verse forms the lives of thirteen female saints between 1443 and 1447 while he was in the Augustinian priory at Clare, Suffolk, which was one of a number of centers in fifteenth-century East Anglia that provided vernacular books to lay audiences. The thirteen legends were collected and copied for Friar Thomas Burgh in 1447 in Cambridge to be presented to a nunnery in the only surviving copy of the collection: London, British Library MS Arundel 327. Bokenham did not compose the lives as a fully-formed legendary, but rather as separate booklets of saints' lives that were often dedicated to lay, female readers, in some cases with the identical names of the holy protagonists of the narratives: to Katherine Denston and Katherine Howard he dedicated his *Life of St. Katherine*; to Agatha Flegge, his *Life of St. Agatha*; and to Elizabeth de Vere, Countess of Oxford, his narrative of Saint Elizabeth. These booklets of female saints circulated among the pious, lay women in East Anglia who served as Bokenham's patronesses before he sent the legends to be published as a whole for female religious. The models provided by the saints in Bokenham's work are applied directly and with a single-minded purpose to the literary tastes of female readers.

The use of saints' lives for both doctrinal instruction and entertainment remained constant throughout the Middle English period, and Caxton's preface to his translation of *The Golden Legend* returns us to the perceived utility of saints' legends, especially for the tutoring of the uneducated reader. As Caxton notes, he began work on this book "to incyte and exhorte men and wymmen to kepe them from slouthe and ydlenesse and to lete to be understonden to suche peple as been not letterd the natyvytees, the lyves, the passyons, the myracles, and the dethe of the holy sayntes" (to urge and exhort men and women to restrain themselves from sloth and idleness and to make comprehensible to people who are not educated the births, lives, sufferings, miracles, and deaths of the saints).[14] Caxton printed his text in 1483 and it was reprinted numerous times to 1527. It is based on a fifteenth-century revision of Jean de Vignay's mid-fourteenth-century French translation of the *Legenda aurea* (of which an earlier translation into English had been published that is commonly known at the *Gilte Legende*), to which Caxton added material from the original Latin collection and the *Gilte Legende* as well. Its nearly 250 legends, composed in an aureate and formal style, can be seen as a fitting culmination of collections of medieval English saints' lives.

Contemplative and devotional writing

Literature focused on the examination of the interior spiritual life and the desire for perfection had developed extensively in Latin since the twelfth century and the great writings on monastic spirituality by the Cistercian authors Bernard of Clairvaux and William of St. Thierry (formerly a Benedictine), and the Victorines Hugh and Richard of St. Victor. At what point the more speculative interests of this theology began to influence writers in England is unclear because so many of the early texts composed by Anglo-Latin writers remain unedited and unstudied. These interests can be registered clearly, however, by the fourteenth century in the work of Richard Rolle and his successors in the practice of "vernacular theology."[15] Like Rolle's texts, almost all of the English works by contemplatives are in prose and have in this way a certain immediacy of style in spite of their often ineffable subject matter. Whereas the critique of ecclesiastical institutions that had developed in hagiographical writings is often indirect, contemplative writers in Middle English are at times outspoken about their political positions, sometimes delivering a clear and uncompromising challenge to the Church hierarchy or, as is the case with Walter Hilton and Nicholas Love, defending the Church against detractors.

Rolle (d. 1349) was active as a self-proclaimed hermit and spiritual adviser in Yorkshire in the 1330s and 1340s. Eventually he withdrew to a cell there in Hampole to be close to Margaret Kirkby, a nun he counseled. His *Form of Living* was composed for her in 1349 on the occasion of her leaving the cloister in order to be enclosed in a solitary cell. Rolle wrote numerous works in Latin early in his career before turning to English near its end. *The Form of Living* and *Ego Dormio*, another tract of advice addressed to a contemplative, give a good view of the ecstatic mysticism counseled by Rolle. The important first step is for men or women to separate themselves from the wretchedness of a life bound to deadly sin. Then they are to open their hearts to God; to pray, meditate, and weep; to avoid temptations or worldly thoughts; and to open the eye of their souls to God – at which point the fire of love (feelingly defined in the poem "Love is life," pp. 42–44) will burn in their hearts and, ravished by it, "þai seth in to heuyn with har gostly eigh" (they contemplate heaven with their spiritual sight).[16] Rolle, the first authority on the spiritual life in England, remained influential far past his lifetime, inspiring such works as *Contemplations of the Dread and Love of God* or *Þe Holy Boke Gratia Dei.*

The importance of contemplative writing to the political and spiritual life in England in the late Middle Ages emerges further in *Piers Plowman*, a poem many scholars have seen as an exercise in lay contemplation. Here, after the failures to regenerate society in the external actions of the Visio section (the disintegration of public morality in Lady Meed's ubiquitous bribery during her visit to the court, the disunity that replaces an initial period of estate cooperation in the plowing of the half acre), the continuing allegorical action turns inward in the Vita section and Will is instructed, in often competing ways, in the stages of spiritual perfection of "Dowel," "Dobet," and "Dobest." These are not to be seen as stages appropriate only for different kinds of life or related to specific sections of the poem, but they mark out steps for all Christians in a spiritual journey owing much to the contemporary literature of interiority – and peopled with such personifications as Kynde Witte, Conscience, and Ymaginatif – that culminates in the vision of the Tree of Charity. Yet, as the apocalyptic and open-ended conclusion of the B- and C-texts, or later, longer versions of the poem, demonstrates (C.22, B.20), Langland viewed the search for spiritual perfection as a continuing and unfinished process, given the corruption within the institution of the Church.

For the author of *The Cloud of Unknowing* and six other mystical pieces in Middle English, the ecstatic imagery of Rolle and Langland's allegory lie far from the essence of the contemplative life: as this proponent of negative theology explains in his Englishing of a Latin translation of Pseudo-Dionysius, *De mystica theologia*, God lies beyond reason and the sense impressions conveyed in imagery, "and his not-vnderstondable ouerpassyng is vn-vnderstondabely abouen alle affermyng and deniinge" (and his incomprehensible transcendence is, in a way not to be understood, beyond every affirmation and denial).[17] But the *Cloud*-author, active in the last quarter of the fourteenth century, finds it as easy to critique academics for their vain curiosity (*Cloud*, chap. 56) as other contemplatives for their failure to transcend sense-bound thinking. His particular audience, like the "spiritual friend in God" to whom the *Cloud* is addressed (pp. 7–8), comprises those who are already recluses and now can move to the final, perfect, stage of spiritual life. Such elitism is very much unlike the work of Walter Hilton (d. 1396) whose *Scale of Perfection* and the works of the *Cloud*-author contain verbal echoes of each other. Both men were active in the East Midlands, but Hilton wrote for audiences that included contemplatives (*Eight Chapters on Perfection*, translated from a lost Latin original, was meant for "men and wommen þat ȝeuen hem to perfeccioun" [men and women who dedicate themselves to achieving perfection]) as well as the laity.[18] For these groups he presents a systematic procedure of what can be achieved spiritually; thus, in the *Scale*, book 1 instructs a beginning anchoress in the foundations of the contemplative life (including the avoidance of the seven deadly sins) before, at the end of book 2, describing the completion of spiritual perfection. The text was versatile enough to be translated *c.* 1400 into Latin by Thomas Fyslake and to circulate widely in this version as well as in the original.

Hilton often defended the institution of the Church against the arguments of the Lollards. Nicholas Love, first prior of the Carthusians at Mount Grace, Yorkshire, in the early fifteenth century, went even further in this regard. A number of the manuscripts of his *Mirror of the Blessed Life of Jesus Christ*, translated and adapted from the *Meditaciones vite Christi* attributed to Johannes de Caulibus, announce that the text has been endorsed by Archbishop Arundel in particular to "disprove heretics or Lollards."[19] Love set out to make his work appealing to the same uneducated laity as he supposed might have been attracted to Lollard arguments by using emotive and affective images of the life of Jesus, since, as he says, the hope for salvation is nourished by the example of the good way of life led by "holy men writen in bokes" (p. 9). The work proved to be very popular, not only with the laity, but also to members of the upper classes and to religious.[20] In Love's text they found training for the "devout imagination," carefully orthodox and appealingly approved, that was focused on the biography of the central figure of spiritual perfection.

What the imagination could look like in its creative and unregulated flights can be seen in the work of two remarkable female visionaries: Julian of Norwich (d. after 1416) and Margery Kempe (d. *c.* 1440). While Julian lay deathly sick at Norwich in May, 1373, a crucifix was held before her eyes and in her heightened imagination it began to bleed and to yield a series of sixteen revelations, many of them concerned with Jesus' wounds during the passion, which she worked to interpret over the next twenty years as an anchoress. The results of her thinking about these visions exist in an early short text, and a later, perhaps uncirculated, long version. Although she describes herself as "leued" (uneducated) in the short text or says that she "cowde no letter" (was unable to read [Latin?]) in the long text, these statements have a self-protective role given the audacity of her visions and her self-interpretive model, especially in an age in which combating heresy had led elsewhere to widespread theological conservatism.[21] In fact, her writings demonstrate that she felt compelled to communicate her visions, and to do so beyond the circle of recluses in Norwich. Indeed, probably in 1413 Margery Kempe was inspired by the anchoress's reputation as a spiritual adviser to visit Julian while in Norwich. Kempe, from the port of King's Lynn in East Anglia, related the incidents of her *Book* to two scribes in the 1430s (one of whom apparently added material of his own to her account); the work survives in one slightly later manuscript (London, British Library MS Add. 61823) that had belonged to the Carthusians at Mount Grace but was unknown in modern times before 1934. Her *Book* is the memoir of her spiritual progress (along with her frequent, loud, and copious weeping), pilgrimages, conflicts with ecclesiastical authorities (who suspected she might be a Lollard), and visions (including her spiritual marriage to Jesus) into the period of the early 1430s. Her highly affective spirituality and her emphasis on Jesus' humanity are characteristics highlighted earlier in Nicholas Love's work, but in other ways, as well, Kempe looks back to previous texts by English contemplatives: as her *Book* notes, she was taught by a priest who read to her from the Bible, but also from works by Richard Rolle, and Hilton's *Scale*, among others. As eccentric as Kempe was, she also stands firmly in a line of English contemplatives who helped define spirituality for both religious and the laity in the late Middle Ages.

Pastoralia

The canons of the Fourth Lateran Council (1215–16) which enjoined education and pastoral duties on the clergy were made more precise in later English ecclesiastical legislation. Archbishop John Pecham's Lambeth Constitutions (1281) specified in article 9 (*Ignorancia sacerdotum*) what the content of pastoral teaching was to be in the province of Canterbury and, later, in York as well (the articles of the faith, the Decalogue, the dual precept of *caritas*, the deeds of mercy, the seven deadly sins and their progeny, the chief virtues, and the sacraments) and it ordered that this syllabus be taught four times a year in English. Archbishop Arundel's Constitutions (1407–09) confirmed this syllabus for the late Middle Ages throughout England. One must keep in mind, however, that the historical development of the outlook institutionalized in Pecham's Constitutions eventually led to the goal of vernacular education in *pastoralia* being achieved not just orally by the confessor or preacher first studying and then communicating doctrinal material to the unlearned, or by a congregant's recitation of convenient formulae in confession or catechetical instruction, but also by the act of reading in environments not specifically ecclesiastical in nature, whether private and solitary or public and communal, in religious communities or in households. The spread of literacy led to the incorporation of the goals of the Pecham syllabus into inspirational reading of many kinds and was accompanied by the enlargement of the original corpus of instruction, as well, such as one finds in the *Lay Folks' Catechism*, an English translation of Archbishop Thoresby's Latin catechism (1357) which supplemented the Pecham Constitutions, or in *The Lanterne of Liȝt* (composed 1409–14), a Wycliffite catechetical work that adds to the normal (and orthodox) corpus of *pastoralia* a Lollard exposition of the true Church.

The most direct, frequently repeated, and often lively method of instruction by the clergy in catechetical matters was through preaching, with its use of short narratives (*exempla*) and similitudes to catch the reader/listener's attention and make the apprehension of doctrine all the easier. Though most sermons from England have been preserved in Latin, whether or not they were preached in English, Latin, or a mixture of the two, an appreciable number of them have been preserved in the vernacular. These represent the full range of Sunday readings in the liturgical calendar, most frequently according to the Use of Sarum (the form of the liturgy used in the diocese of Salisbury that then spread throughout the south of medieval England), but also including texts for saints' days that lie close to the genre of saints' legends, such as John Mirk's very widely transmitted *Festial* (*c.* 1390), or sermons for Lent, such as those mentioned in the fifteenth-century catechetical treatise *Jacob's Well*, or sermons for special occasions (funerals, weddings, etc.). Because instruction in the vernacular was particularly important to the Wycliffites, as witnessed in the large number of their sermons preserved in English, Arundel's Constitutions and the violent suppression of the Lollard heresy had the effect of suppressing the recording of sermons in English from the late fourteenth until the middle of the fifteenth century. The English sermons that survive were often put together from a number of sources, some of them reflecting the popularity of earlier inspirational texts, such as *The Pore Caitif* or *Ancrene Wisse*. In some cases, otherwise orthodox sermons in English reveal their partial (and unconscious) debt to previous Lollard texts: such is the case with the collection of sermons from the late fifteenth century edited by Woodburn Ross which, as has been argued recently, represents the variety of subject matter available to English preachers in that period.[22]

Much of the production of works of pastoral instruction was in the hands of the secular clergy or the friars. They used many of the same techniques seen in the composition of sermons to create works on penance, confession, and treatises on vices and virtues. *A Litil Tretys on the Seven Deadly Sins* by the Carmelite friar Richard Lavynham (d. late fourteenth cent.), for example, is developed from what Lavynham represents as a number of

Scholastic and canonistic sources that he would have become acquainted with during his Oxford education, but its focal point is the popular image of the vices and their sub-sins, as is clear from the author's emphasis in the prologue on constructing his analysis of these elements of immorality around "figuris & ensamplis," that is to say, in particular, around similitudes connecting the vices and animals.[23] Lavynham's text might have been perfectly suitable for use by the laity, in either public or domestic reading, but it seems clear from its careful documentation of source material that it was designed primarily to be employed by the parish clergy or the friars, and more specifically for those clergymen or friars whose grasp of Latin and complex theological issues was limited. Monastic authors, too, early on joined in the education of the laity in matters of catechetical importance. An important example of this tendency is found in Robert Mannyng, member of the Gilbertine order in the late thirteenth and first half of the fourteenth century, whose *Handlyng Synne* (1303) was translated and adopted from the Anglo-Norman *Manuel des Pechiez*. The work is a storehouse of narrative *exempla* designed, as Mannyng points out throughout the long, poetic text, to serve the edification of both the clergy and the laity, for as he notes after his presentation of the sacrament of the Eucharist, he has spoken:

> Nat to lered onely but eke to lewed.
> ȝe lewed men, y telle hyt ȝow,
> Þese clerkes kunne hyt weyl ynow.[24]

[Not only to the educated, but also to the uneducated. / You uneducated people, I tell this to you; / The clergy know it well enough.]

Handlyng Synne is a subtle work, alive to the difficulties of treating sin without becoming mired in sin itself, and aware of the ways in which sins constantly undo the borders between each other or disguise themselves as virtues. Mannyng's work is testimony to the difficulty of any narrative containing, or being contained by, a discursive statement of teaching.

About the religious status of other authors we are unsure. The *Book for a Simple and Devout Woman*, composed *c.* 1400 in the West Midlands and preserved in two manuscripts, was designed with an eye to sacramental needs. Its two most important sources, William Peraldus's *Summa de vitiis et virtutibus* and Friar Laurent's *Somme le roi* (composed 1280 for the use of King Phillippe III of France), played important roles in disseminating material useful for confession. The epilogue of the *Book* addresses the work to an unnamed secular woman and indicates the importance of the sacrament explicitly: "Of penaunce and of hardschip siker buþ þe weyes, and of contemplacion vnstabele and somdel to drede" (the paths of penitence and ascetic living are certain, but of contemplation they are unsure and somewhat frightening).[25] Nevertheless, the epilogue also emphasizes the importance of maintaining a correct internal vision, which demonstrates that for both the author and his intended audience self-examination remained an important contemplative enterprise in its own right. Furthermore, many of the Middle English texts closely affiliated with the *Book* also had more inspirational uses than preparation for confession alone. The author of this text notes explicitly that he wants to guide his simple and devout addressee so that her more wide-ranging contemplation will not lead to spiritual instability (7623–25, p. 300). The epilogue of the *Book* is gendered in an explicit reference to "my dere suster" (7620, p. 300), but much of the text could just as easily have been applied to the laity of either sex (as are many other works of *pastoralia*, such as the more explicitly named *A Myrour to Lewde Men and Wymmen*). The *Book* is constructed along the lines indicated by the third part of Friar Laurent's *Somme le roi*, where the seven heads of the beast in Rev 13:1 serve as an outline for the analysis of the seven deadly sins, but the elaboration of details concerning the sins is most frequently paralleled in Peraldus's *Summa de vitiis et virtutibus* and its many variants and reworkings, including the "Quoniam" and "Primo" texts which also influenced Chaucer's *Parson's Tale*. Other inspirational works in English are closely comparable to the *Book*, especially *Ancrene Wisse*, *Þe Pater Noster of Richard Ermyte*, *Þe Holy Boke Gratia Dei*, and sermons in Oxford, Bodleian Library MS Bodley 95 and other manuscripts related to it. Some of the latter texts demonstrate a close connection with Wycliffite materials, but there is little indication in the *Book* that the compiler had anything but orthodox sympathies. Like much late-medieval vernacular theology in England, the compiler avoided writing about what might have been considered risky questions, emphasizing ethical issues rather than speculative theological matters. As is noted in the epilogue: "Aungeles office hit is heuenliche þyngus to knowe and to wite þe pryuytes þat mow not be departed. Hit is inow to mon to se his owne lodliche synnes" (It is the duty of angels to know divine matters and to understand the secret things that cannot be communicated. It is enough for humanity to see its own hateful sins; 7636–38, p. 300).

The *Somme le roi* is again important, in a version conflated with the *Mirour du monde* (composed before 1280), as the source text translated into the late-medieval dialect of London in *The Mirroure of the Worlde*, transmitted uniquely in Oxford, Bodleian Library MS Bodley 283. The *Mirroure* is a presentation and commentary on the extended Pecham syllabus of catechetical matter: the Ten Commandments, the articles of the faith, the seven sins and the seven virtues, the sacrament of confession, the paternoster, and the gifts of the Holy Spirit. The manuscript of the text has firm connections with London literary culture: it was owned and may have been commissioned by Thomas Kippyng, a draper in the city, and it contains illustrations by an artist from Utrecht who worked in London in the late fifteenth century.

Eventually, secular authors contributed to the composition of major treatises of religious inspiration. Though Chaucer's *Parson's Tale* draws on a number of illustrative texts, there are in large part only two contextual sources of this penitential handbook: lines 80–386 and 958–1080 are based on Raymund of Pennaforte's *Summa de paenitentia* (*c.* 1225–27), while the long treatment of the seven deadly sins and their remedies (lines 390–955) is derived mainly from William Peraldus's *Summa de vitiis* (*c.* 1236) and its offshoots. Thus, the basis for Chaucer's penitential and moral theology in the *Parson's Tale* has a conservative foundation, for it is derived from contextual sources which were roughly 150 years old by the time he adopted them for this treatise. If there is nothing unusual about the form and content of the Parson's penitential manual, it is clear that the context and result of that "meditacioun" do make the work stand out as distinctive. Although we might expect the penitential form to lead to a purely religious confession, as was clearly its primary object as an instrument of institutional policy, we are surprised to find a text of literary penance following the *Parson's Tale*, in the form of Chaucer's *Retractation* (X.1081–92). Not sins, but the ethics of literary works and a literary consciousness are at the center of the "Retractation," as in the same way the *Parson's Tale* itself partakes in the question of literature's usefulness by steadfastly denying fiction a place when it comes to the Parson's turn to narrate in the *Canterbury Tales*.[26] The questions implicated here involve the issue of the possible irony of Chaucer's narration in the *Parson's Tale* and the appropriateness of the Parson's manual as a conclusion to the *Canterbury Tales*. Thus, it is worth noting that the Parson's use of meditative prose can be seen to lead ultimately to Chaucer, the "makere" of the *Canterbury Tales* speaking in his own right in the *Retractation*. There he reveals a remarkable subjectivity and individuality precisely where the reader had come to expect the individual to be subsumed in the impersonally institutional system of ecclesiastically regulated ethics. The privileged position of this penitential manual and meditative treatise on the vices and virtues at the end of the Canterbury pilgrimage may, thus, not be a signal of Chaucer's simple adoption of religious orthodoxy at the end of the *Tales*, but rather may be part of the same careful steps in developing a literary subjectivity with which the journey to Canterbury first began. Chaucer reminds us in a very pointed way that the study of medieval English literature is always also the study of works of religious inspiration.

NOTES

1 Richard Newhauser, *The Treatise on Vices and Virtues in Latin and the Vernacular, Typologie des sources du moyen* âge *occidental*, vol. 68 (Turnhout: Brepols, 1993), p. 14.

2 *Codex* (pl. *codices*) is the term scholars use for the usual form of the book in Western culture since late antiquity, that is, folded sheets bound together.

3 Dan Michel of Northgate, *Ayenbite of Inwyt*, ed. Richard Morris, re-ed. Pamela Gradon, 2 vols., EETS os 23 (1965–79), p. 262.

4 In *Idea of the Vernacular*, p. 240.

5 "Memoriale credencium. A Late Middle English Manual of Theology for Lay People edited from Bodley MS Tanner 201," ed. J. H. L. Kengen (Doctoral dissertation, Katholieke Universitet te Nijmegen, 1979), 235.

6 Ralph Hanna, "Miscellaneity and Vernacularity: Conditions of Literary Production in Late Medieval England," in *The Whole Book: Cultural Perspectives on the Medieval Miscellany*, ed. Stephen G. Nichols and Siegfried Wenzel (Ann Arbor: University of Michigan Press, 1996), pp. 37–51.

7 *Riverside*, p. 67. All quotations from Chaucer are from this edition.

8 *Seinte Marherete þe Meiden ant Martyr*, ed. Frances M. Mack, EETS os 193 (1934; repr. 1958), p. 47.

9 *The South English Legendary*, ed. Charlotte D'Evelyn and Anna J. Mill, EETS os 235 (1956), p. 3, Prol. 59–64.

10 O. S. Pickering, "*The South English Legendary*: Teaching or Preaching?," *Poetica* 45 (1996), 13–14; Annie Samson, "The *South English Legendary*: Constructing a Context," in *Thirteenth-Century England, I: Proceedings of the Newcastle upon Tyne Conference 1985*, ed. P. R. Cross and S. D. Lloyd (Woodbridge: Boydell Press, 1986), pp. 185–95; Klaus P. Jankowsky, "Entertainment, Edification, and Popular Education in *The South English Legendary*," *Journal of Popular Culture* 11 (1977), 706–17; Manfred Görlach, *The Textual Tradition of the South English Legendary*, Leeds Texts and Monographs, NS 6 (University of Leeds, School of English, 1974), pp. 32–50.

11 Sherry L. Reames, "The Second Nun's Prologue and Tale," in *Sources and Analogues of "The Canterbury Tales", I*, ed. Robert M. Correale and Mary Hamel, Chaucer Studies, 28 (Cambridge: D. S. Brewer, 2002), pp. 491–527.

12 Lee Patterson, "'The Living Witnesses of Our Redemption': Martyrdom and Imitation in Chaucer's Prioress's Tale," *Journal of Medieval and Early Modern Studies* 31 (2001), 518.

13 *The Minor Poems of John Lydgate, Part 1*, ed. Henry Nobel MacCracken, EETS ES 107 (1911; repr. 1962), p. 145.

14 William Caxton, *The Golden Legend*, preface, in *Caxton's Own Prose*, ed. Norman F. Blake (London: Deutsch, 1973), p. 89.

15 Nicholas Watson, "Censorship and Cultural Change in Late-Medieval England: Vernacular Theology, the Oxford Translation Debate, and Arundel's Constitutions of 1409," *Speculum* 70 (1995), 822–64.

16 *The Form of Living*, 885–86, in *Richard Rolle: Prose and Verse*, ed. S. J. Ogilvie-Thomson, EETS os 293 (1968), p. 25.
17 *Deonise Hid Diuinite*, 5, in *The Cloud of Unknowing and Related Treatises*, ed. Phyllis Hodgson, Analecta Carthusiana, 3 (Salzburg: Institut für Anglistik und Amerikanistik, Universität Salzburg; Exeter: Catholic Records Press, 1982), p. 128.
18 *Walter Hilton's Eight Chapters on Perfection*, ed. Fumio Kuriyagawa, Studies in the Humanities and Social Relations, 9 (Tokyo: Keio Institute of Cultural and Linguistic Studies, Keio University, 1967), p. 32.
19 *The Mirror of the Blessed Life of Jesus Christ*, ed. Michael G. Sargent (Exeter: University of Exeter Press, 2004), p. 7: "ad … hereticorum siue lollardorum confutacionem."
20 Carol Meale, "'oft siþis with grete deuotion I þought what I miȝt do pleysyng to god': The Early Ownership and Readership of Love's *Mirror*, with Special Reference to its Female Audience," in *Nicholas Love at Waseda*, ed. Shoichi Oguro, Richard Beadle, and Michael G. Sargent (Woodbridge: D. S. Brewer, 1997), pp. 19–46.
21 *Revelations of Divine Love* (short version), 6, in *English Mystics of the Middle Ages*, ed. Barry Windeatt (Cambridge University Press, 1994), p. 189; *A Revelation of Love* (long version), 2, ed. Marion Glasscoe, third rev. edn (University of Exeter Press, 1993), p. 2.
22 H. Leith Spencer, "Sermon Literature," in *A Companion to Middle English Prose*, ed. A. S. G. Edwards (Cambridge: D. S. Brewer, 2004), p. 157.
23 Richard Lavynham, *A Litil Tretys on the Seven Deadly Sins*, ed. J. P. W. M. van Zutphen (Rome: Institutum Carmelitanum, 1956), p. 3.
24 Robert Mannyng of Brunne, *Handlyng Synne*, 10812–14, ed. Idelle Sullens, Medieval & Renaissance Texts & Studies, 14 (Binghamton: SUNY Press, 1983), p. 269.
25 *Book for a Simple and Devout Woman. A Late Middle English Adaptation of Peraldus's Summa de Vitiis et Virtutibus and Friar Laurent's Somme le Roi, edited from British Library Mss Harley 6571 and Additional 30944*, 7633–35, ed. F. N. M. Diekstra, Mediaevalia Groningana, 24 (Gröningen: Egbert Forsten, 1998), p. 300.
26 Lee Patterson, "The *Parson's Tale* and the Quitting of the *Canterbury Tales*," *Traditio* 34 (1978), 345.

4

CHRISTINE CHISM

Romance

Romance was the dominant non-devotional genre of Middle English literature, and its themes permeate medieval literary culture at large. However, because the genre was so ubiquitous and various, it is difficult to define. Romance is the carnival magician of genres, conjuring variety from the same bag of tricks: stock characters, repeated plots, motifs, memes, and overriding themes, right down to the level of verbal formulas and conventional phrases. Individual romances often follow a typical narrative trajectory: exile leading to return, loss redeemed by restoration, complacency goaded by instructive ordeal, innocence riven by experience, the construction of careers and the fall of kingdoms. Its gestures and motifs are equally identifiable – the knight errant, the beautiful endangered lady, the lost heir, the trial of prowess or virtue, the pact gone wrong, the monstrous, magical, and/or disguised challenger, the journey to the otherworld, the joyous return of the prodigal, and the reintegrative celebration.

At the same time, however, the genre is extremely flexible. Its repertoire alters over time as romance writers discard, patch, and adapt their conventional materials so that they can speak more intimately to the on-the-spot concerns of their audiences. Helen Cooper suggests that romance is best conceived as a family, branching and evolving in different directions, rather than as manifestations or "clones of a single Platonic idea," and this family metaphor is useful because it stresses the genre's existence in time.[1] Its mythic, estranged, "once-upon-a-time" mode of telling can actually provide ways of coming to grips with difficult cultural problems – monarchical acquisitiveness, legal corruption, the insecurities of representation and display, commercialism, aristocratic feud – from safer or more elucidating distances. Its exploration of loss and recuperation can speak intimately to the anxieties of its audiences; its fantasies can express yearnings that are profoundly and traceably historical. The genre serves audiences who need simultaneously to be reassured by the traditional and gripped by the urgent and imminent. This flexible timeliness amidst formulaic conventionality explains the centuries-long appeal of romance, and the genre's longevity in post-medieval times despite enormous changes in language and literary tradition. The sheer variety of Middle English romance suggests that it is not something that we should try to domesticate or taxonomize. In fact, its openness invites a particularly rich exploration of the ways genres – and especially medieval genres – work: improvisationally and experimentally rather than as static taxonomies. They are part of the phenomenology of reading: they help readers make meaning in texts from moment to moment as readers traverse them. Genres are themselves generated through histories of reading; readers gather their various experiences of reading into a sense of the central preoccupations of different types of books and then read individual works within and against that set of experiential references. Thus, no work perfectly fits a single genre and the genres themselves change over time as more works play with(in) them. Furthermore, at any given moment the friction created in the reading process – between the reader's accreted sense of the larger genre and her ongoing experience of the individual work – gives the work vitality and immediacy. Readers are often most drawn in when a work tempts, teases, and outrages their generic anticipations. Romance may be such an enduring genre simply because it allows such a breadth of play. In Middle English poetry this play could even cross over into the devotional genres to which romance was so often opposed. Baronial romances such as *Havelok the Dane* and *King Horn* can cast a shimmer of the sacred upon the endeavors of their heroes. Homiletic romances such as *Sir Gowther* and *Guy of Warwick* can assay the ethical imperatives of a culture equally invested in pious self-restraint and secular display. The very conventionality that makes romance instantly recognizable also makes it infinitely quotable: its modes of signification permeate the most significant, generically experimental works of medieval literary culture, from *Piers Plowman* and *The Canterbury Tales* to *Pearl* and *Mandeville's Travels*.

Sources

Many Middle English romances translate or draw from French, Anglo-Norman, or Latin works, and in fact Middle English writing in general is a latecomer to medieval culture. This belatedness is an effect of the Norman Conquest (1066) when William the Conqueror displaced the indigenous English nobility and established a French-speaking monarchy and ruling class, endowing his own nobles and installing Norman bishops and archbishops in England. This long eclipse of literary English means that the first romances written in England were written in Latin, French, and Anglo-Norman. When romance writers began to use English again, it was partly to bring these stories to wider audiences, and partly to retain audiences among the gentility and aristocracy themselves as the native knowledge of French began to dwindle among them. These writers drew, naturally enough, from the stories already circulating both in England and elsewhere in Anglo-Norman, French, and Latin; almost every Anglo-Norman romance has a Middle English version. Yet these were not simple translations but rather free reimaginings of their sources turned to the needs of new situations and audiences. Middle English writers seized upon, redirected, parodied, and criticized the conventions of their sources in an astonishing variety of registers, from the blunt utility of *King Horn* to the intricacy of *Sir Gawain and the Green Knight.*

While translations of continental romances continued throughout the period, many original narratives were also written – *Gamelyn* is one example – adapting the genre to specifically English contexts and audiences. Throughout the period English writers allude to continental romance traditions; the *Gawain*-poet actually allows a character to criticize his hero for not living up to his French romance reputation. The ongoing complexity of literary borrowings makes it difficult to define what sets off Middle English romances from their continental counterparts but two generalizations are possible. Where French romances tend to centralize issues of literary authority and authorship, Middle English romances often thematize the tribulations of literary transmission and the exigencies of their own copying, compilation, and performance; they are more audience-centered. In addition, French and Anglo-Norman romances tend to be more interested in love-induced explorations of individual subjectivity, while Middle English romances, by contrast, tend to abjure such stricken interiorities and instead focus on how subjectivity is enacted through public performance.

Romance preoccupations

Middle English romances are subject-centered; a romance is about somebody.[2] A medieval reader would probably not ask *what* a romance was about but rather *who*. As a result, ideas of identity and subjectivity – the performance of gender, class, and lineage – are at the heart of romance. Romances stereotypically recount the chivalric adventures of a worthy knight in the process of proving his prowess by deeds at arms and of love. However, romances, while drawing upon the practices and ideals of late medieval chivalric culture, could extend as widely beyond chivalry as its writers and readers required. The romance of *Ipomadon*, for example, makes chivalric identity and gender into dramatic challenges for its characters. The poem's heroine and hero wake up, more or less appalled, to find themselves inside a Middle English romance, forced towards roles that at first they have no inclination to fulfill. When we first meet the poem's heroine, the Fere (the proud one), we find that she does not fit the romance stereotype of a distressed heroine in need of chivalric support. Rather she rules her own land, is universally respected, and has made herself all but unavailable by vowing to marry only the best knight in the world. The hero, Ipomadon, seems to be just as disdainful of romance conventions. Rather than courting honor to win her love, Ipomadon takes an intense, perverse pleasure in courting shame. He spends virtually the entire poem in a series of embarrassing disguises – strange servant, queen's official boy-toy, or professional fool – fighting also only in disguise and garnering a chivalric reputation that fastens, in the absence of name, upon his role; he becomes "the nameless knight who was the most worthy." Anonymity, which seemed at first a way of resisting chivalric expectations of reputation-building, becomes a means by which Ipomadon builds his reputation even more effectively.

From *Ipomadon* we can get a good idea of some of the major preoccupations of romance: identity, subjectivity, and strangeness; adventure and risk; gender and sexuality; marriage, family, heritage, and lineage; social hierarchy and social performance; prowess and "trawthe" (trueness, loyalty); and love and friendship. Ipomadon's foregrounding of identity, however, both fulfills chivalric expectations and extends beyond them. Through the Fere's identity-creating pride and Ipomadon's identity-creating anonymity *Ipomadon* makes chivalric worthiness depend less on birth and heritage than on continual challenge: the re-proving of vows or prowess. The worthiness gains authority not because it is entitled (although its entitlement is not incidental) but because it dares to put itself at risk. Yet this investment in risk is not without its stresses and difficulties. As both characters subject themselves to love, they soliloquize their terrifying sense of self-disintegration, their dependence upon each other for any capacity to be or act: thus identity purls in the characters' experiences into a more open, troubled, and narratively gripping subjectivity. The accumulation of these painful and risky performances solidifies over time into an obligation to surpass past deeds and thereby gains a self-perpetuating ethical force. In the end, chivalric performance becomes authoritative only by continually and painfully new-minting "worthiness" itself.

As romances grapple with the acculturations of class, gender, sexuality, and race, they connect heroes and heroines to their social milieu and that of their audiences. They give a local habitation and a name to otherwise elusive dissonances between social values, and offer their audiences dramatic access to crises of coercion, desire, love, labor, mortality, and social justice that implicate their own experience in the world. Romance's focus on identity and performance thus becomes a way of purveying to wider audiences not just the ideals and issues embraced by the aristocracy, but the capacity to investigate self-determination itself, and thus to imagine wider, better polities. It is no accident that Chaucer's Wife of Bath chooses romance as the genre of the tale she offers to the other Canterbury pilgrims. Chaucer performs his understanding of romance's capacity to spin convention and tradition into innovation just as he composites together conventional misogynist texts to create a female narrator who innovatively advocates for women's agency and self-determination. In the course of her tale, the Wife relocates "gentility" from noble birth to noble deeds and makes it available it to all who "liven vertuously and weyve sinne" (l. 320) regardless of their class status. In her Tale, as elsewhere, romance springs from a chivalric ethos only to stretch beyond it to investigate different ideas of social worth. Thus, romance can use chivalric conventions actually to erode aristocratic exclusivity and enact a notional social mobility that speaks powerfully to the continually shifting social networks of fourteenth- and fifteenth-century England.

Style

Alliterative romances such as *Sir Gawain and the Green Knight* display some of the most gorgeous and elaborate poetry in English literature, while metrical romances such as *King Horn* often prefer a gale-force bluntness. However, they are both linked by their formulaic nature; whether brisk as an alliterative battle-sequence or devious as a courtly suitor, a romance works its spell through repetition and variation. Because its verbal surface is unvarying stately, formal, and often beautiful, a romance can lull readers and hearers with a glissade of conventional formulae, even as it underhandedly conducts them into very strange figural territories. It is easy for modern readers (or medieval ones such as Chaucer in *Sir Thopas*) to lampoon the repetitive predictability of the metrical romance style, but this style performed very useful functions: in conditions of oral performance it stabilized listeners, reiterated crucial information to ensure its uptake, and, more subtly, elicited a kind of assent from its audience.[3] The formulaic style eases readers and listeners into a stately world of forms and performances, secured by mystified conventions imbued with the unanswerable force of law, and their difficult negotiation becomes the hero's/heroine's/audience's overriding problem. For example, in the grail romances, Percival neglects to ask the crucial question about the wounded king and spends the rest of the romance striving to make up for that omission; in *Sir Orfeo*, a Fairy King abducts King Orfeo's queen and must be formally dealt with on his own grounds and his own terms; in *Sir Gawain and the Green Knight*, Sir

Gawain must negotiate the compacts he makes in the compacts he makes in mysterious and open-ended exchanges of blows and winnings.

The formulaic style helps give the idea of social convention in these romances an abiding force, but that does not mean that those conventions are not unquestionable. In fact, it is very instructive to try to resist the beauty and dignity of this verbal surface and remain alert to what we are being asked to accept. Oftentimes romances will push their conventions, pacts, and promises to the point of complete incredulity in order to implicate readers in their own acceptance and provoke questions. By showing readers how easily one can be lulled into compliance, it becomes possible to persuade them to wake them up a little to the strangeness of the world such conventions helps to create. To take an extreme example: *Amis and Amiloun* is a romance that tests the validity of knightly friendship as an ennobling convention. Two knights, Amis and Amiloun, swear a youthful friendship to each other and everything in the romance seems to demonstrate that this sworn friendship is an ennobling act that should be respected, accepted, and imitated. However, at one crucial point Amiloun becomes a leper as a result of his loyalty to Amis, and wanders for years as an outcast. When the two friends finally meet again, Amiloun is completely disfigured by the disease, while Amis is prosperously married, with two lovely children. Amis welcomes Amiloun into his house and tends him, but on Christmas Eve, both friends are sent a dream in which an angel tells them how Amiloun might be healed – by bathing in the blood of Amis's children. Without once varying its tone, the romance recounts how Amis walks slowly up the stairs into the children's nursery, agonizes over the value of his friendship and the value of his children, takes up the sleeping children, and, after cutting their throats, tucks their bodies back into bed. When he enters Amiloun's room with the basin of their blood, Amiloun realizes what he has done and is appalled, but Amis reassures him, saying that he can have more children if God wills it, but such a friend can never be replaced. It is at this point that the soothingly formulaic style comes into sharpest counterpoint with what is being depicted.

> He tok that blode, that was so bright,
> And alied that gentil knight,
> That er was hend in hale,
> And seththan in bed him dight
> And wreighe him wel warm, aplight,
> With clothes riche and fale.
> "Brother", he seyd, "ly now stille
> And falle on slepe thurch Godes wille,
> As the angel told in tale;

And ich hope wele without lesing
Jhesu, that is heuen king,
Schal bot the of thi bale." (2341–52)

[He took that blood that was so bright, and washed with it that gentle knight that in the past had been gracious and hale, and then he put him in bed and covered him very warmly with many rich coverlets. "Brother", he said "Lie still now, and fall asleep through God's will, as the angel told in his message, and I hope that without falsehood that Jesus, the king of heaven, will relieve you of your torment."]

Everything in the style of this description is reassuring: the anointing or washing of the gentle knight with the bright blood without any sense of violation, the memory of how gracious Amiloun had been before he was disfigured with leprosy, the rich bedclothes covering him up warmly, the formulaic invocations of God's will, and the angel's tale – all these keep it in the realm not just of the civilized but the sanctioned and holy: a healing act of loving friendship. The style does everything it can to obscure the picture of the bloody leper or the memory of the murdered children. It is quite possible to skim over this episode without really noticing what is going on: a replaying of the bedtime Amis has just given his slaughtered children, made eerier by the juxtaposition of their cold, drained bodies and Amiloun's warm, healing sleep. It is up to the reader to resist the style and make the comparison. Ultimately, the romance rewards Amis's act of friendship by having the children miraculously resurrected on Christmas morning. Even so, however, the doubts raised about the value of a friendship that demands such acts are not dispelled; the picture of the bloody lullaby is too uncanny to forget. Many scholars who compare *Amis and Amiloun* with its Anglo-Norman source find the Middle English poem more skeptical of the friendship it depicts, yoking knightly friendship to divine miracle only with a perceptible strain that the serenity of tone cannot quite eradicate.

This tension – between the smoothness of the formulaic style and the problematic figures and juxtapositions it is able to intimate – is one of the most typical and fascinating of romance's literary habits. And it is at these moments of tension that we can trace the ways romances interrogate the social worlds they depict and implicate their readers. Readers who can resist the stylistic inducement to accept the conventions of such worlds are often well rewarded.

Authors and audience

Although I have been referring in the abstract to writers, audiences, and readers, and the ways that romances implicate them, we really do not know much about the original writers and audiences of romance, or more than approximate dates and locations for their composition. With a few exceptions – and in contrast to continental romances concerned with authorial self-inscription into worthy literary traditions – most Middle English romances are anonymous. It is equally difficult to identify patterns of readership and audience. Individual studies of manuscripts can cast light on particular romances but the sheer social penetration of romance and romance tropes make it impossible to associate romance exclusively with any single set of class imperatives or to identify it exclusively with any exclusive social positioning. Romances are ubiquitous in manuscript compilations throughout the period, bundled next to hagiographies, debates, and histories without any logic discernible to modern scholars, or together with other romances as in the famous Auchinleck manuscript (1330–40). Manuscript quality ranges from expensive, illuminated productions worthy of display in aristocratic libraries, to narrow-margined handbooks, produced in urban workshops for whatever readers could commission them. Romance manuscripts turn up at court, in monastic libraries, baronial households, and London workshops, effectively running the gamut of late medieval English literate society.

Romances do provide us with imagined audiences: one of the most repeated conventions of the genre is to situate itself as an oral entertainment before an audience of post-prandial gentlefolk. We don't know to what extent this is a polite fiction; often the same romances that present themselves as performing for "Princes proude that beth in pres" (1, *Robert of Cisyle*: proud princes gathered together in company) will also refer readers to written sources that would require a knowledge of Latin associated with the clerisy; and many scholars have argued persuasively for the involvement of monastic scriptoria in the production and transmission of romances. The illuminated frontispiece of a manuscript in Corpus Christi College, Cambridge of Chaucer's *Troilus and Criseyde*, a poem that tests the conventions of romance amidst the exigencies of tragic history, depicts Chaucer reciting from his poetry before a courtly audience of noble women and courtiers, but whether romances were predominantly read by courtly aristocrats or women remains an open question. Romances appear in the libraries of forcibly retired queens such as Isabella of France, and king-challenging magnates, such as Humphrey of Gloucester. Kings and nobles seem to exploit romance behaviors for their own ends. Edward I tourneyed in France, and Edward III instituted the order of the Garter in England in a clear appropriations of Arthurian romance, and Susan Crane traces a readiness among the aristocracy and knighthood to imitate and even die for romance ideals.[4] However, the involvement of aristocrats, gentlemen, and urban citizens alike in romance-alluding displays of prowess, gentility, and fidelity – in tournaments, pageants, and processionals – supports the idea that romance tropes were generally associated with an idealized culture of gentility which had been made available to many claimants. In this romance seems always to tread a balance between the glamorously courtly and the irremediably popular.

The varieties of English romance

If romance is best considered as a strange kind of outwardly mobile family, how can we describe its branches and offshoots? Scholars divide Middle English romances into subgroups, with their own characteristic lengths, forms, patterns, and themes, but they disagree as to the best divisions and no one taxonomy has achieved canonical status. Anyone beginning research will encounter the following categories invoked pell-mell across a century of scholarship: the long metrical romance, the Breton lay, the alliterative romance, the prose compilation, the pious or homiletic romance, the historical romance, the romance of antiquity, the family romance, the romance of nation or empire, and the romance of travel, and more. Anchoring the genre is a group of substantial chivalric romances that recount the martial and amorous adventures of a knight, group of knights, or chivalric leader. *Ipomadon* itself is a part of this group, as are *William of Palerne*, *Richard Coer de Lion*, *Bevis of Hampton*, *Amis and Amiloun*, *Kyng Alisaunder*, *Arthour and Merlin*, *Sir Firumbras*, *Lybeaus Desconus*, and *Sir Eglamour of Artois*. Many of these romances are homiletic, while others subordinate penitential themes to the exigencies of aristocratic self-fashioning.

In opposition to these longer chivalric excursions, scholars often distinguish a shorter form: the Breton lay, invented or introduced by Marie of France. Little is known about Marie except that she lived in England, wrote in French, and may have been associated with the Anglo-Norman court of Henry II. Many of Marie's lays were translated (or reinvented) into Middle English, but throughout the thirteenth and fourteenth centuries new poems were also written in the genre she devised. Often Breton lays represent themselves as sung performances of stories from ancient Brittany, and sympathetically depict noblewomen or noblemen who overcome the venalities of aristocratic social practice in the pursuit of true love or a lost identity/heritage. Examples include *Sir Launfal*, *Lay le Freine*, *Sir Degaré*, *Emaré*, *The Erle of Toulous*, *Sir Cleges*, *Sir Gowther*, and the gorgeous *Sir Orfeo*. Overlapping with these length-based subgenres are subgenres based on formal or metrical features: the Middle English metrical romance, the alliterative romance, and the prose compilation (that is, Malory). Middle

English metrical romances use a variety of verse forms. The most notable of the stanzaic forms is tail rhyme, mocked by Chaucer in his deliberately doggerel *Tale of Sir Thopas*, but there is a huge range of metrical forms, from the stanzaic shapeliness of rhyme royal to the briskness of continuous rhymed couplets. (Tail rhyme consists of a rhyming couplet or triplet followed by a shorter line – a tail – that rhymes with other tails; rhyme royal consists of a seven-line stanza with the rhyme scheme ababbcc.) The lines are usually octameters (eight-stress lines) or, more rarely, pentameters (five-stress lines), but "bobs" and "wheels" are also common to break up the narration and underline key ideas. (The latter consist of a single-stress line [the "bob"] and trimeters, or three-stress lines [the "wheel"]). In contrast to metrical forms, Middle English alliterative romances use a meter that harks back to Anglo-Saxon poetry without being traceable to it. In addition to *Sir Gawain and the Green Knight*, the most substantial alliterative romances are the alliterative *Morte Arthure*, *William of Palerne*, *The Siege of Jerusalem*, *The Destruction of Troy*, *The Wars of Alexander*, and *The Awntyrs off Arthure*. However, the opposition between rhymed metrical forms and alliterating forms is misleading; poets often mingled alliteration with rhyme to create an incredible variety of intricate and challenging metrical forms, such as the thirteen-line stanza of *The Awntyrs off Arthure*, which uses alliteration along with a convoluted rhyme scheme abababab-c-ddd-c; it is arguably the most intricate stanza form in English literature. Prose romances and compilations grew in popularity throughout the period. There are prose versions of many verse romances, including the *Morte Arthur*, and *Ipomadon*. However, the most famous romance prose compilation is Thomas Malory's mid-fifteenth-century *Morte d'Arthur*. In this work Malory thoroughly ingests, reimagines, and turns to his own uses an enormous number of French and Middle English Arthurian sources, weaving them into a vast cycle of seven books, arranged like nesting boxes to trace a narrative of chivalric rise and fall.

Overlapping the generic groupings based on length and form are those based on theme or subject matter. Among these are the romances of antiquity concerning the matters of Greece, Troy, Thebes, Rome, Alexander, Charlemagne, and Arthur. These romances negotiate medieval culture's rich ancient and classical legacies. As a group they are ambivalent about historical veracity: some claim historicity, set their events within mappable geographies, and name their source texts or eyewitnesses; while others spurn historicity for fantastic reinvention. Representing Arthur and the matter of Britain are *Sir Gawain and the Green Knight*, *Of Arthour and of Merlin*, *Joseph of Arimathie*, the stanzaic *Le Morte Arthur*, *Lancelot of the Laik*, and the innumerable versions of *The Brut*, the story of the founding and monarchical history of Britain. Alexander the Great emerges as both chivalric exemplar and exotic riddle in *Kyng Alisaunder*, *The Wars of Alexander*, and the prose *Alexander*. Charlemagne is reimagined in *The Sowdane of Babylon*, *The Siege of Melayne*, and the wonderfully earthy *Rauf Coilyear*. Rome is founded in *Eneydos* while Troy and Thebes move to center stage in *The Laud Troy Book*, *The Destruction of Troy*, *The Siege of Thebes*, and, arguably, Chaucer's *Knight's Tale*, and *Troilus and Criseyde*. Closely related to these are romances of English nationhood such as *Richard Coer de Lion*. Other thematic subgroups include the dynastic or family romances which focus on marriage, procreation, lineage, and inheritance: such as *Gamelyn*, *Emaré*, *Lai le Fresne*, *Octavian*, and *William of Palerne*; and the homiletic or pious romances such as *Guy of Warwick* and *Amis and Amiloun* which exploit romance modes in order to instruct their audiences. Two recent studies have even stretched the bounds of romance to include travel narratives, such as Mandeville's *Travels*, which, although it lacks a hero and a series of deeds to make up a plot, succeeds in pulling its readers themselves into the errantry of discovery and the pleasures and monstrosities of a widening world.[5]

I believe these subgroups function most usefully not as an anatomy of the genre but rather as indicators of the mutually determining oppositions that constitute its field of play. In other words, the pious romance becomes pious in opposition to other romances that seem by contrast more concerned with worldly profit; the alliterative romance emerges in opposition to the metrical. But where one scholar might find a deep piety another might see only the seizure of pious conventions in order to ennoble an aspect of lay culture. Furthermore it is important to realize that a single work may promiscuously mix elements from many subgroups at once. Indeed, if one considers how romance worked historically as a genre to its own writers, one finds it flexible, porous, and dialectical. This capacity of generic mixing to spark literary/social questioning merges strongly in some of the greatest Middle English poems that deploy romance conventions while defying generic containment. When William Langland decided to bring a new, exploratory genre into being, he yoked the figural inventiveness of dream vision to the fierce stakes of theological disputation, and the everyday homespun of homily and liturgy to the biting realism of social satire. He then framed the whole heady mixture as a romance quest, a journeying "wide in this world wondres to here" (wide in this world in order to hear of wonders, line 4). His poem comes complete with an errant if drowsy hero, Will, who in the best tradition of romance dons a disguise (the habit of a hermit "unholy of werkes" [line 3]) that, like the knightly disguises in *Ipomadon*, frees him from himself and allows him to take the position of a challenger to those he encounters. Like most romance adventurers Will does not have to go far before he is drawn into "a ferly, of Fairye me thoghte" (a marvel, from Faerie it seemed to me, line 6), which takes the form of a series of marvelous dreams. But when Langland couples the absorption of dream vision to the restless wonderment of romance quest, the result is a visionary errantry at once so penetrating and so adventurous it refuses conclusion. After a quarter century of revision, Langland had not only written *Piers Plowman*, he had also conveyed to some of his readers, inadvertently or not, a desire for social justice so powerful that the name of Piers ended up among the organizational slogans of the rebels of 1381. At the same time Langland instigated a new poetic tradition of social critique through which subsequent writers criticized past government and imagined new utopian polities: the so-called Piers Plowman tradition exemplified by poems such as *Richard the Redeless* and *Mum and the Sothsegger.*

And while *Piers Plowman* exploits the trope of romance quest to induce social interrogation at home, the half-alliterative, half-metrical "visioun"–elegy–homiletic debate of *Pearl* uses it to extend such questioning into the mysteries of the afterlife, leading the errant narrator through a bejeweled and otherworldly romance landscape into more pious climes – the brink of the river of death before the glimmer of heavenly Jerusalem. In a similar way, the travelogue–pilgrimage–encyclopedia of Mandeville's *Travels* seizes on the same quest-trope to entice curiosity about the farthest reaches of the world; it works to instill in readers the desire to dare the unknown, all the while shaping and educating that desire so as to avoid both the pitfalls of mercantile greed, and the too-easy self-gratifications of chivalric love quest. The most urgently read, incessantly copied literary texts of their times – from *Piers Plowman* to Chaucer's *Canterbury Tales*, and *Mandeville's Travels* – consistently put the various genres of medieval writing into intricate and probing dialogue, and within those generic conversations, the voice of romance is key.

Although romance was primarily a literature of entertainment, entertainment performed its own crucial work – the awakening of delight and its instruction. While it was attacked by clerics throughout the Middle Ages for its capacity to distract from more worthy pursuits, the opposition between instruction and entertainment was more ideological than functional. A sixteenth-century annotation at the end of the manuscript of William of Palerne (*c.* 1356) suggests that reading a "goodly story" such as this can "kepe youythe from ydellnes ... wher apon we showld bestow the tym apon the holy day & suche other tymes when we haue lytle or nothynge adoynge elles & In so doynge ye may putawey all ydell thowghtes & pensyffnes [of] hearte" (keep youth from idleness ... whereupon we should bestow the time upon the Holy Day and such other times that we have little or nothing else to do, and in so doing you may put away all idle thoughts and pensiveness of heart). To this late reader, attention to this 200-year-old poem combated idleness and melancholy and became a form of profitable exercise particularly appropriate to a Sunday. Recent studies argue that romance had a much longer afterlife than was previously thought; the genre and its conventions survived changes in language, conceptualization of the literary, and the spread of print culture, and continued to exert widespread appeal well into the seventeenth century. While its popular character has never allowed it to become entirely reputable, in its recognizable successors J. R. R. Tolkien, C. S. Lewis, Philip Pullman, and J. K. Rowling, this carnival magician of genres continues to conjure, weaving familiar conventions into different landscapes of literary pleasure, profit, and cultural fantasy (to the horror of many literati) to this day.

NOTES

1 Helen Cooper, *The English Romance in Time: Transforming Motifs from Geoffrey of Monmouth to the Death of Shakespeare* (Oxford University Press, 2004), p. 8.
2 Paul Strohm, "The Origin and Meaning of Middle English Romance," *Genre* 10 (1977), 9.
3 Susan Wittig, *Stylistic and Narrative Structures in the Middle English Romances* (Austin and London: University of Texas Press, 1978).
4 Susan Crane, *Insular Romance: Politics, Faith, and Culture in Anglo-Norman and Middle English Literature* (Berkeley: University of California Press, 1986); *The Performance of Self: Ritual Clothing, and Identity During the Hundred Years War* (Philadelphia: University of Pennsylvania Press, 2002).
5 Jennifer Goodman, *Chivalry and Exploration, 1298–1630* (Woodbridge, Suffolk: Boydell Press, 1998); Geraldine Heng, *Empire of Magic: Medieval Romance and the Politics of Cultural Fantasy* (New York: Columbia University Press, 2003).

5

STEVEN F. KRUGER

Dialogue, debate, and dream vision

A remarkable number of Middle English works (usually poems) take the form of debate or dialogue; many, too, are framed as dreams. While we may define two distinct genres of Middle English literature – the debate/dialogue and the dream vision – often the two are merged in a single work, with extended debates or dialogues depicted as occurring within a first-person narrator's dream. Indeed, the composite genre of dream-debate/dialogue constitutes one of the most widely used forms in Middle English literature, with a number of the great canonical poems of the fourteenth century – *Pearl*, William Langland's *Piers Plowman*, Geoffrey Chaucer's *Book of the Duchess*, *House of Fame*, *Parliament of Fowls*, and *Prologue to the Legend of Good Women* – being both framed as dream visions and structured around a central dialogue or series of dialogues. In addition, John Gower's *Confessio Amantis*, while not explicitly a dream, shares many of the generic characteristics of the dream vision. Many other Middle English texts also represent debates, dreams, and intersecting dream-debates. The brilliant bird-debate *The Owl and the Nightingale* is usually dated to the end of the twelfth century. Debates between the body and the soul appear in the twelfth and thirteenth centuries, continuing an Old English tradition that extends as well into the Renaissance. Alongside the poems just mentioned, the fourteenth century also produced such alliterative dream-debates as *Winner and Waster*, *The Parliament of the Three Ages*, and Thomas Usk's prose *Testament of Love*. In the fifteenth and early sixteenth centuries, we find a varied menu of debate and dream texts, such as *The Floure and the Leafe*, *The Assembly of Ladies*, *Mum and the Sothsegger*, *The Court of Sapience*, and *Lancelot of the Laik* (the last an odd amalgam of chivalric romance, dream, and advice to princes) and many poems of the "Chaucerian" tradition including works by John Lydgate and the Scottish Chaucerians: James I, William Dunbar, Gavin Douglas, and Robert Henryson. Stephen Hawes, John Skelton, and others bring dream and debate poetry firmly into the sixteenth century. To treat so various a literature in any detail and depth would be impossible in a brief essay. Instead, I here consider the salient features of the intersecting genres of debate/dialogue and dream, sketching their longer history in Western European culture, and try to arrive at a beginning sense of some of the many cultural uses to which these genres were adapted during the Middle English period.

For the purposes of this essay the genres of debate/dialogue and dream vision will be interpreted in broad and inclusive ways. The debate/dialogue genre includes any text constituted wholly or largely by a dialogue between two or more persons or figures (often allegorical personifications like Nature or Love or Philosophy or The Church). Use of both the terms "dialogue" and "debate" in describing this literature suggests that such texts might be more conflictual, on the one hand (debates), or more cooperatively conversational, on the other (dialogues). Sometimes debates or dialogues that contain a multitude of voices have been treated as a separate genre of "parliament," but our definition includes these. The genre stands, obviously, in close relation to *dramatic* forms. The main difference from drama is that the debate/dialogue is framed, via narrative (most often, first-person) or, sometimes, lyric. As a result, rather than see the dialogue directly or immediately enacted, readers encounter a dialogue presented not only in the words of its interlocutors but also through the mediation of a narrator.

The dream vision genre includes any text in which the main narrative (or sometimes lyric) expression is framed by an account of falling asleep and dreaming. Sometimes the dream frame is quite elaborate (as in *Pearl*, Chaucer's dream visions, or *Winner and Waster*), giving a complex sense of the "real-world" situation in which the dream occurs, and hence also a fairly full "characterization" of the dreamer-narrator. At other times, the opening dream frame is spare (as in the Middle English *Debate between the Body and the Soul*, in which the dream follows a minimal, two-line frame: "Als I lay in a winteris night, / In a droukening [troubled mental state] bifor the day, / Vorsothe I saugh a selly [wondrous] syt [sight] ...").[1] Sometimes we have the end of the dream described in detail, as when a sound within or outside the dream causes the dreamer's awakening; thus, at the conclusion of the *Parliament of the Three Ages*, the blowing of a bugle both awakens the dreamer-narrator and recalls the poem's opening, in which that narrator describes himself as a hunter or poacher.[2] The circularity of structure here, with the falling asleep and awakening forming an "envelope" for the dream proper, characterizes many dream poems. Sometimes, however, the end of the dream is ignored altogether (as at the conclusion of one of the versions [F] of Chaucer's *Prologue to the Legend of Good Women*, where the dreamer never awakens). Some visionary texts suggest a dream without making it explicit (for example, Gower's *Confessio Amantis*); others eschew dream seemingly on purpose, emphasizing that the narrator experiences his or her vision while awake and aware. This is the case in Boethius's *Consolation of Philosophy*, and also in Christine de Pizan's fifteenth-century French *Book of the City of Ladies*. Obviously, whenever a dream vision is structured primarily as dialogue or debate (or a debate/dialogue is framed by a dream), a text belongs simultaneously to both genres. These genres contain a remarkable variety of Middle English works, and part of the challenge for critics is accounting for this diversity.

Critical traditions

Individual works of the debate/dialogue and dream vision genres such as *Pearl*, *Piers Plowman*, Chaucer's dream visions, *The Owl and the Nightingale*, and *Winner and Waster* have received extensive scholarly attention. A. C. Spearing's landmark 1976 volume, *Medieval Dream-Poetry* traces classical, Judeo-Christian, and French backgrounds to the Middle English dream vision, develops close readings of a wide variety of poetic texts – moving from Chaucer to the alliterative tradition to the English and Scottish Chaucerians – and recognizes in a subtle, complex way the features of dream vision as a genre.[3] Much subsequent critical work has devoted itself especially to tracing the intellectual and literary lineage of dream vision. Kathryn L. Lynch's 1988 *The High Medieval Dream Vision* argues that we should read dream poetry in relation to the high medieval philosophical traditions out of which emerged such visionary works as Alain de Lille's twelfth-century *Plaint of Nature*, Guillaume de Lorris's and Jean de Meun's thirteenth-century *Romance of the Rose*, Dante's *Purgatorio*, and Gower's *Confessio Amantis*.[4] She also recognizes how medieval philosophy and poetry are both intimately connected to late classical works. J. Stephen Russell's *The English Dream Vision* also appeared in 1988; it puts English dream poetry into the context of classical, late-antique, and medieval currents of thought.[5] Steven F. Kruger's 1992 *Dreaming in the Middle Ages*, while it does not discuss Middle English texts at length, also works to position the genre of dream vision within an intellectual/cultural history that includes late-antique and medieval theories of dreaming; a tradition of "dreambooks" that provide keys for reading dreams; the striking use of dreams in conversion autobiography; and the deployment of dream vision self-consciously to explore the nature of fiction.[6] A snapshot of where things currently stand in thinking about the late-medieval (and early modern) dream text is given in the collection edited by Peter

Brown, *Reading Dreams*; this is introduced by Spearing, and it contains new contributions from Kruger, Lynch, and Brown, as well as David Aers, Peter Holland, and Kathleen McLuskie.[7]

As in the study of dream vision, a consideration of the intellectual and literary backgrounds of the medieval debate genre has been central to the critical enterprise. Thus, there has been much work on the deep influence of Boethius's sixth-century *Consolation of Philosophy*, a visionary dialogue between a first-person narrator and the personified figure of Lady Philosophy. Michael Means, in his 1972 *The Consolatio Genre in Medieval English Literature*, argues that much of Middle English debate and dream literature follows Boethius in emphasizing a movement toward *consoling* the first-person narrator.[8] Michael Cherniss, in his 1987 *Boethian Apocalypse*, shows how patterns of *revelation* established in Boethius underlie much Middle English debate and dream poetry.[9] Thomas L. Reed's 1990 *Middle English Debate Poetry and the Aesthetics of Irresolution* presents the most extensive treatment of the medieval English debate/dialogue genre itself, arguing persuasively that debate is deployed especially to emphasize a failure of resolution;[10] such a reading obviously stands in some tension with Boethian readings that emphasize a firm endpoint of consolation or revelation. Within the larger debate genre, the bird-debates, poems that depict an argument between different species of birds, have received particular critical attention – both because of the relation of Chaucer's *Parliament of Fowls* to the genre and because of the inherent interest of poems like John Clanvowe's *The Cuckoo and the Nightingale* and (especially) *The Owl and the Nightingale*. As this brief survey of critical approaches suggests, scholarly work on both dream vision and debate has, in large part, involved intellectual and literary historical approaches – placing these poetic genres into longer traditions of thinking and writing. With certain individual poems – notably, Langland's *Piers Plowman* – there has also been an emphasis both on the poems' contribution to an ongoing debate about Christian institutions, doctrine, and practice and on their place in social and political history. But there has not yet been a larger attempt to think about the popularity of the genres, and their multiple uses, in relation to particular English religious and sociopolitical controversies and developments (for example, the rise of the "Lollard" heresy or contemporaneous, late fourteenth-century conflicts over the rule of Richard II).

Literary and intellectual traditions

A wide variety of intellectual and literary traditions underlie Middle English debate/dialogue and dream vision. Both genres have been especially strongly linked to Boethius. While the *Consolation of Philosophy* was certainly a crucial shaping force (and one brought directly into the English tradition in Chaucer's translation of *Boece*), other literary models and cultural practices also informed these genres. Middle English debate/dialogue picks up on a wide range of classical, late-antique, and earlier medieval philosophical traditions of dialogue. While Plato's dialogues, so central to our modern conception of philosophy, were – except for the *Timaeus* (translated into Latin by Calcidius in the fourth century) – unavailable to the Latin Middle Ages, Roman and late-antique dialogues ultimately indebted to Plato's Socratic method were read and imitated. Classical works of moral philosophy like Cicero's *De Amicitia* and *De Senectute* were modeled on Platonic dialogues and were available to medieval writers (indeed, both were translated into Middle English in the fifteenth century and printed by Caxton).[11] Late-antique works like Boethius's *Consolation*, Martianus Capella's fifth-century *Marriage of Philology and Mercury* (in which the seven liberal arts of the academic curriculum give lengthy, informative speeches), and Prudentius's fourth-century *Psychomachia* (which depicts an intra-psychic battle between personified Vices and Virtues) helped shape a literature in which personified, and often opposed, abstractions engage in debate. Medieval Latin allegorical and philosophical debate/dialogues, like Alain de Lille's *Plaint of Nature*, along with vernacular offspring like *The Romance of the Rose*, arise from and reshape such earlier traditions, as do Middle English works like *Death and Life* and *Winner and Waster.*

There is also a long Latin tradition of debates focused specifically on the relative merits of the different Western religions, pitting either a personified Church against her Jewish counterpart Synagogue, or individual Christian spokesmen against learned Jews, pagans, philosophers, or Muslims. (One Middle English disputation between a Christian and a Jew appears in the fourteenth-century Vernon manuscript, an important, richly varied compendium of vernacular texts.) Relatedly, Church doctrine was often transmitted in dialogue form – early and influentially in Pope Gregory the Great's sixth-century Latin *Dialogues* between a teacher and student, and then in such medieval Latin works as Honorius of Autun's twelfth-century *Elucidarium* and Caesarius of Heisterbach's thirteenth-century *Dialogue on Miracles.* (Portions of Honorius's dialogic *Elucidarium* were translated into English as early as the twelfth and as late as the sixteenth century.)[12] While such medieval works often focused particularly on developing an orthodox understanding of Christian doctrine, the form of philosophical dialogue was also put to more secular, even profane, uses – notably in Andreas Capellanus's twelfth-century *The Art of Courtly Love*, where exemplary dialogues instruct male readers on how properly to seduce women, as also in the anonymous twelfth-century debate between Helen and Ganymede on the relative merits of male–male and male–female love.

In addition to this rich, complex tradition of Latin literary debate/ dialogue, there were a variety of cultural practices in medieval Europe (as in most societies), that explicitly took the form of debate or dialogue. In the schools and universities, the study of rhetoric might involve the composition of (often playful) debates between opposed entities (for example, water and wine). The public disputation became a rite of passage for more advanced students. And not surprisingly, such pedagogical practices came together with more strictly literary and philosophical traditions – including those sketched above but also such radically new approaches to philosophy as Abelard's twelfth-century *Sic et Non*, structured as it was around the balance of assertion and denial – to produce highly formalized debate structures like the "disputed question." Indeed, from the thirteenth century on, much scholastic philosophical and theological reflection took the form of questions that were first debated from opposing viewpoints and only then given a definitive response.

Legal training and practice – as is still the case today – was also intimately involved with debate, the two sides in a legal dispute each concerned with presenting a persuasive case. And politics involved, then as now, more and less public venues for debate: a powerful figure might privately receive conflicting counsel from his advisers (we see Chaucer parodying such counsel in the Justinus–Placebo debate of *The Merchant's Tale*), and the functioning of a more public forum like the English Parliament was necessarily dialogical. Though we tend to think of ecclesiastical practices as largely monologic, and though Church decrees and doctrine were not lightly disagreed with, official Church positions were arrived at, in synods and councils, through debate and dialogue. And of course there were, throughout the Middle Ages, those who dissented from official doctrine – notably, in the late fourteenth century, the Oxford theologian John Wycliffe and his followers: such dissent might lead to the strongly-skewed "dialogue" of the heresy trial or inquisition. In more everyday ways, too, medieval religious and spiritual practices involved significant dialogic elements. Prayer, after all, is conceived as a dialogue with the divine (if often a one-sided one). Confession, which received increased prominence in Christian practice after the Fourth Lateran Council (1215), is also a dialogue: an extensive penitential literature instructs priests on how best to play their part in the discussion, and sermons and other didactic literature directed lay people on their role in the dialogue. Liturgy, with its interaction between officiant and congregation, also at times takes the form of call and response. And biblical moments – the annunciation, the nativity, the crucifixion – often have a strongly dramatic quality: it is no surprise that medieval texts often re-present these in the form of dialogue, whether in devotional practices like those described by Margery Kempe (where, for instance, Margery imagines herself participating in the events of the nativity) or in lyric and narrative dialogues between the Virgin Mary and Christ, or Mary and Gabriel at the annunciation, or the child Jesus and the Jewish "masters of the law.".[13]

Not all the medieval traditions and cultural practices of debate and dialogue are, however, equally dialogic (in the sense of involving a multiplicity of voices engaged in a true, undecided, and perhaps ultimately undecidable contestation). As we see in our own moment, the *form* of dialogue might be deployed to decidedly undialogic ends: witness the FAQ ("frequently asked questions"), where questions are posed to elicit the correct answers not to open debate. The same is true, at least in part, for medieval dialogues between master and student like those that follow on Gregory the Great's *Dialogues* or for Latin debates between Jews and Christians: while these may raise and consider real, difficult questions, the weight of authority stands firmly on one side. Debate is opened and pursued at least in part to put questions to rest rather than to elicit a variety of equally disputable claims. Even the Boethian dialogue – with its complex back-and-forth between the distressed narrator and Lady Philosophy – moves in large part teleologically, toward a clear, correct outcome determined ultimately by Philosophy's arguments.

But many medieval authors, including many authors of Middle English texts, employed the traditions and practices of debate and dialogue to more truly dialogic ends; as Reed has suggested, *irresolution* is often the achieved effect in Middle English debate poetry. And this effect is often achieved by bringing debate/dialogue together with the dream. (I do not mean to suggest, however, that a dream frame is *necessary* to the achievement of dialogism and irresolution; *The Owl and the Nightingale*, for instance, while lacking a dream frame, nonetheless achieves a complex dialogism.) Like debate/dialogue, medieval dream vision arises from multiple literary traditions, amid a variety of cultural beliefs and practices regarding the dream. Throughout the Middle Ages, in a system of dream theory extending back into antiquity, dreams were understood to be potentially true or false; the result of somatic or psychological disturbance or, alternatively, an intellection of the truth; sent by God or angels (on the one hand) or by demons (on the other). People seem to have used dreambooks – simple keys to dream interpretation – to figure out what their dreams might mean for the future at the same time that these dreambooks were outlawed as superstitious in canon law. Dreams and visions appear in accounts of saints' lives both as demonic temptation and as divine revelation. Similarly, in literary accounts, we can find radically different uses of the dream. Thus, some dream fictions focus in large part on the dreamer's psychological or physical distress, as in the rich store of French dream poems by such writers as Jean Froissart and Guillaume de Machaut that depict a distressed lover dreaming about the cause and course of his love. On the other hand, stretching back to a classical example like Cicero's *Dream of Scipio*, we find dreams that enable a supernatural revelation, showing their dreamers, for instance, the details of the afterlife. (This tradition of revelatory dreams lines up effectively with a revelatory/pedagogical vision and debate tradition like the Boethian.) But while the tradition of medieval dream vision is thus split between the psychological/somatic and the revelatory, in fact, medieval authors often emphasize not one side or the other of the split but instead the dream's ambiguous potential, its connection to both truth and fictionality, both the dreamer's (physical or psychological) distress and the realm of truth in which she or he might find something useful for allaying that distress. The dream frame comes to be used in medieval traditions – both Latin and vernacular – to focus on the crossings and inter-implications of the worldly and otherworldly, to navigate a middle realm of humanness, where both the bodily and the spiritual are acknowledged, and where their complex relations can be explored.

Placing a debate/dialogue within a dream potentially has the powerful effect of putting the questions considered into a frame that emphasizes ambiguity, raising questions about whether the dream will reveal a truth or be empty of meaning. To stage a debate within such a frame, is also to emphasize the debate's dialogism. Even in a work like Nicole Oresme's Latin *Treatise on the Commensurability or Incommensurability of the Heavenly Motions*, which takes up abstruse "scientific" questions, we find a dream frame used to further a debate's irresolution. The work concludes with a dream-debate between personified figures of Geometry and Arithmetic, and a resolution to the debate is promised by Apollo, who serves as judge of the arguments these figures present. But before Apollo can rule, "the dream vanishes," leaving "the conclusion ... in doubt."[14]

The uses of Middle English debate/dialogue and dream

What kinds of difficult questions did the Middle English tradition take up in particular? Previous attempts to characterize the subject matter of dream vision and debate/dialogue have usually depended upon a primary distinction between the religious and the secular. Francis Lee Utley usefully proposes a distinction among "Religious and Didactic Dialogues," "Debates on Love and Women," and "Catechisms on Science and Biblical

Lore" (the last taking up largely religious or philosophical material in a distinctly didactic manner).[15] But, as with dream visions, a strict division of the religious/didactic and secular (here, specifically, the romantic) does not comfortably fit many Middle English examples. Utley classifies the debates between body and soul as religious/didactic dialogue, and certainly they are that; but they also acknowledge the pull of the body and the world. In Utley's schema, *The Owl and the Nightingale* is treated as a debate on love and women, again not inaccurately; but this complex poem also takes on clearly religious questions, and the poem might ultimately be read as quite strongly didactic.

Alongside the classification of Middle English dream and debate/dialogue across the secular/religious binary, it is useful to think about these interlocking genres as considering questions about two large realms of experience, each of which potentially intersects with *both* the secular and the religious. First, we can identify poems centrally concerned with the individual human being, what constitutes him or her (but usually him), what characterizes (and should properly characterize) his/her life in the world, and beyond (after death). These are works akin, for instance, to Prudentius's *Psychomachia*, with its exploration of internal human conflicts, and to Boethius's *Consolation*, examining, as it does, an individual's distress at a particular point of impasse in his life. The Middle English poems of the body/soul tradition, which put into dialogue the recently dead body and its departing soul, explore precisely what it means to be a human being – composed of a mortal, corporeal and an immortal, spiritual part – needing to live in the world, to survive physically, and yet called on to prepare oneself, as a Christian, for the immortal life that continues after death. A poem like *Pearl* takes up similar questions by means of a different dramatic situation, putting into dialogue a still-living dreamer-jeweler, mourning for an earthly loss, and the "pearl" he has lost to death: the poem asks what constitutes the state of life-after-death or salvation, and hence, how one must live in the world – even in and through the despair of loss. Other Middle English poems take up this sort of question not by examining the breach between body and soul or life and death but instead by focusing on the stages of an individual human life. The *Parliament of the Three Ages* puts into dialogue personifications of three stages in the lifecycle – Youthe, Medill Elde, and Elde – exploring through their distinct self-representations the pleasures and dangers of each. A more narrative exploration of lifecycle occurs in the Middle English translations of Guillaume de Deguileville's popular thirteenth-century French dream-dialogue *The Pilgrimage of the Life of Man*;[16] here, an individual pilgrim's journey through his life is depicted, and both the "proper" routes to salvation and dangerous digressions from it traced.

This last tradition provides at least one of the models for Langland's great dream-dialogue poem, *Piers Plowman*, motivated as it is by the questing Will's question, "how I may save my soule."[17]

Second, we can identify works whose main focus is not the individual but the community, social world, and institutions of which she or he is part. Such works emerge from traditions like that of Martianus Capella's *Marriage of Philology and Mercury*, examining, as it does, the institutional division of knowledge into the seven liberal arts, or the interreligious debate, with its explorations of the assumptions of Christian society over against competing religious institutions. Like Capella's poem, the fifteenth-century *Court of Sapience* explores several interlocking systems of knowledge, using a dream dialogue over which the figure Sapience/Wisdom presides. In a very different mode, a courtly poem like *The Floure and the Leafe* puts into dialogue two different approaches to love. A dream vision like Chaucer's *Parliament of Fowls* does similar work, examining different ways of approaching and understanding love and its effects within society; Chaucer's bird-parliament also comments on fourteenth-century political debates and social arrangements (with the different species of birds evoking the various estates of medieval society). In a more explicitly political register, the alliterative dream debate *Winner and Waster* opens by directly raising contemporary social and political issues; it then pits the personified figures of its title against each other, explaining how two very different ways of imagining society and its relations – based either on "winning" (the hard work of earning, but also a frugal stinginess) or "wasting" (profligate spending and consumption, but also generosity) – might be simultaneously attractive and problematic. Again, Langland's *Piers Plowman* is strongly indebted to this social/institutional tradition of dream debate/dialogue (indeed, it several times echoes *Winner and Waster*). Even as Langland's text takes up questions about the individual Will's "pilgrimage of life," it examines a wide range of social practices, institutions, and problems: the relation between ruling and working classes; the messiness of contemporary English society when measured against traditional, ideal visions of the "three estates"; the problematic involvement of the Church in secular as well as spiritual matters; ecclesiastical corruption and political abuses.

Even so, as the example of *Piers Plowman* should make clear, no individual poem will necessarily fit neatly into only one of these two subcategories. The most complex dream visions and dialogues – *The Owl and the Nightingale*, Gower's *Confessio Amantis*, Chaucer's dream poems, as well as *Piers* – most often take up both individual and social/institutional questions. And there will of course be poems that do not fit comfortably into either subcategory. We might, for instance, identify specifically devotional dialogues – between Mary and Jesus or Mary and the Cross – as constituting a subgenre of their own. But insofar as these focus the individual narrator's or reader's attention on the miracle of the Incarnation and the possibility of salvation this makes possible, we might argue that such poems appropriately stand alongside reflections on humanness like the *Debate between the Body and the Soul*. And insofar as they focus attention on the initiation of institutions – the Church, prayer, the possibility of saintly intervention for the sinner, a system of confession and absolution – they resonate with poems that explore society and social institutions.

The recognition that a significant body of Middle English dream debate/dialogues take up primarily questions about the individual, on the one hand, and about society, on the other, provides a useful way of generating critical questions about the genre and its individual poetic instantiations, and especially questions that will help address the need for putting these genres more into dialogue with a historically informed scholarship and criticism. With the poems of the individual, we should recognize (with feminist, queer, and critical race theorists) that defining the category of the "human" always has a political dimension and hence that we need to ask what the limits these poems put upon "proper" humanness suggest about the exclusions that found dominant medieval definitions of the self and the "proper" life. Such exclusions intimately involve religion: the assumed frame for these poems is always a Christian one. But knowing that, in late fourteenth- and fifteenth-century England, at least, there were significant debates about "proper" *Christianitas*, might we need to consider that these poems excluded not only (potential) Jewish or Muslim but also certain Christian readers? (Wouldn't Wycliffites, who called into question the traditional practice of pilgrimage, respond to the "pilgrimage of life" poems differently from more orthodox readers?) Or, recognizing gender as a crucial, if often unspoken, category in poems like the body/soul debates or the *Parliament of the Three Ages* (here, the prototypical "human" is unquestionably male), we need to ask whether and how such poems could speak to women readers.

It has been easier for critics to see in poems like *Winner and Waster* questions that intersect with "real" history, since these are questions made explicit in the text itself. But in other sorts of institutional dream debate/dialogue like *The Court of Sapience* or *The Floure and the Leaf*, we need also to ask politically and historically informed questions. What is at stake, for courtly writers and audiences, in the fine distinctions of love practice in the latter poem (the answer here again might significantly engage with questions about gender, since *The Floure in the Leaf* is one of only a few poems in the Middle English tradition with a female narrator)? And why frame such explorations of society and its institutions so often in the form of dream and/or debate/dialogue? If my earlier argument is right, and the combination of these two forms is especially useful to the Middle Ages for creating areas of uncertainty, ambiguity, and true dialogism, then the posing of significant questions about society, history, and politics in such forms might have provided an important space where commonly accepted verities might be both asserted and called into question – a space, that is, for real political debate, and perhaps even a staging ground for social and political change.

NOTES

1 I cite the text from *Middle English Debate Poetry: A Critical Anthology*, ed. John W. Conlee (East Lansing: Colleagues Press, 1991), p. 20 (with slight alterations to the spelling).
2 *The Parlement of the Thre Ages*, ed. Warren Ginsberg (Kalamazoo, MI: Medieval Institute Publications, 1992), lines 655–57.
3 A. C. Spearing, *Medieval Dream-Poetry* (Cambridge University Press, 1976).
4 Kathryn L. Lynch, *The High Medieval Dream Vision: Poetry, Philosophy, and Literary Form* (Stanford University Press, 1988).
5 J. Stephen Russell, *The English Dream Vision: Anatomy of a Form* (Columbus: Ohio State University Press, 1988).
6 Steven F. Kruger, *Dreaming in the Middle Ages* (Cambridge University Press, 1992).
7 Peter Brown, ed., *Reading Dreams: The Interpretation of Dreams from Chaucer to Shakespeare* (Oxford University Press, 1999).
8 Michael H. Means, *The Consolatio Genre in Medieval English Literature* (Gainesville: University of Florida Press, 1972).
9 Michael Cherniss, *Boethian Apocalypse: Studies in Middle English Vision Poetry* (Norman, OK: Pilgrim Books, 1987).
10 Thomas L. Reed, *Middle English Debate Poetry and the Aesthetics of Irresolution* (Columbia: University of Missouri Press, 1990).
11 On the Middle English translations of Cicero, see Francis Lee Utley, "Dialogues, Debates, and Catechisms," in *A Manual of the Writings in Middle English 1050–1400*, ed. J. Burke Severs, Albert E. Hartung, and Peter G. Beidler, 11 vols. (Hamden, CT: Connecticut Academy of Arts and Sciences, 1967–2005), vol. III (1972), pp. 715–16.
12 On the translation of the *Elucidarium*, see Utley, "Dialogues," pp. 741–42.
13 Utley, "Dialogues," contains summary descriptions of such Middle English biblical dialogues, pp. 673–79, 683–84, 685.
14 Kruger, *Dreaming*, p. 149.
15 Utley, "Dialogues," p. 672.
16 Middle English translations include an anonymous fourteenth-century prose version and John Lydgate's fifteenth-century poetic version.
17 *Piers Plowman*, 1.84.

6

SARAH BECKWITH

Drama

"Middle English Drama" is the conventional, if misleading, category referring to the textual remnants of a vast, expansive, very imaginative performative culture which was largely non-textual. Drama bespeaks authors who write it, theaters in which it might be produced, and conflicts explored in a room with the third wall removed. But the extant texts from the medieval tradition we call "dramatic" have no known authors, and no special, separate spaces in which they are produced. Middle English theater is likely to seem odd and inert when forced into these alien categories of analysis. We must consider it not as a separate aesthetic sphere, but rather, as part of the material organization of public life. Two scenes, both much anthologized, can stand as paradigmatic instances. The first scene can stand for medieval theater's interest in the actor's body as a primary medium of contemplation, interaction, and the creation of community; the second for the uses of theatrical prop as icon, index, symbol, figure.

There are twelve pageants in the York Corpus Christi cycle that concern the passion. These scenes are boisterous and busy (to take up the infectiously alliterative language of the plays), composed of multiple levels and tensions, and scenically enormously complex. But their still center is the *York Crucifixion*, in which Christ's body is ritually tortured in an agonizingly extended sequence culminating in the reconstruction on stage of the central icon of the culture – Christ on the cross, dramatically played as both reenactment of the crucifixion, and a construction of its central representation. Christ is nailed to the cross by a group of soldiers, played by pinners (makers of joining pegs) who mumble and joke about the arduousness of their labor, the labor that constitutes the only action of the play. This action relentlessly translates the theatrical principle that, working through the very medium of the actor's body, the play must process time at the speed of the actor's body. The cross is finally elevated to view and from the cross Christ utters the words of lamentation from the Holy Saturday liturgy (*O vos omnes qui transitis per viam*; O you who all pass along this way). What the spectators "qui transitis per viam" see is that the central icon of their culture has been literally constructed before their very eyes. Throughout the play the soldiers have spoken only to each other. They never speak to Christ but only across him. And Christ neither addresses nor speaks to them. He speaks only to the present audience. The dramatic lines of address thus sideline the original action of crucifixion. What is taking place is not an event long passed to which this action *refers*. Rather, it is happening in a present that exists as a moment of painful and pure communication between Christ and the present audience. It is the soldiers' present that is sidelined in this action. The theatrical lines of address create two times – the past and the present community – and it is the creation of this community that is front and center of this drama. Christ's presence and present and the audience's present and presence are axiomatic, functioning not as a fetishized memorial to an event that has already once happened, but as a perpetually relived and always present enactment. Yet the present and the presence are not givens of the drama – they must be established and paradoxically remembered. Any viewpoint that fails to understand this is unlikely to grasp the rich and subtle significance of this theater. It is actor's theater – a theater of complicity between actor and audience.

But the second scene shows this theater is also extremely interested in how things function as *signs* in performance. It is a cosmological theater preeminently interested in signification rather than representation. The Second Shepherd's play of the Towneley cycle provides us with a wonderful theatrical prop which is also a complex sign in the play. A lamb, stolen by Mak from the group of shepherds, is a little horned ram who typologically signifies the ram substituted for Isaac's sacrifice; the lamb is also the paschal lamb and it has the makings of a tasty supper, relished in anticipation by the hungry Mak and Gil who disguise it as a baby in an effort to protect their stolen property. The shepherds discover the theft when they offer presents to the newborn; that is, as a result of charitable love, not suspicion. This episode then doubles for the nativity play that follows, serving simultaneously as exploration of typology and its rootedness in charitable reading – how a theatrical sign can stand in for something else, be disguised as something else, yet remain a thing which is literally and untransformably itself. Medieval theater is par excellence a theatre of signification. And indeed it must be, for it is above all a cosmological theater where the actors cannot possibly be pretending to be God (a Reformation misreading) but are only signs for him. Medieval plays will be much more accessible with this in mind. They are extremely interested in the communities formed around a present action.

The mystery plays

The mystery plays are the most extensive and elaborate collective theatrical enterprise in English theater history. There are texts of four cycles – York (*c.* 1467), Towneley (*c.* 1500), Chester (1591–1607) and N-town (*c.* 1468–1500; the "N" stands for *nomen*, or "name," the name of any town where any play from the cycle could be performed) in addition to two pageants from Coventry and some fragmentary others. Whether as an idea existing in the mind of the compiler (it is unlikely that Towneley or N-town were ever performed in anything like the form in which they appear in their manuscripts), or as a performance, as in the cases of York and Chester, they each constitute nothing less than a cosmological history of the world in Christian time, from God's creation, through the incarnation, passion, and resurrection of Christ, to the eschaton, the future time of the Last Judgment. They are variously called "mystery" plays because they centrally concern the mysteries of the Christian religion, or because some of them (York and Chester) were produced by the "mysteres" or trade guilds of the cities which produce them as episodic "pageants" processionally performed on pageant wagons in multiple locations. They are also sometimes called "Corpus Christi Plays" because at least the plays of York and Chester were originally produced on Corpus Christi day, the feast instituted in 1264 by Pope Urban IV to celebrate the central sacrament of the Eucharist.

If the mass was a clerically controlled Latin theophany, the mystery plays were produced and performed by lay people in the vernacular at a time when translation of the Vulgate into Latin was a controversial undertaking. But the plays are not so much translations of the Vulgate as engagements with the very modes of presencing of the divine. As such they engage with the apocryphal traditions, and gospel harmonies, with such meditative or visionary texts as *Mirror of the Blessyd Lyf of Christ*, or the *Revelations of St Birgitta*. In spite of their declamatory, demotic appeal and the occasional intricacy of their stanzaic forms, as *texts*, they are often dull and inert. Their fascination and richness derive not from intensity of character, conflict, and plot but from their engagement with the complexities of presence, with the embodiment of forgiveness – and its negation – in the penitential community that is the body of Christ. It is a form of theater that explores theology through the very of logic of performance.

The York plays

Only the York plays can be indubitably linked to the Feast of Corpus Christi. They were probably being performed as early as 1376, and the

York civic records indicate that a processional route seems to have been established as early as 1394. But the only text we have exists in a civic register about a hundred years after the first records of performance. The register is a record of performance, a kind of check list of all the pageants individually performed by the trade guilds. It seems to have been used by the town clerk as he sat at the first station in Micklegate watching the various pageants go by. It is in York that the sheer ambition and complexity of the plays as an incarnational drama of Corpus Christi can best be seen. The records indicate the vast polysemous nature of the performance – as many as 56 pageants performed in sequence at between 10 and 16 stations appointed and approved by the city and played sequentially at each station. As much as a tenth of the city involved in the production – up to 20 Christs, 12 Maries, several different Gods, and a few Satans wandering the city giving multiple performances at different sites. No physical markers separate off a "theater"; rather the fictive localities of Calvary, Jerusalem, Herod's palace, Pilate's dais or Lazarus's tomb are held in active tension with the public spaces of the city. These plays moreover seem to be financed by fines given by members of the trade guilds when infractions to the division of labor established by the dominant mercantile oligarchy occur. They are thoroughly bound up with the political regulation of labor in the city and some of this concern with work can be seen not only in the ascription of the plays to individual crafts – for example, the shipwrights perform the Building of the Ark – but also, as I've already indicated, in the exploration of the work of crucifixion in the *York Crucifixion*. These plays feature a vast rendition of the trial of Christ in which the agencies of punishment are minutely examined and in which Christ is judged as an excommunicant who refuses to recant, someone who could be handed over to the lay arm to be burnt for heresy after the legislation of 1401 (De Heretico Comburendo). Compositely these pageants comprise an extraordinary penitential drama in which the mechanisms of persecution used for heretics are seen to be the same procedures used in the politically organized execution of Christ. The York plays also feature an extended *quem queritis* sequence (literally "whom do you seek?") where they appear to revisit the liturgy of the empty tomb as an exploration of the absent, resurrected Christ. The empty tomb visited by the three Maries is sandwiched temporally between the two scenes going on in Pilate's hall, and spatially by its contiguity to the Visitatio scene. In the Toronto production, the action in Pilate's hall and the scene at the tomb were staged in the same place so that Pilate actually sat on the very stage prop in which Christ later reveals himself to have been hidden in the Resurrection play. Both a political containment of the word and body and a sense of the centrality of absence to the Eucharist are suggested here in a brilliant theatrical economy. These plays then extend the body of Christ into the city as a thoroughgoing exploration of the body of Christ as a penitential community. Confronting the institutions that purport to speak in his name with the explosive, radical presence of his person, they view the Church itself as constituted not so much as a territory to be defended but as a performance of the life of Christ.

The Towneley/Wakefield play

Coventry, Lincoln, and more recently, Wakefield, a manor town in the West Riding of Yorkshire, have all been offered as locations that the Towneley cycle (Huntington Library MS HM 1) has been erroneously located in. Though all these ascriptions are unlikely, the Towneley cycle is most probably a West Riding production. Containing some pageants borrowed from the York cycle and some written anew, the cycle is strikingly a non-urban theater and features in two of its most famous pageants, known as the first and second shepherd's plays (*Prima Pastorum*, *Secunda Pastorum*) a minutely realized world of agricultural labor, bringing it closer to the world of *Piers Plowman* than any of the other cycles. The cycle features some extraordinary pageants unified by their distinctive use of language and probably written by someone given the name of the "Wakefield Master." These plays (*Processus Noe cum filii*, *Prima Pastorum*, *Secunda Pastorum*, *Magnus Herodes*, and the *Coliphizacio*) and others in the which the Wakefield Master may have had a hand (*Mactacio Abel*, *Conspiracio*, *Flagellacio*, *Processus Crucis*, *Processus Talentorum*, *Peregrini*, *Ascensio Domini*, *Iudicium*, and *Lazarus*) are extraordinarily interested in the power of language to name and to deceive, and in some senses, they may be understood as a meta-commentary on the very forms of Corpus Christi theater, and especially on their prototype, the York plays. They explore the linguistic registers of French and Latin, they give some of the personae distinctive speech patterns and idiolects and feature not only the character Titivillus, the folkloric collector of idle language, but also a pronounced interest in what medieval penitential theology classified as "sins of the tongue." As sins of the tongue, language is seen as speech act, a breaking or binding of community. Such sins of the tongue are most evident in the tyrant's rant, in the famous roaring of Herod, and the grandiloquent boasting of Pilate, but also in the forms of false witness and perjury that condemn Christ, and in the words reduced to the breathless brutality of blows in the torture of Christ.

The N-town plays

This East Anglian group of plays is best regarded as a compilation of play-texts composed some time between 1425 and 1450. Some of the plays, such as the astonishing Mary Play, and the two passion plays were no doubt performed separately but the text itself exists as a collection of texts rather than a script for any one composite performance. It is a group of plays extraordinarily interested in the genealogy of the Christ child. Using the Matthean genealogies and the apocryphal legends accreting around Anna and Joachim, the plays explore the notion of the tree of Jesse and are as interested in the life of Mary as they are in the life of Jesus. Indeed there is a concerted exploration of the marriage of Mary and Joseph, including a "trial" involving a series of detractors who doubt the virginity of Mary. There is also an exploration of the childhood of Mary and included here is a ceremonial translation of the gradual psalms of Mary (called *gradual* because going into the temple, they are sung one psalm per step). Unusually, and in pronounced contradistinction to the York plays, a figure "Contemplacio" mediates some of the plays to the audience and this figure has been one of the factors that have led critics to assume that the provenance of the plays may be monastic. Certainly, some of its sources – such as Lydgate's *Life of Our Lady*, indicate that monastic interests at least abound in the play, which also seems very interested in translating and rendering aspects of the Marian liturgy. The N-town play features in addition the debate in the parliament of heaven between the four daughters of God, and it features as well a Christ celebrating the Eucharist (with an "oble," or communion wafer) at the very feast in which this was instituted – Maundy Thursday. The passion plays were staged in fixed locations and they are unusual in supplying an extraordinary number of stage directions which indicate the most complex and intricate piece of simultaneous, rather than processional staging. The scenes of the Last Supper itself are juxtaposed with scenes of the conspiracy, and those actions take place on separate scaffolds which appear to be veiled off until their action occurs. This is a form of medieval cross-cutting which surrounds the historical institution with intense dramatic irony.

The Chester plays

In the post-Reformation banns (verse announcements) to the Chester plays, an ancient lineage is conferred by the attribution to Ranulf Higden (d.1364), a monastic chronicler of Saint Werburgh who wrote the *Polychronicon*, and the Chester plays were thereby passed off as one of the earliest cycles. They are, in fact, the latest redaction of this form, in that all five of the extant texts can be dated after the final performances in Chester in 1575. All the texts of the Chester cycle bear the mark of that lateness in the self-consciousness with which they approach the entire tradition of Corpus Christi in a Reformation climate and context inhospitable to both the Eucharist in the Catholic mass, and to the practice of performing these forms of theater. The Chester pageants, performed initially on Corpus Christi day, are moved to Whitsun (the feast of the descent of the Holy Spirit associated with the very foundation of the Church in an apostolic community) in *c.* 1471–72, and later on still the pageants are performed as part of the midsummer festivities in 1575. In this festive transference might be seen the possibilities and limits of the essentially festive form of the plays. The plays of Chester are marked by a kind of internal self-distancing and in the awareness of a scriptural as much as a performative tradition. They are deeply interested in what constitutes the miraculous and understand this, not as a set of supernatural tricks but as a systematic intervention by God in the world in ways that must be legible as signs. It is the system of signification and legibility then, with which the cycle as a whole seems concerned. It features, for example, an expositor (in plays 4, 5, 6, 12, and 22) who explains much of the action of the plays and acts occasionally as a translator, and it ends with no less a set of authorities than the four evangelists who authenticate the judgments enacted in the Last Judgment play. Moreover, uniquely in the cycle tradition, the Chester plays feature an Antichrist play. In recapping so many of the previous episodes in the pretense and deceit of the Antichrist to cosmic power so that the many pageants we have seen are staged again in his meta-dramas, the plays meditate on the activity of theater itself as imitation. The power of the Antichrist and the danger of his pretense are dissolved by the explosive and miraculous power of the Eucharist held by the prophets Elijah and Enoch which dispels the ambiguity of the signs of Antichrist. They are distinctively concerned with a Trinitarian God and with sign, portent, and the figurative significance of history.

Morality plays

It is a shame that the brilliant and subtle allegorical dramas written for the stage in the late Middle Ages should have been called "morality plays" because criticism has found it impossible to separate the moralist from the moralizer in the adjudication of these plays. The canon critically denoted as "morality plays" comprise only four plays; the brilliant, filthy, and moving play *Mankind* of late fifteenth-century East Anglian provenance; the play *Everyman*, which exists firstly in a printed treatise and is a translation of the Dutch morality play, *Elckerlije*; the vast *Castle of Perseverance* with its multiple scaffold staging; and the play *Wisdom*, a highly polemical psychomachia on the "mixed life" (a form of devotional life espoused by those remaining in the world, rather than in a contemplative order), in which Wisdom and Lucifer struggle for control over Anima, the figure for the human soul. A play less often considered but which should regularly form part of such a group is the stunning morality play *Nature* by Henry Medwall (*c.* 1530), the first vernacular author of a drama in English whose name we actually know.

If these plays share a common theme it is as much their exploration of what it means to be human as any putative shared "morality." For in them humanity (Everyman, Mankind, Humanum Genus) is understood within the context of a nature whose complex faculties are made in the image of God and who therefore has the potential to both mirror and denature that likeness, to render Mankind in the pun of the play *Mankind*, "onkynde." If the Corpus Christi plays concern the remembrance of the life of Christ ("Do this in remembrance of me," Luke 22:19) memory is also an important category in each of the morality plays; for humankind is the kind of creature who forgets who he is and who therefore needs reminders. These plays, then, are profoundly mnemonic. In them remembrance is hard because it involves situating and realizing a life within the horizons of its non-existence. It is striking that all these plays consider the entire life span of a man from birth from which innocence soon departs to death which is evaded and banished only at great cost. Yet the denial of death is also understood as deeply, understandably human too, a fantasy fully natural to men and women.

The plays are deeply interested in the habits of mind, thought, and action that lead to the denaturing of humankind's soul as the image of God. They are remarkable for the way in which interiority, the inner faculties of the soul, are given concrete shape and form and shown in absolutely material interaction in and on the world around them. The plays are also profoundly invested in the idea that human beings are linguistic creatures. The dramatis personae are themselves words and they have a stage-life for as long as they retain the quality that makes them what they are. They walk onto the stage as soon as they are available to the thought of the central protagonist – so, for example, Pride enters in Medwall's *Nature* – "Even the last man that was in my thought," and with his entrance Reason disappears. And Innocence departs as soon as World begins to mediate the World, that is, the unsurpassable horizon of himself, to the central protagonist.[1] Words in these plays are dramatized actions and so the plays work like forms of dramatized speech in which words do things in the world. Because of their interest in language, they develop idiolects for characters. They are, for sure, didactic, expository dramas but their didacticism works not through generalizing abstract qualities, but rather through a thoroughgoing and thoughtful kind of exemplarity in which recognition is absolutely central (see below). But these features – a profoundly linguistic nature; the ability to put, as it were, the very functions of the mind and soul on display; the central concern with a creature who, for good reasons, forgets his own mortality and who needs to be reminded of it – are best exemplified through an analysis of one or two individual dramas that are seen to constitute the tradition, for the plays reveal the incredible possibilities and diversity of the form as performance.

Actors have long understood the power and playability of these dramas. A recent production of *Everyman* revealed something essential to the habit of mind of these plays: that they are, above all, dramas of recognition. In Complicité's brilliant production of *Everyman*, for example, Marcello Magni and Kathryn Hunter found ways of using the characters to discover the virtues and vices as ways of knowing ourselves morally, spiritually and socially.[2] They did this by representing the personae "Good Deeds, Strength, etc." as a concretely realized and imagined community. Good Deeds is a creature who is barely alive, unable to stand up on her own, for example, until Everyman has experienced contrition. The theological point is that good deeds are ineffective without an act of the will. Good Deeds alone helps man into the grave, deserted by all the other personae including his own five wits.

Mankind (*c.* 1465–70) is an exquisitely detailed exploration of the meaning of the words "mercy" and "mankind" in the context of our evasion and recognition of these meanings. Mankind is at first catechized by Mercy and then tempted by three riotous vice characters, Nowadays, New Guise, and the even more brilliantly named Nought, who mock and deride Mercy's aureate Latinate language. Indeed the very capacity of language to denote is at stake here. "Hic, hic, hic, hic, hic, hic, hic, hic" says New Gyse (l. 776) in a parody of the central words of the mass, answering Myscheff's "Mankynde, ubi es?" (where are you?) in a semi-nonsensical hiccough. In a brilliant parody of Mercy's language, the character Myscheff undercuts the eschatologically harsh ultimacy of the winnowing of souls announced by Mercy where the wheat and the chaff shall be separated (Matthew 3:12; Luke 3:17) to "Corn servit bredibus, chaffe horsibus, straw fyrybusque," an economy in which nothing is wasted, all recycled. These dramas have a deep sense of the power of words and are motivated by a penitential understanding of the sins of the tongue and a sense of human responsibility and accountability in words: "for every ydyll worde ye must yelde a reson" (l.173). Mankind is brought to understand that Mercy has broken his neck, and despairing he prepares to kill himself. At this point Mercy exhorts Mankind to ask for Mercy and finally Mankind is brought to utter the words:

> Than mercy, good Mercy! What is a man without mercy?
> Lytyll is our parte of Paradise, where mercy ne were (l. 836–7)

With these words he acknowledges his specific relation to the character of Mercy (that he is direly in need of him), to himself (that *he* is in need) and to God (this is what it means to be one of his creatures, mankind) at one and the same time. Mercy and mankind are co-incidently understood because mankind is a creature in need of mercy. So the point here is that words precisely do not mean independently of our usage of them – that is they mean what they always mean but we do not mean anything by them. So these are word dramas of recognition because the capacity of these words for reference must go through our voicing of them.

Morality play genre explores the exemplary, but this does not mean that it generalizes from a particular case, for it is very possible to generalize from the particular without putting one's subjectivity on the line. But it is impossible to see one's own experience as an *instance* of a more general case without staking oneself in one's claims. It is with such vital distinctions that this genre concerns itself in fascinating and intelligent ways.

The hold and tenacity of the habits of thought explored in the morality play are seen in the use of them made by later playwrights – most famously Marlowe's use of the good and bad angels in *Dr Faustus*, in Jonson's hilarious depiction of the fact that the devil has been utterly outclassed by the urban hipsters of London in *The Devil is An Ass* and in Shakespeare's profound explorations of conscience in *Richard III* and *Macbeth*. These plays are a homage to the morality play tradition, less a supercession of their conventions than a form of loving fidelity to their central thematic concerns.

Miracle plays

The only extant play of the genre we call "miracle plays" is an extraordinary play from the late fifteenth century whose banns located it as being performed in Croxton, a village in Suffolk. *The Croxton Play of the Sacrament* purports to be based on an incident in Heraclia in 1461, and thus is based on one of the numerous anti-Semitic host desecrations in late medieval Christian culture. A host is purchased by a Jew, Jonathas, from a rich merchant, Aristorius, and then tortured to see if it is actually the body of Christ as the orthodox dogma of transubstantiation claims.

This process is conceived both as a reenaction of the mass with Jonathas misquoting the words of consecration "Comedite, corpus meum" (l. 324), and also as a restaging of the passion plays in which Jonathas and his confederates are, as it were, permanently locked in a reenaction of their putative role as the torturers of Christ. The play is interestingly syncretic and also features a folk episode in which a quack doctor attempts to cure Jonathas, who in stabbing the host has induced it to bleed, and to whose hand the bleeding host is stuck. In an effort to separate the bleeding host from his hand, the Jews attach it to a post and pull away Jonathas's hand which then detaches itself from his arm. When the hand with the host attached is plunged into a cauldron, blood runs over the top of it and Christ miraculously bursts out of it uttering the words of Lamentations 1:12: "O mirabiles Judei, attendite et videte / Si est dolor sicut dolor meus" (O you strange Jews, behold and see if any sorrow is like my sorrow). The Jews convert and are baptized by the bishop; the host is returned to the church from which it had been stolen in a Eucharistic procession in which the audience-turned-congregation is led by the bishop to the sound of the "Te Deum." In its ludicrous yet striking and outrageously staged theatrical effects – Christ bursting out of the "oven," then turning back to bread, the detachable hand, the stage blood – *The Play of the Sacrament* indicates the sheer difficulty in communicating the dogma of transubstantiation. As Peter Womack has wittily put it: the sheer violence of the play bespeaks the difficulty in crediting the genre which wrings its miracle, as it were, out of torture. It is a "sabotage of the empirical," a sensational depiction in which the signs subsume their referents. "It is like a man who is so anxious to convince us of the existence of invisible substances that he resorts to assuring us he has seen them."[3]

Saints' plays

Of this genre there appear to be only two extant plays – both of East Anglian origin – the *Digby Mary Magdalen* and *The Conversion of St Paul*. The Digby *Mary Magdalen* is an immensely complex play that incorporates within it virtually every other genre of play – saint's play, miracle play, morality play, conversion, penitential, and passion play. It is a highly allusive work in which Mary is seen as succumbing to sensuality as she is assaulted by the world, the flesh, and the devil. Converted by the raising of her brother Lazarus she becomes a follower of Christ and herself converts the King of Marseilles after preaching to him and his people, and destroying their heathen temple with a fire from heaven. The play is extraordinarily composite but in this it bespeaks the blurring of the very genres of hagiography and romance which were never separable in the first place. Both these plays are plays about conversion as much as they are about sanctity.

This essay has been written with the assumption that plays are to be performed and that it is only within this horizon that their specific languages can be appreciated and understood. As performances, plays are never confined to their time of origin but have the chance to live again in the moment of their reenaction. They thus offer a unique interpretive challenge. If this essay can stimulate such occasions it will have served its turn.

NOTES

1 *The Plays of Henry Medwall*, ed. Alan Nelson (Ipswich: D. S. Brewer, 1980), pp. 107, 109.

2 The Theatre of Complicité production of *Everyman* was part of a "medieval" season played at The Other Place at Stratford, England in 1997 and later transferred to the Barbican in London.

3 Simon Shepherd and Peter Womack, *English Drama: A Cultural History* (Oxford: Blackwell, 1996), pp. 21, 22.

7

ARDIS BUTTERFIELD

Lyric

Westron winde, when will thow blow,
The smalle raine downe can raine?
Christ, if my love were in my armes,
And I in my bed againe.[1]

This famous brief song, which has caught the imagination of many modern readers, encapsulates both the attraction and the complexity involved in interpreting medieval lyrics. The direct, lightly ironic first-person voice speaks so clearly across the centuries that we hear its tone and feel its desire as if the speaker were within hailing distance. This song functions perfectly as a modern lyric: it is short and condensed, it is personal and erotic, it even swears with a modern expletive accent and emphasis. Yet for many readers there will be a nagging doubt about the validity of this description: can a medieval writer really have been as frankly secular as this, so individual, so mockingly post-modern? "Westron wind" must surely be more medieval than it looks. Sure enough, some of these suspicions are confirmed by its sources. Only one copy survives, as it happens with music, in a sixteenth-century Tudor song book (BL MS Royal Appendix 58, fo. 5): it must date from earlier than this, but we have no way of telling how much. All we know is that it also crops up in settings of the mass by the sixteenth-century composers John Taverner, Christopher Tye, and John Sheppard. Such pre-modern liturgical contexts seem a powerful corrective to any sense of the song's self-sufficient erotic secularity.

How then *should* we read "Westron wind"? Much twentieth-century criticism has been rebuking: assuring us that "late Middle English love lyrics were seldom, if ever, purely literary distillations of moments of intense, private emotion."[2] Medieval short verse is essentially practical, formulaic, devoid of intellectual ideas, imagery, or paradox, and above all, religious. The problem is that "Westron wind" and others like it have proved stubbornly resistant to such rebukes: however much they demand to be interpreted historically in one way, they seem to speak in another.

To get closer to an understanding of medieval lyric we need to face this contradiction. We need to keep in tension both ways of thinking about lyric: the instances of short verse that strike us as intense, private, and literary must be set in context with the huge amount of short verse that does not. This essay explores the enduring modern attraction to the medieval lyric and it argues that renewed attention to the medieval lyric will reveal it to be a touchstone for our larger understanding of medieval literature, not a forgotten corner.

Manuscripts and interpretation

The schizophrenia in modern approaches to the material reveals itself in the difference between the way in which lyrics have been edited, and the form that recent research has taken. Modern editors have opted for a thematic approach, creating anthologies with invented categories that largely disregard chronology or context.[3] Yet research in the last two decades has concentrated almost exclusively on questions of manuscript context and compilation, patronage, and readership. The diversity it has uncovered encourages us to reengage issues of critical interpretation that medieval lyrics naturally provoke for modern readers. This diversity may even suggest, once we have let go the post-romantic clutter that still clings to some descriptions of lyric, how much medieval lyric resembles our own.

Manuscript studies must play a part in this. Yet the information they provide is not always as transparently illuminating as we might wish or suppose. We cannot any more behave as if the manuscripts release us from the hermeneutic quandaries that are always present in any text.[4] This point may be clarified by comparing the lyric in England to vernacular lyric on the continent, particularly in French and earlier in Occitan. The vernacular lyric in England resists many kinds of approach that have become central to our understanding of European lyric. If we take the specific topic of personal ("lyrical") feeling, for example, the brilliant work of Paul Zumthor long ago demonstrated for the Occitan and French tradition of troubadour and trouvère song how far this tradition was not bound by a notion of the individual, but shaped by a much broader principle of collective expression.[5] Yet Zumthor's adumbration of a closed or at least highly selective and sophisticatedly manipulated palate of formulas will not work for the lyric in England. There is no broad, recognizable tradition of high art but a much more diverse, messy and undefined, perhaps undefinable range of material. Even a cursory glance reveals how little it resembles a cohesive tradition or even traditions.

Unlike French lyric, English manuscript sources for lyric seem markedly careless and contingent: with the possible exception of Gower, there is a striking lack of control or concern for authorial self-image until well into the fifteenth century. Lyrics occur in a particularly vast number and range of manuscripts: the 2,000 or so poems that have been recorded by modern editors are drawn from around 450 manuscripts from the thirteenth to the sixteenth centuries. The large majority are anonymous with a striking lack of concern for authorial self-image, in spite of a cluster of named authors such as Chaucer, Lydgate, and Hoccleve, and such lesser-known clergy or lay churchmen as James Ryman, William Herebert, and John Audelay. With anonymity comes an extraordinarily diverse set of manuscript contexts, from sermon and preaching material, moral, mystical, and penitential writing, liturgical books, books on law and medicine, romances, chronicles, political tracts, and drama to courtly poetic anthologies, commonplace books, and other miscellanies of prose and verse, as well as songbooks with music. In another contrast with continental lyric, the English setting for lyric is trilingual, characteristically including verse in French and Latin, at least until the fifteenth century. All this diversity makes it hard to posit a clear sense of an audience or audiences.

The sheer miscellaneous variety of these contexts suggests that the surviving form of the medieval English lyric is evidence in general of a weak and struggling vernacular, not given to self-consciousness and without much sense of itself as a coherent literary language. Yet that very weakness may have very rich implications for our broader sense of literary language in England in the Middle Ages. Lyric language in Middle English functions both as high art and as a more transparent medium full of formulas, repetition, and citation; it requires us to consider questions of the whole and the fragment; of linguistic identity and plurality; of the relation between words and music; of lyric's possible meditative, didactic, liturgical, and political functions; and of memory, writing, and oral performance. This essay will consider these questions as it works selectively through the main types of source for short verse in the period, in rough chronological order.

Origins: 'authentic' survivals

The earliest surviving lyrics in English occur in manuscripts of the late twelfth and early thirteenth centuries. They have acquired a semi-mythical status in the modern period. The title of "oldest"' lyrics goes to three short sets of verse attributed to Saint Godric, who died in 1170 after a life spent first on pilgrimage and then in isolation as a hermit near Durham. The poetry occurs in several manuscripts, mostly as part of biographies written by the monks of Durham: like Caedmon, Godric apparently received these songs, words, and music from heavenly instructors, in this case Mary,

Saint Nicholas and accompanying angels. Three of the manuscripts contain music, and several provide a Latin translation of the English lines:

Sainte Marye Virgine,
Moder Jesu Christes Nazarene,
Onfo, schild, help thin Godric,
Onfang, bring heyilich with thee in Godes Riche.

Sainte Marye, Christes bur,
Maidenes clenhad, moderes flur,
Dilie min sinne, rix in min mod,
Bring me to winne with the self God.

(Davies, No. 1, p. 51)

These songs are full of interest for several reasons: not only are they at the cusp of post-Conquest change in the English language, they are also provided with a story of spiritual inspiration which confers on them originary status. At the same time, both from the music (to which I shall return) and the Latin translation, there are intriguing signs that the form in which we read them has already been modernized and improved by scribes determined to give them even more spiritual authority.

The issue of authenticity is even more pressing in perhaps the most well-known medieval song of all, "Sumer is icumen in." Surviving uniquely in a mid-thirteenth-century manuscript from Reading Abbey, the song is written out with music above two lines of text, in two languages, English on top in black, Latin underneath in red. In English, the song is a celebration of spring with a cuckoo's call in the refrain ("Sing, cuccu, nu!"); in Latin it is a moving and dignified hymn with pastoral overtones ("Perspice, Christicola" [See, O Christian]). Instructions in black with separate notes in red indicate that the song is a round (*rota*) or canon: it can be performed by two singers, or perhaps as many as twelve. No other piece with this degree of canonic repetition exists in the thirteenth century, either in England or on the continent.

All this complexity is awkward (and usually ignored in modern literary editions). English audiences over the centuries have overwhelmingly preferred to assume the lyric was originally English: the Latin words added later to give the secular song a pious afterlife. Yet, as musicologists have long explained, there are no grounds at all musically or metrically for deciding conclusively that the English comes first. The dilemma is a remarkable reminder of how powerful the desire to choose one version of the song over the other has been for modern audiences. By contrast the manuscript encourages us to think dually and flexibly. "Sumer is icumen in," that iconically English song of the countryside, turns out to invoke far wider cultural meanings than subsequent, narrower ideas of Englishness have implied. It also opens up questions about the linguistic borders between the religious and non-religious.

Preaching manuscripts and related religious books

Such questions continue throughout the period. From the mid-thirteenth century onwards, large numbers of lyrics can be found in manuscripts associated with preaching, preaching aids, and sermon notebooks, as well as actual sermon collections, many of them compiled by Franciscans and Dominicans. Sermon collections are sometimes organized alphabetically by topic or, like the Franciscan *Fasciculus Morum*, according to a structure such as the seven deadly sins. The preaching context is important for many reasons. Most immediately, it shows how misleading the modern anthology can be. Some of the lyrics most frequently chosen for modern editions, and presented as miracles of miniature, poetic concision, are actually found embedded – often almost imperceptibly – in prose works. And here they may contribute in very specific ways to the larger prose structure. The most underlying of these is their use to mark the structural divisions, which medieval sermons employed according to careful rhetorical principles. The following comes from a sermon on Christ as knight, teacher, physician, and judge; the divisions first given in Latin are announced in English verse as follows:

A knyht of pris to ffyth for man.
A clerk ful wyse and techyn he can.
A scley leche þat brynges oure hele.
A streyt domes-man oure met to dele.[6]

Verses can also act as a means of formulating didactic material, arguments and messages in a way that can be easily memorized. For example, there are verse versions of the Decalogue, or Ten Commandments, and verse summaries of the five kinds of lechery, given first in Latin and then in English. Less catechistically, verse will be used to summarize the moral lesson of a story in a rhetorically arresting and dramatic way, or to express the moralizing thoughts spoken by a character in an exemplum. Verse inscriptions are quite common, as are proverbs, versified prayers, and verse renderings of biblical quotations.

The question of their status as English verse – verse in English – is intriguing. Most of the sermons and sermon material containing verse are in Latin, and the bulk of the English verses are the result of translation from Latin. Thus, a great deal of this verse needs to be understood as embedded not just structurally within a larger prose surround, but linguistically within a liturgical and para-liturgical Latin culture. To take one of the most anthologized examples:

> Now goth sonne under wod:
> Me reweth, Marye, thy faire rode.
> Now goth sonne under Tre:
> Me reweth, Marye, thy sone and thee.
>
> (Davies, No. 6, p. 54)

This classic example of an ostensibly intensely literary lyric actually occurs in a thirteenth-century Anglo-French treatise by Saint Edmund of Abingdon called *Le merure de Seinte Eglise* (*Speculum ecclesiae*), dedicated to the monks of Pontigny.[7] In chapter 24 Edmund urges his readers to think on Mary as she waits and watches her son dying on the cross. Edmund uses this lyric as the third in a sequence of citations, the first two of which are in octosyllabic French couplets. First, Mary addresses herself in the words of Naomi:

> E pur ceo poeit el dire de soi
> Ceo ke dist Neomi:
> "Ne me apelez des or ne avant;
> Kar de amerte e dolur grant
> M'ad replenie le tot pussant."

[And because of this she can say of herself what Naomi said: "Do not call me by name from this time on, nor from before, for the Almighty has filled me with bitterness and great pain."]

Next a citation from the *Song of Songs*:

> Meimes cele tenuire
> Dit ele en le chancon de amur,
> "Ne vus amerveillez mie
> Que io su brunecte e haslee
> Car le solail me ad descoluree."

[She utters the same theme in the following love song: "Do not marvel that I should be brown and sunburnt for the sun has discoloured me."]

Finally, and unexpectedly, Edmund turns to English:

> E pur ceo dit un Engleis en teu manere de pite:
> Now goth sonne …

[And because of this an Englishman says in this way out of pity …]

After Mary speaks through two well-known biblical female figures of woe, the move to a male voice ("un Engleis") – implicitly the male preacher

Edmund speaking for his male audience of monks – positions the English lyric as part of a biblical history of female grief, speaking for Mary and not just about her. The lyric's use of English has a special force: it attempts to make this grief newly and immediately accessible to its present audience. The weight of puns (sun/son; wood/cross/tree; cross/face) in the densely accretive repetitions of the English words comes partly from that linguistic shift, and the sense of an emotional and metaphoric journey in which language has acquired increasing significance. "Thi faire rode" gains the meaning of "haslee" and "descoluree" ("tainted" and "discoloured"), just as "sonne" has become threatening and powerfully transforming ("le soleil me ad descoluree"), itself a metaphorical realization of "de amerte e dolur grant / M'ad replenie le tot pussant." The manuscript context of "Now goth sonne" and the textual support already provide by its medieval commentator does not thwart a modern close reading but gives it new depth and richness. The lyric's English is the product of a wider process of exegesis in which the English words have a hinterland of French and Latin writing.

Perhaps surprisingly, some lyrics in sermons or other preaching contexts are by no means narrowly religious. The theme of a sermon may be based on a dance-song, or the preacher may refer during his address, sometimes with wry humor, to love songs that he characterizes as well known to his audience. In one example, the early thirteenth-century Archbishop of Canterbury, Stephen Langton, based a sermon on the French *rondet de carole* "Bele Aelis" (pretty Alice): each line of the song is written out separately in large red letters and followed by a detailed theological exposition. The following couplet is used in another thirteenth-century sermon to show how, like Christ, we must wrestle with our spiritual enemy:

> Atte wrastlinge my lemman I ches,
> And atte ston-kasting I him forles.[8]

Songs like these were often used, along with proverbs and short narrative anecdotes, to introduce a sermon, or provide material for giving authoritative weight to a moral point. Sometimes the preacher will explain with often exaggerated scorn (as in one of the sermons that cites "Atte wrastlinge") that this sort of song is sung by "wild women and wanton men in my country when they dance in a ring, among many other songs they sing, which are worth little" (214);[9] but at others, he may introduce a song neutrally, even with implied respect. A sermon on human ingratitude and lack of faithfulness ascribes a love song to Christ whom the preacher imagines might address the soul in the same way as a cuckolded husband might complain to his wife. Thus the Lord, when he is abandoned by the soul as a cuckold is abandoned by his wife, could after Easter use this love song:

Ich aue a loue vntrewe,
Þat [is] myn herte wo.
Þat makez me of reufol hewe
Lat[e] to bedde go.
Sore me may rewe
Þat eure Hi louede hire so.[10]

Such references show that a preacher may not only be aware of well-known secular songs but may be on the inside rather than the outside in using them as a frame of reference for his sermons. They also show that sermons give us access to more than one type or register of verse. Some of the verse is directly drawn from Latin, from the liturgy, antiphons, prayers, and hymns; some is composed to add a vernacular counterpoint to the Latinate rhetorical structure of a sermon or set of preaching notes; and some is from a wider, less specifically ecclesiastical world of heard and repeated verse that the preacher wants to appropriate. Rather than see the latter as a battle between sacred and secular as modern scholars of lyric have often been inclined to do, or else, more romantically, as a means of discovering a lost world of folk song, we might, through the manuscripts, take our cue from the diverse responses of the preachers themselves.

Earlier household collections of verse and prose

Household collections constitute a further group of thirteenth- and early fourteenth-century manuscripts in which questions of register, language, and cultural context are particularly prominent. Recent research on the most well known among them, London, British Library, MS Harley 2253, has shown that most of the book was copied *c.* 1340 by a professional scribe who probably put the material together as a household book for the Ludlows of Stokesay.[11] Other related collections include Oxford, Bodleian Library, MS Digby 86, Oxford, Jesus College MS 29 and Cambridge, Trinity College MS 323. Harley 2253 has a special status for scholars of the medieval lyric because – unlike any other book containing lyrics from the period – its lyrics were edited separately in 1948 by G. L. Brook. Yet although this edition drew pioneering attention to the manuscript source of these lyrics, and has subsequently given them the cachet of their own name "The Harley Lyrics," it also misrepresented it and them since Brook included only secular or religious lyrics written in English. In fact, Harley 2253 is a trilingual miscellany, in which secular and religious lyrics in English are to be found in amongst very varied writings in prose as well as verse, in French as well as Latin.

The English lyrics often occur in a mixture of mini-sequences interspersed with prose and verse pieces in French and some macaronic verse, that is, verse written in a mixture of French, Latin, and English. In one intriguing cluster in Quire 7, nine of the English lyrics mingle with a political poem, a verse narrative about a cross-dressed monk called Marina, a semi-religious poem on repentance, the raunchy dramatized French fabliau *Gilote et Johane*, and a French prose tract on pilgrimage. Susanna Fein has argued that these pieces are an "inventive collage" on the topic of female sexual appeal:[12] this makes convincing sense of songs in which women are depicted as themselves a collage of physical features:

Hire rode is ase rose that red is on ris;
With lilie-white leres lossum he is;
The primerole he passeth, the perwenke of pris,
With alisaundre thareto, ache and anis.
Cointe ase columbine such hire cunde is,
Glad under gore in gro and in gris;[13] (p. 21)

Hire browe browne, hire eye blake;
With lossum chere he on me logh,
With middle small and well imake.
(Davies, No. 13, p. 68; p. 23)

This barrage of details obscures and fragments their female subject. In the larger comically knowing context, they demonstrate that the broader language of female description crosses genres in often ironic and disrupting ways. The compiler of Harley 2253 does not view lyrics as either exclusively English or narrowly "lyric." He often intermixes lyric with narrative, verse with prose, English with French, politics with piety and unrestrained sexual humor.

Later fourteenth-century religious books

Lyrics play a role in the huge Vernon manuscript, one of the most important religious collections of the latter half of the fourteenth century. The largest surviving book of Middle English works, the Vernon manuscript weighs nearly 50 lb (22 kg), and was made from the hides of over two hundred calves. It is too heavy and bulky to transport easily, and so, like a musically notated mass book (the only kinds of contemporary books in England comparable to Vernon in size) must have rested on a ledger as a one-volume library, probably for the daily devotional use of a community or institution such as a nunnery wealthy enough to have commissioned it. The place of lyrics in this volume differs strikingly from that of Harley 2253 some fifty years earlier. The earlier sections of the book contain some very long, major works, such as the *Speculum Vitae*, the *South English Legendary*, the *Prick of Conscience* and *Piers Plowman*, alongside much shorter pieces, hymns and prayers. Lyrics are gathered together principally in the last quire, twenty-seven altogether. Of this number, twenty-three use stanza forms borrowed from French ballades, including refrains.

As I wandrede her by weste
  Faste under a forest side,
I seigh a wight went him to reste;
  Under a bough he gon abide.
Thus to Crist ful yeorne he criyede,
  And bothe his hondes he held on heigh:
"Of povert, plesaunce, and eke of pride,
  Ay merci, God, and graunt-mercy!"

(Norton, No. 104, p.105)

In contrast to Harley 2253, the lyrics are perceived as a distinct genre, one with a place in an exclusively English-medium book.

Richard Rolle (d. 1349), whose work appears in the Vernon manuscript, wrote intense, spiritual tracts punctuated with songs of love directed at Jesus. These widely circulated tracts encouraged much other affective writing, including lyrics. Rolle's sensuous lyrics convey a first-person speaker who breeds emotional fervor in repetitive, yearning lines:

I sitt and sing of luve-langing
That in my breste es bredde.
Jesu, Jesu, Jesu,
When war I to thee ledde?

(Davies, No. 36, p. 109)

This is clearly personal and emotional verse: yet is it "lyrical"? We need a descriptive language that can allow for the intensity and privacy of Rolle, and yet includes much more than the merely "lyrical." Rolle uses language that is not his, since it is part of the wider world of vernacular piety and common discourse. It is constructed of phrases that can be widely, and often exactly, paralleled across other verse, and also other genres. The language of the *déjà-dit* is not only rife at this time but vital since it creates the base of popular response to religion. This language is also the language of love. Rolle's distinctive habit of fusing these common languages, of generating a gradually more vivid spiritual experience through accretive effects marks him out not merely as "lyrical" but as a writer who extended the power of the first-person voice to move and stimulate his reader or listener into deeper pieties.

Author collections

The only substantial author-based lyric collection in Middle English is attributed not, as one might expect, to Chaucer, but to the French poet Charles d'Orléans. John Gower produced a collection of ballades in French along the lines of the sophisticatedly crafted author-centered books of lyrics produced on the continent. However, the lyric in English was only sporadically organized into authorial collections, more usually being caught up in a haphazard fashion in quite separate publishing ventures. Even Chaucer's lyrics, though usually attributed and copied in short sequences, are set into larger anthologies rather than presented as discrete authorial publications. English writers do not begin to imitate their continental counterparts until later in the fifteenth century when Lydgate, Dunbar, and Skelton take more control over the material character and layout of their lyric writings. The inspiration for this change may ultimately lie with Chaucer. In spite of their sporadic manuscript status, the difference in Chaucer's lyrics is palpable: the higher style, the pretensions toward classical status and the brilliant ease with which he redirected the current of a highly confident French lyric mode into English are written all over his few surviving examples of lyric verse:

> Hyd, Absolon, thy gilte tresses clere;
> Ester, ley thou thy meknesse al adown;
> Hyd, Jonathas, al thy frendly manere;
> Penalopee and Marcia Catoun.
> Make of youre wifhod no comparysoun;
> Hyde ye youre beautes, Ysoude and Eleyne;
> My lady cometh, that al this may disteyne.[14]

Later household and commonplace books

Lyric copying proliferates in the fifteenth century. Characteristically, lyrics are collected in books which have extremely varied contents and seem to have been put together either through an individual's exercise of personal taste and convenience, or a household's desire to have some central repository for written information and entertainment. Well-known examples include *The Commonplace Book* of a Norfolk churchman Robert Reynes of Acle (Tanner MS 407) (compiled *c.* 1470 to 1500) and the books of London grocer Richard Hill and London mercer John Colyns. The material in these books ranges from court proceedings, terms for food rents, directions for blood letting, notes on hexachords (six-note sequences of tones) and London street locations, to chemical and cookery instructions (on dyeing cloth, how to kill rats, or make ink), arithmetical puzzles, riddles and card tricks. Lyrics seem to have been regarded in this context as domestic fare rather than high art.

It is gud for dronkyn men
A raw lek to ete, & comfortyth the brayn[15]
He pat stelys this booke
shulbe hanged on a crooke;
He that this booke stelle wolde
sone be his herte colde:
That it mow so be
seip amen, for cherite.
Qui scripsit carmen Pookefart est sibi nomen
Miller jingatur qui scripsit sic nominatur.
(Robbins, No. 89, p. 85)[16]

Other books of this type, such as the "Findern" manuscript, and Fairfax MS 16, seem to take lyric more seriously. They also shed further light on fifteenth- and early sixteenth-century reactions to Chaucer's lyric verse. They show a taste for love poetry and its anthologizing properties: whole poems are copied, such as Chaucer's *Parliament of Fowls* but also extracts, single stanzas or short sections of longer works, chosen seemingly for their didactic or proverbial qualities. The Findern MS adds a new and rare phenomenon: lyrics probably written by women directly into convenient spaces in the book. It is always difficult to identify women's writing in the Middle Ages: even where it is not anonymous, it may have been copied and transformed by a male scribe. These lyrics are tantalizingly likely to be the homely work of women in the Findern household: full of the familiar courtly phrases used by lovers, on separation, longing and loyalty.

Lyrics and music; songbooks

The survival of music for the English vernacular lyric is scarce, especially in the thirteenth and fourteenth centuries. We have some two- and three-part polyphonic settings of short stanzaic verse, such as the song "Bryd one brere" which occurs on the back of a legal document, and "Worldes blis" found in a fragmentary state in the binding of a Cambridge manuscript.[17] Apart from such scattered scraps, the most revealing information comes indirectly from an Irish manuscript, the so-called Red Book of Ossery. This contains sixty religious Latin songs composed by the Bishop of Ossery (in office in southern Ireland from 1317–60). He tells the reader that his aim was to ensure that his priests did not pollute their throats by singing "frivolous, lewd and worldly songs" (*cantilenis teatralibus, turpibus et secularibus*). The incipits of sixteen of them are then written by the side of his pious words, indicating that he was quite happy for their melodies at least to be reused (although unfortunately this is an unnotated manuscript).

Once we move into the fifteenth century, songbooks survive, several with music; these are largely of carols, stanzaic songs with a burden or refrain, the topics of which include political propaganda, lullabies, Christological and Marian devotion and sexual comedy as well as Christmas feasting. Carols thus have a strong musical connection: they seem to have been largely generated from monastic institutions such as Worcester Cathedral, Bury, and Meaux Abbey, and perhaps give us an indication of the less structured activities of monks and clerics, probably in company with lay associates. Early Tudor songbooks, such as the Fayrfax MS, or Henry VIII's MS, in which we come back full circle to "Westron winde," have a broader range of repertoire, including instrumental pieces, puzzle-canons, and rounds as well as continental songs, and have a more directly courtly ambience and function.

Conclusions

The medieval English lyric makes us engage heavily with anonymity, largely freeing us from the weight and bias of author-dependent criticism, so marked in modern responses to Chaucer. In being forced to turn to the texts without that particular prop, we find ourselves, paradoxically, much closer to the social and physical circumstances of people quickly scribbling in margins and in spare sections of parchment pages, making notes for their professional duties as teachers, preachers, choirmasters, and spiritual directors. We come closer, in other words, to a less exalted and abstract notion of authorship, one that involves the working practice, and also forms of relaxation, of a very broad cross-section of the literate population. Medieval English lyrics have much to teach us about the nature of public language, about the ways in which a whole community can have access to a common culture and how educated writers can speak to and on behalf of that culture. In such a textual world, the notion of a single text or for that matter a single voice seems inadequate.

Chronology, too, becomes an often elusive guide to a text's meaning, since a lyric may be repeated, and transformed, across several centuries. The fifteenth-century lyric "I sing of a maiden" (Davies, No. 66, p. 155), for example, has been remodeled from a longer thirteenth-century piece "Nu þis fules singet" (Brown, No. 31, p. 55). Public language, language cited across specific literate communities, speaks more broadly than we are often prepared to allow: and, as in the Findern lyrics discussed earlier, however poignantly and indeed autobiographically a lyric text may sound, it is always expressing that sense of singleness within a context of known public access to such forms of utterance. No individual lyric is impoverished by our recognition of this, and neither need any seem oddly out of place in its modernity; rather lyrics teach us to value the power of a collective sense of language, in all its forms, throughout the Middle Ages and into our time.

NOTES

1 R. T. Davies, ed., *Medieval English Lyrics: A Critical Anthology* (London: Faber and Faber, 1963), [hereafter Davies], No. 181, p. 291.

2 T. G. Duncan, ed., *Late Medieval English Lyrics and Carols 1400–1530* (Harmondsworth: Penguin, 2000), p. xxiv.

3 Carleton Brown's edition of *Religious Lyrics of the Fourteenth Century*, 2nd edn (Oxford: Clarendon Press, 1957; 1st edn, 1924) [hereafter Brown] is the only one that groups lyrics according to author and manuscript rather than theme.

4 See Andrew Taylor, *Textual Situations: Three Medieval Manuscripts and their Readers* (Philadelphia: University of Pennsylvania Press, 2002).

5 Paul Zumthor, *Essai de poétique médiévale* (Paris: Editions du Seuil, 1972).

6 Siegfried Wenzel, *Verses in Sermons: "Fasciculus Morum" and its Middle English Poems* (Cambridge: Medieval Academy of America, 1978), p. 83.

7 H. W. Robbins, ed., *Le Merure de Seinte Eglise by Saint Edmund* (Lewisburg: University Print Shop, 1925).

8 Siegfreid Wenzel, *Preachers, Poets and the Early English Lyric* (Princeton University Press, 1986), p. 213, note 20.

9 For discussion of ecclesiastical disapproval of French *caroles*, see C. Page, *The Owl and the Nightingale: Musical Life and Ideas in France 1100–1300* (London: Dent, 1989), pp. 110–33.

10 Wenzel, *Preachers*, p. 220, note 36.

11 Carter Revard, "Scribes and Provenance," in *Studies in the Harley Manuscript: The Scribes, Contents, and Social Contexts of British Library MS Harley 2253*, ed. Susanna Fein (Kalamazoo: Medieval Institute Publications, 2000), pp. 21–109.

12 Susanna Fein, "A Saint 'Geynest under Gore': Marina and the Love Lyrics of the Seventh Quire," in *Studies in the Harley Manuscript*, p. 353.

13 Maxwell S. Luria and Richard L. Hoffmann, eds., *Middle English Lyrics* (New York: Norton, 1974) [hereafter Norton], No. 26, p. 21.
14 *Prologue* to *The Legend of Good Women*, *Riverside*, F 249–55.
15 R. H. Robbins, ed., *Secular Lyrics of the Fourteenth and Fifteenth Centuries*, 2nd edn (Oxford: Clarendon Press, 1955) [hereafter Robbins], No. 80, p. 77; San Marino, Huntington MS HU 1051, fo. 85r.
16 London, British Library MS Royal 18 A XVII, fo. 199r.
17 See E. J. Dobson and F. L. Harrison, eds., *Medieval English Songs* (Cambridge University Press, 1979).

8

RITA COPELAND

Lollard writings

The heterodox movement known as Lollardy produced a great many writings in Latin and English. To group these writings together as a "literature" or literary tradition is a retrospective formation, although as we will see, a valid one. But those who wrote the texts would not have seen their writings as contributing to a "literary" culture in any formal sense, even though at times they appropriated certain standard literary forms or traditions to their own purposes. These writings do not fall easily into aesthetic categories of the "literary," in the sense of observing literary modes (drama, poetry, forms of fictive narrative) or genres (romance, epic, history, lyric), although there are many examples among them of rhetorical genres such as sermons, polemic, and personal testimonies. Lollard writings productively test the limits of what might commonly be understood as the "literary," because they constitute a textual culture embedded in political, religious, and even intellectual argument. To the extent that Lollard writings reflect upon their own literary forms or formation, it is in the interests of vernacular literacy itself: Lollard writings in English often present an acute self-consciousness about transferring a technology of critical literacy to a vernacular audience imagined as participating in a continuing process of textual interpretation and correction.

Lollard writing presents a particular set of themes that, when taken together, express dissent from orthodox religious teachings and practices. Dissent in itself is not a literary genre or form or theme: it is a posture in relation to a certain historical occasion or condition. We find many different historical developments that produced oppositional writing: among these are the rebel letters of the 1381 Peasants' Uprising; bills, libels, and similar public documents associated with moments of acute unrest, such as Cade's Rebellion of 1450; and more persistently, a long tradition of social satire and complaint against corruption of the clergy, which might have been acidic in its attack but was not necessarily suppressed. Lollard writing at times shares certain themes or forms with these kinds of polemical texts (as does *Piers Plowman*), and in fact the boundary between what was considered heretical dissent and what was tolerated as satire could sometimes be rather porous. But nevertheless Lollard writings do have a very distinctive history of their own, emerging in response to specific historical circumstances, and engaging certain core theological issues. Later Lollard writings also demonstrate a great sense of continuity with earlier Lollard texts, which is not surprising, given that most writing by Lollards was produced within a period of thirty years, from the last decades of the fourteenth century to the early years of the fifteenth century. This essay will focus on Lollard writings in English, treating them as a relatively coherent textual tradition.

Lollardy had its origins in the heterodox thought of the Oxford theology master John Wyclif (d. 1384). (The term "Lollard" came to be applied to Wyclif's followers around the time of his death. The term derives from Dutch "lollen," to mumble, and was a term of opprobrium applied to eccentrics and vagabonds.) In its earlier phase it was an academic movement, limited to Wyclif and his circle of younger academic followers at Oxford. In the 1370s Wyclif had gained notoriety (and, for a time, some powerful political support from no less a figure than John of Gaunt) for advocating disendowment of the clergy in temporal goods (that is, land holdings and other wealth). But Wyclif also gave enormous attention to doctrinal questions, most importantly in his attacks on the doctrine of the transubstantiation of the Eucharist. In 1382, the Blackfriars' Council, a council of clerics and theologians convened by the Archbishop of Canterbury, determined that certain propositions found in Wyclif's writings were heretical or erroneous. This council can be seen as a historical dividing line between the academic and popular or lay phases of the heretical movement. After 1382, the movement slowly began to lose its academic foothold, as the authorities of the Church turned their attention to purging Oxford of adherents to Wyclif's thought, over the next two decades forcing some to recant, driving others underground, and persecuting new or remaining adherents. In 1401, the statute *De heretico comburendo* declared heresy a capital offense, and created a very dangerous climate for adherents of the sect. In 1407 and again in 1409, Archbishop Thomas Arundel imposed his *Constitutions*, which sought to suppress the Lollard heresy by rooting out its causes, and prohibited unlicensed possession of vernacular Bibles and of any writings associated with the heresy, as well other manifestations of the heresy. The *Constitutions* established detailed and comprehensive terms for the prosecution of Lollard suspects, responding with particular force to the textual and pedagogical character of the movement.

For Wyclif, scripture is the "book of life" and the only real ground of truth, and thus "every Christian must study this book."[1] This theme in Wyclif's writings would enable the continuation and expansion of his movement into the popular sphere, in spite of the loss of its academic core and more general repression: Wyclif's advocacy of vernacular and lay access to Scripture and to theological discourse gave the impetus for the production of an astonishing corpus of vernacular Wycliffite writings, including the translation of the whole of the Bible into English, perhaps the greatest achievement of textual culture in medieval England. In the years after the Blackfriars Council of 1382, while religious authorities suppressed the movement's academic core, many Wycliffite intellectuals took their work beyond Oxford, quite literally translating it into an English textual environment. The strong links they established with lay communities would carry the movement forward through the fifteenth century and into the sixteenth long after the influence of the academic center had waned.

Other aspects of Wycliffite reformism, both doctrinal and ecclesiological, also provided a focus for popular anticlericalism. Wyclif's argument against transubstantiation, the orthodox doctrine that the bread and wine consecrated during the mass change their substance into the body and blood of Christ, proved to have especially strong appeal among lay communities. The mystery of the Eucharist seemed to epitomize the authority vested in priests because of their sacramental role, an authority that could be used to mislead lay people who were denied their own independent access to the genuine theological truths of Scripture. According to the *Twelve Conclusions of the Lollards*, a text that documents Lollard beliefs (which survives only because it was either copied or compiled by adversaries of the Lollards), "the feynid [*feigned*] miracle of the sacrament of bred inducith alle men but a fewe to ydolatrie," for they are made to think that just by virtue of the priest's words the substance of Christ's body is enclosed in a little piece of bread that "thei schewe to the puple." Rather, they should believe what Wyclif taught, that the material bread is the body of Christ by convention only, not in substance: "for we suppose that on this wise may euery trewe man and womman in Godis lawe make the sacrament of the bread withoutin oni sich miracle."[2] The force of this opinion derives from two related ideas: that the real ground of spiritual truth is found, not in the external performance of the sacraments, but in Scripture itself, and that all people – both men and women – who are guided by virtue, faith, and contrition constitute a "priesthood of all believers" who should not be dependent upon clerical mediation of the truths that are fundamental to salvation. The inevitable corollary of these ideas – a theme pursued relentlessly throughout Lollard polemics – is that the people must have access to the word of God, the Scripture, in their own language. Lollardy was a heretical movement fueled above all by the production and circulation of theological texts in the vernacular. While Lollard teachers and preachers could exert charismatic influence over individual communities of Lollard adherents, the attraction that sustained the Lollard movement through repeated persecutions was the empowering idea of reading and interpreting the Bible, independent of priestly oversight. The prospect of unsupervised, individual lay interpretation of Scripture was in turn particularly threatening to official orthodoxy.

With this interest in the vernacular in view, we can begin classifying Lollard "literature." The central and monumental achievement of the Wycliffite Lollard movement was the translation of the Bible.[3] This was achieved in two versions. The first, known among modern scholars as the Early Version (EV) was a very literal translation, an unapologetic attempt to render the Latin word for word, and thus to stay as close as possible to its literal sense. The second version, known as the Later Version (LV), is a more idiomatic rendering which retains the literal meaning of the original while also achieving great elegance and power in its language, syntax, and prose rhythms. The work on the Bible translation must have spanned the last two decades of the fourteenth century, beginning somewhere around 1380, with the LV reaching completion some time in the late 1390s. It was a collective effort, and the names of the writers involved in it are not known: despite a tradition of assigning Wyclif's name to it, there is no evidence to link him with its production. As to where it was produced, Anne Hudson concludes that it was probably carried out at Oxford, the most likely place because it had a scholarly community and a concentration of books for study;[4] moreover, the established network of Wycliffite adherents was there. It is remarkable to think that the period of steadily mounting pressure on the academic circle of Wyclif was also the period of the most intense productivity of these radical scholars and preachers.

The Wycliffite Bible, in part or in whole, survives in over 250 manuscripts, the greatest number of copies of any Middle English text, more than double the number of copies than the *Prick of Conscience*, and almost five times as many as the *Canterbury Tales*. This degree of survival is especially notable when we consider that possession of the Lollard Bible was prohibited after 1409. Readers of the vernacular Bible ranged across social classes, from noble sympathizers with Wycliffite ideas to learned laity, and to the artisanal communities in towns across England, among whom the Lollard heresy established strong footholds during the fifteenth century. The fact that many manuscripts are not complete, but contain one or more sections of the Bible (for example, copies of the Gospels alone, or the New

Testament alone) may suggest the practise of laypersons commissioning a copy of one portion of the Scripture.

The Wycliffite Bible represents a crucial phase in the development of English prose, perhaps the greatest monument of English prose before the Renaissance. It is also a culminating point for the history of what Ralph Hanna calls "Ricardian translation," the large projects of Englishing history, philosophy, and theology in the fourteenth century.[5] The General Prologue to the Wycliffite Bible, found in eleven copies of the Bible, shows how the translators understood their project and used the completed text as an occasion for sustained theoretical reflection on the issues of vernacular translation and the nature of scriptural interpretation. The writer of the Prologue links the objective of stylistic and linguistic clarity in translation to the desire for interpretive accessibility: "At the bigynnyng I purposide with Goddis helpe to make the sentence as trewe and open in English as it is in Latyn, either more trewe and more open than it is in Latyn." Here the notion of clarity ("open") applies to both language and meaning.

The Prologue also presents a self-consciously historicizing perspective on biblical translation. Chapter 15 directly addresses official opposition to Bible translation (in the 1390s, such opposition was not yet formally legislated, but the pros and cons of Bible translation were being vigorously debated in Oxford). The writer of the Prologue (who was also involved in the work of translation) sets forth a historically sophisticated response to the opponents of vernacular translation of Scripture by noting that the Latin Vulgate Bible was itself nothing more than a "vernacular" translation of its own era, and that the modern English translators are simply following in the footsteps of Saint Jerome by translating Scripture into their own vernacular.

> For Ierom, that was a Latyn man of birthe, translatide the Bible bothe out of Ebru and out of Greek into Latyn, and expounide ful myche therto ... And Latyn was a comoun langage to here puple aboute Rome and biȝondis and on this half, as Englishe is comoun langage to our puple ... And the noumbre of translatouris out of Greek into Latyn passith mannis knowing, as Austyn [*Augustine*] witnessith in the secounde book of *Cristene Teching* [*On Christian Doctrine, or. De doctrina christiana*]
>
> ... Lord God, sithen [since] at the bigynnyng of feith so manie men translatiden into Latyn and to greet profyt of Latyn men, lat oo [one] symple creature of God translate into English for profyt of English men!

Moreover, the Bible has been translated into other vernacular languages, so there is nothing exceptional about a modern English translation:

> For if worldli clerkis loken wel here croniclis and bookis, thei shulden fynde that Bede translatide the Bible and expounide myche in Saxon, that was

> English either comoun langage of this lond in his tyme. And not oneli Bede but also king Alured [*Alfred*], that foundide Oxenford, translatide in his laste daies the bigynnyng of thte Sauter into Saxon, and wolde more if he hadde lyued lengere. Also Frenshe men, Beemers [*Bohemians*] and Britons [*Bretons*] han the Bible and othere bokis of deuocioun and of exposicioun translatid in here modir langage.[6]

In this argument we see the true character of Lollard "radicalism": "radical" properly means "proceeding from the root" (Latin *radix*), and while it may now connote unorthodox deviation, Lollard arguments on behalf of their reformism always claim that theirs is a desire to return to the roots of the Church, to purge the Church of its recent corruptions and return it to its original purity. This argument extends to the Englishing of the Bible: rather than defending vernacular translation as something new (and necessary), they present vernacular translation as something that is as old as Christianity itself, and that has a long and honorable tradition. It is the current opposition to translation that is unprecedented and perverse.

Along with the translation of the Bible, there emerged two other signature forms of Lollard scriptural production: the texts known now as the *Glossed Gospels*, and the vast English sermon cycle. Both of these may be said to constitute forms of a pedagogical genre. We can take the example here of the *Glossed Gospels*, which were a smaller-scale production than the sermons. Surviving in nine manuscripts, the *Glossed Gospels* were an attempt to provide authoritative commentaries, in English, elucidating the literal sense of Scripture. They are based on a form of the EV translation, and they all follow a similar format: they quote a passage from the Gospel, break the text into shorter passages to be glossed (*lemmata*), and then follow it with an English commentary based on standard, orthodox sources (usually the Church Fathers, Bede, Bernard, and Aquinas). But most interesting is the way that the *Glossed Gospels* reveal their purposes and intended audiences through the prologues that accompany some of them. These prologues explain the layout of the text in the form of a "user's guide" to the visual organization of the page, as if the compiler assumed that his audience would have little or no familiarity with the way that text and commentary work together on a page, and set out to teach them:

> First in glos a word of text is vnderdrawen; thanne cometh glos and the doctour seyinge that is alleggid in the ende of the glos. And aftir that doctour, al the glose suyinge is of the next doctour alleggid, so that the glos is set before, and the doctour aleggid after, who it is and where.[7]
>
> [First, a word of the text is underlined; then comes the gloss and the name of the learned authority [who is being quoted]. After the citation of that learned doctor, the following gloss is from the next authority being quoted, so that

the gloss is set out first, and the name of the authority is given after [the gloss derived from his writing] – who said it and in what work he said it.]

Such a text brings scholarly exegetical practices to a non-academic, lay audience, teaching readers how to recognize and use these academic textual procedures (glosses and citations of authorities keyed to short passages). Many lay Lollards, especially from the artisanal classes, participated in underground reading circles (conventicles), and from the records of investigations and trials throughout the fifteenth century, we know that some Lollards acquired their literacy through the Bible readings conducted in these illegal reading groups. The *Glossed Gospels* appear to be directed to the needs of such lay readers, providing the tools of scriptural interpretation as well as technical introductions to the use of those tools.

The cycle of 294 English Wycliffite sermons may also have been used for group study, although by no means limited to this, as is suggested by the ambitious and professional character of the manuscripts, and by their sometimes erudite content. They may also have been intended for public use, as alternative homiletic material for preaching in established churches.[8] The sermons are grounded in readings from Scripture (although the biblical text used in the sermons is independent of the EV and LV translations), and as Kantik Ghosh has shown, their character is in large part exegetical (in ways that derive from the disputative complexities of Wyclif's own work) rather than overtly polemical.[9] A number of sermons that are outside the cycle offer a more direct insight into the circumstances of their use. One of these is a sermon on mendicancy from the early fifteenth century, the "Omnis plantacio" sermon, based on Matthew 15:13. It appears to have been delivered by an itinerant preacher, with the closing passage suggesting a strong relationship between the preacher and a community of readers: "Now siris [*sirs*] the day is al ydo [*done*], and I mai tarie ȝou no lenger, and I haue no tyme to make now a recapitulacioun of my sermon. Netheles I purpose to leue it writun among ȝou, and whoso likith mai ouerse [*peruse*] it."[10]

Investigations of Lollard suspects and trial proceedings against them produced a variety of textual genres: catalogues of Lollard beliefs prepared by adversaries, as well as their counterparts, instructional *schedulae* or lists of tenets prepared by Lollards for their own instruction (although these survive only in the adversarial record); records of trials and the evidence given by or against individual Lollards, sometimes comprising extended narratives as well as confessions; and personal testimonies of interrogation. These records (mostly in Latin) provide much of our evidence for the views of lay Lollards, and sometimes give us the voices of women, such as the remarkable testimony about Margery Baxter and the confession of Hawisia Moone, both of the Norwich diocese.

Two magnificent texts represent this last genre: Richard Wyche's letter of 1403 (in Latin), and the *Testimony of William Thorpe*, which is set in 1407, although whether it was written then or a few years later cannot be known with certainty. Both Wyche and Thorpe were itinerant Lollard preachers, among the few remaining members of the core Wycliffite intellectuals. Richard Wyche was imprisoned in Durham from 1402 to 1403, during which time he was periodically interrogated by the Bishop of Durham. Late in this process he composed a long letter to a friend in Newcastle, in which he detailed how he was questioned and urged to recant and affirm his faith in orthodox teaching.[11] Although he did recant shortly afterwards, he continued his heretical activity up until 1440, when he was burned as a relapsed heretic. His letter is dramatically constructed, relating a story of how a knight came to his cell one day and offered him a deal: he can make a public abjuration of his heretical beliefs without compromising his conscience by swearing his oath with "mental reservations." But the deal is a trap, as he discovers to his dismay, and in his subsequent appearances before the bishop he summons up all the evasive techniques that we might expect of a former academic trained in the skills of disputation. The *Testimony of William Thorpe* stages disputational technique with even greater force. It purports to be Thorpe's own narration of his interrogation at the hands of Archbishop Thomas Arundel over three days in 1407 (there is no external record of Thorpe's arrest and interrogation on this occasion, and there is little documented evidence of Thorpe's career outside this very "literary" autobiography). Thorpe shows himself getting the better of Arundel at almost every juncture in the interrogation, which builds to a dramatic, angry climax. But Thorpe's *Testimony* is also important for its evocation of the circle of Wyclif and his disciples at Oxford some thirty years earlier. Thorpe places himself among this group (possibly as a younger member of the circle); from his present position as a persecuted preacher of Wycliffite ideas among the laity, he looks back at Wyclif's charismatic leadership and the power of his teaching, which his disciples spread beyond the walls of the university:

> Ser, in his tyme maister Ioon Wiclef was holden of ful many men the grettist clerk that thei knewen lyuynge vpon erthe. And therwith he was named, as I gesse worthili, a passing reuli man and an innocent in al his lyuynge. And herfore grete men of kunnynge and other also drowen myche to him, and comownede ofte with him. And thei sauouriden so his loore that thei wroten it bisili and enforsiden hem to rulen hem theraftir; and for thi, ser, that this forseid lore of maistir Ioon Wiclef is ȝit holden of ful manye men and wymmen the moost acordinge lore to the lyuynge and to the techynge of Crist and his apostlis.[12]

The last categories of vernacular Lollard writings that we will consider here are the polemical tract, the legal document, and the verse satire. It is difficult to classify such texts according to genre; it is better to say that they attach themselves to available genres through parody, imitation, and even interpolation. One important example is the *Tretise of Miracles Pleyinge*, an attack on the mystery plays. Another is the *Lantern of Light*, which was written soon after the imposition of Arundel's *Constitutions* and their prohibition of the translation of any text of Scripture in any form. The *Lantern* is an overt and harsh response to the repressive effects of the *Constitutions*, an affirmation and exposition of Lollard positions on theology, ecclesiology, and lay access to Scripture. It is also an important piece of evidence for our understanding of lay education, and of the legal measures taken to suppress the heresy. In 1415 the London skinner John Claydon was brought up on charges of heresy, and his ownership of the *Lantern* was the main incriminating evidence against him. According to the records of the case, Claydon had commissioned a copy of the book. But Claydon was illiterate, and the record recounts that he had his servant read the book to him. Claydon had been convicted once before for heresy, and with these new charges he was condemned as a relapsed heretic and burned with his book.[13]

The category of legal document is not an absolute one, since Lollard polemics as well as catalogues of tenets have legal orientations or have their origin in confrontations around canon law; by the same token, the testimonies of Wyche and Thorpe are profoundly concerned with questions of legal compliance and interpretation of the law. The category is made more ambiguous by the problem of Lollard hostility to legal documents, especially indulgences and letters of fraternity, and by Lollard appropriations of some literary forms of legal documents, notably the devotional image of the Charter of Christ.[14] But one important text that enters directly into the field of legal discourse is the Lollard Disendowment Bill, which was probably presented to Parliament in 1410, at a point at which it was still possible for Lollards to engage legitimately in the public sphere. The text is preserved in both English and Latin in several chronicles. It purports to be a petition presented by the commons, and calls upon the king to confiscate all the temporal holdings of "bisshopes, abbotes and priours" as well as of colleges, chantries, cathedrals, and the like; the king will be able to put these new resources to better use, including endowing new universities and enabling each town to care for its poor. As implausible as its claims may seem, it was a carefully constructed and well-researched production.

Lollard verse satire attaches itself to existing forms and traditions: this is nowhere better illustrated than in *Pierce the Plowman's Crede*, a poem of the 1390s, which offers itself both as an imitation of *Piers Plowman* (in the manner of other social satires that were not regarded as heterodox) and as a reinterpretation of the pedagogical genre of the primer, with its catechetical teaching. The *Crede* is itself a primer in Lollard ecclesiological reformism. The speaker seeks instruction from the friars (like the narrator in passus 8 of Langland's poem), in the hopes of learning the Creed, that is, the principles of true belief. As in the tradition of Langland's poem, the only competent teacher is the humble Plowman, whose own rhetoric – rejecting any magisterial authority – resembles that of the teacher's voice in the Lollard *Glossed Gospels*. The poem is notable, not only for its systematic denigration of the mendicant orders, but for its sympathetic references to figures in the Lollard movement, Wyclif himself (528–32) and the layman Walter Brut, tried for heresy in 1393 (657–62), and for the outrage it expresses about the prosecution of Lollards.[15]

If the year 1382 represents an important turning point in the history of the Wycliffite Lollard movement, marking the beginning of its gradual transformation from an academic sect into a long-lived popular movement, so six centuries later the year 1988 might be seen to mark a significant transformation in modern literary scholarship on Lollardy. In this year, Anne Hudson published *The Premature Reformation: Wycliffite Texts and Lollard History*, the first great book in more than half a century devoted to the textual culture of the movement, and the most complete account of Lollard history and writing ever produced. Where previous scholarship on the Wycliffite Lollard movement had dealt with particular aspects of it (for example, Wyclif's own theology, or the role of the movement in fourteenth- or fifteenth-century politics, or later Lollardy, or the Lollard Bible, or specific questions of manuscripts and their provenance, or specific questions of Lollard writings and more "mainstream" literary texts), Hudson's encyclopedic study assembled the results of her own and others' research to paint a broad picture of the origins, spread, and continuing power of Wycliffite ideas, the means of their purveyance, and their role in the histories of lay piety and of lay education. Most important, Hudson's book was able to substantiate a strong claim about Lollardy: that it had a literature, and constituted a literary tradition. The appearance of the book was the impetus behind a sudden efflorescence of Lollard research in Middle English studies, a new sense of the importance of Lollard textuality within English literary history, and an emergent sense of continuities between the medieval and early modern periods, now understood to be linked through common traditions of ecclesiological reform. From being a relatively specialist scholarly interest just a decade or so earlier, Lollard literature began to emerge as a key focus in Middle English studies, in tandem with new approaches to *Piers Plowman* and other vernacular traditions of reformist satire and spiritual piety. An important facilitator – and tracker – of this renaissance of Lollard studies has been the formation of the Lollard Society, originally organized by Jill Havens, which has also maintained an up-to-date bibliography compiled by Derek Pittard (www.lollardsociety.org). Within literary studies, there have been relatively few new monographs devoted entirely to Wycliffite Lollard texts; but the conception of Middle English literary history has been so thoroughly reshaped by the field of Lollard textuality that Lollard writings figure now in many book-length studies of later Middle English literature, as scholars seek to understand the interaction between heterodoxy and orthodoxy, and more important, the often fluid boundaries between the two.

NOTES

1 John Wyclif, *De veritate sacrae scripturae*, ed. Rudolf Buddensieg, 3 vols. (London: Wyclif Society, 1905–07), vol. I, p. 109; trans. Ian Levy, *John Wyclif: On the Truth of Holy Scripture* (Kalamazoo: Medieval Institute Publications, 2001), p. 98. See also Anne Hudson, *Selections from English Wycliffite Writings* (Cambridge University Press, 1978), p. 162, and Steven Justice, "Lollardy," in *CHMEL*, p. 666.

2 Hudson, *Selections*, p. 25

3 Josiah Forshall and Frederic Madden, eds., *The Holy Bible ... Made from the Latin Vulgate by John Wycliffe and his Followers*, 4 vols. (Oxford University Press, 1850).

4 Anne Hudson, *The Premature Reformation: Wycliffite Texts and Lollard History* (Oxford: Clarendon, 1988), pp. 240–41, 246–47.

5 Ralph Hanna, "The Difficulty of Ricardian Prose Translation: the Case of the Lollards," *Modern Language Quarterly* 51 (1990), 319–40; David Lawton, "Englishing the Bible, 1066–1549," in *CHMEL*, pp. 454–82.

6 Hudson, *Selections*, pp. 70–71; the complete General Prologue in Forshall and Madden, eds., *The Holy Bible.*

7 Rita Copeland, *Pedagogy, Intellectuals, and Dissent in the Later Middle Ages: Lollardy and Ideas of Learning* (Cambridge University Press, 2001), pp. 133–34, cited from Oxford, Bodleian Library MS Laud Misc. 235, fo. 2r.

8 Hudson, *Premature Reformation*, pp. 197–200. For the entire corpus of sermons, see Anne Hudson and Pamela Gradon, eds., *English Wycliffite Sermons*, 5 vols. (Oxford: Clarendon, 1983–96).

9 Kantik Ghosh, *The Wycliffite Heresy: Authority and the Interpretation of Texts* (Cambridge Univeristy Press, 2002), pp. 112–46.

10 Hudson, *Selections*, p. 96. The complete sermon is edited in Anne Hudson, ed., *The Works of a Lollard Preacher*, EETS os 317 (2001).

11 Wyche's letter is edited in F. D. Matthew, "The Trial of Richard Wyche, 2 *English Historical Review* 5 (1890), 530–44. On this text, see Copeland, *Pedagogy*, pp. 151–90.

12 Hudson, *Selections*, p. 32; the complete text is in Anne Hudson, ed., *Two Wycliffite Texts*, EETS os 301 (1993). See Copeland, *Pedagogy*, pp. 191–219.

13 Hudson, *Premature Reformation*, pp. 211–14; *The Register of Henry Chichele, Archbishop of Canterbury, 1414–1443*, ed. E. F. Jacob and H. C. Johnson, 4 vols. (Oxford: Clarendon, 1938–47), vol. III, pp. 132–38.

14 Emily Steiner, *Documentary Culture and the Making of Medieval English Literature* (Cambridge University Press, 2003), pp. 201–11.

15 Helen Barr, ed., *The Piers Plowman Tradition* (London: Dent, 1993); see especially the introduction, pp. 8–14. Most surviving copies of the poem date from the sixteenth century. Another group of satirical texts in verse and prose, *Jack Upland, Frair Daw's Reply*, and *Upland's Rejoinder*, ed. P. L. Heywood (London: Oxford University Press, 1968), dates from the earlier part of the fifteenth century.

PART II

Authors

9

RALPH HANNA

William Langland

In a volume such as this one, a chapter entitled "William Langland" is uniquely paradoxical. While not an anonymous (like "the *Gawain*-poet"), Langland remains alone among Middle English poets in failing to exist, in any meaningful way, outside his poem. Eloquent testimony to this liminal status appears in the frequent confusion, robust until well into the sixteenth century (and still occasional in modern critical discussions), in which this poet's title character, Piers Plowman, is often construed as the authorial (and not simply the authoritative) centre of his poetic work. As "William Langland," this poet has no known biography. Reliable early fifteenth-century evidence indicates that the name may well be a pseudonym, assumed by one William Rokayle, from a gentry family with its seat at Shipton under Wychwood (Oxfordshire). He was probably the man of that name who was ordained to "first tonsure," the lowest clerical order, in the Worcester diocese *c.* 1339 to 1341. Given canonical restrictions, this means Rokayle/Langland might have been born as late as 1331 to 1333, a period consonant with the date, 1325 to 1335, that may be inferred from the poem (in the B version, see Passus 11, line 47, and Passus 12, line 3).

We know nothing of Langland's life-occupations beyond what the poem itself implies: residence in London (cf. C 5.2, as well as citations from perhaps in-progress materials by London writers 1376–86) and an intense familiarity with clerical – not simply religious but also legal, administrative, and parliamentary – culture. Indeed, the only evidence for Langland's protracted life comes from the survival of his poem in three distinct forms – A, B, and C versions – a first taste of the work's many confusing multiplicities. The A version, the earliest, consists of three visions, conveyed in approximately 2500 lines, divided into ten sections or *passus* (Latin for "steps"), along with a prologue. The B version adds eight more dreams and ten more passus, in addition to reworking and expanding some of the material in the earlier passus, for a total of some 7,700 lines. The C version is about 350 lines longer than B, but constitutes an extensive reworking, including a different division of passus, which yields 22 rather than 20. (This essay mainly restricts itself to the B version, customarily read by students.)[1] From his use of a parliamentary statute of 1388 to shape a passage customarily taken as "autobiographical" (C 5.1–104), Langland was still alive at the end of the 1380s, but we do not know for how long after.

This problematic status of the "author" signals many other unique aspects of *Piers Plowman*. Although customarily discussed in the context of other late fourteenth-century poetry, Langland's interests are distinctly "precanonical." He does not seem to have much interest in poetry for its own sake, and although he may have lived until *c.* 1390, his work differs markedly from that of his "contemporaries." He relies upon literary procedures of the period preceding and leading up through his youth, *c.* 1270–1340. This was a culture intensely trilingual (reflected in the poem's frequent reliance on Latin and – much less frequently – French, quotation) and one in which English writing was regionally, not nationally, based, most particularly in the West of England. This culture often remained impervious to continental influences that "Ricardian" writers like Chaucer, Gower, and the Gawain-poet take for granted. In form, *Piers Plowman* is fundamentally a dream narrative (and thus analogous to many "Ricardian" and later poems). But alone among dream poetry, the poem is not a single dream but a succession of them: eight in four paired sets, the two central examples punctuated by "inner" dreams (in which the sleeping poetic figure falls asleep again). The eight visions present a bewilderingly discontinuous succession of diverse narrative movements. Individual dreams often begin by bruiting issues their predecessors had seemed to resolve. And confusion does not end here. Characters disappear from the narrative and reappear in different guises: in passus 4, Witty is a sharp grafter but Wit in passus 8–9 is seemingly an authoritative speaker; in passus 4, Peace is a wronged peasant but in passus 18 a merciful female personification of virtue.

Although the poem rebuffs continuous narrative, and with it, narrative summary, it does display a general movement. The first two dreams, framed as a search for Truth (God), take up topics prominent in early alliterative poetry, West of England writing, "the [parlous] condition of England." The first dream emphasizes problems of courtly life, relations of kings and magnates, and the second agrarian ones, those of peasants and their directors in the fields. The second pair of dreams, in which the object of the search has become (defining) "Do-well," largely consists of academic debate, much of it confusingly addressing the value of academic discussion itself. Following one resolution of these difficulties early in the first dream of the next pair (Anima, the soul, integrates all the disagreeing faculties of the previous dreams), most of the remainder of *Piers Plowman* is generated from actions of the second inner dream. This concluding movement renarrates the New Testament, primarily the gospels and Acts of the Apostles. The final dream, redolent with allusions to the Apocalypse, the end of the New Testament, designedly returns the project to its beginnings in contemporary English deviation from gospel precept.

This bare summary may indicate, just as does the profusion of dreams here, Langland's predilection for episodic form. While the poem is narrative, it is only fitfully, and sometimes apparently repetitively, so. Surprisingly for a poem that gestures so often at the need for spiritual renewal, Langland chooses as narrative model what many medieval religious writers considered their depraved literary enemy, the knightly romance. Although the poem prominently identifies itself with pilgrimage-narrative, in its handling, Piers rebuffs the expected progression (advance in understanding or virtue) inherent in a pilgrimage-allegory and replaces it with a fuzzier sense of quest through a trackless landscape. And Langland further derives from romance his interest in narrative proliferation and divagation.

Yet narrative fitfulness fails to explain everything about the poem. The primary thrust of *Piers Plowman* remains thoroughly consonant with dream narrative – not romance marvels and encounters, but endless conversations. *Piers Plowman* is overwhelmingly imbricated in talk, which suspends and retards narration and which often seems, in its diverse spiritual, political, and social subject matter, at odds with the romantic narrative medium. Morton Bloomfield indicated this particular uniqueness in a famous statement that reading the poem "is like reading a commentary on an unknown text."[2] In so doing, he drew attention to the tendency of *Piers Plowman* to be filled with talk but not with a narrative recognizably associable with any conventional literary genre. Indeed, this inability to link the poem clearly to some subject or referent provoked Bloomfield's effort to create a genre for it, the "apocalypse." But this literary type, as Bloomfield himself admitted, has no recognized status, and he was forced to present *Piers* as a compound of six separate literary forms. The problem Bloomfield astutely framed now is usually seen as one of the poem's multiple discourses. Langland proves especially confusing because, unlike Chaucer, he tends not to parcel his diverse voices out among clearly delimited social sites. He constantly reproduces conversation because, in what he regards as a social emergency, the language which might direct and regulate behavior, spiritually and socially, has become ineffectual and fractured. England has lost its coherent centre and become a range of contending voices.

In this formulation, the poem addresses a problem most particularly spiritual because medieval regulative language traditionally depends upon Latin-based clerical instruction. But in the situation Langland addresses, clerical instruction has lost its attraction; too many priests ignore the basic responsibility of caring for souls or have found other, more salubrious pursuits: government administration and high theologizing, for example. Regulation of linguistic, and thus social and spiritual, behavior has become ineffectual. In this situation, any self-anointed individual might set up shop as an apparently viable teacher, and the very language of regulation itself falls under scrutiny and becomes the subject of debate.

Both these topics are broached in the narrator Wille's self-description of the opening lines:

> I shoop me in shroudes as I a shepe weere,
> In habite as an heremite, vnholy of werkes ...

As a speaker, Wille is fundamentally unrooted and identity-less, always "as" or "like." He presents himself as assuming a state traditionally blessed, poverty, but questionably so: although dressed in rough woolens (sheep-clothes), he might be, following on the gospels, only a costumed wolf preying on a flock/audience. (Cf. Matthew 7:15: "Beware of false prophets, who come to you in the clothing of sheep, but inwardly they are ravening wolves.") As hermit, he may express an intensely private religious fervor; yet equally, this status appears self-created, unregulated, and thus perhaps a symptom of (rather than cure for) social malaise, an anomalous religious order including only himself. (Much later in the poem the character Hawkin, in his pride, is described as "Yhabited as an heremyte, an ordre by hymselue, / Religion saunz rule and resonable obedience," 13.284–85).

As this opening continues, the speaker "wander[s] wyde in this world wondres to here" and identifies "this world" with the western Malvern hills. These references imply a poem most broadly about "the condition of England," the romance land of marvels. But as an opening, to say this is to signal "the condition in which I as a poet find myself." Wille is first presented as an ambivalent and identity-less speaker, a figure for a poet coming to write, after some undesignated other career and at a preternaturally advanced age, perhaps forty (at some point toward 1370 or perhaps later). The wonders he "hears" (not, one must insist, the more conventional "sees") point to the need for linguistic recuperation of a better England. But simultaneously, laying "wonders" (prodigies, perhaps monstrosities) out for a reader requires taking on a new, surely undefined and perhaps improper social identity. Through this act of self-recuperation, Langland always implies a desire to remake not simply society but the speaker into a better self/citizen/soul. *Piers Plowman* is most basically a dream (and thus far from unique in its gross form). But its dreams fail to achieve a closure convincing to the poet – hence their profusion. Multiplicity is also a recurrent property of the poem's individual dreams. Unlike other dream visions, typically given over to authoritative instruction of a more or less willing naive auditor, *Piers Plowman* rebuffs authority and closure.

The episodes at the head of the poem's two major sections provide salient examples. That at the opening of passus 8 almost functions as a signature, having inspired the first of several deliberate Piers-imitations, the Lollard onslaught on the friars called "Pierce the Plowman's Crede."[3] In this waking episode, Wille meets a wandering pair of Franciscans; they offer him perfectly traditional, orthodox, and sensible instruction, to be ratified at numerous later points in the poem. But he rejects the friars' information angrily, not for its content (on which he offers no commentary) but because put off by these figures' (quite real) sanctimonious self-righteousness. In passus 1, the dreamer meets and is put off by the overbearing and unsympathetic Holychurch, who should ostensibly be the source of basic spiritual answers. Both these episodes indicate that, whatever the content of the conversations would suggest, traditional and popularly sanctioned religious ideas do not form the center of the work, but only provide a place from which its trajectory may begin. Confusingly, the dreamer's distaste is not predicated upon the message he receives from Holychurch (which persists in the poem as basic given) but rather upon the drama of conversation. He responds negatively to medium and manner, the narrativized and personalized way in which authoritative instruction is offered. This repeated form of portrayal underwrites the poet's own title for his endeavors, "Dialogus Petri Ploughman." The generic marker "dialogue" implies a conditioned and argumentative approach toward truth, in which no speaker or statement might stand without qualification.

The poem's unique multiplicity of dreams requires that a reader always begin, start over again. But, less obviously, dream visions conventionally present a poet's memory of imaginative/imagined experience. Thus, Wille's C version "autobiography" is introduced as "romynge in remembraunce" (5.11). The poem is engaged not just in a constant movement of forward-looking, often frustrated, expectation, but equally always of recursive memory of the dream(s) that have gone before. And if the dreamer is to remember, this demand equally extends to the poem's readers, who can only capably follow the argument if they can recall the terms and conditions of its past interrogations of repeated topics. Thus, although Langland's primary narrative metaphor is the pilgrimage, this never clearly fulfills the progressive model one might expect. Although a specialized version of the knightly quest (one could compare the two parts of the earlier London romance Guy of Warwick), rather than reaching a destination, Truth's tower for example, pilgrimage in the poem just as often proves recursive, reconsidering and rewriting (as, at a larger level, Langland's revisions between textual versions do) the poem's own construction. Indeed, manuscript rubrics suggest that the poet may have designated the second part of his poem "inquisiciones," querulous searchings, a term that lacks any implication or promise of closure.

Piers Plowman himself powerfully invokes the pilgrimage narrative in this spirit. He elaborates a clearly linear track that, he alleges, will lead to the court of Truth (heaven, salvation). Yet the description of one's entry rebuffs the very metaphor in which the narrative has been couched:

> And if Grace graunte þee to go in in þis wise
> Thow shalt see in þiselue Truþe sitte in þyn herte
> In a cheyne of charite as þow a child were,
> To suffren hym and segge noȝt ayein þi sires wille. (5.605–08)

A lengthy linear, and ostensibly developmental, model concludes with the rejection of progression altogether. As Piers describes it, the narrative metaphor that implies travel through a landscape has only described introspective movement (to visualize the heart and its contents). Pilgrimage cannot form a sequence of acquiring knowledges but a memorial act, a return to a childish knowledge already present. There is, in this formulation, nothing to move or develop from, only and always the loving "kind knowing" Holychurch has argued is implanted in the heart at its creation (cf. 1.137–43). Yet simultaneously and typically, the actual detail of the progressive pilgrimage narrative has been neither elided nor erased from the poem. Most importantly, Grace the gateward makes a concerted reappearance at 19.199–335 in association with the poem's enigmatic emblem of salvation, Piers's pardon.

Moreover, the poem is itself predicated upon other memories. Critics have frequently described it as being socially conservative, and at least part of this conservatism is a desire to return to an older (and mythologized) England. The character Anima incidentally laments the decline of grammatical knowledge (the very clerical regulation of language itself), at one point (15.376) citing, among present-day failures, the loss of competence in reading Anglo-Norman, the traditional legal/administrative language of England. Anglo-Norman had also been a precocious literary medium but was by the later fourteenth century in literary eclipse.

Remembering or reviving features of this culture lies very near the heart of Langland's peculiar modes of poetic operation. Like Anglo-Norman literary practices common at the time of the poet's birth, *Piers Plowman* constantly straddles a divide between the clerical (in the sense of "cure of souls"), and governmental, employing a clerical discourse which moves naturally and at an instant between social practice (especially as legalistically conceived), legendary and romance history, biblical narrative or citation, and moral comment. The poem overtly remembers examples of this cultural practice with some precision. For example, Conscience's moralization of Saul's regal rapaciousness (3.259–83) recalls an analogous use of the same biblical locus in the *Vita Edwardi Secundi* (*c.* 1326). Again, the affecting account of the peasant Peace's despoliation by suppliers for a magnate household (4.47–60) takes up a complaint presented through heroic and gospel history in William of Pagula's *Speculum Regis Edwardi III* (early 1330s). The loss of such discursive linkages and proprieties, now displaced by other clerical pursuits, contributes to the emergency that generates the poem.

Piers Plowman also looks to specifically English models, which are equally antiquated, more testimony to that recycling and resurrection in a new context one would associate with memory. Langland's most obvious inspiration, at least early in the poem, is perhaps the most modern of these, the alliterative debate/satire, *Winner and Waster* (1350s), but older texts, for example, *The Simonie*, a satire of the social estates responding specifically to events of the early 1320s, may be more pervasive in their influence. Winner's speaker identifies himself as a "westren wy," from a locale like the envisioned Malvern, and the intensely trilingual culture of the Welsh Marches, best exemplified in the collection British Library, MS Harley 2253 (*c.* 1340), also lurks very near the inception and procedures of the poem. In the Harley MS and collections like it, Langland would have found a developed literature of political complaint and, especially pregnantly, a depiction of a laboring, but put-upon Husbandman. This figure, nearly uniquely in earlier English writing, anticipates Piers the Plowman. Given agrarian discontents (and eventually the Peasants' Revolt of 1381), fourteenth-century accounts usually denigrate, rather than idealize, the rural workforce. The figure also anticipates yet other unique features of the poem. How many title figures are so peripheral to their narratives? How many so present only through allusion? For Piers is, in some sense, only narratively focal in a single episode, passus 5–7.

Like all Langland's other personifications, Piers is provisionally defined by his name, and the narrative action of the poem directed to spelling out the implications of the name. He appears first and preeminently as a plowman, an agrarian laborer whose industrious and committed fieldwork might be socially conceived as model for communal regeneration. (In one of Langland's prominent narrative echoes, 6.1–58 rewrites Pro. 112–22 in a new, socially inverted vein.) By his opening words, Piers indicates his intimate connection, through labor, with Truth, the poem's usual identification of the divine:

"Peter!" quod a plowman, and putte forþ his hed:
"I knowe hym [i.e. Truth]
as kyndely as clerc doþ his bokes."(5.537–38)

The second line should be translated, "I know Truth in the same intimate/natural way as a clerk, who is by nature/definition a learned man, knows books." This claim foreshadows the poem's most enigmatic (and, embarrassingly for both Wille and his readers, generative) moments, where an unlearned and naturally instructed plowman squares off, as it were, against the entire world of learning. In the most prominent of them, Piers, driven to rage by a priest's officious interjections, tears the pardon sent from Truth (7.107–43a). Equally disruptive, and equally opposed to clerical instruction, is the embarrassed report, offered by the personification of learning, Clergy, of Piers's resolution of the great academic dilemma that has animated passus 8–12, how to define "Do-well" (13.120–30).

This presentation points to yet another rather antiquated foundation of the poem. For a sequence of London works of devotion, composed *c.* 1300–40 and transmitted as a group in Cambridge, Magdalene College, MS Pepys 2498 (*c.* 1365–75), displays an intense interest in laypeople pursuing "God's law," the Truth of the gospel. The texts encourage them to cultivate an evangelical commitment, at best loosely subjected to clerical supervision – and in the English vernacular (cf. 7.136–41). Certainly, such potentially holy lay actuation of the gospel message lies close to the conception of a Piers Plowman. As industrious plowman-hero, Piers enacts Holychurch's injunctions to express divine service, gratitude for God's gifts, through work, honest labor (cf. 5.539–53 with 1.85–93). In this activity, he enacts clear biblical antecedents, most particularly in the sequence of gospel parables that present agrarian labor as a similitude for the kingdom of heaven (for example, Matthew 13:24: "The kingdom of heaven is likened to a man that sowed good seed in his field"; and Matthew 20:1: "The kingdom of heaven is like to an householder, who went out early in the morning to hire labourers into his vineyard"). But simultaneously, Piers's status as model Everyperson has more troubling, equally biblical sources. Labor is necessary to human life because man is of the earth and must return to it; if a rewarding occupation and necessity for all, its universality depends upon God's curse upon the fallen Adam, the first plowman (Genesis 3:17–19). As Piers discovers in trying to organize fieldwork in passus 6, both his and Holychurch's optimism is predicated upon a suppression or omission: work should express, at some level, not a genial hope of heaven, but an omnipresent possibility for damnation. The poem expresses this possibility in the stains one will see in passus 13–14 on the coat, once the clean baptismal garment, of the work-obsessed Hawkin "the active man."

Piers's Christian name addresses these concerns and becomes the progressively more active figure for the character after passus 7. For Piers is the Frenchified nickname for the apostle Peter, and the portrayal shifts toward playing out the implications of Jesus' address to him in Matthew 16:18–19. Jesus gives the keys to the kingdom to Peter, as the rock on which the Church is founded (retrospectively, the motte upon which sits Truth's romance tower, the tabernacle of Psalm 14 and Psalm 15 in the King James version). These conventionally are the keys to the papal "treasury of grace" (Peter the rock is the first and founding pope), the Church's capacity to absolve sin, the habit inherited from our Adamic antecedents, through the sacraments. Like all late medieval catechesis, from the moment Piers renounces a thorough immersion in the world's work (7.120–35), the poem insists most strenuously upon one sacrament, that penance by which one atones to God and man and, in return, receives salvific grace.

The implications of the Christian name become fused with the generic "plowman" in the grand spiritualized reformulation of the plowing allegory in passus 19. Here Piers is intimately associated with Grace (his double, as porter of heaven at 5.595), and they, momentarily at any rate, enact a thorough inversion of the laboring allegory of passus 6. On the earlier occasion, where the capacity of work to express virtue initially seemed unproblematic, one sought to win a crop (and "wasting," not contributing to the endeavor, as it had since line 22 of the Prologue, was the consummate sin). But at this late point in the poem, the smooth connection of production–consumption has been turned on its head. Labor here expresses the consciousness of debt, of necessary penitential atonement for sin. The injunction to attend to debt, couched in the Latin "Redde quod debes" and presented allegorically as "purchase" of that pardon Piers had earlier received from Truth, harks back to the confessions of passus 5. The Latin first appears as a text scrutinized by Robert þe Robbere in 5.461; Repentaunce badgers Covetise ceaselessly on the point at 5.260–95. Perfect penance requires restoration of all ill-gotten gains (and as a more distant implication, trying to repay God/Jesus for the injuries sin has done him). The argument perfectly inverts the getting and spending emphasis of passus 6; at the poem's end, one labors to surrender, not to invest, consume, or entertain (which implicitly queries the value of poetic labor, in the poem addressed in Ymaginatif's criticism of the entire endeavor, 12.3–28). But, in a world where Piers and Grace remain only immanent, always off plowing Truth, these economically unnatural imperatives are forgotten in the Apocalypse narrative that provides the poem's cataclysmic final passus.

Much of the poem's gospel narrative chronicles an effort to move Piers between the two figural positions, Adam/Peter. After another protracted absence from the poem, the character reappears when Anima associates him with Charity: "Wiþouten help of Piers Plowman," quod he, "his persone sestow neuere," a linkage quickly succeeded by *Petrus, id est Christus* (15.196, 212: "Peter, that is, Christ"). These enigmatic hints associate, yet do not identify, Piers with the incarnate Jesus/Charity. They become fully elaborated in the moving Passion/Harrowing narrative of passus 18, where Piers provides the visible flesh honest and loving enough to invest the deific romance conqueror (and following 15.199–200a, the straw-boss's scrupulousness that understands actions well-intentioned enough to receive pardon):

> Oon semblable to þe Samaritan [who is Charity] and somdeel to Piers þe Plowman
> Barefoot on an asse bak bootles cam prikye. (18.10–11)

Hence, Jesus' great outburst of love, his longing to invert Eucharistic miracle and to drink souls for their salvation, is ultimately couched in a language of loving concern Piers himself has first introduced in the poem:

> For blood may suffre blood boþe hungry and acale
> Ac blood may noȝt se blood blede but hym rewe
> (18.394–5; cf. 6.207–09)

Reading the poem requires a threefold attentiveness. First, the text demands extensive local attention. Because of Langland's propensity for dialogic voicing, for putting non-congruent discourses into collision, one must grasp the bare sense argued by Langland's speakers (including their frequently tacit logic), and also ascertain the seriousness to be accorded any statement. As the title "Dialogus" would imply, most propositions bruited are far from unqualified in their cogency, yet infrequently marked as such. The cacophony of the first inner dream (passus 11), integral to Langland's development of Piers's penitentialism as "patient poverty," displays the technique at its fullest and most vertiginous. Second, because Piers Plowman is at least incipiently narrative, any constructive reading further requires an extensive sweep across the poem's whole arc, the ability to lay passages against their echoes and recurrences. Langland's debt to romance tradition includes a reliance on a narrative technique common in that genre, the symbolic type-scene. The poem re-presents the same action in a variety of different contexts, for example Wille's despairing swoon at the juncture of passus 10 and 11 as a reprise of Piers's anxieties when he tears Truth's pardon. Such scenic echoes require the reader to recognize similarities and assess differences; in the example cited, Wille fails to sustain Piers's faith in divine benevolence (cf. 7.120), even when that divinity is confronted with human sin. Third, because of Langland's propensity to revise his work, any full reading requires comparing in depth Langland's multiple presentations. Rather generally, the B version often works upon A by expanding suggestions of the earlier text through large interpolations. C also employs this technique, but its revisions are characterized by far more meticulous and precise argumentative development than its predecessor.

One can instantiate these suggestions by a single brief example. At the end of his description of the pilgrimage to Truth's castle, Piers addresses the question of sin. He argues that recidivism, backsliding into one's old ways, will get one banished from the premises. But, he argues, such banishment may be only temporary. The castle's posterns are kept by welcoming guardians, seven ladies, the virtues that traditionally remedy the seven sins, and gracious Mercy will also allow reentry (for those who appeal to these virtues and thereby show contrition). At this crucial moment, Piers's account is interrupted:

> "Ac who is sib to þise seuene, so me God helpe,
> He is wonderly welcome and faire vnderfongen.
> But if ye be sibbe to some of þise seuene
> It is ful hard, by myn heed, any of yow alle
> To geten ingong at any gate, but Grace be þe more."
> "By Crist!" quod a kuttepurs, "I haue no kyn þere."
> "Nor I," quod an apeward, "by auȝt þat I knowe."
>
> (5.625–31)

The information Piers presents here is utterly basic catechetical lore, frequently offered (as in the fifteen independent Middle English translations of Lorens of Orleans's *Somme le roi*) as a pattern of sevens that outline the route to salvation. Moreover, the same castle/postern/maiden allegory occurs in the popular Anglo-Norman poem "Chateau d"amour" by Robert Grosseteste, Bishop of Lincoln (d. 1253). But in this context, even the conventional encounters resistance.

The poem's language indicates the difficulty, one that goes to the very heart of Langland's project. The professional designations cutpurse and apeward (as well as the waferer, pardoner, and whore who eventually join them) do not imply spiritual acumen or desire for virtuous action. But the figures cannot just be passed off as inherently sinful and spiritually obtuse (cf. the extended reprise and analysis of the wafermaker as Hawkin in passus 13–14). The problem is more complicated; in raising the issue of "kyn," cutpurse *et al.* hear and respond to Piers's own repeated language, the roughly synonymous "sib(be)." Piers doesn't mean this as a literal statement; both he and the poem at large ceaselessly rely on metaphors of relationship (for example "Abstinence myn aunte," 5.383).

Piers intends "sib" to have strictly metaphorical force; "be sib to" simply means "be in a relationship with." The phrase gestures at, while not describing in any detail, something like "come to contrition" or "practise virtue again." But this gestural evocation of an attenuated spiritual sense does not correspond with what Piers's interlocutors hear. They conceive of Truth's castle as quite literally that, a large stone edifice on a hill, and, socially aware, they know that castle inhabitants get to live there because of their "kyn," their bloodlines. The nobility that inhabit castles aren't just anyone, but members of chosen noble families (for example designated by inherited blazons). For the rascals who here desert the pilgrimage, the literal narrative implications of romance presentation supersede the second-level moralizations Langland's allegorical form supposedly encourages and supports. Socioliterary responses overwhelm and thereby query what the poem's most efficacious and exemplary instructor, Piers, considers plain moral discourse.

One of the great litmus moments in the poem, the passage provides a commentary on the poet's entire endeavor. Two conflicting discursive responses to the same information come into direct confrontation. The failure of Piers's instructional metaphor here represents the failure of the literary discourse that would seem central to Langland's entire project. For Piers's metaphoric figure is the literary technique that underwrites (personification) allegory, traditionally the form of dream narrative and of authoritative statement. The world's languages, on which the poem must necessarily draw, simultaneously rebuff and display the necessity of writing this kind of poem.

At the same time, one must see this moment as one of particular poetic specificity and openness, not one entirely sui generis in the poem. In B, the account (and passus) ends with some characters bailing out of pilgrimage altogether. (Cf. "I ne woot where þei bicome," 5.642). But such scenes of turning from the path, eschewing moral imperatives, occur repeatedly, for example the failure of some to labor (to follow the plough, in the Middle Ages, significantly for Piers Plowman, a circular or spiral track) in passus 6; in passus 17, Faith and Hope turning aside from the man fallen among thieves; or the downfall of Contrition in Unity (the Church Militant, worldly version of Truth's tower, the Church Triumphant) at the poem's end. Yet that last passage also retrospectively rewrites voiding the castle. At poem's end, Conscience, like the pardoner and whore, abandons the great house, now visualized as a tithe-barn, and wanders off one knows not where ("as wide as þe world lasteþ," 20.381). But he has a goal, if the perplexingly indefinite one the poem has always sought, to elicit Clergy's help (20.228–9, 375, fulfilling the conversation of 13.198–210) in finding Grace and the pardon-guarding Piers.

A quick glance at the antecedents and progeny of the B account I have described will offer further revelations. The A version is typically truncated; while it includes B's discursive conundrum, it ends (A 6.123) with some soupçon of hope, Piers's second hortatory injunction, not wandering pardoner and whore. C 7.292–308 significantly expands and explicates the conclusion; rather than Truth's court being abandoned by those declassé and socially suspect, a sequence of Latin citations connects the refusal of pilgrimage with those too engrossed in the world's business, the guests who decline the invitation to the Lord's feast in the parable of Luke 14:16–24. These include in 299–304 a character Active who intensifies connections with B's Hawkin – as well as with the dreamer's "autobiography," unique to C 5; but also (305–06) a character Contemplation, whose presence implies (equally a false step) that pilgrimage might proceed with minimal involvement in worldly labors.

But the C revision more powerfully resituates the episode. Uniquely in this version, the confession of Sloth is split off from the remainder of deadly sins (C 7.1–118) and stands isolated at the head of this narrative unit. In the later versions, Sloth is presented, in part, as a trivial (romance) poet ("I kan rymes of Robyn Hood and Randolf erl of Chestre," 5.395), and in C, this association is intensified by a lengthy and largely metaphorical discussion of a licit divine minstrelsy (C 7.81–118), here moved forward from its original placement in B passus 13. Insofar as this passage tries to formulate the nature of licit poetry (cf. "God Friday þe geste," the subject of passus 18, climax of the poem), Piers's instruction, at the framing conclusion of the passus, comes to stand as a dispiriting test case. But typically, his intrusive entry into the poem transforms, within the metaphorical mode here described as failing to communicate, pilgrimage, from the literal tourist jaunt envisioned by the palmer Piers has succeeded as instructor, to its catechetical roots as satisfaction for sin.

This example should indicate, far more thoroughly than a narrative summary, some qualities of a compelling intellectual statement – and a very great poem. In Piers's instructions, one can see Langland's local attentiveness to language and its valences, spiritual and social, and the way in which linguistic implication complicates and retards any pursuit of T/truth. Yet equally, the passage is far from isolated; my analysis should suggest something of the care and meticulousness with which Langland has plotted out his echoic (and progressively specifying) narrative at a thematic level. And in the layered revisions to his poem, he displays a concerted attentiveness toward at least elaborating, if not defining, the need, nature, and difficulty of renewing England and himself.

NOTES

1 All citations are from the magisterial "Athlone edition": William Langland, *Piers Plowman: The Three Versions*, George Kane, gen. ed., 3 vols. (London: Athlone Press, 1960–97). I have adjusted punctuation and capitalization to accord with modern usage, and I occasionally report the unanimous reading of all B version manuscripts, rather than the edited version of Kane and E. Talbot Donaldson.
2 Morton W. Bloomfield, "*Piers Plowman*" *as a Fourteenth-century Apocalypse* (New Brunswick, NJ: Rutgers University Press, 1962), p. 32.
3 For all these works, datable *c.* 1401–15, see Helen Barr, ed., *The Piers Plowman Tradition* (London: Dent, 1993).

10

SARAH STANBURY

The *Gawain*-poet

Cleanness, one of two homilies attributed to the *Gawain*-poet, ends on a wild night of partying, spectral apparitions, and mayhem. Embellishing an episode from the Book of Daniel, *Cleanness* tells how King Belshazzar invites his own demise through his sacrilegious use of holy vessels and candelabra that his father, Nebuchadnezzar, plundered from the Temple of Jerusalem. Not only are we told about Solomon's holy vessels, as in the biblical Book of Daniel, but we are also shown them in a description of exceptional visual coherence. The gold cups are worked to resemble castles, with gilded turrets and pinnacles encrusted with parrots and flowers made of gems. The candlestick, so massive it must be brought in on a cart, is cast in gold in the shape of a tree, its branches filled with colorful birds. Like the vessels, the candlestick embodies spiritual, material, and aesthetic value. Its beauty is its truth and its truth its beauty. It is, that is, a symbolic object as well as a merely useful or beautiful one. Belshazzar's failure, his "uncleanness," lies in his failure to see these relationships. He uses the vessels at a drunken party, and hence he dies.

Although Belshazzar makes a fatal error in his assessment of the power of sacred objects, he is correct in his appreciation of their beauty. Delight in the aesthetic qualities of things not only marks the account of holy vessels in *Cleanness*, but also characterizes descriptions of many types in all four of the poems that are normally identified as the work of the anonymous *Gawain*-poet. The four late-fourteenth-century poems of British Library Cotton Nero A.x., *Cleanness*, *Pearl*, *Sir Gawain and the Green Knight*, and *Patience*, the other homily, are generally believed to be the works of a single poet. This consideration is based partly on their compilation together in one manuscript copied by a single hand and illustrated by a single illuminator, but also on the predominance of shared themes and habits of style, among them long passages of descriptive enumeration that present, in great detail, in the surface textures of the pleasurable, and especially courtly, world. Indeed, descriptive passages often interrupt the action and may seem, to modern tastes, protracted. Arthur's feast in *Gawain* is a gorgeous picture of excess – so many dishes there is hardly room for them on the table. Other objects of the rich life detailed in these poems include gems and jewelry; textiles, including tapestries and high-fashion clothing; architectural interiors and castle facades; and chivalric equipment, such as armor and tack for horses, as witnessed in the account of green trappings on the Green Knight's steed. Rural landscapes and urban architecture are also described – the menacing forest of Wirral in *Gawain*; the transformed garden in which the narrator wanders in *Pearl* and the New Jerusalem that he is shown by the maiden; or the violent storms that afflict Noah in *Cleanness* or Jonah in *Patience*. And as with the holy vessels in *Cleanness*, surface textures can veil meaning. Things of the world appear as if organized by the gaze of viewers in the text, yet those viewers are repeatedly cast as innocent, or like Belshazzar, even ignorant about the significance of what they see. The *Gawain*-poet engages his characters, and readers as well, in an interpretive project or, we might say, visual hermeneutic, where places and objects are known and presented through acts of perception. In a world of brilliant and even illusory surfaces, the individual is very much alone.

The vivid descriptions, particularly of places, clothing, and furnishings that might speak to courtly, aristocratic tastes, have long been noted by scholars, some of whom have looked to that material world for clues about the poems' dates or authorship. While readers have agreed that the poems are unusual in their presentation of a coherently visualized world, they have offered different explanations of its purpose or achievement. Early commentators suggested that description is essentially ornamental in service of purely aesthetic goals. Subsequent studies recognized that the technique of organizing space around a point of view of a character within the text seems to offer us a commentary not only on the world but also on the mind of the perceiver within the text. Parlayed through an eyewitness point of view, description, especially in *Gawain*, turns the world seen into an objective correlative of a character's mind or commentary on his emotions. Yet, as several critics have noted, there are tensions between the spatial coherence the descriptions present and the eyewitness, who is after all a product of the text. These tensions quickly generate problems in interpretation. Discernment becomes a central challenge both to the protagonist and to the reader. In *Gawain*, it even becomes part of the narrative's elaborate game. Description, organized according to the mechanics of perception, works to dramatize the limits of human vision. The search for "trawthe" (honor; fidelity) in *Gawain* or for spiritual consolation in *Pearl* is circumscribed by the workings of the gaze.[1]

Recent work has also drawn particular attention to the consonance between spiritual crisis and the picture of courtly life. While some readers have argued that the visual theatricality of the poems, especially in *Gawain*, levels a critique at the artificiality of courtly manners and fashion, more have felt, to the contrary, that the material culture of courtly life as described in these texts illustrates the system of ethics that they promulgate and even speaks to a particular readership, illustrating an allegiance, as one reader puts it, to "high-medieval feudalism."[2] The concern with expensive objects and clothing, with feasting, and with behaviors marked by elaborate rituals of courtesy speaks to the interests of well-to-do lay readers. The depiction of courtly pleasures in these poems is designed to appeal to aristocratic patrons and even, it has been suggested, to occlude the very ethical crises the poem present. Helen Barr notes *Pearl*'s "mercantile consciousness" and Felicity Riddy suggests that the poem, through its emphasis on pearls, becomes itself an aesthetic object.[3] Both of these arguments accord well with John Bowers's contention that the poem's aristocratized values were targeted specifically for Richard II, hypothesized as the poet's royal patron, who was reputed to be fond of jewels and ornament.[4] Even starkly critical of the courtly values in the four poems, David Aers argues that all of them envision a perfect consonance between the Church and aristocratic values, submerging possibilities of real personal transformation in the idealization of courtliness. The poet's Christ, he writes, would be "a divine Sir Gawain."[5]

The ethical demands exacted in these texts may be consonant with the structures of late medieval chivalry, but the extent to which individuals change remains an open question in these texts. Does the *Pearl*-dreamer truly move into a new state where he understands divine grace? Does Sir Gawain attain a meaningful Christian humility? Does Jonah learn patience? The theatrical presentation of material culture actually sharpens the focus on individuals, particularly Jonah, Gawain, and the *Pearl*-dreamer, who respond to ethical demands articulated in confrontations between human and supernatural or divine beings. It may be, as well, that poetic techniques of lexical accumulation through multiple synonyms, elaborate numerology, and complex prosody in rhyme scheme and alliteration also further a picture of a world that is both intricate and ordered and in which heaven seems to mirror courtly life – the divine court a refraction of the royal one. The individual who reads visual signs does so in the world, not against it, accommodating himself to the disciplines of courtly Christianity. The personal trial or quest framed by the known world – even when the familiar locations morph into exotic places – is one of following spiritual commands while living the good life.

In presenting detailed, spatially coherent descriptions of the natural world and courtly life, the four alliterative poems of Cotton Nero A.x. are similar to other late medieval English poems that rely on alliteration as a principle of form and meter. Like other fourteenth-century alliterative poems written in the north and northwest of England specifically, these poems also display, with exceptional skill, a distinctive "ornamental verbal density."[6] Indeed, verbal density may be not only a thematic or topical characteristic of alliterative poems but also a special property of alliterative prosody. Alliteration, which tends to draw on the same distinctive vocabulary, often regional and often originating from Anglo-Saxon words, requires a rich stock of synonyms. Lists, which often occur within descriptive passages in the *Gawain*-poems, make particular demands on language in alliterative verse. Lists are taxonomic, groupings of items in categories that lay out the world in its order and also its multiplicity. Lexical demands increase even more when terms for those objects also begin with identical sounds. In the list of gemstones decorating the holy vessels in *Cleanness* we see this kind of elaboration: "Ande safyres, and sardiners, and semely topace, / Alabaundarynes, and amaraunz, and amaffised stones, / Casydoynes, and crysolytes, and clere rubies ..." (lines 1469–71) (And sapphires and cornelians and lovely topazes / Alamandines and emeralds and amethyst stones / Chalcedonies and chrysolites and clear rubies).[7] In alliterative poetry, language itself partakes in the sumptuous variety and pleasures of the world.

The very quality of accumulation or descriptive density in these poems also works to underwrite, however paradoxically, a sense that material or bodily things are ephemeral. The practice of organizing descriptive passages according to the real or implied gaze of textual eyewitnesses has the effect of both joining the world to the viewer and also of limiting knowledge of the world to what that viewer can see. As with the holy vessels in *Cleanness*, physical objects or structures present their own fantastical or spectacular surfaces independent of how we might understand or use them; yet the poems' protagonists are also spiritually accountable for their response to those surfaces. David Lawton has noted that important characteristics of alliterative poetry are the goal of penance, and the struggle to live up to Christian and courtly ideals.[8] Penance is dramatically expressed at the end of *Gawain* when Gawain adopts the green girdle as his own personal baldric of shame. Penance also emerges powerfully in the other poems as well. The *Pearl* dreamer, lectured by the maiden on the importance of accepting divine grace, finally discovers himself excluded from heaven; Jonah in *Patience* faces the narrow discipline of following divine law; and the reader in *Cleanness* is witness to repeated examples of hairline distinctions separating the clean from the unclean. Penance and courtly accumulation work in a kind of synergy. Penance, of course, requires a temptation and often then a world to renounce; and as we see in the bedroom scenes of *Gawain* the vivid descriptions can in some cases offer up the courtly life as a trap or seduction. Lexical accumulation – or we might say the *materiality* of these poems – gives dramatic framing to private acts of penance. This is not to say that the *Gawain*-poet subjects the material world to a moralizing or penitential critique. Far from it; the poems are remarkable for the pleasure they take in recording the physical, and especially courtly world. Description, then, poses a riddle, as characters within these narratives struggle to live up to Christian ideals while surrounded by distracting places and things. Without denying the senses, how can we "steer the heart," to borrow a phrase from *Patience*, in a world that is so rich in its pleasures?

Pearl

Pearl, first in the manuscript, gives this question dramatic play in its story of a lost object, framed as the story of a jeweler who has lost a pearl in a garden. In this dream vision, told as are all medieval dream visions through first-person narration, the jeweler steps from the garden where he "lost" his pearl into a dream-like landscape where familiar objects are quickly defamiliarized. As he searches for his pearl and then finds it again in radically changed form, we learn that the pearl is in fact a dead two-year-old girl, most likely his daughter, and the work of the poem is the work of mourning and acceptance. An allegory of spiritual discovery in the tradition of Dante's *Divine Comedy*, the poem is situated in a lush and transforming landscape, its topography shifting from a spice garden to an Eden-like landscape and finally to a vision of the New Jerusalem, the heavenly city as described in the Book of Revelation. Each of these locations is described with a rich accumulative vocabulary of delightful things: the spot where his pearl was lost is now covered with "gilofre, gyngure, and gromylyoun" (line 43; gillyflower, ginger and gromwell); the dream-landscape is adorned with tree trunks of indigo, the gravel "þat on grounde con grynde" (line 81), comprised of oriental pearls; and the twelve foundations of the New Jerusalem are each a single stone – jasper, sapphire, chalcedony, emerald, and more.

Pearl uses a hybrid versification and exploits techniques of rhyme, verbal concatenation, and even numerological ordering to achieve a complexity unmatched in Middle English poetry and perhaps rivaled only by Dante's *Comedy*. Each of the poem's 101 stanzas – a number that evokes both perfection and flaw – has twelve lines that not only alliterate and rhyme, but also connect through a repeating word, a technique called concatenation. Words repeat but also change in meaning in an elaborate punnology.[9] In the first stanza group, for instance, the link-word *spot* means place and blemish; *date* in the ninth stanza-group means both limit and time of year or day; in group 16, *mote* means castle or city as well as stain. Alliteration, rhyme, and concatenation build the paradox of accumulation and change into prosody; words and sounds repeat in nearly every line but at the same time they transform. Poetic form does the work of mourning by returning, in haunting recapitulations, to the lost thing and then moving on.

Above all, *Pearl* – along with the other poems in the *Gawain* manuscript – is courtly. Dialogue in the poem is couched in formalities that underscore a hierarchal vision of both human as well as spiritual relationships. When the maiden first greets the dreamer she bows low and removes her crown, a gesture that marks her status as his daughter and not as a queen; a bit later, when she rises up, puts her crown back on, and begins to lecture him on his errors, she asserts her status as queen of heaven through this gesture of command.[10] Heaven is equally courtly in its structure and principles. Mary is the "queen of courtesy," and the dreamer's visual theophany when he sees the New Jerusalem pictures a centripetal kind of worship. The bleeding lamb, or Christ, is centered on high amid its worshipers. As one reader remarks, the social order of heaven is a fully "aristocratized theology" specifically targeted to appeal to a lay readership.[11] The physical world described in the poem also seems magnificent in ways designed to appeal to the tastes of a worldly gentry interested in aesthetic pleasure. Some readers, arguing that *Pearl* was written in the 1390s, have based the case in part on the consonance between Richard II's love of luxury and his "courtly francophilia."[12] *Pearl* could be, that is, not only a Christian consolation but also an elegy targeted to a particular worldly court.

By organizing its quest through the gaze of a narrator who is, at the end, excluded, the poem heightens the emotions of longing, linking penance with desire, both for things of the world and for the afterlife. Is the dreamer transformed by his visionary quest, or is he still in a state of desire, even though the object of desire may have changed from a lost pearl or girl to heaven? The narrator is excluded from heaven in part because of his acquisitiveness; he longs to hang on to his pearl – his daughter – even after he knows she belongs to heaven. In the final stanzas, after he awakens, the narrator accepts the daily sight of the Eucharistic wafer during the mass as a substitute vision, but his acceptance may not convince all readers of the poem. "More and more," the refrain of the third stanza group, could well serve as the refrain for the poem as a whole. Longing, however changed in its goals, remains the poem's enduring emotional and thematic arc.[13]

Cleanness

Cleanness and *Patience*, alliterative homilies that retell Old Testament stories to illustrate a single virtue, seem on the surface very different from *Pearl* in structure, genre, and tone, though the poems are similar enough to each other that it seems probable they were written or compiled as paired texts. Yet like *Pearl* and *Gawain*, both advocate behaviors that would be fully legible to men and women of the fourteenth-century gentry. Both picture relationships with God in terms of courtly behaviors and ethics. *Cleanness* is structured according to a complex numerology, a feature it shares with *Gawain* and *Pearl* and one that seems targeted to an unusually well-educated audience.[14] Both homilies, furthermore, visualize places and objects with close attention to detail and to the mechanics of visual perception. Even though *Cleanness* differs from the other three poems in telling a series of narratives rather than a single story, it also organizes descriptions according to visual logic, a technique that makes conduct a matter of perception and response; comportment and ethics are a matter of how we see, know, and use the world of things.

In *Cleanness*, the equation between "clean" conduct, courtliness, and religious rectitude is explicitly evoked through alliteration, as the words "clean" and "court" repeat as a pair throughout the poem. The goal, we are also told repeatedly, is to see God in his court, a reward that will come from clean acts; the punishment for moral or especially bodily filth is exile from that home. This rather severe disciplinary narrative, drawing on the Bible as well as on the liturgy, retells three Old Testament stories that illustrate uncleanness, acts defined primarily by the violation of literal or figurative bodies: Noah's Flood, brought as a punishment for bodily sins against nature; the destruction of Sodom, punishment for sodomy; and the death of Belshazzar and the Chaldeans, destroyed as fitting retribution for their idolatrous uses of the holy vessels. The emphasis throughout on images of vessels or containers and on feasting suggests that "body" in this text also has an allegorical dimension as Christ's body, or the Eucharist, and that violations of the body are also sacramental perversions. The pointed denunciation of sodomy, an attack furthered through the poem's highly unusual praise of non-procreative heterosexual pleasure (lines 701–08), may be, as some readers have argued, directed explicitly against homosexual priests, represented as unfit for handling the Eucharist.

The norm against which clerical or bodily perversions are measured, however, is courtly life. As Elizabeth Keiser has argued, the poem's indictment of sodomy and celebration of heterosexual pleasure both work to idealize the properly masculine courtier, a "connoisseur and practitioner of the festive decorum which makes the good life imitate art."[15] The perfect example of this good life is the feast, whose rituals of decorum are violated by the serf in rags. In the story of the wedding feast that opens the poem, cleanness is exemplified by seating arrangements in which each guest is seated according to his rank (lines 115–17); filth, embodied in the guest who arrives in his rags straight from the fields, violates the festive life. Peasant labor intrudes into the halls of the rich – peasant labor, "fyled with werkkez" (soiled with work), that makes no effort at concealing what it is. The holy vessels abused by Belshazzar at his feast at the end of the poem extend the performance of magnificence broadly to encompass both liturgical performance and also aesthetic reverence. The ideal courtier is also a devout and obedient parishioner who values aesthetic beauty in the service of Christian ritual. The rich man, the poem seems to say, takes the surest way to the kingdom of heaven, particularly if he obeys the laws of the Church.

Patience

In *Patience*, a much shorter homiletic narrative also based on a text from the Beatitudes, courtliness is manifested not through beautiful things but through the poem's central didactic goal: restraint. Patience or "steering the heart," the goal named in the poem, is also the practise of self-mastery that is a central goal of courtliness.[16] In failing to obey God, Jonah fails to demonstrate patience as well as obedience to the commands of a superior. The ethos of aristocratic comportment is also evoked in accounts of distinctly non-courtly spaces. Descriptions of place dramatize exile from God's court by picturing alternative interiors: the hold of the ship, the whale's belly, and the little hut made of ivy. Like *Pearl*, *Patience* uses description to align a central character, through the logic of his perception, with the world as he experiences it. A look at one short passage can serve to illustrate techniques of alliterative wordplay that guide the aesthetic of the poem as a whole. In the belly of the whale, one of the great descriptive passages in Middle English literature, the poet leads the reader through the sensory world that Jonah touches but cannot, in the dark, even see:

> He glydes in by þe giles þurȝ glaym ande glette,
> Relande in by a rop, a rode þat hym þoȝt,
> Ay hele ouer hed hourlande aboute,
> Til he blunt in a blok as brod as a halle.
>
> (lines 269–72)

> [He glides in by the gills through slime and filth,
> Rolling in by the gut, which seemed to him a road,
> Constantly heel over head hurling about
> Until he stopped in a compartment as wide as a hall.]

This passage conveys movements of Jonah's body, gliding, rolling, hurling. When he stops, the verb is "blunt," a word that as an adjective can mean "stunned" or "dazed." Clearly those meanings are also present here. Alliteration, richly accumulative, aligns Jonah rolling body with the whale's interior, as verbs depicting his motion pattern with nouns parsing the whale's anatomy: "relande in by a rop," "blunt in a blok." Alliteration emphasizes relationships of physical scale – Jonah's small helplessness and the whale's massive gut – and also underscores likenesses, and again these are likenesses to the court, or at least human habitation. When Jonah comes to a halt, it is in a place as broad as a hall, the great room in a manor or castle. Description visualizes his body within the whale; it also tells us what he knows or how he compares things, which is to roads and halls. At this point in time, this is all he can feel and ascertain.

The geography of sensory exile, of course, personalizes the fault of impatience. It makes Jonah's actions and the consequences of those actions, as we say, very real. A penitential voice, a feature of alliterative verse in general, emerges with particular power in this section, and it comes through forcibly because exile has been so graphically evoked. Lodged in the whale, Jonah says a long mournful prayer in which he acknowledges his distance from God's temple and promises obedience. If this prayer convinces – and it apparently convinces God, who orders the whale to cough up Jonah on the spot – it does so in part because the conditions of his exile have been graphically detailed. Features of late medieval alliterative poetry – lexical richness, descriptive precision, and a thematic emphasis on penance – work together brilliantly in this passage, as they do throughout the poem in general, through the agency of perception. Jonah's regret or penitential moment is fueled by his love for and exile from the world.

Sir Gawain and the Green Knight

Of the poems attributed to the *Gawain*-poet, none is more descriptive or penitential than *Sir Gawain and the Green Knight*, one of the best-known poems in Middle English. In many respects *Gawain* builds on familiar romance conventions, borrowing narrative elements from Celtic sources but most directly from French romances that develop from those of Chrétien de Troyes. Many elements of the plot are familiar from Arthurian tradition: the sidelining of Arthur to focus instead on one of his knights; the dramatic challenge that happens on a feast day; elements of magic; the quest and test of the hero's masculine honor; inscrutable and dangerous women. As Ad Putter says, romances were "simply the most popular form of literary entertainment for the higher strata of society," and *Gawain* is brilliantly crafted to appeal to this small market.[17]

What sets *Gawain* apart from his French sources as well as from other romances in English is the synergy between lexical accumulation, an eyewitness point of view, and alliteration, though it is more correct to say partial alliteration. Groups of alliterating lines are punctuated with short rhyming codas, called "bobs and wheels," that give the romance a stanzaic form. Like *Pearl* and *Patience*, things of the world appear to us as they appear to the protagonist; and as in those poems perceptual logic organizes descriptions of people, objects, and places. With the exception of the hunting episodes, which occur in Gawain's explicit absence, the narrative unfolds much as Gawain sees it. His challenge or test is to perform as a perfect courtier in a world in which he has only immediate visual or sensory information. The long and detailed description of the Green Knight's clothing when he shows up at Camelot on Pentecost offers the first of many dazzling visual traps for the eye: like Gawain, we survey him but can't quite figure him out: Why is he green? Why does he hold a holly sprig as well as an axe? And why no armor? He seems constructed as a blazon of mysterious visual cues. In spite of his monochromatic greenness, he is also a model of late fourteenth-century court fashion, and hence the challenge he directs to the court invites the viewer to an interpretive game. Gawain's penitential self-loathing at the end of the poem when he returns to Camelot, a response many readers find excessive, becomes credible if we see it, at least in part, as his response to his own performance in the game. He has, after all, failed completely to figure out the nature of the test and the trick.

The poem produces a particularly English picture of chivalry that is both contemporary and nostalgic, both native and continental. The alliterative long line, a traditional English form, domesticates its imported sources, reprising French source material with a native prosody. *Gawain*'s narrative is itself backward-looking, making us aware of history and inviting us to speculate on nationhood and on national identity. The poem begins with the founding of Britain, lending the poem an historical consciousness from the outset, and it imagines its ideals of honor, "trawthe," and fidelity as qualities belonging to a glorious past. However, the poem's descriptions give its nostalgia a highly contemporary patina. Though the story takes place in sixth-century Britain, its elaborations of fashion, home furnishings, hunting rituals, and castle design belong to the fourteenth-century scene. The canvas is a local one melding legendary English heroes with an English landscape and late fourteenth-century baronial splendor. The poem's eyewitness technique, particularly as parlayed through its rich alliterative vocabulary, both personalizes and generalizes this drama of aristocratic masculine restraint; the hero's personal quest bespeaks much broader concerns about national identity and the performance of the noble life.

Gawain's attention to English geography and to the trappings of late fourteenth-century aristocratic life may even comment directly on political relationships in the last years of the fourteenth century. The striking contrasts between two courts, one a distant baronial court in north Wales and the other a royal castle, between a wild man and a knight, between wilderness and hall, suggest the poem may be commenting as well on tensions between centralized authority and baronial power, between London and the northwest Midlands or Wales. If the poems emerged within the patronage system of Richard II's court, their disappearance may also have been a strategic erasure following Richard's murder in the Lancastrian usurpation. These poems, for all their brilliance, appear to have been largely unknown to subsequent readers until *Gawain* was first transcribed in the nineteenth century. Theories of patronage and then suppression are consistent with arguments that early fifteenth-century language policies promoted Chaucer as poet laureate for a new dynasty and London English, as opposed to regional dialects, as the language of the realm. With the ascendancy of Henry IV, the new court may have exacted a repression of signs of the deposed king, including poems, such as those of Cotton Nero A.x., written in the Cheshire dialect and perhaps even commissioned under his patronage.

These speculations, provocative as they are, have as yet no solid evidence to support them. The authorship and history of the manuscript before its appearance in the library of a Yorkshire collector in 1614 remain a major unsolved literary mystery.[18] It is thus even more tempting to search for the patron and writer in the techné of description: textiles, armor, hairstyles, and castle ornament. Yet even here evidence is slippery. The poems offer an extraordinarily rich picture of fourteenth-century aristocratic life, but whose life, exactly, or when it was lived remains uncertain, except to say that the poems were produced in Cheshire between the middle and the end of the fourteenth century. More certain are the dual concerns of four poems with an ethics of self-mastery that follow laws of the Church as well as laws of table, hall, and hunt. The author – learned, familiar with both the Bible and with the liturgy as well as with continental romances, dream visions, and lyric forms – must have been a cleric, almost certainly one who was attached to a baronial or even royal house; and in that identity we can find a writer well poised to explore the difficult accommodations between often antithetical codes of behavior. Certainly these poems bring the physical world to life in ways that brilliantly dramatize the challenges of attending to Christian doctrine as well as to social rules. The quest for consolation, *trawthe* or patience is a quest to love the world.

NOTES

1 Sarah Stanbury, *Seeing the Gawain-Poet: Description and the Act of Perception* (Philadelphia, PA: University of Pennsylvania Press, 1991).

2 Charles Muscatine, *Poetry and Crisis in the Age of Chaucer* (Notre Dame: University of Notre Dame Press, 1972), p. 40; D. S. Brewer, "Courtesy and the *Gawain*-Poet," in *Patterns of Love and Courtesy: Essays in Memory of C. S. Lewis*, ed. John Lawlor (Evanston, IL: Northwestern University Press, 1966), pp. 57–66.

3 Helen Barr, "*Pearl* – or 'the Jeweller's Tale'," *Medium Aevum* 69 (2000), 61; Felicity Riddy, "Jewels in Pearl," in *Companion to the Gawain-Poet*, ed. Derek S. Brewer and Jonathan Gibson (Cambridge: D. S. Brewer, 2001), pp. 143–55.

4 John Bowers, *The Politics of Pearl: Court Poetry in the Age of Richard II* (Cambridge: D. S. Brewer, 2001), p. 158.

5 David Aers, "Christianity for Courtly Subjects," in *A Companion to the Gawain-Poet*, p. 100.

6 Ralph Hanna, "Alliterative Poetry," in *The Cambridge History of Medieval English Literature*, ed. David Wallace (Cambridge University Press, 1999), p. 493; Larry D. Benson, *Art and Tradition in Sir Gawain and the Green Knight* (New Brunswick, NJ: Rutgers University Press, 1965), p. 171–84.

7 Citations from the texts are taken from *The Poems of the Pearl Manuscript: Pearl, Cleanness, Patience, Sir Gawain and the Green Knight*, ed. Malcolm Andrew and Ronald A. Waldron, rev. edn (Exeter University Press, 1987).

8 David Lawton, "The Unity of Middle English Alliterative Poetry," *Speculum* 58 (1983), 92.

9 Sylvia Tomasch, "A *Pearl* Punnology," *JEGP*, 88 (1989), 1–20; Ad Putter, *An Introduction to the Gawain-Poet* (New York: Longman, 1996), pp. 147–51.

10 J. A. Burrow, *Gestures and Looks in Medieval Narrative* (Cambridge University Press, 2002), p. 30.

11 Nicholas Watson, "The *Gawain*-Poet as Vernacular Theologian," in *Companion to the Gawain-Poet*, p. 312.

12 Bowers, *Politics*, p. 81; Ardis Butterfield, "French Culture and the Ricardian Court," in *Essays on Ricardian Literature*, ed A. J. Minnis, Charolotte C. Morse, and Thorlac Turville-Petre (Oxford: Clarendon Press, 1997), pp. 82–120.

13 Maria Bullon-Fernandez, "Beȝonde þe Water: Courtly and Religious Desire in *Pearl*," *SP*, 91 (1994), 35–49.

14 Donna Crawford, "The Architectonics of *Cleanness*," *SP*, 90 (1993), 29–45; Russell A. Peck, "Number as Cosmic Language," in *Essays in the Numerical*

Criticism of Medieval Literature, ed. C. D. Eckhardt (Lewisburg, PA: Bucknell University Press, 1980), pp. 15–64.

15 Elizabeth Keiser, *Courtly Desire and Medieval Homophobia: The Legitimation of Sexual Pleasure in Cleanness and its Contexts* (New Haven: Yale University Press, 1997), p. 8.

16 A. C. Spearing, "The Subtext of *Patience*: God as Mother and the Whale's Belly," *JMEMS* 29 (1999), 296.

17 Ad Putter, *Sir Gawain and the Green Knight and French Arthurian Romance* (Oxford: Clarendon Press, 1995), p. 2

18 On the manuscript, see A. S. G. Edwards, "The Manuscript: British Library MS Cotton Nero A.x.," in *Companion to the Gawain-Poet*, pp. 198–219.

11

DIANE WATT

John Gower

"And for that fewe men endite ..."

In the early to mid 1470s, George Ashby's *Active Policy of a Prince* ranked the poet John Gower, his more famous contemporary Geoffrey Chaucer, and Chaucer's successor John Lydgate as the "Primier poetes of this nacion."[1] Ashby celebrated them as vernacular writers, responsible for rhetorical, linguistic, and formal innovations, which he associated with the formation of an English identity and saw as the starting point of a distinctive English literary tradition. Ashby's views were not unique, and, although gradually tastes changed to Gower's disadvantage, Gower, Chaucer, and Lydgate continued to be viewed as a triumvirate well into the sixteenth century. But how accurate is Ashby's appraisal of Gower's achievement, and is he justified in linking his name not just to Chaucer, but to Lydgate, and thus implicitly to other of Chaucer's disciples such as Thomas Hoccleve?

Relatively little is known about Gower's life. We are not certain when he was born (his birth date is taken to be 1330), or where he was brought up. We do not know anything definite about his education, or even about his choice of career, but the consensus, based largely on the evidence of "insider" knowledge displayed in his poetry and of surviving records of various property dealings, is that he trained as a lawyer. We do know that in the 1370s he moved to the Priory of St. Mary Overeys in Southwark, that in 1378 Chaucer granted him power of attorney when he traveled to Italy, that in 1398 Gower married, and that shortly after he went blind, and that in 1408 he died. It is also clear that toward the end of his life, Gower benefited from the patronage of Henry of Derby both before and after he became king. Gower's surviving poetry seems to have been written in the second half of his life, up to around 1400.

Our lack of knowledge about Gower makes it more difficult to place his poetry. Critics have tended to locate Gower within a similar social milieu to Chaucer. Certainly, the official record indicates the two knew each other well. Furthermore, both poets refer to each other in their work. Chaucer dedicates his *Troilus and Criseyde* to "moral Gower" (V.1856) and playfully alludes in the Introduction to the Man of Law's Tale (78) to the sort of "wikke ensample" found in Gower's *Confession Amantis*, while Gower in turn in the unrevised *Confessio Amantis* (VIII.*2942) describes Chaucer as the "poete" of Venus.[2] But unlike Chaucer, Gower does not seem to have been employed by either the court or the government, and there is little solid evidence to connect him with other members of Chaucer's circle. The exception is Thomas Usk, whose *Testament of Love* (which dates to the mid-1380s) advertises its dependency on Chaucer's poetry at the same time as it borrows from without crediting Gower's *Vox Clamantis*. Yet Usk, who was executed in 1388, may have been at best a marginal member of Chaucer's coterie. Furthermore, the literary projects of Chaucer and Gower followed significantly different trajectories. The most striking difference between the two is that Gower composed his poetry not just in English, but also in Latin and Anglo-French. In fact each of Gower's three major poetic enterprises – *Mirour de l'Omme*, *Vox Clamantis*, and *Confessio Amantis* – is written in a different language.

Amongst Gower's earliest poems is the *Mirour de l'Omme*, composed before 1378. It is an expansive treatise concerned with sin, salvation, and the ills of society. His other Anglo-French works are balade collections. The first, the *Cinkante Balades*, is a sequence of poems describing a love affair and may be of a similar date to the *Mirour*. The second, the *Traitié pour Essampler les Amantz Marietz*, includes Latin notes and seems to have been written after and in response to *Confessio Amantis*, from which it takes its exemplary narratives. Gower's most extensive Latin work is his *Vox Clamantis*, originally completed before 1381, but subsequently expanded some time between the early- and mid-1380s, and further revised in the 1390s. It shares with the *Mirour* a preoccupation with vice and corruption, and similarly focuses on questions of good governance and the failings of the three estates. In the form it has come down to us, revised after 1381, it includes in its opening book Gower's famous nightmare vision of the Peasants' Revolt. In his revisions, he becomes increasingly critical and condemning of Richard II. The *Cronica Tripertita*, written after Richard II's deposition in 1399, is an overtly partisan political work written in support of Henry IV seizing power. It can be usefully considered alongside the English poem *In Praise of Peace*, written at the same time in justification of Henry IV's claim to the throne. There are also a number of short Latin poems. But the work to have gained the most attention over the centuries is *Confessio Amantis*, completed between 1390 and 1393, which, like the *Vox*, was substantially revised by its author. This long poem is often referred to as Gower's major "English" work, even though large parts of it, including prose commentaries and verses that introduce sections and subsections throughout the poem, are written in Latin.

It should be clear from this brief summary of Gower's works that Gower, unlike Chaucer or Lydgate, was not only or even primarily an "English" poet, in the sense of writing poetry through the medium of English. Nicholas Watson's observations about Chaucer in relation to vernacular poetry are useful: "What made Chaucer so important ... may have had less to do with any belief he had in himself as the founder of a self-conscious vernacular poetic tradition than with his *invention* as a founding figure."[3] Taken out of context, these comments seem all the more apposite when applied to Gower, who, in choosing to write *throughout* his literary career in Latin and Anglo-French as well as English, surely conceded some of his status as literary and linguistic ground-breaker. Yet at the same time, Gower, even more than Chaucer, recognized the connection between vernacular poetry, politics, and patriotism that would be picked up on and celebrated by later writers such as Ashby. In the revised opening of *Confessio Amantis*, Gower explains his decision to compose in the medium of English:

> And for that fewe men endite
> In oure englissh, I thenke make
> A bok for Engelondes sake. (Prologue, 22–24)

By means of such careful self-fashioning as an English poet, Gower guaranteed the survival of his reputation into the fifteenth century and beyond. But did he also succeed in securing the preservation of his poetry, or, for later poets, was his name simply one with which to conjure? Having considered further the *Confessio Amantis* itself, I will go on to examine the extent to which the poem influenced the work of Hoccleve and Lydgate.

"wisdom ... and pley"

According to the first version of *Confessio Amantis*, the poem was written at the request of Richard II, to whom Gower says "belongeth my ligeance / With al myn hertes obeissance" (Prol.*25–26). Gower recalls how he once chanced upon the king on the River Thames. Having been invited aboard the royal barge, Gower was instructed by the king to write "som newe thing ... / That he himself it mihte loke" (Prol.*51–52). This sort of commissioning claim is conventional enough, and there is no way of knowing if the episode is based on an actual event. It is perfectly in keeping with the end of the unrevised poem which includes a prayer for Richard II, "my worthi king" (VIII.*2986) in whom are combined the virtues of justice, pity, largesse, and charity (VIII.*2989–90). When Gower reworked the poem, he removed the lines in praise of Richard, and replaced them with a dedication to Henry of Derby, the future Henry IV. It is now that Gower reports that he decided to compose his poem, apparently on his own initiative, "for Engelondes sake" (Prol. 24). Gower also changed his conclusion, replacing the prayer for Richard with a prayer for the country.

The prologues and conclusions to Gower's poem, with their foci on the evils of division, the corruption of society, and the duties of kingship, bear a close relationship to the structurally foregrounded Book VII. The *Confessio* is organized in eight books, each corresponding to a different "deadly sin" with the exception of Book VII, which gives an account of Aristotle's education of Alexander the Great, and which conforms to the popular medieval genre of the "mirror for princes" or *Fürstenspiegel.* Yet, although the inclusion of dedications in a poem such as this is quite standard, their content is less so. As Larry Scanlon explains, "Normally the occasion for the compiler of a *Fürstenspiegel* to display his dependence on the prince he is advising, these dedications tend to show the opposite, both in their content, and by the very fact there are two of them."[4] While Gower may owe "obeissance" to Richard II, he presents himself as dependent on neither the king, nor for that matter Henry of Derby. His celebration of the earl is almost curt: Henry, we are told, is "Ful of knythode and alle grace" (Prol. 89). Gower is primarily concerned with developing his own role as a patriotic vernacular poet and as a bluff, honest adviser. His main interest is the state of the nation, and he is willing to speak on matters of kingship and self-governance, even though he has to do his best "With rude wordes and with pleyne" (VIII.*3068, cf. 3122).

Many critics believe that the revised dedications reveal Gower's changing political allegiances and it is certainly true that in the 1390s Gower became disaffected with Richard II. Throughout *Confessio Amantis* the king is implicitly compared to Alexander the Great, an ambiguous figure, who is a mighty conqueror, a chaste and honest ruler, and at the same time a rash tyrant. While Richard II is mirrored in Alexander, Gower's alter ego is Genius, the priest to whom Amans (the lover referred to in the title and the poem's protagonist) makes his confession. On a number of occasions the voice of Genius slides into that of the poet-narrator, especially in his discussions of the authority of the Church (II.2803–3071), and world religions and Christianity (especially V.738–1830), with its attack on Lollardy (V.1803–19). In Book VII, Gower/Genius plays Aristotle to Richard's Alexander. Nevertheless, as such Gower reveals his awareness of his responsibilities and his sense of his own inadequacies in such a role.

Aristotle may be a philosopher teacher worthy to advise his prince, but he is not without flaws (especially VIII.2705–13). In the climax of *Confessio*, Gower further undercuts his own status as disinterested councilor when he identifies *himself* with Amans (VIII.2321), now finally exposed as an old man and incapable of love, and describes himself as "feble and impotent" (VIII.3127).

While possible to resolve to some extent, the tension between the dedication to Richard II and that to the man who was to overthrow him is indicative of other conflicts within the poem. In the opinion of some readers, *Confessio* uneasily combines political and ethical concerns with the conventions and subject matter of courtly romance and with lurid stories taken from classical and other ancient writings. Book I begins as if it were a dream vision, but recounts events that take place when Amans, its narrator, is awake. It opens with a discussion of love, which holds sway over the world. Amans declares that he will tell of his own encounter with love, and goes on to describe how he set out walking in a wood one day in May, and came upon "a swote grene pleine" (I.113). Lamenting because he was "further fro my love / Than Erthe is fro the hevene above" (I.105–06), he fell to the ground in despair. Upon waking, he uttered a prayer to Cupid and Venus, only to find them standing in front of him. Eyes averted in fury, Cupid picked up "a firy Dart" (I.144) and pierced him through the heart, before vanishing. No less angry, Venus demanded to know what he was and what ailed him, and, remaining doubtful about his claim to be one of her own servants, deserving of pity and reward, instructed him to make his shrift. *Confessio* then continues as a dialogue between Amans and Genius, with Genius illustrating various classifications and subclassifications of sins against love and also many virtues with an encyclopedic series of exemplary narratives.

While Gower himself tries to resolve the apparent disunity in his poem – the dual foci on the ethical-political and the erotic – by making explicit the connection between microcosm and macrocosm, between "this litel world" that is the individual and "the grete world" of the cosmos (Prol. 957–58) – many internal contradictions remain. The penitential scheme of the work is interrupted by the analysis of good government and self-conduct in Book VII. It is then further disturbed when "Lust" is replaced by "Incest" as the topic of Book VIII. At no point is this substitution mentioned, far less, explained, although the theme of incest is clearly crucial to *Confessio* as a whole. Genius, for example, is compromised in his position of priest to Venus and Cupid, when he finds himself not only describing but also condemning their incestuous relationship in his account of the pagan gods (V.1382–1446). Gower's versions of the Tale of Apollonius of Tyre

(VIII.271–2008), which begins with a father's seduction of his daughter, and the Tale of Canace and Machaire (Book III.143–336), which tells of an affair between a brother and a sister, seem to have very quickly achieved some notoriety. Chaucer's Man of Law dismissed both stories as immoral and disgusting, "swiche unkynde abhomynacions" (88).

It would be wrong to place much faith in the opinions of Chaucer's Man of Law or to assume from his words that Gower's stories lack conventional moral frameworks. Nevertheless, Gower's portrayal of Canace is famously sympathetic to the plight of the woman who, after her relationship with her brother has been discovered, is forced by her father to kill herself, knowing her baby will almost certainly die. In other medieval versions Canace's story is told under the heading of "mad passion,"[5] but Genius introduces it to illustrate the sin of wrath: Amans is to learn from the error of Canace's father (III.134–42). Genius goes to considerable lengths to exonerate Canace and her brother, who, we are told, are young and isolated and are driven by natural urges to engage in a relationship that is contrary to nature (III.148–78). Karma Lochrie contends that even while he explores sexual "perversions" Gower adheres to a conservative gender ideology.[6] Yet in his sensitive and complex portrayal of Canace as victim of her own actions, circumstance, external forces, and unjust and inequitable punishment, Gower is not as anti-feminist as Lochrie implies. Furthermore Gower offers no easy solutions to the problem of sex. In his discussion of chastity (VII. 4215–37), Genius explicitly praises heterosexual desire, exclaiming "The Madle is mad for the femele" (VII.4215), and goes on to praise marriage and condemn adultery. Nevertheless, the resolution offered in Book VIII, following the completion of lover's confession, seems sadly inadequate. At the end of the poem, Amans – now identified as John Gower himself – does not find himself a wife or even a lover, but remains aged and alone, "And in this wise, soth to seyn, / Homward a softe pas y wente" (VIII.2966–67). Marriage may be answer, but not, it seems, for Amans.

Chaucer, in applying the epithet "moral" to Gower, and then effectively taking it away again when the Man of Law decries his stories as immoral, can be seen to be responding to Gower's own poetry. "Divisioun," sin or evil, is a recurring concern of Gower (cf. Prol. 849–1052) and the corruption of society and humanity is reflected in the fissures in *Confessio Amantis* itself. In other words, the poem, like the world, is divided. Nevertheless, some of the unresolved difficulties in *Confessio* can also be understood in terms of Gower's playfulness. Such playfulness, or *ludus,* combined with the sort of moralizing we might more readily expect to find in such instructive works, is inherent in the genre of the mirror for princes.[7] Gower simply develops it to its fullest extent in his own poem. From the start Gower warns that wisdom "dulleth ofte a mannes wit" (Prol. 14) and again and again he stresses that he is concerned with "ernest *and* game" (VIII.3109, my italics). This is after all a poem that from its first conception was intended as "wisdom to the wise / And pley to hem that lust to pleye" (Prol.*84–85). But to what extent did Chaucer's literary sons follow their father's lead and identify in Gower's works both wisdom and play?

"Hast þou nat eeke my maister Gower slayn"

The posthumous influence of *Confessio Amantis* is first seen in Hoccleve's *Regiment of Princes*, written between 1410 and 1412. Hoccleve represents himself as an unworthy heir to Chaucer, who "fayn wolde han me taght; / But I was dul, and lerned lite or naght" (*Regiment of Princes*, 2078–79).[8] For Hoccleve, Chaucer is "The firste fyndere of our faire langage" (4978). His death is lamented (1961–74 and 2080–2107), and Hoccleve determines to preserve his image (4992–98). Yet while Gower is praised for his "vertu" (1976), *his* demise is passed over quickly – "Hast þou nat eeke my maister Gower slayn" (1975) – and there is no acknowledgment of Hoccleve's debt to his poetry. Yet this debt is manifest in the body of Hoccleve's *Regiment*, which, like *Confessio Amantis* VII, takes the form of advice offered to a prince, sharing some of the same sources and exemplary tales.[9] Furthermore, the overlap between Gower and Hoccleve can also be seen in the extended prologue to the *Regiment*, which resonates with the penitential frame of *Confessio Amantis*, combining wisdom with sardonic humor.

Similarly to *Confessio Amantis*, the prologue to Hoccleve's *Regiment* sets up expectations that it is a dream vision only to confound them. Here the narrator tells how his troubles prevented him from sleeping, and on the following morning he set out walking in the fields where he was engaged in conversation by a beggar. This "poore olde hore man" (122) resembles Gower's Genius.[10] In *Confessio Amantis*, Book I, Amans pleads with Venus, asking whether she wants him to be healed or to die, and Venus, having asked him to reveal his "maladie" (I.164), entrusts him to Genius's care. In Hoccleve's *Regiment*, the beggar offers to "cure" the poet-narrator's suffering (Prol. 161), playing on the medical and pastoral senses of the word. From early in their dialogue, the beggar addresses Hoccleve, as Genius addresses Amans, as "My sone" (Prol. 143), and insists that if Hoccleve follows his teaching he will escape from his melancholy (Prol. 214–17). Eventually Hoccleve shares the cause of his distress, and explains that at its root are financial problems, exacerbated by the fact that he has a wife to support. In this respect Hoccleve's poetic persona, who otherwise is reminiscent of Gower's youthful and frustrated Amans, seems quite distinct from his antecedent. Nevertheless, in the beggar's digression on marriage, he expands on the theme of marriage found in *Confessio Amantis*. Hoccleve's beggar examines much more explicitly than Genius the nature of matrimonial love itself (Prol. 1555–1764). In so doing, he addresses an omission in Gower's poem, resolving some of its difficulty, but sacrificing some of its playfulness in the process.

Hoccleve's *Regiment* also answers Gower's *Confessio Amantis* on a political level. In the *Regiment*, it is the Beggar who commissions the poem, for the benefit of the future Henry V. He instructs Hoccleve to pen a poem "fresh and gay" (1906) that might amuse the prince, and also bring the poet the patronage he so desperately needs. He goes on to suggest that Hoccleve should translate a "tretice / Groundid on his estates holsumnesse" (1949–50). Compared with *Confessio*'s unusual reticence, the *Regiment* is much more conventional in its fulsome address to its patron (2017–30). However, Hoccleve also indirectly compares Alexander to Prince Henry, and in so doing he, like Gower, introduces a note of warning, as, for example, in the story of the knight who reproaches Alexander for his "lust, bestial and miserable" (3503). While Alexander may acknowledge his sin, and resolve to reform himself, he is clearly also mortal rather than divine, capable of ill as well as good. As the *Regiment* moves toward its climax, the advice given to the prince becomes more urgent as it merges into a request for favor. At the same time Henry blurs with the beggar (who, we have been told, spent his youth in the tavern playing dice, swearing oaths, and womanizing [610–58]). When Hoccleve finally acknowledges his follies and repents of his "mysrewly lyfe" (4376) he does so not to the beggar but to the prince.

On the whole, Hoccleve's political position is more straightforward than that of the Gower responsible for *Confessio*, and closer to that of the Gower of the late, pro-Lancastrian propaganda poem, "In Praise of Peace." In the latter poem, Gower declares to Henry IV, shortly after his overthrow of Richard, that "Thi title is knowe uppon thin ancestrie" (12). Hoccleve details Prince Henry's lineage through references to Henry IV (816–26, 1835, 3352–53), John of Gaunt (3347–51 and 3353), Henry of Lancaster (2647–53), and Edward III (2556–62). The ill-fated Richard II is only alluded to when the poet-narrator records how "Me fel to mynde how that, not long ago, / ffortunes strok doun threst estaat royal / Into myscheef" (22–24). However, even here Hoccleve's mention of Richard's fall actually has the effect of bringing his poem much closer to *Confessio Amantis*. Overtly, Hoccleve's narrator is drawing a parallel between his own position and that of the former king. But as Scanlon observes, the allusion draws our attention to the uncertainty of the prince's own future, "for it not only makes Hoccleve and Richard indistinguishable, it also makes Henry and Richard indistinguishable."[11] As in Gower's poem, the complex play with doubles and alter egos has a serious message.

"In moral mateer ful notable was Goweer"

John Lydgate's longest work, the *Fall of Princes*, was written between 1431 and 1438 or 1439. Like both Gower's *Confessio* and Hoccleve's *Regiment* it follows the advice to princes format. It is claims to have been commissioned by the younger brother of Henry V, Humphrey, Duke of Gloucester, Protector of England during Henry VI's minority. Lydgate describes his poem as a translation of a French version of a poem by the Italian author, Giovanni Boccaccio,[12] but its genesis is in reality more complex and it draws on a range of other sources, including the work of Chaucer and Gower. Like Hoccleve's *Regiment*, the *Fall of Princes* makes use of a number of the same stories as *Confessio Amantis*, including the famous Tales of Lucrece and Virginia as well as other political narratives. Second, Lydgate, like Gower, includes lengthy discussions of vice and virtue. Third, as in Hoccleve's *Regiment* and *Confessio Amantis*, Alexander the Great features prominently in the *Fall of Princes*, but as a more flawed and less divine figure. In Gower's Tale of Diogenes and Alexander (*Confessio Amantis*, III.1201–1330), Alexander listens to the old philosopher with courtesy and respect (III.1263–64 and 1293–97), and Diogenes is represented as having "enformed" Alexander (III.1313), suggesting that Alexander is at least open to instruction. In Lydgate's version (*Fall of Princes*, I.6224–79), Alexander is summarily dismissed as one whose reason was "vnder thobeisaunce / Off flesshli lustis fetrid in a cheyne" (6254–55).[13] Not surprisingly, Lydgate carefully avoids suggesting comparisons between Alexander and Duke Humphrey.

This reticence brings us to a further and more unexpected aspect of Gower's influence on Lydgate: their shared fascination with salacious stories. In the *Fall of Princes*, Book I, Lydgate freely expands his named source in order to pick up on Gower's preoccupation with incest. Lydgate does not make use of Gower's Tale of Apollonius of Tyre, but retells the related story of Oedipus (I.3157–3815). Moreover, Lydgate includes the story of Canace and Machaire (I.6833–7049), recounted only briefly in his main source, alongside other Ovidian narratives concerned with incest and the related sin of self-love: Narcissus, Byblis, and Myrrha (I.5552–5775). Although Lydgate does not slavishly follow Gower's version of Canace and Machaire – most notably he does not attempt to explain away the brother and sister's relationship in terms of their youthfulness and the contradictions inherent in nature – there are clear parallels between the versions. Whereas in Ovid's *Heroides*, XI, the entire story is narrated in epistolary form, both Gower and Lydgate make Canace's letter to her brother only part of the story.[14] Furthermore, Lydgate's envoy follows *Confessio Amantis* in that the story ostensibly illustrates the sin of ire (*Fall of Princes*, I.7057–63). Strikingly, Lydgate borrows from Gower, albeit in simplified form, the poignant image of the child bathing in its mother's blood (*Fall of Princes*, I.7033–35; *Confessio Amantis*, III.312–15).

While Lydgate owes as least as much to Gower as does Hoccleve, he is even less willing than Hoccleve to admit it. In the Prologue to Book I, praise of Lydgate's "maister Chaucer ... cheeff poete off Breteyne" (I. 246–47) appears alongside an extensive list of Chaucer's works (I.274–357). His appreciation of Chaucer finds its fullest expression at the poem's climax in his envoys to his patron and closing farewell to his book. In an elaborate reworking of the famous ending to *Troilus and Criseyde* ("Go, litel bok, go, litel myn tragedye ..." [V.1786ff.]), Lydgate alludes to Chaucer's moral Gower (*Fall of Princes*, IX.3410). In this, the *only* direct reference to Gower in Lydgate's entire poem, Lydgate is more concerned with imitating and responding to Chaucer, and with establishing his own place within the same classical and vernacular tradition, than with actually admitting his own literary genealogy. In fact, Lydgate makes it clear that within the emergent English canon at least, Chaucer is the only "Laureat" poet whom he is willing to acknowledge. When Lydgate celebrates Chaucer as one who "excellyd al othir in our Englyssh tounge" (IX.3407), he willfully overlooks Gower.

"In englesch forto make a book"

It is tempting to attempt to understand Hoccleve's and Lydgate's failure to acknowledge Gower in terms of literary competitiveness. Rather than recognize Gower as their antecedent, Hoccleve and Lydgate trace their genealogy directly to Chaucer, seeing themselves as inheriting and going beyond the tradition they ascribe to him. Perhaps it is because they judge Chaucer to be the better poet that they want to claim him as their predecessor, but a more convincing explanation lies in the interaction of vernacularity, politics, and patriotism discussed earlier. As critics such as David Lawton and Scanlon have shown, Gower, Hoccleve, and Lydgate adopt very similar stances as poets, and share common political and ethical concerns.[15] Gower's authorial representation as a forthright councilor and his claim to lay rather than clerical textual authority had a significant impact on his fifteenth-century followers when they came to write about kingship and government. Furthermore, Gower, Hoccleve, and Lydgate all share anxieties about the threat to the security of the nation offered by Lollardy and by war, and actively promote suppression of heresy and the maintenance or establishment of peace.

Nevertheless, in one crucial respect, Hoccleve and Lydgate diverge from Gower. It is clear that when Gower resolved "In englesch forto make a book" (VIII.3108), he saw *Confessio Amantis* as a development of his previous work in French and Latin, not as a break from it. The Latin colophon to *Confessio* envisages Gower's three major works as part of a single design. For Gower, writing in three languages does not detract from his undertaking or achievement. On the contrary, it adds to it. For Hoccleve and Lydgate, however, writing in English is presented as the only option. In the *Regiment*, the poet-narrator has to be cajoled into writing in English, having refused the beggar's demand that he "Endite in frensch or latyn" (1854). In the *Fall of Princes*, Lydgate claims, as part of his apology for the flawed state of his "translation," that he is not particularly skilled in French (IX.3329–30). Underlying such modesty is an awareness of the nature of their audiences, Hoccleve's "Lettered folk" (Prol. 155), whose literacy might well not extend beyond English. But, in Lydgate's poem at least, there is also a hostility to France (see IX.3134–3238), and thus implicitly to the French language, that reflects the political climate of the fifteenth century and the ongoing struggle for the French throne. Hoccleve and Lydgate were concerned with policing the linguistic as well as ideological borders of fifteenth-century literature. Chaucer represented a vernacular integrity that Gower, despite his willingness to intervene in politics and his engagement with ethics, *was* seen to compromise, at least by those poets most indebted to his "English" poem. Nevertheless, in terms of real, if unacknowledged influence, Gower remained second to none.

NOTES

1 George Ashby, *Active Policy of a Prince* in *George Ashby's Poems*, ed. Mary Bateson, EETS ES 76 (1899), Prologue, l. 2.

2 References to Chaucer's poetry are to *Riverside*. References to Gower's English poetry are to *The English Works of John Gower*, ed. George C. Macaulay, EETS ES 81, 82 (1900, repr. 1979). Following Macaulay, quotations from the unrevised *Confessio Amantis* are indicated with an asterisk. References to Gower's French and Latin poetry are to *The Complete Works of John Gower*, ed. George C. Macaulay, vols. III and IV (Oxford: Clarendon Press, 1899 and 1902).

3 Nicholas Watson, "The Politics of Middle English Writing," in *Idea of the Vernacular*, p. 347.

4 Larry Scanlon, *Narrative, Authority, and Power: The Medieval Exemplum and the Chaucerian Tradition* (Cambridge University Press, 1994), p. 252.
5 C. David Benson, "Incest and Moral Poetry in Gower's *Confessio Amantis*," *The Chaucer Review* 19 (1984), 105.
6 Karma Lochrie, *Covert Operations: The Medieval Uses of Secrecy* (Philadelphia: University of Pennsylvania Press, 1999), pp. 223–25.
7 Siân Echard, "Introduction," in *A Companion to Gower*, ed. S. Echard (Cambridge: D. S. Brewer, 2004), p. 4.
8 References to Hoccleve's *Regiment of Princes* are to *Hoccleve*'s *Works*, ed. Frederick J. Furnivall, vol. III, EETS ES 72 (1897).
9 Hoccleve acknowledges two direct sources which he shares with Gower: the Pseudo-Aristotelian *Secretum secretorum* and *De regimine principum* of Giles of Rome, but, whereas Gower also makes use of the *Livres dou Trésor* of Brunetto Latini, Hoccleve's third source is the *Ludus shachorum* of Jacobus de Cessolis.
10 Scanlon, *Narrative, Authority, and Power*, p. 304.
11 Ibid., p. 303.
12 The immediate source is Laurence de Premierfait's *De cas des nobles hommes et femmes*, a reworking of Giovanni Boccaccio's *De casibus*.
13 Reference is to *Lydgate*'s *Fall of Princes*, ed. Henry Bergen, 4 vols., EETS ES 121–24 (1924–27).
14 Ovid, *Heroides and Amores*, ed. and trans. Grant Showerman, rev. G. P. Goold, Loeb Classical Library (London: Heinemann, 1977).
15 David Lawton, "Dullness and the Fifteenth Century," *ELH*, 54 (1987), 761–99; Scanlon, *Narrative, Authority, and Power*, esp. pp. 245–350.

12

LARRY SCANLON

Geoffrey Chaucer

In the *House of Fame* Chaucer's visionary alter-ego encounters a maze of literary monuments. Kidnapped by an abusive eagle – a comic emblem of Dante – and deposited unceremoniously before a cliff of ice, he makes his way up to a palace of beryl consisting almost entirely of windows and "pynacles." There he discovers Lady Fame herself, high above milling crowds, on a dais supported by pillars, each displaying a great poet or historian, Josephus the Hebrew, Statius, Homer, Guido della Colonna, Geoffrey of Monmouth, Virgil, Ovid, Lucan, Claudian, and many others. As he exclaims, the hall was as full of authors of "olde gestes" as trees are full of rooks' nests. With Chaucer's characteristically sly, self-deprecating irony, this whimsical *ekphrasis* aptly figures the vicissitudes of poetic authority. The pillars Chaucer's narrator envisions are mainly made of iron, serviceable and dependable; nevertheless they stand in a radically uncertain structure, founded on the illusory solidity of a cliff of ice. Whatever the strength of its own intrinsic value, the sources and effects of poetic authority must remain framed by uncertainty. The poetry of the present or of the recent past, here embodied in the figure of Dante, leads the reader to the durable wealth of the more ancient past. Yet taken in its entirety previous tradition overwhelms, precisely because it endures so long and because what endures is so rich and profuse. The profusion overwhelms even the minimal level of human organization by the House of Fame and can be made intelligible only by recourse to the natural world. The forest of rook's nests is a figure of renewal, but one that is slightly macabre. These are the nests of scavengers, incubators of new life out of a past in decay and putrefaction.

Geoffrey Chaucer is the most monumental of English poets – more monumental even than Shakespeare, as he is the more ancient. While hardly the most ancient – that honor traditionally goes to Caedmon, the Anglo-Saxon cowherd half a millennium his senior – Chaucer is the oldest English poet to be read continuously from his own time to the present.

Chaucer's monumentality gives his work an authority current readers can neither evade nor assimilate with any ease, especially as irony is its most constant hallmark. This passage from the *House of Fame* is hardly isolated. Throughout his long and varied career Chaucer returns regularly to the problem of poetic authority. As we have just seen, he anticipates postmodern anxieties regarding previous authority and the value of tradition. There is no doubt that Chaucer's lasting centrality began with the canonizing efforts of Thomas Hoccleve, John Lydgate, and others, nor that this literary initiative was underwritten in part by the political needs of the house of Lancaster. Nor is there any doubt that a century and a half later the English Renaissance would turn Chaucer's centrality against his successors and contemporaries, saving Chaucer and jettisoning most of the rest. The field of modern Middle English studies has devoted significant labor to undoing these longstanding historical consolidations and exclusions. Some medievalists feel Chaucer is still too hegemonic, that he still attracts too much scholarly attention, and that the field needs some fundamental restructuring to insure he plays an appropriately reduced role in the future. A less drastic approach to the problem might lie in reconsidering Chaucer's authority in all of its historical and conceptual complexities: what was it in particular about his poetry that inspired his successors to claim him as the founder of their tradition? The answer to that question obviously begins with Chaucer himself and his ambivalent meditations on poetic authority and the durability of tradition.

Geoffrey Chaucer was born about 1340 in London, the son of a prosperous wine merchant, who was also a deputy butler to Edward III. By his late teens, he was already being trained at court, beginning in the household of Prince Lionel, one of Edward's younger sons. In 1359 he served briefly in the Hundred Years War, captured and ransomed the next year. Between 1360 and 1378 he traveled to the continent with some regularity for various diplomatic purposes, including a trip to Genoa and Florence in 1372–73, and one to Milan in 1378. It is generally assumed that these journeys introduced Chaucer to the Italian authors Dante, Petrarch, and Boccaccio, all of whom would exert major influence on his work. Implicit in this simple, material fact are two others which are equally important but less remarked. Whatever their feelings about his poetic talents, Chaucer's royal sponsors clearly recognized his linguistic skills at a very early date, and trusted him to represent their interests. Although the official language of diplomacy in the later Middle Ages was Latin, most courtiers were more comfortable in their native vernaculars. Diplomatic work thus required a constant process of translation in informal as well as formal terms and in representing his own political community, Chaucer the diplomat would have needed to be attentive to the linguistic nuances and complexities of the communities with which he was negotiating.

In 1374, Edward III appointed Chaucer the Controller of Custom, a post he held until 1386, although his active involvement had probably tailed off a few years before when he was granted permission to appoint deputies. He continued as a public servant for the rest of his life. In 1385, having taken up residence in Greenwich, he was appointed Justice of the Peace in Kent, and the next year he was elected to Parliament as knight of the shire, or member of the House of Commons. In 1389, Richard II appointed him Clerk of the King's Works, and in 1391 he became deputy forester of the royal forest of North Petherton in Somerset. These later duties obviously did not involve translation in the literal, linguistic sense. However, they did require mediation and mediation that occurred largely through the use of language. Chaucer was representing a central form of authority, the Crown, from which he, as a commoner, was sharply differentiated. The initial audience for his poetry was probably commoners like himself in royal service.[1] But the social composition of his audience quickly expanded, an expansion no doubt facilitated by his own complex medial and mediating social position.

Thus it is not surprising that Chaucer's poetry involves translation in both the literal and more extended senses. Many modern scholars have viewed Chaucer as a European rather than an English poet. There is some accuracy in this claim. For although Chaucer's status for much of his posterity as the father of English poetry would make him quintessentially English, as a matter of actual poetic practice, his Englishness was largely a matter of translation. Like most of his Middle English contemporaries and predecessors, Chaucer was broadly influenced by Latin traditions, both those of the Christian Church and of classical antiquity. But he was virtually alone in the broadness of his engagement with other vernaculars. He essentially introduced the Italian tradition to England, but he also drew widely on more different French writers and traditions than anyone else. His poetic line was always syllabic, a prosody ultimately derived from French models. He was hardly the first to work with such a line; syllabic poetry in English began in the twelfth century. Nevertheless, when Chaucer began writing in the late 1360s, alliterative verse was still the dominant form of prosody. And none of the previous practitioners of syllabic verse could match Chaucer's demonstration of its range and versatility. Moreover, previous syllabic verse tended to be octosyllabic, closer to standard French models. Chaucer himself wrote in octosyllables in the *Book of the Duchess* and the *House of Fame*, but thereafter he adopted the hitherto much rarer decasyllabic line, frequently employing it in rhyming couplets. The decasyllabic couplet would go on to become a mainstay of narrative poetry in English for the next five centuries; in essentially inventing it, Chaucer was obviously seeking in French prosodic models a variation that best fit the specific needs of his own vernacular. We can make a similar observation about his broader engagement with other European works and traditions. His continual, wide-ranging adaptation and translation of these works and traditions monumentally enlarged the poetic capacities of the language to which he was offering them. Whether he consciously intended to imitate Petrarch's laureateship, which, he has his Clerk declare, "Enlumyned al Ytaille of poetry" ("illuminated all of Italy with poetry"), the effect was similar.[2] Writing in a language largely marginal to current European culture, lacking the literary prestige not only of Latin, but also of Italian, and especially French, Chaucer's engagement with the centers of European literature brings those centers back to his periphery.

Chaucer's first three major poems, the *Book of the Duchess*, the *House of Fame*, and the *Parliament of Fowls*, are all dream visions, one of the central genres of later medieval poetry. Like most dream visions, they are allegorical. Chaucer renders the visionary landscape of each of them a concise encylopedia of previous poetic tradition. He makes each of them literally texts constructed out of previous texts, and he is particularly interested in the experiential dimension of this process. Both the *Book of the Duchess* and the *Parliament* begin with Chaucer's account of reading a particular text before falling asleep. That text will then structure the account of the dream. In the *Book of the Duchess*, it is the story of Ceyx and Alcione from the eleventh book of Ovid's *Metamorphoses*. Ceix was a king who lost his life in a shipwreck, and Alcione, his queen, long left without word of his fate receives in a dream his drowned body from Morpheus the god of sleep. Ovid's narrative anticipates the loss of the Black Knight, whom Chaucer the dreamer discovers apart from a hunt, lamenting his beloved White. (In all likelihood, Chaucer wrote this poem to commemorate John of Gaunt's wife, Blanche, the Duchess of Lancaster, who died in 1369.) Chaucer assumes he is following a story of a conventional disappointment in love, even though the Black Knight declares early on that Ovid offers no remedy for his woe (568). Moreover the poem raises the stakes of this confusion by drawing as well on Guillaume de Machaut's *Judgment of the King of Bohemia*, a fourteenth-century French poem featuring a debate on the question of whether the loss of a love to infidelity was worse than to death. It is not until the very end of the poem that the Knight reveals to him, and to Chaucer's readers, that White has died. This intrusion of the irremediable loss of death offers a stark counterpoint to the shaping power of previous poetic discourse. As the poem gives Machaut's debate an actual referent, the anticipation of the ending by the Ceyx and Alcione story brings no lasting solace. The conventions of love poetry which the Knight's dialogue works through, in spite of their power to call for and shape erotic desire, founder on this final rupture.

The *House of Fame* begins by rewriting the most famous *ekphrasis* in all of Western tradition, Virgil's description of the paintings in Juno's Temple in Carthage in the first book of the *Aeneid*. Hidden in a cloud and spirited into the Temple by Venus, his mother, Aeneas finds himself confronted with scenes from the fall of Troy. In transforming poetry into architecture, Virgil is obviously affirming poetry's capacity to monumentalize the past, but in making Aeneas himself a witness to this transformation, he also suggests the monument necessarily ruptures its connection to the past it preserves. In the *House of Fame* Chaucer the dreamer finds himself surveying moments from the *Aeneid* in a "temple ymad of glas" (120), but this time the witness is Dido. This shift gives the gap between historical experience and its written monuments both greater poignancy, and a political depth. In a speech for which Chaucer alleges "non other auctor" but himself (314), Dido complains her name is "lorn": fame is "so swift" that "though I myghte duren ever, / That I have don rekever I never" (345–60). Chaucer has restored to Dido, the archetypal woman betrayed, the voice which the narrative trajectory of the *Aeneid* silences and the point of view it ignores as it pursues its account of Aeneas's founding of Rome. In fact Chaucer adapts Dido's speech from Ovid's *Heroides*, a collection of verse epistles from famous women, but even this irony serves his larger purpose, which is to recover that which Dido claims is irrecuperable, that part of the past which poetry, or any written text, fails to preserve. He suggests throughout this poem that the key to poetic authority lies in its relation to the unauthorized and non-authoritative, and as he seeks the center of that authority, he does so from the periphery. The dreamer exits the temple and finds it is located in an arid desert. After the encounter with Lady Fame the dreamer wanders to the House of Rumor, an embodiment of the totality of everyday conversation in all of its gossipy banality. The poem was never finished, and ends irresolutely with the enigmatic appearance of "A man of gret auctorite" (2158).

In the *Parliament of Fowls* the problem of authority becomes explicitly political. Parliament emerged as a distinct political force in the latter portion of the fourteenth century, and became the chief institutional battleground for the reign of Richard II, as control veered back and forth between the royal factions and their baronial opposition. While the poem's conceit assumes the institution's basic ideal as a deliberative arena where all the estates of the kingdom could have their say, this ideal remains largely in the background. In what will be a keynote of the rest of his career – already implicit in the treatment of Dido – Chaucer will frame general questions of politics through the specific dynamics of gender and sexuality. The poem turns on the problem of female desire. Its main antecedent is the *Romance of the Rose*, a thirteenth-century French work and the most widely disseminated vernacular poem of the entire Middle Ages. Before sleep Chaucer reads Macrobius's fourth-century commentary on Cicero's *Somnium Scipionis*, or "Dream of Scipio," a work the *Romance of the Rose* summarizes in its opening lines. Scipio appears in Chaucer's dream to lead him to the park modeled on the *Rose*'s Garden of Earthly Delights. There, on Saint Valentine's Day – that date's first known association with love – the goddess Nature convenes an assembly of birds to help a "formel" (female) eagle decide among three "tercel" (male) eagles who are wooing her. After representatives of each class of birds – water-fowl, worm-fowl, seed-fowl, and the noble "foules of ravyn" (birds of prey) – have their say, Nature decrees that the choice is to be left to the formel alone. The formel requests and receives a year's respite to make the decision. The poem ends in that state of suspension, perhaps as a way of emphasizing the formel's agency.

Chaucer was prolific and versatile. During the course of his career he produced a small but impressive and varied body of shorter poems. He translated Boethius's *Consolation of Philosophy* and portions of the *Romance of the Rose*. He is also one a very few Anglophone poets with a scientific work to his credit, albeit one that is unfinished and somewhat elementary. He addressed the *Treatise on the Astrolabe* to his son Lewis; parts one and two offer a description of the instrument and directions for its use. The work's introduction promises more technical information in the final three sections, but those Chaucer apparently never completed. Nevertheless, the work remains extant in thirty-one manuscripts, an impressive total that testifies to its popularity. Chaucer's later career was dominated by three major works: *Troilus and Criseyde*, the *Legend of Good Women*, and the *Canterbury Tales*.

Troilus and Criseyde is an epic, or a fusion of epic and romance. The secret love affair between the two title characters, the Trojan prince, Troilus, younger brother of Hector and Paris, and the noble widow, Criseyde, takes place against the background of the Trojan War. As a retelling of one of Western culture's oldest stories, the poem provides Chaucer with the opportunity for another, much more extended meditation on the past. There is the specifically poetic problem of the literary past, and the more general historical question of pagan antiquity; for medieval culture the originary epoch preceding the coming of Christ. Chaucer will refract these two ways of imagining the past through a narrative of erotic desire and a politics of gender which that narrative reveals. Although most of the characters can be found in classical sources, the narrative itself is a medieval invention, first appearing in the twelfth-century French poem, *Roman de Troie* by Benoît de Sainte-Maure, then redacted in 1287 in Latin prose by Guido delle Colonne as *Historia destructionis Troiae*. Chaucer's immediate source was Boccaccio's *Il Filostrato* from the late 1330s. Chaucer never acknowledges Boccaccio – perhaps because he considered Boccaccio too recent and insufficiently authoritative – inventing instead a fictive authority he names Lollius (1.394, 5.1653).

Chaucer radically reshapes Boccaccio's poem, making the story at once more public and more private. He makes it more public by amplifying its historical and political dimensions, and he makes it more private by developing more fully the three main characters, Troilus, Criseyde, and Pandarus, Criseyde's uncle, who acts as the go-between. He foregrounds the complicated interiority that both Troilus and Criseyde bring to the affair, and emphasizes the instrumental role played by Pandarus as matchmaker. Pandarus is ubiquitous and intrusive to the point of voyeurism, thus making Chaucer's readers aware of their own voyeuristic pleasures and desires. Nor is the poem's implication of its readers confined to its erotic dimensions. The narrative's turning point occurs when the Greeks, persuaded by Calchas, Criseyde's father, who has already defected to them, offer to return the recently captured Antenor in exchange for Criseyde. During the "parlement" in which the Trojans decide to accept this exchange, Troilus must stay silent or betray his secret love, while Hector, noting Criseyde is "no prisonere" objects that in Troy, as a civilized society, "We usen here no wommen for to selle" (4.179, 182). Hector's blunt assessment of Trojan behavior on this occasion points to a larger and even more uncomfortable truth. All aristocratic societies do in fact depend on the exchange of women. Troilus and Criseyde's secret love is a medieval courtly romance set in ancient Troy; but the political circumstances that bring it to an end characterized the nobility of the Christian Middle Ages no less than they did that of pagan antiquity.

The *Legend of Good Women* was Chaucer's final dream vision. Although he never completed it, he began work on it some time in the 1380s, after he had finished the *Troilus*. It shows many of the same preoccupations of the earlier dream visions. However, it is also an anthology held together by a frame tale, thus constituting an important anticipation of the *Canterbury Tales*. Long considered an artistic failure the poem has been taken much more seriously during the last twenty-five years, largely in response to the emergence of feminist criticism. It begins with a dream of Cupid and of

Alceste, a queen of classical legend who persuaded the gods to accept her into the underworld in place of her husband. In Chaucer's retelling she is transformed into a daisy. Cupid reproves Chaucer for having translated *The Romance of the Rose*, and for having presented Criseyde unfavorably in *Troilus*. Alceste intervenes on Chaucer's behalf. She recites a canon of his work, then commands him to make "a glorious legende / Of goode wymmen, maydenes and wyves" (F 483–84; G 473–74). A number of recent scholars have these passages as indirect registrations of the responses of Chaucer's contemporary audience; some even as the figuration of female patronage. In any case, Chaucer clearly intends "legend" to be read in its medieval association with hagiography. He tells the stories of nine women: Cleopatra, Thisbe, Dido, Hypsiplye, Medea, Lucretia, Ariadne, Philomela, and Phyllis. The incipits and explicits (beginnings and endings) of two of the poem's six substantially complete manuscripts describe the first six women as martyrs. Although inspired by Boccaccio's *De claris mulieribus*, Chaucer draws the bulk of his material from Ovid and other classical sources. With the exception of Thisbe, all of these women are betrayed by their lovers. Yet the exception is telling. For Chaucer is less interested in either the perfidy of the men or the sheer suffering of the women than he is in their fidelity, their devotion as lovers in spite of betrayal. Once again he returns to the classical to undercut the idealizations of medieval romance. In contrast to the (characteristically male) lover of romance, who proclaims to be dying in the cause of love, a number of these heroines actually do die. The poem's emphasis on their fidelity thus grounds itself on a grim recognition of the political constraints on female desire.

Chaucer began work on the *Canterbury Tales* in the mid-1380s and presumably continued to work on it for most of the rest of his life. Some scholars have taken the Retraction, which occurs at the very end of the collection, and disavows those tales that "sownen [tend toward] into synne" (X, 1085), to indicate that Chaucer had already stopped work on the poem some time before he died in 1400, perhaps when he took up residence at Westminster Abbey in the last year of his life. Extant in 83 complete or partial manuscripts, and six pre-1540 print editions, the collection has basically come down to us in ten fragments. The first includes the General Prologue and the first four tales, ending with the incomplete *Cook's Tale*. In the most widely accepted order, that of the Ellesmere manuscript, seven of the fragments contain at least two tales with prologues, or introductions linking one tale with the next. Even the three containing a single tale also contain prologues, introductions or endlinks connecting each of the tales to the frame tale in some way. It is true that this order is only one among many and in other manuscripts even the number and content of the fragments vary. Indeed, some recent scholars have provocatively suggested Chaucer intended the collection as a kind of the anthology with even the order of the tales left up to the reader.[3] However, the evidence of the fragments – jumbled and contradictory though it is – tells a different story. Chaucer clearly wanted his readers to think of the individual tales in the Canterbury collection as inserted into a larger narrative – a narrative that to be a narrative must have a coherent temporal order. While it seems unlikely we will ever recover that order, the text itself, in all of its extant manuscript variations, demands we continue to seek as much of it as we can.

This paradox is only one part of the much larger ambiguity that confronts a reader of the *Canterbury Tales* in the twenty-first century. As Chaucer's greatest work, and one of the greatest literary works ever composed in English, the *Canterbury Tales* bears the lion's share of the responsibility for Chaucer's enduring poetic authority and reputation. Yet nowhere is this elusive poet more elusive and more eager to disavow his own authority. Until the advent of the novel, there are few if any works so consistently interested in perspectives of the politically marginal, be the basis of that marginalization class, gender, or sexuality. In his frame tale, Chaucer offers representatives from each of the Three Estates of traditional medieval political theory: the Knight and the Squire for the nobility, or those who fight, the Monk, the Parson, and others for the clergy, or those who pray, and the Ploughman, and the Miller for the peasantry (*laboratores*), or those who work. He adds to these important female voices, the Prioress, Wife of Bath, and Second Nun. He also adds representatives of newer social positions not easily absorbed into the more traditional conception: for an emergent lesser nobility, the Yeoman and the Franklin; for an emergent urban patriciate, the Merchant, the Shipman, the Guildsmen, and others; for an expanding legal and clerical bureaucracy, the Man of Law, the Summoner, the Pardoner, and others.

The trope of pilgrimage enables Chaucer to bring together a wide variety of narrators and narrative perspectives. It also gives the collection a more explicitly devotional cast than any of his other works, with the exception of a few of the lyrics. It suggests a specific interest in the penitential, a suggestion reinforced by the collection's final tale, the *Parson's Tale*, a penitential manual, and the Retraction. The nature and degree of Chaucer's piety has been a perennial concern of modern scholarship. During much of the post-war period this concern could almost be said to have constituted the field in its totality, dividing it neatly between "exegetical" critics who argued that Chaucerian irony must always be read according to a traditional Augustinianism and formalist critics who took such irony as end in itself, an expression of a larger humanist generosity. Since the 1980s the field has moved beyond its concentration on this single question. It has also set aside a corollary assumption: that a poet's religiosity must necessarily express itself in a stable text, consisting of determinate meanings. The Canterbury collection's frame tale neatly illustrates the fallacy of such a presumption. The story of a pilgrimage, it necessarily entails, like all pilgrimages, what Peter Brown has memorably called the "therapy of distance": ground must be covered; obstacles must be overcome.[4] Without such resistance the pilgrims have no way to demonstrate their devotion. The sacred destination that constitutes their goal must be separated from them by a geographical space that must be substantial, but must also be non-sacred, that is, must otherwise be entirely random. Pilgrimage is a devotional exercise with a determinate, sacred goal whose determinate, sacred meaning – paradoxically, but inescapably – depends on indeterminacy.

Chaucer intensifies this structural paradox by making the pilgrimage the occasion of a tale-telling contest, one which originates as a tavern game. Taverns were a necessary evil which the social economy of medieval pilgrimage could not do without. The goal of the Canterbury pilgrimage is Canterbury Cathedral and the shrine of Saint Thomas à Becket. However, the tale-telling contest, as proposed by Harry Bailly and accepted by the pilgrims, entails tales told on the way back as well as the way out. Its goal is Southwark and the Tabard Inn; where the pilgrimage is linear, the tale-telling contest is circular. At its simplest the plot of the frame tale has competing goals and a radically divided trajectory. It is built around an irresolvable ambiguity and the irresolution is inescapable. By mapping the tale-telling contest onto pilgrimage's therapy of distance, Chaucer makes tale-telling (and by extension, poetry itself) a worldly, non-sacral enterprise, or even a profane one – as we might expect of a tavern game. Nevertheless, without the pilgrimage there would be no tale-telling; the worldly contest is indissolubly linked to the sacral; the collection's narratives always hold out the possibility of sacral significance, even where they seem most profane. As Chaucer himself declares in the *Prologue to the Miller's Tale*, there are plenty of tales in the collection that "toucheth ... / ... moralitee and hoolynesse" (I, 3179–80), and thus express the abundant aspects of Chaucer's piety. Where some modern scholars have erred is not in seeking signs of piety even in the tales that "sounen into synne," but in assuming piety can only be expressed through textual stability. As a result they have been less interested in actually exploring the piety of such tales than in denying the tales' undeniable indirections – denying that is, the narrative ambiguities and indeterminacies that constitute their surest link to the sacral.

As befits the social cross-section of tellers, the collection constitutes something of an encyclopedia of late medieval narrative genres. The game begins with the Knight, the pilgrim of highest social rank, who tells an epic reminiscent of *Troilus and Criseyde*, but on a smaller scale. Most modern Chaucerians have taken the Miller's subsequent drunken interruption of the Monk, to whom Harry had turned as the next in social rank, as registering Chaucer's desire to expand the range of serious poetry. The Miller will tell a fabliau; though he proclaims it a "noble tale" Chaucer will redesignate it a "cherles tale" consisting of "harlotrye" (I, 3126, 3169–84). The collection includes five or six fabliaux: the *Miller's Tale*, the *Reeve's Tale*, the *Cook's Tale*, the *Merchant's Tale*, the *Shipman's Tale*, and, according to some scholars, the *Summoner's Tale*. Chaucer's extensive use of this genre constitutes something of a revival. The fabliaux were a French genre, flourishing in the twelfth and thirteenth centuries: short, comic, and often obscene tales, typically, though not always, set in lower-class milieux. The collection also includes at least four romances, the Arthurian *Wife of Bath's Tale*, the *Franklin's Tale*, a Breton lay, the possibly parodic *Squire's Tale*, and the definitely parodic *Tale of Sir Thopas*; two fables, the *Nun's Priest's Tale*, and the *Manciple's Tale*; at least four exempla, the *Friar's Tale*, the *Squire's Tale*, the *Physician's Tale*, the *Pardoner's Tale*; an exemplum collection, the *Monk's Tale*; an anti-Semitic Miracle of the Blessed Virgin, the *Prioress's Tale*, a philosophical treatise, the *Tale of Melibee*, a penitential manual, the *Parson's Tale*; three fictional autobiographies, the Wife of Bath's and Pardoner's Prologues, and the *Canon's Yeoman's Prologue and Tale*; a hagiography, the *Second Nun's Tale*; and finally, two hard to classify tales that might be romances or exempla, but which Chaucer seems to have regarded as secular hagiographies, the *Man of Law's Tale* and the *Clerk's Tale* (the *Prioress's Tale* might be added to this group).

Modern critical reception of the *Canterbury Tales* has tended to structure itself around individual tales, with the *General Prologue*, the *Knight's Tale*, the *Miller's Tale*, the *Wife of Bath's Prologue and Tale*, and the *Pardoner's Prologue and Tale* consistently attracting the most attention. That makes them not only the most analyzed and documented poems from later medieval England, but also among the most analyzed and documented across the entire span of Anglophone tradition. It also illustrates, in perhaps a somewhat exaggerated form, an important feature in the hermeneutics of major canonical works. As canonization privileges a few texts above others, it also privileges key portions of the texts canonized. The past three decades have seen a noticeable diffusion of critical attention across all of the *Canterbury Tales*; perhaps ironically, this change expresses the same interest in canon expansion one finds in the rest of Middle English studies, sometimes in explicit opposition to Chaucer's preeminence. Benefiting as well from the profusion of new critical approaches, neglected tales such as the *Monk's Tale*, the *Tale of Melibee*, the *Parson's Tale*, and the *Second Nun's Tale* received sustained critical attention for the first time. Some tales, like the *Nun's Priest's Tale* which, with its explicit interest in Christian exegesis, had been at the center of exegetical/formalist debates, suffered a diminution in interest. A variety of others, including the *Man of Law's Tale*, the *Clerk's Tale*, and the *Prioress's Tale* attracted increased attention in response to the discipline's general interest in issues of politics, gender, and cultural and racial identity.

Even in this era of canon expansion, Chaucer has remained the single most important author in the field. As a result, until very recently, much – though by no means all – of the most innovative scholarship has tended to cluster in Chaucer studies, and it was through Chaucer studies that leading trends in the discipline of literary studies as a whole tended to enter literary scholarship in Middle English. That was certainly the case with both feminism and the "new" historicism. New historicism proper began in Renaissance studies with the appearance of a special issue of *Genre* in 1981. Its considerable impact on the field of Middle English was anticipated from within by the appearance in 1973 of Jill Mann's *Chaucer and Medieval Estates Satire.* Arguably the most important reading of the *General Prologue* ever produced, this volume, by means of an extended meditation on the *General Prologue's* generic affiliations to estates satire, combined a formalist interest in the resources of irony with a thoroughgoing commitment to social and intellectual history. Mann demonstrated that historicism need not predicate its inquiries on the assumption of a semantically stable text. Her interest in the social anticipated a robust resurgent historicism that was equal parts formal analysis of textual complexity and synthetic social history. Notable instances include Paul Strohm's *Social Chaucer* (1989), Lee Patterson's *Chaucer and the Subject of History* (1991), and David Wallace's *Chaucerian Polity* (1997).

Feminism entered Chaucer scholarship earlier and somewhat less obtrusively; charting it is a bit more difficult. Certainly it constituted an active, if under-recognized presence in the field by the 1970s.[5] Feminism's interest in the politics of gender offers an obvious point of contact with the political edge of recent historicism. The two converged in a groundbreaking 1981 essay on the Wife of Bath by Mary Carruthers.[6] Nevertheless, as both trends developed, this contact has as often been a matter of contention as of agreement. The most influential feminist studies include Carolyn

Dinshaw's *Chaucer's Sexual Poetics* (1989), Elaine Hanson's *Chaucer and the Fictions of Gender* (1992), and Susan Crane's *Gender and Romance in Chaucer's "Canterbury Tales"* (1994). To the consternation of some, gay and lesbian studies established an early beachhead with Monica McAlpine's 1980 essay "The Pardoner's Homosexuality and How it Matters," which set off a storm of controversy that has yet to subside. The past decade has seen a variety of queer readings of Chaucer, of which Glenn Burger's *Chaucer's Queer Nation* (2003) is probably the most notable. Historicist, feminist, and other theoretically inflected work tended to assume more dispersive models of authorial intention than obtained on either side of the formalist/exegetical debates of the 1950s and 1960s. The purest expression of this trend could be found in H. Marshall Leicester's *The Disenchanted Self* (1990), in my view an underrated work that offers extended readings of three of Chaucer's narrators influenced both by deconstruction and Lacanian psychoanalysis. Psychoanalysis, traditionally a medievalist *bête noire*, has, if anything, grown in influence in the past fifteen years, as L. O. Aranye Fradenburg's *Sacrifice Your Love* (2002) powerfully demonstrates.

The welcome attention to other aspects of Middle English literary culture has not meant an appreciable slackening in work on Chaucer. Indeed, from post-colonial critique to thing theory to aesthetics to ethics it is hard to find a current trend in the discipline as a whole that is not having an impact on Chaucer studies. Two very recent trends bear special mention. The first is the sustained explorations of Chaucer's *nachleben*, as exemplified in Steve Ellis's *Chaucer at Large: The Poet in the Modern Imagination* (2000), and Stephanie Trigg's *Congenial Souls: Reading Chaucer from Medieval to Postmodern* (2001). The second is the welcome return of language study, also exemplified in two recent studies, Christopher Cannon's *The Making of Chaucer's English* (1998) and Simon Horobin's *The Language of the Chaucer Tradition* (2003).[7] Nearly a century ago, George Lyman Kittredge, the founder of modern Chaucer studies, began his 1915 volume *Chaucer and His Poetry* by declaring Chaucer "the most modern of English poets."[8] This honorific may seem a bit quaint; perhaps it should be dismissed as an empty formula. But surely the more historically responsible course is to read it to the letter, to acknowledge its stark, unapologetic anachronism. Kittredge makes Chaucer's canonical authority the measure of modernity. When contemporary scholars read a Chaucer text in response to some current critical debate, they are doing exactly the same thing. Whatever else the future brings to the study of Chaucer, that seems unlikely to change.

NOTES

1 Paul Strohm, *Social Chaucer* (Cambridge, MA: Harvard University Press, 1989).

2 *Clerk's Prologue* in *Riverside*, p. 137, IV, 33. All subsequent quotations are from this edition. Line numbers will be given in the text.

3 Seth Lerer, "Medieval English Literature and the Idea of the Anthology," *PMLA* 118 (2003), 1254; Derek Pearsall, *The Canterbury Tales* (London: Routledge, 1993), pp. 22–23.

4 Peter Brown, *The Cult of the Saints: Its Rise and Function in Latin Christianity* (University of Chicago Press, 1981), p. 87.

5 See, for example, Arlyn Diamond, "Chaucer's Women and Women's Chaucer," and Maureen Fries, "'Slydynge of Corage': Chaucer's Criseyde as Feminist and Victim"; both in *The Authority of Experience: Essays in Feminist Criticism*, ed. Arlyn Diamond and Lee Edwards (Amherst: University of Massachusetts Press, 1977), pp. 60–83, 45–59.

6 Mary Carruthers, "The Wife of Bath and the Painting of Lions," *PMLA* 94 (1979), 209–22.

7 For the bibliographical details of all the works cited in this paragraph and the one preceding, see the Guide to Further Reading.

8 George Lyman Kittredge, *Chaucer and His Poetry* (Cambridge, MA: Harvard University Press, 1915; repr. 1970), p. 2.

13

LYNN STALEY

Julian of Norwich

Julian of Norwich, the fourteenth-century mystic and writer whose *Showings* recount a series of visions she had when she was "thirty and a half," has gained in appeal throughout the late twentieth and early twenty-first centuries. With her description of God as both mother and father, her unwillingness to dwell upon sin and judgment, her carefully articulated discussion of divine love, and her refusal to claim for herself any special status, she speaks to the devotional needs of many who find themselves weary of the hegemonies of gender and power. She is a subtle theologian of quiet daring and one of the early masters of Middle English prose. Like other late fourteenth-century writers such as William Langland and Geoffrey Chaucer, she understood and exploited the inherent flexibilities of the vernacular as a medium of common and uncommon speech. In so doing, Julian at once drew upon a vigorous tradition of vernacular devotional prose and employed that tradition to reformulate the terms with which the divine nature and the human flesh it took as its clothing are understood.

The textual history of the *Showings* suggests both the extraordinary care she took as a writer and the vulnerabilities to which manuscript culture was subject. There are two sets of manuscripts. Julian wrote a Short Text recounting her visionary experience some years before she completed the Long Text of the *Showings*. The Long Text is a significant expansion of the earlier version, but it is also a careful reading and exposition of the visions she originally described that testifies to her growing sense of authority as a writer and a thinker. The Short Text survives in a mid-fifteenth-century collection, possibly of Carthusian provenance, of devotional texts, including some by Richard Rolle of Hampole, the important mid-century Yorkshire mystic, whose achievements in the vernacular almost match those of Julian. The Long Text survives complete in three seventeenth-century manuscripts; excerpts of it appear in a mid-fifteenth-century Westminster Cathedral manuscript, which also contains excerpts from *The Scale of Perfection* by her contemporary, Walter Hilton.[1] As Edmund Colledge and James Walsh have pointed out in their edition of *The Showings*, we owe the preservation of Julian's work to the devotion of English Benedictine convents on the Continent, where the Long Text was copied and disseminated.

Our knowledge of Julian is frustratingly partial. The Short Text opens by announcing, "Here es a visionn schewed be the goodenes of god to a deuote womann, and hir name es Julyan, that is recluse atte Norwyche and ȝitt ys onn lyfe, anno domini millesimo CCCC xiij ..."[2] That there was indeed a recluse named Julian living in Norwich can be corroborated from bequests made to such a person in four separate wills, which date from 1394 to 1416. In *The Book of Margery Kempe*, Margery describes a visit she made to an "anchoress," in Norwich, a "Dame Julian," who gave her counsel about her revelations (chap.18). The Long Text supplies further internal dating. There, Julian begins her account by saying that the revelation came to her on May 13, 1373. In chapter 86, she writes that fifteen years later, she was told that the meaning of the revelation was love. In chapter 51 she says that "twenty yere after the tyme of the shewyng save thre monthys" she had further inward teaching about the original revelation that allowed her to understand the mysterious parable of the Lord and the Servant, which appears in the fourteenth showing.[3] Though she was not necessarily an anchoress when she had the visions, by 1394, one year after she had further inward teaching, she was enclosed and had enough of a reputation for sanctity to be left two shillings by Roger Reed (Short Text, vol. 1, p. 33). Her internal references to time also serve to emphasize the process of vision and understanding that for her validates the Long Text. Where the Short Text presents itself as a faithful account of one woman's visionary experience, in the Long Text, Julian foregrounds the intellectual process by which she came to be able to expound her own experience.[4]

Julian makes other changes in the Long Text that indicate the broader scope she saw it as having. The Short Text assimilates itself to the traditions of female devotional literature. As a narration of the visionary experience of one woman living as a "recluse atte Norwyche," it does not claim more for itself than plain narrative. During the mortal illness that Julian says preceded her visions, her mother waits with others near her bed (p. 234), at one point putting her hands to Julian's face to see if she is alive. At a crucial moment, her curate, accompanied by a boy carrying a cross, enters the room and says to her, "Dowȝtter, I have brought the the ymage of thy sauioure" (p. 208). Once she does as she is bidden and focuses her sight upon the image on the cross, she begins to experience the series of showings. Not only does the Long Text omit the reference to her mother and to the sex of the author, as well as a later description of herself as a feeble and frail woman (p. 222), but Julian alters the dynamic between herself and her curate by deleting his address to her as "daughter." With such personal details omitted, the Long Text's detailed and assured account *and explanation* of visionary experience at once guides a reader through that experience and offers a reader ways of "seeing" Christ in the world's homely reality.

To some extent, Julian's self-assurance as a writer and a thinker may owe something to Norwich itself. The prosperous center of England's cloth trade, the nucleus for a variegated and thriving religious culture, and a contact point with the mercantile and devotional life of the continent, Norwich was one of the places in England where a mind such as Julian's might have found nurture. The second most populous city in England, Norwich had around 10,000 inhabitants and 46 parish churches, a far larger proportion than neighboring towns. Norwich was the seat of the bishopric, but the Benedictine Cathedral Priory also had a power that extended throughout the city and its suburbs. Most of the lands surrounding the city were owned by religious institutions – the bishop of Norwich, the Priory, or the nunnery of Carrow. Carrow is associated with the anchorhold in the church of St. Julian, occupied from the twelfth century, where Julian herself lived as a recluse. Norwich was a city containing more than churches and merchants: there were more hermits and anchorites in Norwich than in any other English town, as well as a community of lay women vowed to a common religious life, not unlike the "beguine" communities to be found in the Low Countries, and a rich culture of craft guilds and confraternities whose pageants and devotional practices helped shape the civic life of East Anglian towns.[5]

Julian was also nurtured by the textual culture to be found in Norwich. Though she describes herself as unlettered, the evidence of her writings suggests an active engagement with both Latin and vernacular spirituality. The picture she fashions of herself as unsophisticated serves her, as it serves Chaucer, as a screen behind which she could explore topics that might be conceived of as heterodox or potentially inflammatory. Though the late fourteenth century was less constrictive than the fifteenth, Julian could, nonetheless, be disciplined for writing anything that might seem heretical. At a time when the views of John Wyclif about clerical purity and authority, auricular confession, and unlicensed preaching were exciting the attention of English bishops, Julian could not risk the loss of her anchorhold that suspicions of heresy or dissent might entail. The many assertions of her obedience to "mother church" that punctuate *The Showings* attest to her awareness that speech is a form of action and thus subject to social penalty. But what a use Julian makes of her mask of intellectual humility! By tackling such issues as the nature of sin, salvation, and divinity, she gestures toward her own informed reading.[6]

The table of contents describing each of the sixteen revelations Julian received, locates the Long Text of *The Showings* within a textual tradition of mystical prose, but this table of contents does not hint at the complex reasoning that Julian employs to understand the meaning of her experience. The revelations begin by focusing on the physicality of the Passion – the red blood under the crown of thorns, the face on the crucifix held before her that summons up recognition of Christ's buffeting and scourging, the drying out of Christ's flesh during the crucifixion, the wound in Christ's side. Julian's focus upon the tactile in her account of these early revelations is not designed as a means of denying sensual reality in favor of spiritual, but rather of linking and affirming both.

Revelation 1 epitomizes Julian's seamless weaving together of technique and theology. She begins with the "sight" of the "reed bloud rynnyng downe from under the garlande, hote and freyshely" (8). The adverbs here work to mitigate the tendency to focus simply on Jesus' physical pain and, instead, suggest the generative nature of his suffering. The sight of Jesus' blood, which we might expect to lead into a prolonged description of the crown of thorns or the nails that pierced hands and feet, is succeeded by Julian's description of the Trinity, which "fulfilled my hart most of ioy."[7] She understands that the Trinity is God, our maker, our keeper, our everlasting lover, and our endless joy and bliss and is understood through Jesus Christ. She here anticipates the account in Revelation 14 of Jesus as father, mother, and lover. Next, Julian sees with her "understanding" the "Ladie Sainct Mari," who appears spiritually in "bodily lykenes" as a simple maiden. After this succession of images, Julian declares that at the same time that she saw the head bleeding, she had a sight of the good Lord's "homely loving." She then employs an image that unites the apparently disparate scenes she has just recounted: "He is oure clothing, that for love wrappeth us and wyndeth us, halseth us and all becloseth us, hangeth about us for tender love, that he may never leeve us" (9). The verbs describing Christ – wrap, wind, embrace, enclose – are feminine, belonging to Mary's care for her child, who is wound in Mary's flesh as his mortal clothing.[8] The mortality signified by the bleeding head, the fecundity implicit in its hot fresh trickling, the joyfulness sparked by the Trinity, and the tender reverence of the young Mary are each present in Julian's understanding of a Lord who, wearing mortal clothing, is nonetheless our immortal dress. As in the "sight" of "all that is," lying in the palm of her hand, the size of a hazelnut and round as a ball (9), the realm of matter is not seen as distinct from that of the spirit, but as the source of our understanding, potentially the source of our glory.

Julian stresses in this first revelation that its "lesson of love" (12) was shown in all that followed, that the "strenght and the grounde of alle was schewed in the furst sight" (12). Her comparison of God's goodness in showing her this revelation to the honor a great lord does to a poor servant foreshadows the parable of the Lord and the Servant she explores in Revelation 14. Similarly, her statement that God loves all that he has made, that "in man is God and in God is alle" (16), occasions the first of her assertions that she believes what the Holy Church teaches. Her credal statements of orthodoxy, however, establish a tension between what she "sees" and what she has been taught that at once tempers her prose and serves to mark her own independence of thought. Her later formulations of the concept of the "godly will" of the elect, the hints of her awareness of the concept of universal salvation, and her presentation of God as androgynous are all carefully couched in the terms of orthodox theology and buffered by her assertions of her fidelity to the Church's teachings.[9] What she has "been shown" in three manners – by bodily sight, by words formed in her understanding, and by spiritual sight – she attempts to resolve with the tenets of orthodox doctrine, but she cannot deny her experience in favor of a truth, taught but unseen.

One of the more striking characteristics of *The Showings* is Julian's refusal to employ binary terminology to explain her spiritual experience. The revelations do not trace a linear path from material to spiritual but constantly negotiate the interdependence of the two realms, thus suggesting her unwillingness to negate one reality in favor of another. For example, Revelation 2 focuses on the face of the figure on the crucifix, and Revelation 3 is the sight of God "in a point," or God as all things. Moving from this abstraction, back to the concrete world, the next two revelations concern the face of the crucified. Revelations that describe pain are followed by those that describe her apprehension of joy and God's pleasure in suffering for us until in Revelation 12 she is shown God as "glorified," filled with joy, courtesy, blessedness, and light. In the next revelation, Julian makes a move that for many readers has seemed electrifying. Confronted with God's glory, she is also confronted with her longing, which is the distance between her soul and its maker. She thus sees nothing but her sin that prevents her from being "like" God. God's reply to a sorrow that in the literature of moral theology might lead into a minute discussion of contrition, the fallen human realm, and the particulars of sin alerts us to the full scope of Julian's intent: "Synne is behovely, but alle shalle be wele, and alle shalle be wele, and alle maner of thynge shall be wele" (39). "Behovely," meaning necessary, of benefit to someone, appropriate, was more often used to describe the necessity or benefits of peace or wisdom or the sacrifice of Christ. Julian uses it to characterize sin, that "nakyd word" that to her means "alle that is nott good."

As Denise Baker has demonstrated, Julian's decision to inquire into the nature of sin places her in dialogue both with dualistic solutions to the existence of evil, such as those propounded by the early Manichaeans and the later Cathars, and with the orthodox solution articulated by Saint Augustine.[10] Her inquiry suggests her rejection of any dualistic notion that evil is an actual force opposed to God and the divine plan, but it also suggests her discomfort with the idea that human beings, in choosing to disobey God, brought evil into the world by their choice and, with evil, judgment for sin. The heart of her argument about sin, and thus about the divine nature, occurs in Revelations 13 and 14, both of which are vastly expanded from the versions in the Short Text. Her rejection of dualism is cast in orthodox language: she did not see sin because "it had no maner of substaunce" (40). On the other hand, she struggles a good deal with the orthodox understanding of evil as issuing from the disobedience of God's creatures. Rather than seeing depictions of human depravity and divine punishment, she sees much evidence of Christ's compassion and God's mercy.

It is important here to emphasize that Julian does not deny her own sense of sin or the mental suffering her awareness of it produces. However, rather than devote her efforts to cataloguing her shortcomings, she seeks to understand how sin functions, what meaning it has in relation to her understanding of God as encloser, lover, wrapper, and maker. She is accordingly taught that sin is no shame but "worship" to man (52), that even as sins result in diverse sufferings, so sins result in diverse joys in heaven. She here recalls such examples as Mary Magdalene, Saint Paul, and Saint Thomas, each of whom suffered through sin and reaped a reward in the awareness of God's love. Their sins become their glories, not their shames. In chapter 39, she defines sin as a "scourge" for the soul, rather than describing the soul as scourged by God for sin. In other words, pain is not the punishment *for* sin but the symptom *of* the awareness of sin and is thus beneficial ("behovely").

Despite the care with which she explores the function of sin, steering between the relatively simple answers inherent in dualism and the more complicated arguments worked out through Augustinian theology, Julian can end her account of Revelation 13 only with the statement that God is an endless comfort. She has not yet explored the divine nature in relation to or as implicated in the sufferings attendant upon knowledge of sin. Revelation 14, the most mysterious and famous of her revelations contains her fullest exposition of her new understanding of the divine nature. Though portions of it appear in the Short Text, the Short Text does not really prepare us for the startling leaps she makes and the arguments she presents in the Long Text version of Revelation 14. Here we find both her "parable" of the

Lord and the Servant and her description of Christ as our mother. At the beginning of the revelation, she announces that they are two "conditions" of what God showed her about prayer, rightful prayer, and certain trust. If prayer is the means by which we are united ("onyd") to God, and God is "grounde" of our beseeching, our very search for God, which is our distance from God, takes place in and through God. Prayer – the signifier of our lack – at the same time witnesses to our wills' residence in God, despite our sin (chap. 43). How then can Julian reconcile her growing understanding of a God who takes joy in us, who is the very ground of our being and the source of our desire, with the Church's teachings about God's harsh judgment for sin: "A Lorde, Jhesu, kyng of blysse, how shall I be esyde? Who shall tell me and tech me that me nedyth to wytt, if I may nott at this tyme se it in the?" (69). She cannot "see" God's judgment, but she is given a showing that, by her own account, took her twenty years to be able to analyze.

In her account of the Parable of the Lord and the Servant, she dramatizes the process by which she comes to substitute an understanding of suffering for her previously held belief in judgment.[11] In so doing, she learns to identify Christ in the face of the servant who wears the foul clothes of human toil. When she first "sees" the lord and the servant, she sees only a story she partially comprehends. The lord sends his servant on an errand; in the act of seeking to do his lord's bidding, the servant falls into a dell, where he remains in sorrow, unable even to turn his head to see his lord's face. Julian enumerates the ways in which the servant suffers and notices the constantly loving look the lord directs toward his fallen servant and his intention of rewarding the servant with endless bliss. Then the showing ends, and Julian is left with a preliminary understanding of its pictures. She deduces that the servant stands for Adam, but she also feels there are details she does not understand. Twenty years, "save thre monthys" later, she receives inward teaching, directing her back to her original sight of the lord and the servant. In so doing, she replays in her memory the scene she first "saw" so long ago. She recalls the vision in technicolor, recounting the color and drape of the lord's clothing, the tone of his skin, the place where he sat, the amazing tenderness of his gaze on his servant, and the servant's stained and sweaty clothing:

> Outward he was clad symply as a laborer whych was dysposyd to traveyle, and he stod full nere the lorde, nott evyn for anenst hym, but in perty a syde, and that on the lefte syde. Hys clothyng was a whyt kyrtyll, syngell, olde and alle defautyd, dyed with swete of his body, streyte fyttyng to hym and shorte, as it were an handfull beneth the knee, bare, semyng as it shuld sone be worne vppe, redy to be raggyd and rent. And in this I marvelyd gretly,

> thynkyng: "This is now an unsemely clothyng for the servant that is so heyly lovyd to stond in before so wurschypfull a lord." (74)

If Julian plays and replays her showings, pausing over a picture she has seen, teasing out its many levels of meaning, we can only pay her the same amazed attention. Here, she presents not simply a careful picture of the servant, but a picture of herself watching the picture and decoding its signs. He stands near the lord, slightly to the left; his clothing is old, stained with the sweat of labor, short, looking already worn out. This picture contrasts sharply with that of the lord, who sits, wearing flowing blue robes. She then indicates her reaction to the picture, initially judging the servant harshly, expressing a conventional disapproval at the "unseemly clothing" the servant wears before a lord so deserving of worship or honor. She thus not only conveys her acute awareness of social degree, but transfers the heavy blame of her own sense of sin to her reading of the servant. The servant's clothes are at once those of the churl and Adam's fleshly tunic. But the servant is also "heyly lovyd" and "inward in hym was shewed a ground of love, whych loue he had to the lorde, that was evyn lyke to the love that the lord had to hym" (74–75). In seeing the servant's love for his lord, she begins to move away from the concept of punishment for sin and toward her growing understanding of suffering because of sin.

She accomplishes this move by coming to a new awareness of love. In seeking to understand why her original thought that the servant was Adam was not the complete explanation of the parable, she focuses upon the servant as a willing and loving agent in his own fall:

> Ther was a tresoure in the erth whych the lorde lovyd. I merveyled and thought what it myght be. And I was answeryd in my understandyng, "It is a mete whych is lovesom and plesyng to the lorde." For I saw the lorde sytt as a man, and I saw neyther meet nor drynke wher with to serve hym. (75)

Where the Parable of the Wedding Feast in Matthew 22, which frames this scene, provides a standard of judgment and punishment for lapses, Julian's parable suggests that this man wearing foul clothes is, in fact, Jesus, that he labors as a gardener in order to serve a feast to his lord. Once she begins to see Jesus in the churl, she comes to understand that his fall into the earth, his sorrow and suffering are also the willed suffering of love. If Jesus can be found in Adam, Adam's crime may be understood in terms of the suffering we all endure for our separation from our lord. In the passages following her recognition of love, Julian offers a dazzling allegorical reading of her parable that appears to come to her with all the urgency of a problem suddenly solved. The garment looking soon to be ragged is the flesh soon to be scourged and torn, a sign of the rent flesh she sees in an earlier revelation. From the Parable of the Lord and the Servant, she moves swiftly into her revelation of the motherhood of God, "And thus I saw that God enjoyeth that he is our Fader, and God enjoyeth that he is our Moder ..." (79). Judgment or punishment is not denied, but it is superseded by her sight of suffering. God is father *and* mother, spouse *and* wife. The two "conditions" of prayer (rightful prayer and certain trust) that she uses as the rubrics for Revelation 14 are embodied in the loving looks between lord and servant and in the secure love between a God who is all things and His lost and beloved child. The fleshly clothes we wear are signs of that love.

In this Revelation and the two following Julian evinces her growing trust in the truth of what she has been shown. In Revelation 16, she stages a moment of self-doubt, the fear that she has been "raving," but it is followed by continual assurances of God's love, of his pity for the servant. In the final chapter she admits that for years after she received the showings, she desired to know what God's meaning was. She received an answer fifteen years later: "Wytt it wele, love was his menyng. Who shewyth it the? Love. Wherfore shewyth he it the? For love" (124). A ringing affirmation of love is the final sentence in the book: "In oure makyng we had begynnyng, but the love wher in he made us was in hym fro without begynnyng, in whych love we have oure begynnyng. And alle this shalle we see in God with outyn ende" (125). In echoing the opening of the Gospel of John, which describes the Creation as proceeding from Christ, the Word, who is the life and the light of men, Julian reaffirms the relationship between humankind and God, grounded from before time in creative love.

In the *Showings* Julian goes well beyond any contemporary vernacular treatment of God and his immanence in human nature. If we turn to the vernacular religious culture with which she was no doubt familiar, its texts seem to insist that the realm of matter is less the medium of our likeness to God than the source of our unlikeness. *Ancrene Wisse*, the important thirteenth-century guide for anchoresses, shows us how to temper the flesh, to discipline it with understanding. *The Pricke of Conscience* encourages a self-scrutiny that opposes the cleanness of heaven to the fleshly filth of earth. The works of Richard Rolle likewise are designed to chasten any fondness we might have for the material and physical. Walter Hilton in *The Scale of Perfection* grounds his discussion of and guide to the contemplative life in a distrust of our physicality. Chaucer's Parson, like each of these authors, looks forward to the clean and perfected body we shall receive in Paradise. By chastening ourselves in the awareness of God's wrath for our sins, we reorient ourselves, seeking to abandon the flesh for the spirit. I do not mean to suggest that these works do not possess integrity or intelligence or subtlety, but Julian seeks to do something other than guide us through the murk of our darker selves. In searching out the nature of God, she avers the links between God and humankind, Adam's body, Christ's body, Mary's clothing, our rags that are our badge of honor.

Julian's habits of composition focus upon the difference between truth that is "taught" and truth that is understood, deployment of the vernacular as a serious medium of inquiry, and mining of homely detail and plain speech she shares with her contemporaries, William Langland and Geoffrey Chaucer. *Piers Plowman* she might well have known, and her reading of it may have served as a stimulus for her own evolving inquiry into types of truth. Julian, like Chaucer, may owe a good deal to Langland, whose poem circulated throughout England and in so many varieties of manuscripts during the crucial years when both were gaining mastery over their crafts. For each of these writers, a world containing roof tiles, hazelnuts, tunics, sweat, and ditches is the site of our suffering, our searching, and our potential renewal. Julian's presentation of the world as redeemed in and through God's loving look toward us and our anguish at our incapacities suggests an engagement with the material as profound as those we find in *Piers Plowman* or the *Canterbury Tales*. From Langland's hawkers' cries of "Hot pies," "Good geese," "white wine," to Harry Bailey's admission that Goodelief, his wife, wears the sword in the family, our efforts to apprehend truth are woven into the details of daily life. Julian may have removed her mother from the room where she lay ill, but she did not ignore the ordinary world where we must learn about love.

NOTES

1 For manuscript information, see Edmund Colledge and James Walsh, *A Book of Showings to the Anchoress Julian of Norwich*, 2 vols. (Toronto: Pontifical Institute of Medieval Studies, 1978), pp. 1–10; Nicholas Watson and Jacqueline Jenkins, eds., *The Writings of Julian of Norwich* (University Park: Pennsylvania State University Press, 2006), pp. 31–43. Many thanks to Denise N. Baker for reading and commenting upon this essay.

2 Colledge and Walsh, *Showings*, vol. 1, p. 201. All quotations from the Short Text refer to this edition and will be cited in the text by page number.

3 Denise N. Baker, ed., *The Showings of Julian of Norwich* (New York: W. W. Norton & Co., 2005), p. 72. All quotations from the Long Text refer to this edition and will be cited in the text by page number.

4 On distinctions between the two texts, see Barry Windeatt, "Julian of Norwich and Her Audience," *Review of English Studies*, 28 (1977), 1–17; Denise Nowakowski Baker, *Julian of Norwich's Showings* (Princeton University Press, 1994), pp. 135–64; David Aers and Lynn Staley, *The Powers of the Holy: Religion, Politics, and Gender in Late Medieval English Culture* (University Park: Pennsylvania State University Press, 1996), pp. 138–39; Watson and Jenkins, *Writings*, pp. 1–4.

5 Norman P. Tanner, *The Church in Late Medieval Norwich, 1370–1532* (Toronto: Pontifical Institute of Medieval Studies, 1984), pp. 2–3, 140–43, 58, 73. See also Gail McMurray Gibson, *The Theater of Devotion: East Anglian Drama and Society in the Late Middle Ages* (University of Chicago Press, 1989); Marilyn Oliva, *The Convent and the Community in Late Medieval England: Female Monasteries in the Diocese of Norwich, 1350–1540* (Woodbridge, Suffolk: Boydell Press, 1998). An anchorhold was the space, usually within or attached to a church, where a recluse (anchor or anchoress) lived a vowed life, removed from the world and devoted to prayer. Such persons and places were under the governance of ecclesiastical authority.

6 Aers and Staley, *Powers of the Holy*, pp. 107–78.

7 See ibid., pp. 77–104, for Julian's manipulation of affective traditions.

8 See Gibson, *Theater of Devotion,* pp. 156–66, for an evocative treatment of Mary as Christ's clothing.

9 Baker, *Julian*, pp. 107–34; Nicholas Watson, "Visions of Inclusion: Universal Salvation and Vernacular Theology in Pre-Reformation England," *JMEMS* 27 (1997), 145–87.

10 Baker, *Julian*, pp. 40–134.

11 The section on the Lord and the Servant is drawn from my essay, "The Man in Foul Clothes and a Late Fourteenth-Century Conversation About Sin," *SAC* 24 (2002), 31–36.

14

ETHAN KNAPP

Thomas Hoccleve

One of the great pleasures of reading Thomas Hoccleve's poetry is the fact that we have reason to feel closer to a known individual than is often the case when reading medieval literature. As a clerk in the Privy Seal, one of the three great writing offices in Westminster, it was first of all Hoccleve's profession which ensured that he would appear in the surviving archival records of this period more frequently than many of his contemporaries. During Hoccleve's lifetime, the Privy Seal underwent a crucial transformation, leaving the king's household and becoming one of the machines for generating, tracking, and storing the vast quantities of documents that were necessary for the increasing extension of centralized state power. Many of these documents were receipts, and enough of these survive recording payments to Hoccleve to give us a good outline of his official career. Most abundantly, we find notices of annuities and grants stretching from 1391 to 1426.[1] These annuities would have constituted the most reliable part of his wages, and they, in turn, would have been supplemented by small gratuities expected from anyone who needed to have a document produced. We also find reimbursement for supplies (ink, livery, and parchment) and two notices certifying the fact that Hoccleve had agreed to serve as *mainpernor*, the guarantor, for a fee, of a given individual's appearance at court. Lastly, the records register transactions relating to two corrodies, or guaranteed lodging in monastic houses often provided to aging servants. One of these corrodies was transferred in 1400; the other was given to an Alice Penfold in 1426, with the note that she was to hold it in the same way as "Thomas Hoccleve now deceased."[2]

The surviving documents show that Hoccleve entered the Privy Seal between 1387 and 1391 and served there until very near his death in 1426. His position, as he grew in seniority, became important enough that he had several junior clerks working under him, but his financial situation was never entirely secure, at least not to his satisfaction. His wages were substantial but were paid out with troubling irregularity. And we can see that he shared with other clerks of the time a resourcefulness in producing supplemental income through extra commissions or by using the information that passed through their office to spot an advantageous deal in forfeited real estate. The account we can reconstruct through these documents is both reinforced and supplemented by the striking number of autobiographical references in his poetry. For convenience sake, we might divide Hoccleve's poetic output into three stages: an early period of around 1402–09 in which he wrote shorter poems of mixed genres; a middle period from 1410–16, during which he turned to more political verse, producing his most popular work, the *Regiment of Princes*, as well as several shorter poems addressing important issues of state; and, lastly, a final period in which he wrote the sequence of poems usually referred to as the *Series*. The autobiographical strand in Hoccleve's work runs through all of these periods, from the early confessions of debauchery in "La Male Regle" to the fretting about income in the dialogue that prefaces his *Regiment of Princes* to that most distinctive moment, his wrestling with madness and alienation as the point of departure for the *Series*. Unlike some medieval biographies that smack more of convention than lived experience, Hoccleve's autobiographical poetry seems to be confirmed in many of its details by the materials of the documentary record. His anxieties about money can be mapped onto the disconcerting irregularities of payment in the Privy Seal, and his bout with what he called his "wyld infirmytie" appears to correspond to a period in which there is a gap in the payment of his annuities (Michaelmas, 1414).

Hoccleve is also brought closer to us through the condition in which his works survive. Rarely do students of medieval literature have a sure sense of what an author would have presented as a finished work, or even whether these authors thought their poetry ought to be set into a single definitive version. However, Hoccleve left behind a manuscript of much of his work in his own hand, a compilation so unusual as to lead John Bowers to call it the first "collected poems" in the English language.[3] In part, the production and survival of this manuscript is due, no doubt, to the fact that he was a professional scribe, one skilled in the complex business of producing a manuscript in the world of vellum and ink. We know, in fact, that Hoccleve wrote not only countless documents for the Privy Seal but also worked as a copyist on manuscripts of Middle English verse produced for the book market in London.[4] Unlike many medieval poets, Hoccleve was a writer by profession, a writer in the most material sense, and the survival of the products of his craft give us an unusually rich context within which to understand his strictly poetic output.

Early career

Much of the poetry of the early fifteenth century has long been categorized as Chaucerian, a poetry of imitation rather than of innovation. Hoccleve himself claims to have known Chaucer and even suggests that Chaucer tried to teach him the art of poetry.

> My deere maistir, God his soule qwyte,
> And fadir, Chaucer, fayn wolde han me taght,
> But I was dul and lerned lyte or naght.[5]

In this famous passage from his *Regiment of Princes*, Hoccleve laments the death of Chaucer and the fact that his death has left the nation bereft of its great master of rhetoric, philosophy, and poetry. As a reflection in miniature of this loss, Hoccleve also grieves that he himself was able to learn so little from Chaucer because of his own dullness. But, as so often in this period, such confessions of dullness can easily have a double edge. By 1410, the likely date of composition of these lines, Chaucer had been dead for ten years, and Hoccleve was writing them both as an act of public mourning and also as a claim to having inherited Chaucer's place as an important writer in the newly consolidated tradition of English verse.

This passage encapsulates a number of motifs that will be important throughout his career. First, we might note the delicate balance between humility and self-promotion, a balance achieved in much of Hoccleve's work through a style of aggressive self-denigration, a habit of camouflaging the broadest claims to textual authority beneath apparent confessions of inadequacy. Second, we can see here a prominent interest in poetic genealogy, appropriate for a writer who makes so visible the strands of intertextual influence that fed into his work. Lastly, we should note the simple prominence of Chaucer, Hoccleve's metaphoric "father" and "master". Hoccleve's earliest work can be seen as an apprenticeship in the Chaucerian style, a close engagement with a set of topics and styles that were central to Chaucer's work. On the stylistic side, Hoccleve's debts to Chaucer ranged from fundamental prosodic forms to the use of both framed narratives and an identifiable, and pseudo-autobiographical, persona. On the topical side, Hoccleve inherited a sense that the central materials of poetry were those that had been fixed by the French models of Machaut and the *Romance of the Rose*, supplemented perhaps by the proto-humanism of Hoccleve's own contemporaries in early fifteenth-century Paris (figures like Christine de Pizan and Jean Gerson). This was a poetic tradition of philosophical and civic ambition, one which blurred the line between allegory and mimetic realism through the persistent use of narrative fragments as exempla, and one which most often approached both psychology and ethics through the dynamic and sophisticated vocabulary of love.

These Chaucerian features run through all of Hoccleve's earliest poems. The best known of these is probably "La Male Regle," a mock penitential confession in which Hoccleve laments the time and money he has spent in the tavern, and the sickness and poverty to which it has led him, praying to the god "Helthe" to aid him and heal both body and purse. It is a deft autobiographical experiment, particularly striking in the way that it extends the wryly self-deprecating Chaucerian persona into a richly and specifically autobiographical figure, a "Thomas" whose history establishes the generic grounding of the text (misdeeds requiring confession) and whose potential futures organizes its ethical trajectories (will he be redeemed or no?). In addition to "La Male Regle," it seems likely that Hoccleve produced in these years some portion of the undatable lyrics that we find attributed to him in both the holographs and other manuscripts. Like "La Male Regle," they too show strong signs of Chaucer's influence, particularly in the Marian focus of the sacred material and the playfully sardonic tone of the petitionary works.

Perhaps the most interesting work from this period is Hoccleve's first datable poem, the "Letter of Cupid," a translation of Christine de Pizan's *Epistre au Dieu d'Amours*. A versified royal letter written by Cupid in response to a petition from women complaining about false lovers, the poem fictionalized the sort of document Hoccleve would himself have been responsible for in the office of the Privy Seal, adapting the bureaucratic form to the poetic world of love. Christine's original draws on other literary "defenses of women," such as Boccaccio's *On Famous Women* and Chaucer's *Legend of Good Women*, but Hoccleve develops this tradition in two striking directions in his "Letter," both developments circulating around his key term of "doubleness." First, Hoccleve shifts the focus away from the traditional homology between the fallen world and the divided psychology of the inconstant man, substituting instead a new link between the internal divisions of erotic inconstancy and the fictiveness of poetic utterance. As Cupid explains

And passying alle londes/ on this yle
That clept is Albioun/ they moost conpleyne
They sayn þat there is croppe and roote of gyle
So can tho men dissimulen and feyne
With standing dropes in hire yen tweyne
Whan þat hire herte/ feelith no distresse
To blynde women with hir doublenesse[6]

The doubleness of the men of Albion does not lie in their willingness to profess love and then abandon their lovers, the obsessively reiterated dynamic of inconstancy exemplified Aeneas' betrayal of Dido and replicated through countless Ovidian complaints. Instead, it rests on a single element of affective deception, the ability to manufacture false distress. As Cupid's account continues, it becomes clear that this false distress is most dangerous when turned to false speech: "Hir wordes spoken been so sighyngly / And with so pitous cheere and countenance" (22–23). In other words, the doubleness of these men lies precisely in their ability to produce the oral genre we know as the complaint.

The importance of this gesture is clarified by Hoccleve's second revision. In addition to entangling the dishonesty of the lover with the untrustworthiness of the poet, Hoccleve also moves to undermine the customary ethical gravity of such charges, replacing the ontological tragedy of Boethian inconstancy with a more localized and psychological gesture. A typical example of this alteration occurs at the moment at which Cupid explains the cause behind men's betrayal of women.

> Ful many man eek wolde for no good
> Þat hath in loue/ spent his tyme and vsid
> Men wiste/ his lady/ his axing withstood
> And pat he were of his lady refused
> Or waast and veyn were/ al þat he had musid
> Wherfore/ he can no better remede
> Buyt on his lady/ shapith him to lie (120–26)

Men's accusations that women are also inconstant are not here given any of the gravity of ecclesiastical satire; nor are they made part of a general Boethian lament against the fickleness of worldly fortune. These men's accusations are instead accounted for as simply a response to the injury of their own pride at any woman's refusal. Moreover, this effect is compounded by a witty refusal to specify exactly what is refused. This ambiguity penetrates even through the depiction of the character of Cupid, who becomes momentarily flustered at the conclusion of the poem, when his praise of women's virtue and purity leads him to an encomium praising the martyred Margaret, a figure of virginity, at which point he has to pull himself up sharply to remind that audience that he is, after all, Cupid, and cannot really advocate virginity *per se*. In both the protestations of Cupid and the vacillations of the men of Albion we are meant to see doubleness not as an inescapable ontological condition so much as a specific psychological state, one that might be best evoked by thinking of Hoccleve's project here as the anatomization of that particular form of internal doubleness we call embarrassment. One might, in fact, go so far as to think of embarrassment as the figure in the carpet of Hoccleve's early verse – to use Henry James's famous metaphor. We see it in the doubleness of the "Letter to Cupid"; it binds the varied petitionary lyrics into a joint statement of necessity; and it is invoked time and again in "La Male Regle" (most vividly in the tavern scene). In the rich satiric traditions of medieval poetry, there is no shortage of figures who become the object of ironic treatment, but the element of embarrassment is something distinct, and crucial, to Hoccleve's poetics. With embarrassment we encounter a form of irony that is internal to the subject, a form of internal fragmentation that disputes the governing regimens of both ethical and epistemological correction.

Mid-career

In 1410 Hoccleve began his most ambitious work, the *Regiment of Princes*, the most popular of his poems, and one of the most widely circulated of all the major Middle English texts, surviving in more than forty copies. Political topics had always simmered near the surface of Hoccleve's work, but usually only in metaphorical form: the title of "La Male Regle" is based on a punning connection between the conduct of the individual and wise governance; similarly, even the world of *amor* in the "Letter of Cupid" is colored by Cupid's frequent reference to treason, a topic Hoccleve adds to Christine's original. But in the years from 1410 until at least 1416, the world of governance comes explicitly to the front and center of Hoccleve's work, to the extent that some have speculated that he was serving as an unofficial laureate poet for the Lancastrian regime. The *Regiment of Princes* was addressed to the Prince, and this work was followed by a cluster of four occasional poems written for King Henry in the first three years of his reign, along with the *Letter to Oldcastle* in 1415. The larger portion of *Regiment of Princes* is organized by subdivision into a sequence of short sections rubricated as *de fide*, *de justitia*, *de pietate*, etc., sections meant to advise Prince Henry on the requisite virtues that would ensure good governance through the ethical perfection of the sovereign. This interest in governance takes a specifically Lancastrian turn in Hoccleve's diatribes against Lollardy, a topic that colors a number of the sections of the *Regiment* and one that motivated the *Letter to Oldcastle*. But beyond these topical concerns, the political verse of his middle period is perhaps most distinctive in Hoccleve's attempt to craft a public poetry that continues to foreground the autobiographical concerns established in his earlier work. Here we might consider Hoccleve's chief predecessor to be not Chaucer but Langland. Very much as Langland's *Piers Plowman* is shaped by the guiding presence of Will, so Hoccleve's *Regiment of Princes* is shaped by the somewhat prickly interruptions of Hoccleve himself, a figure carefully named in the initial section of the work.

The *Regiment of Princes* is a hybrid in both its source materials and its structural composition. It draws materials from the pseudo-Aristotelian *Secreta secretorum*, from the *De regimine principum* by Giles of Rome, and from Jacobus de Cessolis' *De ludo scaccorum*. These texts were all well known in Hoccleve's day, and all were part of a well-established tradition of mirrors for princes, works offering counsel to the sovereign on the virtues and practises necessary for good rulership. As Nicholas Perkins has pointed out, Hoccleve's use of his sources is arranged, in part, to highlight his own role as counselor: a large number of his borrowings from all three of the source texts consist of exemplary stories or commentary about the proper sorts of speech to offer a ruler and the proper responses a sovereign might make to this speech.[7] The structure of the work also highlights this concern with the proper scope of dialogue between sovereign and poet-counselor. The poem is divided into two major sections, with the first 2,016 lines constituting a pseudo-Boethian dialogue between Hoccleve and an unnamed Old Man, in which Hoccleve complains of his poverty and anxiety and the Old Man advises him to write a poem for the Prince as a cure, and the remaining 3,448 lines being first a brief prologue addressing Prince Henry and then the Mirror of Princes proper, the series of largely expository treatments of sovereign virtues. This structure has meant that the major interpretive crux in the poem has typically been that of determining the relationship between the autobiographical dialogue and the Mirror for Princes proper.

Speaking broadly, the relationship between the two halves of the poem seems calculated to address the issue of poetic authority. The opening dialogue serves to justify the composition of the Mirror proper, as it stages both the Old Man's injunction to write and the complaints of poverty that are to be solved by the composition. Moreover, the centrality of poetic authority is emphasized by the presence of dual eulogies to Chaucer, positioned just at the moment at which the opening dialogue ends and pivots into the prologue. These passages serve to implicitly answer Hoccleve's own protestations that he is not the man to write advice to a prince, claiming at least the displaced credential of being Chaucer's heir. Of equal importance to the discourses of authority Hoccleve chooses to cite (the Boethian model of consolation and the descent of authority through a poetic genealogy) is the particular discourse of vulnerability he uses to evoke the anxiety of one who would offer counsel to the prince. Authorial anxiety is invoked here through three interlocked topoi: first, a persistent set of rhetorical self-accusations that his speech is worthless, that, to use one of his favorite verbs, he "clappeth"; second, of all the virtues and vices treated in the *Regiment*, one of the most central is the danger of flattery, or "favel," the vice that particularly involves the relationship between the prince and the poet who would make him a dupe through the doubleness to which all poets are prone; lastly, and most eccentrically, Hoccleve turns again and again to the simple fear that one must feel in addressing the prince. And here his account is remarkable not only for the emphasis on the affective register but also because he channels this account of affect through an analogy with the gendered hierarchies of the world of love. In the pivotal stanza that assents to the Old Man's advice to take up his pen (and which serves as the introduction to the first Chaucer eulogy), Hoccleve describes his feelings as such:

> With herte as trembling as the leef of asp,
> Fadir, syn yee me rede to do so,
> Of my simple conceit wole I the clasp
> Undo and lat it at his large go (1954–57)

The simile of trembling in fear like the leaf of the aspen is one that he almost certainly borrowed from Chaucer. It occurs in none of the other major Middle English poets of the period (not even Gower with his fondness for such similes), and the simile cannot be traced before Chaucer (though it must derive from the Latin name for the tree – *populos tremula*). Chaucer himself used the simile three different times, once in reference to anger (the Summoner who is too enraged to speak after the *Friar's Tale*), and twice in reference to fear (Hypermnestra's fear when her father gives her a knife to kill her husband in the *Legend of Good Women*, and Criseyde's quaking when she and Troilus are finally brought together in Book III of *Troilus and Criseyde*). The vivid simile of quaking like an aspen thus appears, in Chaucer's work, to be a specifically gendered response. Hoccleve's additional specification that it is his *heart* that quakes seems calculated to reinforce the parallel with Criseyde in particular, the suggestion that he plays a fearful Criseyde to Henry's Troilus, shaking in trepidation, yet, knowing, as Criseyde says, that he is only at the present juncture because he truly yielded to it long ago.

Late career

Hoccleve's next major work, the *Series*, was begun in 1419 and completed most probably in 1421. The *Series* is a poem in five parts. It opens with a "Complaint," a lament that he had been struck by what he calls his "wilde infirmite," a madness that drove away his wits and his friends. The "Complaint" moves seamlessly into the next section, the "Dialogue with a Friend," in which Hoccleve's solitary lamentations that he has been abandoned are interrupted, quite comically, by a knock on the door and the arrival of a Friend, who first tries to dissuade him from publishing his "Complaint" (now suddenly revealed to be the text we have been reading) only to then relent and suggest that Hoccleve write something for the potential patron Humphrey, duke of Gloucester. The final sections then constitute a three-part offering for Humphrey: a translation from the *Gesta Romanorum* concerning the "Tale of Jereslaus' Wife"; a translation of a dialogue on confession and death entitled "How to Learn to Die"; and, lastly, another translation from the *Gesta Romanorum*, this concerning the "Tale of Jonathas." In its structure, then, the *Series* bears remarkable similarities to the *Regiment of Princes.* The opening two sections provide an autobiographical framework, explaining how the work came to be written and offering it up to a potential patron.

But there are also major differences between the two works. First, while the initial dialogue of the *Regiment* is also a formal complaint, treating Hoccleve's financial anxieties and the omnipresent burden of "thought" itself, the opening movement of the *Series* takes on an even darker tone in its invocation of the "wilde infirmite." Hoccleve says in his "Complaint" that this episode had occurred five years previously, or in 1414, and there is circumstantial evidence that some real crisis did indeed occur in these years, as his payment from the Privy Seal was interrupted in 1414 and we have no datable surviving poems from the period between 1413 and 1415. It is tempting to read this crisis as a turning point in his poetic career as well. The *Letter to Oldcastle* was written in 1415 and the short lyric "To Henry V and the Company of the Garter" in 1416, but, these aside, there is a silence in the poetic record from the period of his infirmity up to the initiation of the *Series* that seems to match the protestations voiced in the "Complaint" by both the Hoccleve character and the Friend that any speech or writing coming from Hoccleve will be useless now, as it will simply be turned into further proof of his madness. Indeed, Hoccleve seems to be adapting the events of his life to a script indebted partly to Boethius and partly to the Book of Job, shaping them into a narrative of social ostracism and silence. In this context, we can see that the *Series* offers a certain ambivalence about the task of writing: it is by writing a book for Humphrey that Hoccleve and the Friend seek to bring him back into his former dignity, but the book offered never leaves behind a fretting anxiety about being misunderstood or giving offense.

In addition to this difference in the tone of the autobiographical frames, there is also a dramatic alteration in the materials chosen for the main bodies of the two works. Where the *Regiment of Princes* draws its materials from largely expository sources, using stories only as brief exemplary illustrations, the *Series*, for the first time in Hoccleve's career, takes narrative as its chief object. This difference in emphasis can be seen most vividly in the apparatus that organizes the structures of each work, the rubrications and composition on the page: put simply, whereas narrative in the *Regiment* is subordinated structurally to an organization via topics, in the *Series* narrative itself becomes the dominant structuring device. This new emphasis urges a simple question upon us: why narrative? When we look back over Hoccleve's career we find that it is peculiarly bare of narrative. This claimant to the Chaucerian mantle is perhaps most un-Chaucerian in his marked lack of interest in storytelling, preferring in his early and middle career the modes of satire and of philosophical counsel. Why should Hoccleve turn so sharply to stories now, at the end of such a career? The answer, I think, is to be found in the two structuring systems that Hoccleve uses to shape the *Series*: first, the two-part distinction between autobiographical prologue and the triptych of stories putatively meant for Humphrey (that is, "Jereslaus' Wife," "Learn to Die," and "Jonathas"); and, second, the neat, chiastic balance among the stories of gender and justice that form the triptych itself.

As in the *Regiment*, the relationship in the *Series* between autobiographical frame and the rest of the work is one of careful displacement, but its metaphoric system is much more complex than the earlier work, being meant to register on at least three levels. First, the presence of "Learn to Die" in the center of the triptych anchors much of the *Series* thematically around the importance of penitence and confession, radiating out into both climactic confessional moments in the *Gesta* narratives and also back to Hoccleve's need to surmount the silence into which madness had locked him.[8] Second, whereas Prince Henry had appeared as the sole audience for the *Regiment*, the dedication of the *Series* to Humphrey of Gloucester is immediately undermined by the much more charged and extended consideration of another audience – the women who will read the work. As the Friend counsels him to avoid giving further offense to the women who had disliked his earlier works, Hoccleve crosses the boundary between frame and narrative by creating a parallel between the rejection of his company chronicled in the "Complaint" and the rejection of his poetry by this imagined audience. This paranoid figuration of courtly readership as essentially feminine and essentially hostile to the powerless male poet serves, as it will also in so much later courtly literature, to fix the identity of the poet within a world in which patronage is imagined to be as precarious and fleeting as the affections of a cruel lover. Lastly, and most importantly, the relation between the two parts of the *Series* hinges on the putative exemplarity of the narratives, on the sense that narrative will redeem the crisis of the "Complaint" by demonstrating Hoccleve's ability to present an edifying tale.

It is this final dynamic which is complicated by the balanced arrangement of the stories in the triptych, particularly by the relation between "Jereslaus' Wife" and "Jonathas." The first is the story of an absolutely virtuous woman. The wife of the Emperor Jereslaus resists entreaty after entreaty to be unfaithful to her husband, although the result is exile from home and wanderings in anonymity through strange lands. Finally, having become a great healer through her spiritual purity, she triumphs by healing the very men who had injured her, forcing them to confess their deeds. The other is a story of a woman without virtue, one meant to serve as a warning to the Friend's fifteen-year-old son: here a young man, Jonathas, inherits three magic items from his dying father and has the items stripped away one by one as his false lover, Fellicula, persuades him to let her "guard" them for him; he reclaims the objects, and, having also become a great healer, uses his medical skills to exact vengeance on her. As even this very brief sketch should indicate, these two stories mirror each other through a complex set of parallels. In form, each is organized as an episodic romance, in which an essentially reiterative structure demonstrates the same point repeatedly (the necessity of refusing the uxorious man who inevitably appears in any refuge/the need to understand that the trusted girlfriend who has lost your magic ring might not be the best steward for your magic brooch). The narrative engine of both plots is the tension between secrecy and revelation; events move forward only as a consequence of things not said, and this dynamic channels the libidinal power of such suspense into a resolution via penitential confession at the end of each story. Lastly, the virtues represented by Jonathas and Jereslaus' wife (the knowledge he acquires and the pity she enacts) come to be physically enacted through their parallel development as healers.

But it is with this point that the two narratives diverge sharply. In the climactic scene of "Jereslaus' Wife," the evil and uxorious men who have troubled the Empress appear at her nunnery, each stricken with some terrible disease, and have to confess and beg her pity before she heals them and reveals herself to her husband. The conclusion here is clearly meant to illustrate the inevitable, though long-delayed, triumph of pity and virtue over malice, even drawing the villains within the benign ending through the act of healing. By contrast, Jonathas becomes a healer not through piety and virtue, but by discovering two pools of water and fruit from two trees while wandering in exile. The fruits and water are fruit and water *in bono* and *in malo*: one fruit inflicts leprosy, and the other will cure it; one water will make the flesh fall from the bones and the other will restore it. When Fellicula returns to Jonathas stricken with disease and confesses and repents for cheating him, Jonathas offers her not the good fruit and water but the bad, causing her an agonizing death. Thus the pity of the first narrative, its sense that justice might be seamlessly achieved for all, is reversed into simple revenge, emphasized by Hoccleve's narration of Jonathas' unrestrained glee at the recovery of his goods and by the emptiness of the penitential gestures in this account (her confession and suffering produce no forgiveness or pity – only pleasure at her fate).

Like the fruit that can cure or kill, the *Series* ends with stories that seem utterly opposed to each other in significance. And it is in this sharp opposition that I think we can see the meaning of narrative for Hoccleve. These stories are themselves a dialogue, a reflection of Hoccleve's tendency to bifurcate all his expository and philosophical models into dialogic forms. As the redundant narrative structures of both *Gesta* translations attest, stories are endlessly expandable combinations of events, of causes and outcomes that we have seen since Aristotle as being ethically descriptive of the world. The world of Boethian instability that anchors the *Series* is one in which the sure and singular pairing of an event with its ethical significance could never obtain, in which the exemplarity of narrative is a symptomatically elusive mirage. They mirror back the madness of the opening "Complaint," showing narrative as no cure but only another version of the dispersal of meaning.

NOTES

1 For a list of these documents and transcription of their contents see John Burrow, *Thomas Hoccleve* (Aldershot: Variorum, 1994), pp. 33–49.

2 Ibid., p. 29.

3 John M. Bowers, "Hoccleve's Huntington Holographs: The First 'Collected Poems' in English," *Fifteenth-Century Studies* 15 (1989), 27–51; see also *Thomas Hoccleve: A Facsimile of the Autograph Verse Manuscripts*, ed. J. A. Burrow and A. I. Doyle, EETS ss 19 (2002).

4 See A. I. and M. B. Parkes, "The Production of Copies of the *Canterbury Tales* and the *Confessio Amantis* in the Early Fifteenth Century," in *Medieval Scribes, Manuscripts, and Libraries*, ed. M. B. Parkes and A. G. Watson (London: Scolar Press, 1978), pp. 163–203.

5 *Thomas Hoccleve: The Regiment of Princes*, ed. Charles Blyth TEAMS Middle English Series (Kalamazoo: Medieval Institute Publications, 1999), p. 100, lines 2077–79. Subsequent citations are to this edition; line numbers are given in the text.

6 Thomas Hoccleve, "Letter of Cupid," in *Poems of Cupid, God of Love*, ed. Mary Carpenter Erler and Thelma A. Fenster (Leiden: E. J. Brill, 1990), p. 176, lines 15–21. Subsequent citations are to this edition; line numbers are given in the text.

7 Nicholas Perkins, *Hoccleve's "Regiment of Princes": Counsel and Constraint* (Cambridge: D. S. Brewer, 2001), pp. 85–125.

8 Christina von Nolcken, "'O, Why Ne Had Y Lerned for to Dye?': *Lerne for to Dye* and the Author's Death in Thomas Hoccleve's *Series*," in *Essays in Medieval Studies*, vol. X, ed. Allen J. Frantzen (Chicago: Illinois Medieval Association, 1993), pp. 27–51.

15

JAMES SIMPSON

John Lydgate

Study of the writings of John Lydgate offers attractive, multiple challenges for scholars of Middle English at all levels. Certainly the bibliographical and textual work on the Lydgate corpus done in the first half of the twentieth century made critical reassessment possible. And certainly the readiness of historicist scholarship, over the last twenty or so years, to define the cultural function of literary (and non-literary) texts has opened new paths to Lydgate's work. These paths were closed as long as New Criticism was the gatekeeper of scholarly interest, since Lydgate's many larger-scale works responded poorly to detailed formalist analysis. The correlative extension of interest in Middle English studies from the late fourteenth into (in one development at least) the fifteenth century has, further, prepared the ground for renewed consideration of Lydgate's oeuvre. Despite these enabling scholarly advances, the challenges offered by Lydgate remain under-exploited and attractive: consideration of so much of the large corpus remains inchoate, and, for those who enjoy the challenge of persuading readers that a previously ignored or dismissed text deserves attention, there is plenty of enjoyment to be had.[1]

A brief bio-bibliography will help situate this writer.[2] John Lydgate (*c.*1371–1449) was born in Lydgate, Suffolk, from which he took his name. He entered the Benedictine abbey of Bury St. Edmunds as a boy. Between 1389 and 1397 he passed through the range of orders from acolyte to priest. Lydgate is not recorded as having taken a degree, but he was certainly in Oxford at Gloucester College, *c.* 1406–8, possibly much longer. His connection with Prince Henry began before Henry's accession as Henry V in 1413: already in 1412 Lydgate began his ambitious narrative of the Trojan War, the *Troy Book*,[3] finished in 1420. His intensely lyrical account of certain episodes in the life of the Virgin, *The Life of Our Lady* and his short anti-Lollard polemic *A Defence of Holy Church* were also written during the reign of Henry V (1413–22).[4] The *Siege of Thebes* (sometimes known as the *Destruction of Thebes*), which narrates catastrophic Argive intervention in the civil war of Thebes, seems to date from 1421,[5] but may date from just after the death of Henry V in 1422.

In 1423 Lydgate was appointed as prior at Hadfield Regis, a small Benedictine priory in Essex, but had ceased to be prior by 1429–30, and was permitted to return to Bury in 1434. Throughout the 1420s he seems to have been exceptionally mobile for a monk, being present, for example, in Paris as part of an English occupying English force. The *Title and Pedigree of Henry VI* (1426, written for Richard Beauchamp, earl of Warwick),[6] the pungent dance of death, known as *Danse Machabré* (*c.* 1426),[7] and, possibly, the allegorical spiritual narrative, the *Pilgrimage of the Life of Man* (1426, dedicated to Thomas Montacute, earl of Salisbury) derive from the Parisian sojourn.[8] During this very active period he also received commissions for both secular and religious works from a wide range of both courtly and civic figures. These include a royal entry for Henry VI, commissioned by the Lord Mayor on behalf of the City of London (1432),[9] and a series of Mummings, or dramatic pieces, written for the Sheriffs of London, the London Mercers, and the Goldsmiths.[10]

In 1431 he began work on his huge translation: *The Fall of Princes* (whose ultimate source is Boccaccio's *De casibus virorum illustrium)*, under the patronage of Humphrey duke of Gloucester, uncle to the young King Henry VI (1422–61).[11] In the period after his return to Bury, he continued to work on the massive *Fall* up to 1438, as well as producing some large-scale saints' lives: the *Lives of Saints Edmund and Fremond* (1434–36) were commissioned by William Curteys, abbot of Bury St. Edmunds, as a gift to the boy Henry VI when he visited the abbey in 1433–34,[12] while the *Lives of Saints Alban and Amphibal* (1439) were commissioned by John Wethamstede, abbot of St. Albans.[13] In this period he seems also to have written for the household of William de la Pole, earl (later duke) of Suffolk; the *Virtues of the Mass* (after 1430) was written for Alice, countess of Suffolk (Chaucer's grand-daughter).[14] In his last years he may also have written his ostensibly autobiographical *Testament* and, what was apparently his last work, a translation of the *Secreta secretorum* (?1446–49), the section of which written by Lydgate simply stops mid-text at a line appropriately about the power of death to consume everything, even Lydgate.[15]

Lydgate worked within social networks both distinct from and much wider than any prior poet writing in English. The only examples of Chaucer's poetry with named or almost named patrons are *The Book of the Duchess* (*c.* 1368) and the "Complaint to His Purse" (*c.* 1399). Significantly, both these poems are addressed to Lancastrian patrons (respectively John of Gaunt and his son, Henry IV). Once the Lancastrians took power, they cultivated English poets and poetry in ways without precedent; Lydgate was their poet of choice. Perhaps profiting from this royal cultivation, Lydgate also enjoyed patronage from an exceptionally wide and deep range of English society. He was patronized by, or addressed poems to, other members of the royal family (e.g. by Humphrey duke of Gloucester); by other great nobles, both men and women (e.g. Richard Beauchamp and by Isabella, countess of Warwick); by abbots (Wethamstede and Curteys); by London livery companies and by London bureaucrats (e.g. John Carpenter, Town Clerk of London, who commissioned the *Danse Machabré* to be painted on the wall of a chapel of the Virgin Mary on the north side of St. Paul's in London). He produced verses for pining lovers (e.g. *The Temple of Glass*,[16] and *The Complainte of the Black Knight*),[17] and for devotional readers (e.g. *The Dolerous Pyte of Crystes Passioun*).[18] He even produced verses for laundresses, with tips on how to remove stains.[19]

On the face of it, Lydgate should be very significant in literary history for these reasons at least: (1) he is the first "official" poet writing in English; (2) he is Chaucer's immediate successor, and he addresses the Chaucerian oeuvre more consistently and energetically than any other writer except perhaps Henryson; (3) in addition to his deep engagement with Chaucer, he also enlarges the range of reference available to English poets, both from the English and continental traditions; (4) his engagement with earlier, twelfth-century French humanist narratives of city-state catastrophe (Troy and Thebes) is more thoroughgoing than any other later medieval English poet except perhaps Chaucer; (5) his engagement with a newer, Latin-based humanism derived from Italy (and especially from Boccaccio) is by far the most committed in the English medieval vernacular tradition; and (vi), almost alone in that vernacular tradition, he capitalizes on his authority as monk (an authority both spiritual but more especially historical) to produce ambitious vernacular texts for an exceptionally wide social range of readers.

For all that, Lydgate has suffered badly in literary history. In the two great periods of pre-twentieth-century English literary history (i.e. the sixteenth and the later eighteenth centuries), Protestant or Enlightenment hostility to Catholicism consigned Lydgate to the shadows, or worse: as one Enlightenment reader had it, Lydgate was a "voluminous, prosaick, and drivelling monk"; he wrote "stupid and fatiguing productions"; he "disgraces the name and patronage of his master Chaucer", and his works should be consigned to "base and servile uses."[20] In the twentieth century, too, both New Criticism and New Historicism have consigned Lydgate to the same dark place: critics working in the mode of New Criticism defined his lack of stylistic and structural tension as a medieval, periodic rule, against whose measure they were able to calibrate Chaucer's incomparable and ahistorical genius. And New Historicist critics produced a version of the same argument, driven by a different axiom. Because Lydgate was complicit with Power, and because that power was illegitimate, Lydgate was at his most interesting only when the contradictions of power became impossible to manage. Lydgate's own concerted exercise of control over his text fails at interesting moments, so as to expose, despite Lydgate's best efforts, the illegitimacy of the Lancastrian regime, which had come to power via a *coup d'état* in 1399.

From the middle of the sixteenth century, then, the comparison between the two poets has routinely been made to Lydgate's detriment: he is pitched against Chaucer in a hopeless agon, which he is bound to lose badly. Lydgate proves the rule of medieval darkness and, in Lydgate's case, medieval dullness. He is doomed to imitate Chaucer but equally doomed only to fail in the attempt. Lydgate generously provides grist for an exclusionary mill, and the bulk of Lydgate scholarship is generated by a logic of exclusion. Thus, for example, Lydgate's work is *not* rhetorically adept, *not* proto-Protestant, and *not* subversive. Lydgate wanders forever in a *regio dissimilitudinis*, or region of either Protestant, Enlightenment, or liberal unlikeness.

Answering a challenge of that kind would require thoroughgoing consideration of Lydgate's entire corpus. That is clearly impossible here. Instead, I devote the rest of this chapter to the way in which Lydgate confronted the two most significant historical challenges as he or his patrons saw them, civil war on the one hand and Lollardy on the other.

The recent example of France was both the biggest opportunity and the biggest potential nightmare on the English horizon in the early fifteenth century. With the onset of insanity in Charles VI of France (1380–1422) in 1392, France was subject to civil war among rival factions. In 1407 partisans of John the Fearless assassinated Louis of Orléans, which precipitated a full-scale civil war between factions known as the Armagnacs and Burgundians. This was, in the first instance, a great opportunity for England's militarist class: Henry V allied England to the Burgundian faction of John the Fearless, and his victory at Agincourt in 1415 depended on the fragility of France subject to ferocious civil division under an insane king. That victory paved the way for the Treaty of Troyes (1420), by whose terms England gained greater ascendancy than at any other point in the so-called Hundred Years War between 1337 and 1453: Charles VI was to disinherit his son, the Dauphin, and Henry V was to marry Katherine of Valois (daughter of Charles VI), thereby becoming king of both England and France.

Civil war in France was, then, a golden opportunity for the English militarist class. For English writers with longer historical memories and a sharper awareness of the way in which external war can very easily provoke internal crisis, it was a disaster waiting to happen. Fortune's revolving wheel did in fact produce a very different and far more treacherous outcome for England from the one projected by the Treaty of Troyes. Henry V died prematurely in 1422, leaving an eight-month-old child, Henry VI, as king of both England and France. This was already, then, a challenging project, but later an impossible one as Henry VI, no less than his French royal grandfather, displayed mental incapacity. The fatal sequence of events that was to lead to bloody English civil war between 1455 and 1485 was far in the future when Lydgate began his translation of the *Troy Book* in 1412. Despite the impossibility of foreseeing just how disastrous imprudent militarism against France would turn out to be, Lydgate's *Troy Book* does nevertheless offer a blueprint for the catastrophes that ensue from blind militarism, catastrophes that befall apparent winners as much as evident losers. The *Troy Book* also offers a blueprint for Lydgate's authorial confidence, across the rest of his career and in a variety of genres, to rebuke his powerful patrons.

It's true that the Prologue of the *Troy Book* begins with an invocation to Mars; it's also true that Lydgate says that the translation was commissioned by Prince Henry, in order that the "noble story openly wer knowe / In oure tonge, aboute in every age, / And ywriten as wel in our langage / As in latyn and in Frensche it is" (Prologue, 112–15). These gestures might suggest that Lydgate is a poet captive to the militarist and nationalist culture of his patrons. Before we accept the framing gestures of this large work (both Prologue and triumphalist Envoy, or "send-off") too readily, however, we might also notice that the second invocation is to Othea, goddess of Prudence (38). Prudence is the capacity to see the past, the present and the future, the difficult skill of understanding the ways in which known events will shape and be shaped by unknown events. The story of Troy as translated by Lydgate is a narrative of one catastrophe after another. This is primarily a sequence of military disasters, in which everyone is a loser: Troy is utterly destroyed twice, and all the Greek heroes, including Ulysses, are themselves murdered in a variety of ways when they try to return after their victory. But it's not simply a question of military disasters; more precisely, these were avoidable disasters produced by poor diplomatic procedures and even worse processes of political consultation in which military leaders stupidly refused to listen to prudential voices. Diplomatic missions are poorly executed, contrary to the ostensible wishes of executive power, and counsel sessions badly conducted.

The narrative cries out for prudential voices to bridle aristocratic militarists, and yet such voices that urge prudential caution are silenced. The most powerful scene in which prudential voices are raised only to be dismissed is in Book 2 (worth reading as a unit in itself). Lydgate, following his source, gives a detailed narrative of a committee at work, deliberating on matters of enormous gravity. History is in the balance; the narrative of decision-making is gripping as we watch the wrong decision being taken, despite the reiterated articulation of powerful and prudential anti-war positions. Hector begins by confirming the justice of vengeance. He articulates a militarist, chivalric ethics, which is a remarkably simple ethical system, with very few categories: birth, shame and violence, where the only category that admits of gradation is birth. The higher born one is, the greater the need to avenge insult. Hector, however, is an expert rhetorician, and his defense of a chivalric response turns out merely to be a way of capturing the good will of his audience, before he proceeds to dismiss that very response:

> But first I rede, wysely in your mynde [advise]
> To cast aforn and leve nat behynde, [consider]
> Or ye begynne, discretly to adverte [before]
> And prudently consyderen in your herte
> Al, only nat the gynnyng but the ende,
> And the myddes, what weie thei wil wende. (2.2229–34)

The key word here is "prudently": prudence is the central virtue of the so-called cardinal virtues (prudence, temperance, justice and courage), a classical ethical system known throughout the medieval period through, among many other sources, compendia of Cicero's *De officiis*. Like the chivalric system, this ethical construct is concerned with action in the world; unlike the chivalric system, it is concerned with survival. All other considerations are secondary to the primary goal of completing a sequence of actions materially better off than when one started, with one's probity intact. Hector argues very forcefully here that the Trojans will be worse off for this war, and they need only consider the strategic situation to recognize that. Even if the Trojans can count on the support of all Asia, the Greeks hold the balance of power, with Europe and Africa behind them. If Troy initiates a war, Hector argues, the Trojans will be put "alle to destruccioun." So, he recommends, the Trojans should act "by dissymulacioun," by which he means that they should pretend that no injury has been done, and thereby avoid the need to activate the entropic forces of war. Having articulated the chivalric position by speaking like a knight, that is, Hector looks to the future and speaks as a prudent, secular cleric.

This *miles/clerus* (knight/scholar) opposition runs deep through the *Troy Book* and, indeed, throughout Lydgate's other tragic narratives.

In Book 2, however, prudential counsel utterly fails: willful old Priam is swayed rather by willful young voices of Paris, Deiphebus, and Troilus. Each voice promoting prudence is sidelined. Hector is ignored; Helenus is dismissed as he foresees the total destruction of Troy; and in a later session of the Trojan parliament, the philosopher Pentheus is hounded for daring to suggest that the mission is utterly foolish. His failure gives way to the impassioned but useless prophecy of Cassandra, and, finally, to the rueful voice of the poet himself, who reflects that if the council had been swayed by Hector, Helenus, Protheus and Cassandra, Troy would still be standing (2.3295–3318).

If these societies of the past were destroyed for want of philosophical reflection, the work presents itself as saying, then *contemporary* readers might be able to avoid the same mistakes by attending to this very work, and to the prudential voice of its author and translator. This voice, it should be stressed, does not, on the whole, promote specifically Christian morality. The narrator voices prudential and practical wisdom, and not, for the most part, Christian morality. It proposes more effective political action, rather than Christian counsel to turn aside from a deceptive world. This is, in short, not so much the narrative of great kings and warriors ending in military disaster; it is that narrative as commented on and arranged by a distinct, clerical voice, capable of intervening in and shaping it for persuasive ends. The clerical voice of the narrator holds up to aristocratic readers the spectacle of their own downfall, cast down by their own readiness blindly to mount the turning wheel of Fortune.

Lydgate's first large-scale work presents, then, a powerfully antimilitarist voice that pitches itself in terms its audience cannot avoid. This is not the voice of Christian morality, but rather of prudential wisdom arguing extreme caution in committing a nation to the hazards of war, mainly because it will end badly. Isolation of that voice serves to highlight its presence across the rest of Lydgate's oeuvre, answering to different historical exigencies. It certainly appears in the *Siege of Thebes*, written either immediately before or just after the death of Henry V in 1422. The narrative tells the story of catastrophic fratricidal war that destroyed not only Thebes, but also the well-intentioned Argive force that comes to the aid of Polynices, unjustly deprived by his brother of the kingdom of Thebes. It stresses above all the need to listen to prudential voices before it is too late; being on the side of justice is no guarantee against Fortune's treacherousness. If this was written before the death of Henry V in 1421 (as the astrological dating would suggest), it was preternaturally prescient about the tensions between Henry V's brothers as they vied for power in the vacuum created by Henry's death. And, in the 1430s, we can hear that prudential, confident voice again, as Lydgate composes the *Fall of Princes*. To be sure, the text is punctuated by calls for payment from Lydgate's patron, Humphrey duke of Gloucester, and Lydgate gives very high profile to the theme of the poet patronized by the powerful in the *Fall*. For all that, the basic premise of the text is that patrons need poets much more than poets need patrons: one after another, phantoms of the now dead and powerful come begging Boccaccio in his study to portray their fame in a positive light. The poet's study becomes the site in which posterity's power is distributed: patrons are insistently reminded that the poet's power outlasts theirs. The theme of poets courageously addressing and correcting lords also surfaces in very sophisticated ways in other genres. In an animal fable, the delightful *Churl and the Bird*, for example, we see Lydgate in less explicitly public mode, where the issue is less how to advise kings about war, and more how to advise the powerful *per se*. More than any other of Lydgate's texts, this is about the exercise of rhetoric itself, where the dull churl stands in for poetic patrons, the mercurial bird for poets.

Throughout all of his works of counseling lords, then, Lydgate consistently occupies an oppositional position, and consistently explores the rhetorical modalities of effective counsel. This is by no means a subversive position: Lydgate imagines himself on speaking terms with those in power. For all that, the discursive position is nonetheless clearly distinct from that of the powerful, and one from which Lydgate underlines the need for courageous, rhetorically skillful, and prudential counsel.

What of the second major historical challenge as Lydgate saw it, that of Lollardy? It's true that Lydgate does not often address the question of Lollardy directly. His one explicitly polemical religious text, *A Defence of Holy Church* (before 1422), encourages Henry V to destroy those who falsely make war against their own "mother" (126). Even here, however, he does not mention Lollardy by name, but refers only to "these sectys newe" (93). In this reticence he is very unlike his much more strident contemporary Hoccleve, who attacks Lollardy in sustained and explicit ways in both the *Regement of Princes* (1412) and in *To Sir John Oldcastle* (1415). That said, I will be arguing here that Lydgate's engagement with Lollardy is fundamentally a question of style; that it continues throughout Lydgate's career; and that it provokes him to develop wholly new stylistic possibilities in English and Scots poetry.

Lydgate has often been damned for stylistic imprecision, both in syntax and lexis: his syntax is, scholars have repeatedly argued, imprecise, and his lexical choices (described as "aureate," to use Lydgate's own term) disagreeably florid and mannered. A recent essay provides a very forceful rebuttal of the syntactic charge,[21] but the lexical charge remains unaddressed. The first point to make is that Lydgate's aureate style is very restricted in usage, and does not at all characterize his narrative poetry (i.e. most of his output). Compare these passages. The first, from the *Troy Book*, describes the throne in Priam's new Troy:

And al above, reysed was a se,
Ful curiously of stones and perré [precious jewels]
That called was, as chefe and principal,
Of the regne the sete moste royal.
To fore which was set by gret delyt
A borde of eban and of yvor whyt, [ebony]
So egaly ioyned and so clene,
That in the werk ther was no rifte sene. (2.995–1002)

This passage describes an object of beauty and skilled craftsmanship. Its own craftsmanship is, nonetheless, entirely straightforward both syntactically and lexically. This is characteristic of a middle style, designed to sustain the long march of narrative. It is entirely characteristic of all Lydgate's narrative works, which constitute the vast bulk of his output.

Compare that style with, say, the following hymn of praise, Lydgate's version of the Te Deum:

Te deum laudamus! To the lord sovereyne [We praise thee God]
We creaturys knowlech the as creatoure;
Te, eternum patrem, the peple playne, [You, eternal father]
With hand and herte doth the honoure;
O femynyn fadir funte and foundoure, [fount]
Magnus et laudabilis dominus, [great and praiseworthy Lord]
In sonne and sterre thu sittyst splendoure,
Te laudat omnis spiritus.[22] [every spirit praises you]

Here Lydgate shapes a static, formal address in exceptionally courtly, mannered form previously untried in English. The most obvious formal quality is the mixture of Latin and English, with the Latin worked into the metrical and rhyme structure of the English. The next stanza's "*Tibi* curiously *cantant celi celorum*" (11) expresses the "curiousness" (in the earlier sense indicated here, of "mannered, ingenious") of the whole effect of Latin worked in with English. But the English is itself unwilling to leave its Latinate source, with each rhyme word drawn from a Latin root. The very metrical structure is pulled into a pattern determined here by the Latin refrain (*Te laudat omnis spiritus*) whose four stresses characterize each line. No one tradition of English verse is, indeed, sufficient to the task in hand, for if the fact of rhyme is characteristic of English metrical practise derived from French models, the regular use of alliteration and the four-stress line harnesses the energies of English alliterative poetry, generally eschewed by southern and eastern late medieval English poets. With the figures of speech (of rhyme and alliteration), Lydgate gives very high profile to the sonic patterning of words; the stanza is no less dense in figures of thought: "O femynyn fadir funte and foundoure," deploying both paradox ("femynyn fadir") and metaphor ("funte," fountain, spring).

What has this style to do with Lollardy? In the *Defence of Holy Church*, Lydgate targets the Lollards especially for their dislike of ornament: they would deprive her of "hir ornamentes," and withdraw her "rich paramentes" (127–30). Correlative with that distrust of ecclesiastical ornamentation among Lollards is a distrust of any but a plain written style (not to speak of a distrust of literature itself): if texts are to be open and readable by all, they must be stylistically plain. It seems to me that Lydgate's aureate style is designed to meet and to counter the Lollard challenge on stylistic terms. Lydgate is on the crest of a translational wave as he begins his career, when English gained authority as a language of both official business and of literary discourse. Lollardy, however, posed an acute problem for anyone wanting to write Christian matter in the vernacular, since, by the terms of the anti-Lollard Constitutions promulgated by Archbishop Arundel in 1409, no one must translate Scripture into English. And that prohibition on scriptural translation created a larger sense of potential danger associated with any vernacular treatment of theological material. Writers responded to this pressure on the vernacular in a variety of ways: Nicholas Love's *Mirror of the Blessed Life of Jesus Christ* (*c*.1410) adopts a plain narrative prose style focused on the suffering and humanity of Christ; in mid-century Bishop Reginald Pecock crafted a plain argumentative prose style shorn of all affective resources. Some other writers (Capgrave, for instance) chose to write quite sophisticated vernacular theology in the apparently innocuous genre of hagiography. Lydgate, by contrast, shaped an aureate style. That florid style absolutely and immediately distinguishes Lydgate's incorporation of biblical matter and biblically derived hermeneutics from Lollard writing.

We need, in short, to historicize Lydgate's style in his theological writing. Once we have the characteristics and determinants of that style in focus, we can trace it across large tracts of Lydgate's poetic career. It is already visible in, for example, his accomplished and ambitious early work, the *Life of Our Lady* (1413–22); his psalm versions; his translations of hymns; his *Virtues of the Mass*; his prayers to saints; and in his prayers to the Virgin. Once distinguished from Lollard textuality by style, Lydgate is free to write biblical matter of much greater poetic intensity and much greater hermeneutic sophistication than was otherwise possible. Take for example his *Procession of Corpus Christi*, a text, like many other Lydgate texts, designed to accompany, record, and recreate a dramatic procession.[23] Lydgate moves through the entirety of scriptural time – Hebrew scriptures, New Testament, and the entire period of scriptural reception up to Aquinas (d. 1275) – suggesting the way in which images of food figure forth the Eucharist. Thus reference to the Old Testament Melchisedech (Genesis 14.18) as the type of the priest offering the Eucharist gives access to the wholeness of scriptural time, both wholly available and temporally distinct:

> Remembreth eeke in youre inwarde entente
> Melchysedec, that offred bred and wyne,
> In figure oonly of the sacrament,
> Steyned in Bosra, on Calvarye made red,
> On Sherthorsday to-fore er he was ded,
> For memorial mooste sovereyne and goode,
> Gaf hees apostels, takethe here off goode heed,
> His blessed body and his precyous bloode.
>
> (lines 17–24)

This single stanza compresses an astonishing historical range of reference into a single, short vision: the priest and king of Genesis, Melchisedech, is read figurally as a priest offering the Eucharist. But that reference is made via Christ instituting the sacrament at the Last Supper. That reference, in turn, is enriched by a citation from Isaiah 63:1–7 to the blood-stained conqueror, taken to be a figural reference to Christ. This web of historical references is all held together by the present "inwarde entente" of the viewer/reader. Such a rapidly constructed historical web puts pressure on syntax, pressure most evident and most revealing in the implied identity of the "sacrament" on the one hand and Christ "Steyned in Bosra, on Calvarye made red" on the other. Lydgate's stylistic pyrotechnics permit intellectually demanding, hermeneutically complex biblical variations. His style distinguishes an intellectually and poetically demanding practise from the plainness of Lollard discourse; it also protects such a practise from the repressive response to Lollardy.

NOTES

1 Though see the two recent collections, *John Lydgate: Poetry, Culture, and Lancastrian England*, ed. Larry Scanlon and James Simpson (Notre Dame, IN: University of Notre Dame Press, 2006); and *Lydgate Matters: Poetry and Material Culture in the Fifteenth Century*, ed. Lisa H. Cooper and Andrea Denny-Brown (New York: Palgrave Macmillan, 2008).

2 What follows is dependent on Derek Pearsall, *John Lydgate (1371–1449): A Bio-Bibliography*, English Literary Studies, 71 (Victoria, British Columbia: University of Victoria Press, 1997).
3 *Lydgate's Troy Book*, ed. Henry Bergen, 4 Parts, EETS ES 97, 103, 106, and 126 (1906, 1908, 1910, and 1935). All citations are to this edition. Line numbers will be given in the text.
4 *A Critical Edition of John Lydgate's "Life of Our Lady"*, eds. Joseph A. Lauritis, Ralph A. Klinefelter, and Vernon F. Gallagher (Pittsburgh: Duquesne University Press, 1961); *A Defence of Holy Church*, in John Lydgate, *The Minor Poems*, 2 Parts, ed. Henry Noble MacCracken, EETS ES 107, 192 (1911, 1934; repr. 1961), Part 1, no. 10. All citations to this edition. Line numbers will be given in the text.
5 *Lydgate's "Siege of Thebes"*, ed. Axel Erdmann and Eilert Ekwall, 2 vols., EETS ES 108, 125 (1911, 1930; rpr. 1960).
6 *Minor Poems*, Part 2, no. 28.
7 *The Dance of Death*, ed. Florence Warren, EETS OS 181 (1931).
8 *The Pilgrimage of the Life of Man*, ed. F. J. Furnivall, and K. B. Locock, 3 Parts, EETS ES 77, 83, 92 (1911–34).
9 *Minor Poems*, Part 2, no. 32.
10 Ibid., Part 2, nos. 40, 45, and 46 respectively.
11 *Lydgate's Fall of Princes*, ed. Henry Bergen, 4 vols., EETS ES 121, 122, 123, 124 (1924; rpr. 1967).
12 "S. Edmund und Fremond, von Lydgate," in *Altenglische Legenden: neue Folge*, ed. C. Horstmann (Heilbronn: Heninger, 1881), pp. 376–445. See also *The Life of Saint Edmund King and Martyr: John Lydgate's Illustrated Verse Life Presented to Henry VI: A Facsimile of British Library MS Harley 2278*, introduction by A. S. G. Edwards (London: British Library, 2004).
13 *Saint Albon and Saint Amphibalus*, ed. George F. Reinecke, Garland Medieval Texts, 11 (New York: Garland, 1985).
14 *Minor Poems*, Part 1, no. 17.2.
15 Ibid., Part 1, no. 68, and *Lydgate and Burgh's Secrees of Old Philosoffres*, ed. Robert Steele, EETS ES 66 (1894).
16 *Lydgate's Temple of Glas*, ed. Joseph Schick, EETS ES 60 (1891).
17 *Minor Poems*, Part 2, no. 11.
18 Ibid., Part 1, no. 47.
19 Ibid., Part 2, no. 52.
20 Joseph Ritson, *Bibliographia Poetica: A Catalogue of English Poets* (London: Roworth, 1802), pp. 87–88.
21 Phillipa Hardman, "Lydgate's Uneasy Syntax," in *Lydgate: Poetry, Culture*, pp. 12–35.
22 *Minor Poems*, Part 1, no. 7, lines 1–8
23 Ibid., Part 1, no. 11.

16

REBECCA KRUG

Margery Kempe

Margery Kempe was born *c.* 1373 in prosperous circumstances in Bishop's Lynn (now King's Lynn) in Norfolk. Her father was a prominent burgess and served five times as mayor. Although she traveled widely, on pilgrimage, and for other spiritual purposes, she resided all of her life in Lynn, where she married and raised children, dying *c.* 1440. Modern scholars have settled upon the term "autobiography" to describe the genre to which *The Book of Margery Kempe* belongs. This seems quite sensible given that Margery Kempe is both the *Book's* author – in collaboration with her scribes – and its subject. Further, the work's autobiographical aspects extend beyond subject and authorship to structure and style. For example, although the narrative is not strictly chronological, it is loosely arranged around events in Margery's life. Similarly, although it is told from third-person perspective rather than first (Margery refers to herself as the "creatur"), it reflects the author's point of view, offering moral and personal commentary on her experiences.[1] Finally, the *Book's* frequent use of direct discourse makes it seem as if Margery "re-speaks" her own words for the reader's benefit. As a genre, autobiography holds out the promise that we can know and feel what the author experienced – what she was *really* like. Modern enthusiasm for Kempe's *Book* suggests that it is a promise many readers feel her *Book* keeps.

Yet as fitting as it is for us to think of the *Book* as autobiography, use of the term probably tells us more about modern interests and inclinations than it does about medieval ones. Margery Kempe and her scribes never used the word to describe her writing: they could not since it did not come into use until the late eighteenth century. Nor do they choose what would seem to be the closest Middle English approximation, "life." Instead, they refer to her work as, straightforwardly, her "book" – a long piece of writing – or, more particularly, her "tretys." In Middle English, "treatise" could be a synonym for book, but it was also frequently used to indicate that a text addressed a particular subject of study. So, for example, Chaucer wrote a treatise about the astrolabe to show his son the art of using this device to navigate the stars; Lanfranc composed a treatise on surgery to teach his readers that skill.[2]

Treatises explored particular topics and invited readers to learn to use the knowledge provided in their own lives. Not limited to teaching pragmatic skills, they frequently offered readers instruction in spiritual matters. The *Prick of Conscience*, for example, a poetic meditation on the four last things (death, judgment of the soul, the pains of hell, and the joys of heaven), calls itself a treatise that explains why believers should fear God. It sets out to teach those unable to muster the proper "dread" how to do so.[3] Similarly, the *Lay Folk's Mass Book*, another treatise, teaches the reader how to hear mass with an attentive spirit. The *Pore Caityf*, a compendium of biblical, devotional, mystical, and catechetical material, describes itself as a treatise that points readers toward "the right way to hevene."[4] If, as I am suggesting, Margery Kempe wrote a treatise rather than an autobiography, what was the subject of this treatise and what methods does it teach? And more broadly, why does it matter to think of the *Book* in this way if we want to know about Middle English literature?

In this essay, I argue that Margery Kempe's *Book* teaches its readers strategies for managing the emotional, and ultimately spiritual, damage brought on by feelings of uncertainty, unworthiness, and despair. The *Book*, like other Middle English treatises, approaches its subject by assuming that readers need to be able to use the material they read. In this case, Margery Kempe's life is the subject of the treatise and the method for using that life involves experimentation with the reader's self-understanding. As a treatise, Margery Kempe's *Book* can be understood as less concerned with the factual history of the author's life and more focused on its readers' use of the work in their lives. In this way, the *Book* challenges modern understandings of autobiography as a genre concerned with the particularity of individual (the author's) experience. It offers, instead, a model of "life-writing" that extends beyond the text's autobiographical subject to its readers.

Critical history

Given the critical history of the *Book's* reception, it is little surprise that we now look at it as an autobiography. Probably composed in the 1430s and first rediscovered in 1934, the *Book* has come to be viewed as the most important evidence of women's involvement in late medieval literary culture. This was not always the case. In the first decades after its reappearance, it was often treated with condescension. Scholars sometimes exhibited hostility toward the *Book* because they were frustrated by its lack of similarity to mystical writing by men. Some critics felt that it was too concerned with lived experience to qualify as a serious discussion of religious understanding.[5] Scholars sympathetic to the *Book* were, therefore, put in the position of defending Margery Kempe, first, as a woman, and second, as a religious writer.

In the 1970s and 1980s feminist scholars began to explore the *Book* for insights into women's history. In the first full-length study of the *Book*, Clarissa Atkinson argued that scholars needed to consider the kinds of religious, social, and psychological experiences that would have been common to women living in fifteenth-century England.[6] Studies such as Atkinson's sought to place Margery Kempe in a social context, and the *Book* became a source of information about the life of a real, historical figure.

In the 1990s, literary critics became interested in studying Margery Kempe as a medieval woman writer. Scholars including Karma Lochrie and Lynn Staley turned their attention to the "textual" nature of the *Book*. Lochrie (1991) challenged the ways in which traditional writing about medieval mysticism had excluded Margery Kempe on the grounds that her *Book* was too concerned with the "mundane and untranscendent."[7] Lochrie advanced a "re-examination of our critical categories" that included women's physicality as part of mystical experience, and she explored the ways the *Book* reflected its author's experience of female bodyliness.[8] Staley, too, was concerned with Margery Kempe as an author, and she in turn challenged assumptions about the "artlessness" of the *Book*, proposing that scholars distinguish between the historical person, "Kempe," who composed the *Book*, and the figure "Margery," who functions as a character in the *Book*.[9] Both Lochrie and Staley rejected straightforward readings of the *Book* as autobiography, but both, nonetheless, found the work's significance and power in Margery Kempe's experiences as a woman writing in opposition to patriarchal society.

Preoccupation with Margery Kempe's life continues to characterize writing about the *Book*. This is perhaps because, as Barbara Newman suggests, the author herself seems to be "fascinated by her own experience."[10] Readers of the *Book* are attracted by the sense that this lived life *mattered* to its author and to the people around her. As Newman observes, the Book reflects a feeling of excitement, "sacred awe, a delighted satisfaction … sheer wonder at what it is possible for a human being to know of God."[11] It is this intensity of experience that, I think, makes us want to think of this as autobiography but which, I believe, might be more effectively understood if we read the *Book* as a treatise. The difference between autobiography and treatise is, at one basic level, in the effect on the reader. In this essay I argue that Margery Kempe's *Book* describes her fascination with her life not so readers will admire her or familiarize themselves with her life history, but, rather, so they might find such fascination in their own spiritual lives.

The *Book* as treatise

Treatises were written with their audiences in mind, and the *Book* begins by addressing its readers directly. Calling them "synful wrecchys," a phrase that associates personal unhappiness with their fallen natures, the *Book's* prologue draws attention to its readers' emotional experiences (pp. 17–21). According to the prologue, these readers lack "solas and comfort." They feel inadequate and incapable of comprehending Jesus' "hy and unspecabyl mercy," and, because of these feelings, they need to be reminded that God is an active presence in their lives. Jesus is not, according to the prologue, merely a historical, biblical figure but, rather, a "sovereyn Savyowr" who intervenes "now in ower days." This inclusive "our" makes it clear that the scribe counts himself among the "unworthy" in whose lives Jesus, despite that unworthiness, "deyneth to exercysen hys nobeley and hys goodnesse." The scribe explains that he and the *Book's* readers need this "short" and "comfortabyl" "tretys" because its contents will relieve their misery by providing them with an example of God's "wonderful werkys."

It might seem, then, that Margery Kempe, the recipient of God's wondrous mercy, would be represented as distinct from the *Book's* readers. This is not, however, the case. Although it is true that the *Book* differentiates Margery Kempe's experience of special grace – her understanding of "secret and prevy thyngys" (p. 18) and her direct, sensual apprehension of God's presence, for example – from more pedestrian religious encounters, in doing so, it aligns her emotional condition directly with the emotional experiences of her readers. Like her *Book's* "wretched" readers, like her scribes, Margery Kempe, despite the special grace shown to her, experienced repeated episodes in which she felt "gret hevynes" (p. 206). In pointing out the "forme of [Margery's] levynges" (p. 19), the *Book* imagines its readers as taking part in those experiences through shared understanding of emotional distress. Margery's methods for managing such emotions are offered to the readers as means by which they too can overcome their own "heaviness" and find, as the prologue promises, emotional stability and comfort.

For readers to "use" Margery Kempe's experiences, they needed to understand their own life in relation to Margery's. The *Book's* first chapter promotes this sense of affinity by insisting on the ordinariness of Margery's emotional responses and situation. She is, according to the opening chapter, a typical woman of her time who, at twenty years of age, married a "worschepful burgeys" and quickly became pregnant "as kynde wolde" (p. 21). Like many women, Margery had a difficult pregnancy. She was repeatedly stricken with debilitating illnesses and, shortly after the baby was born, she became seriously depressed. The *Book* treats this in a matter-of-fact manner, and, given the state of medieval health care, this was no doubt an all too common result of pregnancy. Tired, ill, and despairing for her life, Margery, according to the *Book*, called for a priest in order to confess her sins. The sympathetic reader, familiar with the dangers of childbirth, might easily identify with this young mother's sickness and depression.

Having established familiarity between reader and subject, the chapter goes on to heighten the identification between the two by describing Margery's fear of confession. No longer simply representative of her "kind," that is, women who bear children and become ill, in the rest of the chapter, Margery takes on the role of every believer who has been afraid to confess her sins. Margery, the reader learns, is guilty of a secret, unconfessed sin. When she was in "good heele" she had believed she "nedyd no confession" (p. 21) for this secret sin. Embarrassed by her guilt, she felt too ashamed to tell her priest what she had done. Instead, she convinced herself that she could do "penawns be hirself alone" and if she did "all schuld be forgovyn" since God is "mercyful inow" (p. 22). At the point of death, she finally acknowledges that she must confess the sin and asks to see a priest.

The *Book's* reader, if the process of identification has worked, feels linked to Margery through a common understanding of shame and self-deception. She feels Margery's intense, emotional turmoil over her unconfessed sin and has no trouble understanding the ways in which this fear escalates during the subsequent conversation with the priest. When Margery falls silent after the priest's arrival, terrified, on the one hand, of damnation and petrified, on the other, by the harshness of the priest's "sharp reprevying" (p. 22), the sympathetic reader, familiar with the discomfort of exposing her own sins, shares Margery's pain. The complete mental breakdown that follows this failed confession must seem, to the reader who has allowed herself to think of her own experiences as she reads of Margery's, almost inevitable.

But that sense of inevitability is exactly what the *Book* tries to teach the reader to resist. Without warning, Margery experiences a miracle. Jesus appears to her as she lies in bed and asks a simple question: "Dowtyr, why hast thow forsakyn me, and I forsoke nevyr the?" (p. 23). Unable to accept that God (and her priest) can forgive her for her secret sin, Margery, according to Jesus, has withdrawn from his presence. He suggests that Margery has left him out of exhaustion, sickness, shame, and self-hatred. Once she is reminded that she has an emotional obligation to him – he has never left her – she quickly recovers. Sin, according to the *Book*, can lead to overwhelming shame, and it is shame, not sin itself, that has kept Margery from God.

Pastoral writers acknowledged the dual nature of shame's effect on believers. Although it was considered necessary for recognizing one's sinfulness and achieving forgiveness, shame could also become a spiritual stumbling block. John Mirk, for example, relates the story of a woman who had committed a sin so grievous that she felt she "myght neuer, for schame, shryuve hyr therof."[12] In Mirk's story, the woman, like Margery Kempe, lies in bed and has a vision of Jesus. Jesus asks her why she has not confessed the sin, and when she replies that she is too ashamed to do so, Jesus takes her hand, places it in his wounded side, and tells her as he draws out her bloody hand, "Be thou no more aschamed to opyn the hert to me, then I am to opon my side to the."

Mirk's story appears to anticipate Margery's, but it diverges from her account in important ways. In his account, the woman's first response is to the blood: she is "agrysed," that is, horrified, by the blood and tries to wash her hand. She has no success – "scho myght not, be no way" cleanse her hand – until she goes to confession. After she is shriven, "anon the hand was clene as that othyr." The woman learns that the practise of confession is the vehicle for overcoming sin: opening one's heart to Jesus means confessing one's sins. In contrast, Margery Kempe's *Book* omits further discussion of confession. Instead, she tells a story that draws on the power of affective relations and self-understanding. Margery and her readers find the solution to sin by relinquishing the sense of shame that holds the sinner captive. In its first chapter, the *Book* establishes a method for doing this: in place of Margery's shame-induced despair, she focuses instead on God's presence.

The *Book* does not tell Margery (or the reader) to ignore her feelings of shame and replace them with faith. Instead, it offers her methods by which she can overcome emotional responses that restrict her spiritual life. By reimagining herself according to God's point of view rather than her own, Margery learns to move beyond constrictive, human definitions. In particular, she discovers, as Jesus tells her on two separate occasions, how to think of herself as Jesus does: not as she "hath ben" but instead as she "wyl ben" (p. 59). What the reader needs to learn, as Margery does, is to think of herself as perfected in the future rather than limited by the present and the past.

Virgins and wives

Margery's struggle with female bodiliness is pivotal in developing this theory precisely because that condition seems to define her existence most pointedly. In the first of the two passages about future perfection, Margery is embarrassed by the fact that she is pregnant. Virgins were seen as spiritually superior to married women, and Margery tells Jesus she is "not worthy" to engage in intimate conversation with him (p. 59) because she continues to have marital relations with her husband. Jesus does not dismiss her concerns but instead assures her that it is his will that she should bear more children. Although this sounds like traditional, clerical advice to laywomen, Jesus goes on to complicate the definition that ties women's spiritual worth to their sexual identities. Rather than restating the traditional view, he reassures Margery with a paradox: Jesus tells her that virgins *are* worthier than other women *and also* that he loves Margery "as wel as any mayden in the world" (p. 59). This paradoxical statement is framed by Jesus' challenge to human definitions of divine love: "Ther may no man let me to lofe whom I wele and as mech as I wil" (p. 59). Jesus claims the right to love without regard to rules that define who is most lovable, even if those rules have divine authority behind them.

Margery and the *Book's* readers confront a logical problem: how can virgins be superior to wives such as Margery (the orthodox understanding) if at the same time Jesus tells pregnant Margery he loves her as well as a virgin? When Jesus explains that to love him "best" she needs to "have mende" of her "wykydnesse" and "thynk on" Jesus' "goodness," she can only respond by declaring her unworthiness all over again (p. 59). Unable to understand Jesus' reassurance about his love and stricken, it seems, by his attention to her "wickedness," Margery fails at first to see beyond her bodily condition. However, she is able, eventually, to think through the paradox. She can do this only after Jesus reframes his admonitions. When she repeats that she is "the most unworthy creatur that evyr thow schewedyst grace unto in erth," Jesus replies, "A, dowtyr ... fere the nowt, I take non hede what a man hath ben, but I take hede what he wyl ben" (p. 59). Margery's concentration on her present, physical condition is set aside in this way: if Jesus is able to look at Margery as perfected, then Margery must also relinquish the present version of herself in favor of an understanding of her identity as "future" Margery, that is, as the Margery she "will be."

Having "mind" of her wickedness is necessary just as shame is in the opening story: it keeps her from misunderstanding her sinful condition. But, like her earlier sense of shame, Margery's feelings of unworthiness are useful only if they are not obstacles to spiritual growth. Insofar as such emotions limit her ability to love God, they lose their effectiveness. Jesus' insistence on his love for Margery as uninflected by her past and present underscores the *Book's* sense that God attends to individuals in the conditions in which they find themselves. The reader who feels, like Margery, dismayed by her physical existence, is encouraged to look beyond such emotions in order to imagine herself from God's perspective. The reader's task is, then, to discover what it means to see herself as God does.

Bodily understandings are not the only ones that can limit spiritual growth. In the second revelation concerning future perfection, Margery has become "stuck" in her identity as a devout laywoman. This sequence begins with God the Father's decision that Margery should be "weddyd to my Godhede" (p. 91). Margery is unhappy about this because "al hir lofe and al hir affeccyon was set in the manhode of Crist" and she was "ful sor aferd of the Godhed" (p. 91). Margery, as a laywoman, feels most comfortable with affective devotion, that is, love for Jesus that is focused on his human nature. God does not allow her, however, to restrict her understanding to this aspect of divine love. Instead, a reluctant Margery is married to God the Father and comes to experience the "fyer of love" (p. 93) as a prelude to learning that God wants her to reject the limitations of lay religiosity. God encourages Margery to move beyond recommendations that she, as a laywoman, should perform outer devotions exclusively. Rather, he explains, she should embrace a life of inner *and* outer devotion. Although Margery does not live in a religious enclosure, he assures her that she can adapt the rules of contemplative practise to the situation in which she finds herself. In place of a cell, Margery has a bed, and God tells her to lie in it and think "in thi mende" (p. 94). Margery is to use what she knows as a mother, wife, and daughter to do this, and she should feel confident in her love because, as he reminds her, he takes "non hed" of what Margery has been but thinks of what she will be (p. 94).

Spiritual gifts

Just as fixed understandings of one's sinful nature, body, and position in life can hinder spiritual fulfillment, so too can feelings about divinely sent gifts. At the end of the first book, we learn that, especially in the early years of her visionary experience, "drede" of her "felyngys was the grettest scorge" Margery "had in erde" (p. 206). Like her fear of robbers, rapists, the weather, and disease, Margery's anxiety concerning her "feelings" is based on uncertainty about the future. Each of her spiritual gifts – her uncontrollable sobbing; waking visions and conversations with divine and biblical figures; visionary dreams; prophetic knowledge; and auditory signs – troubles Margery because she is unsure about its validity in predicting things to come.

Unable to feel secure until she "knew be experiens" whether her "feelings" were true or not (p. 206), Margery was plagued by doubt as she began to look for deeper spiritual understanding of her relationship with God. This was because, at least in part, those around her were concerned with this subject. Late medieval writers composed texts that explained ways in which the validity of revelatory experience might be determined, and these texts are relevant to Margery's experiences. In the *Book* she encounters a Carmelite friar who shows familiarity with writing about the "discernment of spirits." He assures her that she has not been "dysceyved be any illusions" (p. 52). Similarly, Julian of Norwich, in Margery's meeting with the anchoress, declares that Margery can be sure of her feelings because, as the writing on the discernment of spirits states, the things that God "put in hir sowle" were not "ageyn the worshep of God" and were to the "profyte of hir evyn christen" (p. 53). The *Book* portrays Margery as seeking out authorities to verify her religious experience, and critics have shown how important such validation was to the "authorization" of Margery Kempe's spiritual life.[13]

However, as important as this verification is to the *Book*, the unceasing search for evidence is shown to be spiritually crippling. In her interview with Margery, Julian of Norwich shows sensitivity toward Margery's insecurity, but she also emphasizes the importance of putting uncertainty aside. Drawing on the biblical Epistle of James (1:6–8), Julian compares the person who is "evyrmor dowtyng" with the "flood of the see" because both are "unstablyl and unstedfast" (p. 53). Just as the sea is borne about by the wind, the "dubbyl man," according to Julian, has his feelings tossed about and, despite God's "tokens," fails to "stedfastlych belevyn that the Holy Gost dwellyth in hys sowle" (p. 54).

Relying on the wrong kind of evidence pushes aside the importance of the lived moment in favor of final outcomes, and the *Book* presents a number of episodes in which people who choose to do so are clearly mistaken. One of the most striking involves the "gret lordys men" who "sworyn many gret othys" and who ask Margery if it is true that she can tell them whether they "schal be savyd er damnyd" (pp. 134–35). Margery's answer makes it clear that the men need to think about their question differently. She says, "Ya, forsothe can I" but then, rather than predicting their futures, tells them if they continue to swear oaths they will be damned and if they confess their sin and "levyn it [their sin] whil [they] may" they will be saved (p. 135). The men are disappointed with Margery's conflation of present practice and future fate and respond, "What, canst thu noon otherwise tellyn us but thus?" (p. 135).

Margery does, of course, prophesy. She predicted, for example, who Lynn's new prior would be (pp. 164–65) and she knows when the plague will come (p. 177). The *Book* states very clearly that when her predictions were confirmed it "strengthyd hir mech in the lofe of God" (p. 177), and her ability to foretell the future is represented as a sign of special favor that validates her revelatory experiences. Yet even as the *Book* presents Margery's prophetic gifts as examples of God's mercy, it diminishes the importance of the prediction in favor of what is learned in these situations.

Those people in the *Book* who want to know the future are shown to err in that desire. One of Margery's scribes, a priest, for example, presses her to prove herself, asking her "qwestyons and demawndys of thyngys that wer for to komyn" and yet, when she does prove herself, against her will, he nevertheless "wold not alwey gevyn credens to hir wordys" (p. 64). The *Book* follows this observation with a story about the priest's misguided notions about evidence. A young stranger visits the priest to ask for help. He tells the priest a jumbled story of his predicament, explaining that he had been about to take orders as a priest but, having to defend himself against attackers, he "smet a man or ellys tweyn" (p. 64). Despite the vagueness of the story (how could the young man not know if he'd killed one man or two?), the priest gave "credens to the yong mans wordys" because he was "an amyabyl persone, fayr feturyd, wel faveryd in cher and in cuntenawns" (pp. 64–65). Margery warns the priest that, despite his "ful fayr" appearance, the young man is not to be trusted. The priest learns his lesson only after lending him money that is never repaid.

The story validates Margery's authority, but it also calls into question the priest's reliance on appearances. In his eagerness to draw conclusions, he mistakes a handsome sociopath for an impoverished Christian. More than simple verification of Margery's prophetic abilities, the episode calls on the *Book's* readers to notice the connection between the priest's evidentiary demands and his inability to evaluate evidence. Perhaps even more to the point, it calls on readers to embrace the idea that although certain things are "hidden" from view, they can, nonetheless, be understood through the application of faith. God, as he himself reminds Margery, is a "hyd God" and because of this she should be "the mor besy" to search for him (p. 194). Instead of searching for evidence about the world's affairs, the attentive reader is encouraged to pay attention to "signs" of God's presence.

Experimentation

It is possible to argue that the *Book* teaches the reader to move from simple, outer devotional practices to more complex, contemplative engagement. "Future perfect Margery" would, then, be a Margery who concentrates on her inner experience and her relationship with this "hidden" God. There were, certainly, treatises such as Nicholas Love's *Mirror of the Blessed Life of Jesus Christ* that sought to teach lay readers how to adapt meditative principles to secular lives, and the *Book* shows obvious acquaintance with Love's work.[14] However, in contrast with Love's *Mirror*, which promotes visualization of and meditation on events from Jesus' life, Margery Kempe's *Book* eschews a single, consistent methodology. Barbara Newman observes that Margery "seems self-consciously to have experimented with every spiritual practice she encountered in every book she could persuade her clerical friends to read to her."[15] Scholars have noted the influence of a range of devotional writing on the *Book* including the works of Hilton, Rolle, and Bridget of Sweden. Yet what is perhaps most interesting about these influences is the fact that the *Book* makes no attempt to synthesize them.

Rather than teaching contemplation, it seems, Margery Kempe's *Book* offers enthusiastic endorsement of experimentation. It is only when Margery relinquishes her desire for fixed answers that she seems to be able to think of herself, at least in approximate terms, as she "will be." Trying out various "positions" in relation to God is shown, in the *Book*, to be the best way to experience God's mercy because it keeps the believer from assuming a constrictive, static, identity. It is perhaps for this reason that the model for many of Margery's experiences with the divine is conversation. Because conversation is fluid and malleable, it lets Margery express her fears without feeling trapped in them. As long as she remembers not to get tangled up in her own sense of herself, Margery can talk her way to God.

Conversation also, most importantly, allows the *Book's* readers to use Margery's experiences without making revelation the expected outcome of religious devotion. In the *Book*, different people experience God's mercy in different ways. Critics have tended to understand Margery's representation of her special gifts as another way in which she claims social and religious authority, yet we might as easily see it as an expression of individual particularity. Read this way, Margery's gifts are special and peculiar to Margery, but her exceptionality does not exclude or denigrate her *Book's* reader. Instead, the reader is reminded she has her own spiritual gifts. They are different from Margery's but are just as fully expressions of God's grace. The reader, like Margery, can converse with God, through her reading, through her prayers, and through her openness to unexpected religious experiences.

The significance of thinking of Margery Kempe's *Book* as a treatise is in what it tells us about medieval literary culture. Generic distinctions are often imprecise, and in some ways, whether we call this "autobiography" or "treatise" matters less than it might seem. What does matter is that these categories help us to understand the literature we study. Using the term "treatise" to describe Margery Kempe's *Book* lets us see the ways that the

Book's readers, scribes, and author thought about written texts as means by which people might change their lives. For the *Book's* readers as much as for the *Book's* subject, the "solas and comfort" that reading offered was less about knowledge of a particular individual life and much more about understanding that life in order to find one's way through difficult times.

NOTES

1 *The Book of Margery Kempe*, ed. Lynn Staley, TEAMS Middle English Texts (Kalamazoo: Medieval Institute Publications, 1996), p. 21. Subsequent citations are to this edition. Page numbers will be given in the text.
2 *A Treatise on the Astrolabe* in *The Riverside Chaucer*, pp. 661–84; *Lanfrank's Science of Cirurgie*, ed. R. V. Fleischhacker, EETS os 102 (1894, repr. 1988).
3 The prologue is printed in *Idea of the Vernacular: An Anthology of Middle English Literary Theory 1280–1520*, eds. Jocelyn Wogan-Browne, Nicholas Watson, Andrew Tayler and Ruth Evans (Exeter University Press, 1999), pp. 241–44.
4 *The Lay Folk's Mass Book*, ed. Thomas Frederick Simmons, EETS os 71 (1879, repr. 1968); the prologue to the *Pore Caityf* is printed in *Idea of the Vernacular*, pp. 239–41.
5 David Aers, *Community, Gender, and Individual Identity: English Writing 1360–1430* (London and New York: Routledge, 1988), pp. 73–80.
6 Clarissa W. Atkinson, *Mystic and Pilgrim: The Book and the World of Margery Kempe* (Ithaca, NY: Cornell University Press, 1983).
7 Karma Lochrie, *Margery Kempe and Translations of the Flesh* (Philadelphia: University of Pennsylvania Press, 1991), p. 226.
8 Ibid., p. 8.
9 Lynn Staley, *Margery Kempe's Dissenting Fictions* (University Park, PA: Pennsylvania State University Press, 1994).
10 Barbara Newman, "What Did It Mean to Say 'I Saw'? The Clash between Theory and Practice in Medieval Visionary Culture," *Speculum* 80 (2005), 33.
11 Ibid.
12 *Mirk's Festial: A Collection of Homilies*, ed. Theodor Erbe, EETS ES 96 (1905), pp. 90–91.
13 Rosalyn Voaden, *God's Words, Women's Voices: The Discernment of Spirits in the Writing of Late-Medieval Women Visionaries* (Suffolk, UK: York Medieval Press, 1999).
14 *Nicholas Love's Mirrour of the Blessed Lyf of Jesus Christ Oure Lord*, ed. Michael Sargent, Garland Medieval Texts 18 (New York: Garland, 1992).
15 Newman, "What Did It Mean," 32.

17

DAVID WALLACE

Sir Thomas Malory

Sir Thomas Malory's *Morte Darthur* evokes a Middle Ages of expiring time, a culture bequeathing one last literary testament as it fades from view. The sense of loss suggested by Malory's languorous prose, particularly that of his final *Tale*, resonates with many succeeding English generations. So too does the half-hope of Arthur's return from the dead, or from Avalon (p. 716), at the nation's hour of need; or that the imperial project of the *Morte*, achieved and then lost by the end of the text, might come again.[1] Readings of Malory also accompany the long-sustained and ultimately frustrated project of carrying English aristocratic rule to the world. This begins with the naming of Henry VII's first-born son as Arthur. It continues in 1522 as Henry VIII, assuming his dead brother's mantle, escorts Charles V, Emperor-elect of the Romans, to a London pageant starring "the ryght noble and victorious emprowr Kynge Arthur with a crowne imperiall"; Charles is then led to Winchester to see, in the Round Table portrait, Arthur repainted in Henry's image and likeness.[2] All this ends with the Somme and associated slaughters of the First World War: that massive loss of a chivalrically minded youth that, had they not stumbled into the age of barbed wire and machine guns, might have sustained English global *imperium* for a little while longer. Malory's *Morte* thus figures in England as a national epic with a dying fall: a text that might inspire even Milton to consider matters Arthurian before settling on the neo-biblical landscapes of *Paradise Lost*.[3] And yet, simultaneously, the *Morte* is romance: a text that, foreknowing its inevitable end, opens spaces for play and diversion; for time off the teleological clock. Like the *Canterbury Tales*, the *Morte* anticipates the heavy curtain of repentance and death, social disintegration and final judgment. Yet, like the *Tales*, it keeps *thought* at bay through pleasurable dilation; through the art most brilliantly exemplified by Chaucer's Wife of Bath, another teller of Arthurian tales, as "wandrynge by the weye."[4]

For most of its history, the experience of reading Malory proved unproblematic: versions varied, according to target audience, but they all derived from the editions of Caxton (1485) and Wynkyn de Worde (1498). But everything changed in 1934, with the discovery of the manuscript at Winchester. T. E. Lawrence, who had campaigned through Arabia with Malory in his saddlebags, hoped that he might edit Winchester: but that honor fell to Eugène Vinaver (first edition, 1947). Scholarship, it might be thought, would adjust fairly easily to these new circumstances: after all, a text surviving in one manuscript (written by two scribes) and in one first printed edition (surviving in two exemplars, one complete and one not) surely offers little scope for controversy. But not so: a volume of 420 pages called *The Malory Debate* sees nineteen critics arguing intensively over editorial practises and preferences.[5] *A Companion to Malory* (1996) frankly acknowledges the inconsistencies and possible confusions of its own citational practices: qualities that, we are told, are "at least a reflection of the general situation."[6] Today it is possible to read Malory in the tradition of Caxton through which he was long received, or in a modernized-spelling version of the same.[7] The manuscript, now generally locked away in a British Library vault, may be approached via paper or digitized facsimile,[8] or in one of the various editions deriving from it (offering various permutations of modernization, abbreviation, or original-spelling completeness). The standard work is currently Vinaver's three-volume third edition, revised by Field (1990). A fourth edition is on the way, but many critics refer chiefly to the second since it is the only complete text in original spelling in paperback; the 2004 Norton edition is changing things again.[9] The complexities now spun between Caxton and the Winchester manuscript, it is now realized, go back a long way: for although Winchester did not form the basis of Caxton's edition, it was actually in his printing shop at some point in the period 1480–83. Caxton worked on Malory with a strong editorial hand (he was "dangerously full of initiative," according to Vinaver).[10] But even here it is disputed whether certain changes to the text – as in the "Roman War" section – reflect Malory's own revisionism (in a version now lost) or Caxton's.

Not every reader of Malory need be detained long by such scholarly conundrums; the *Morte* is a text that loves and repays reading in any form. It is best engaged, in my opinion, through a full-length, original-spelling version that does not occlude the distinctive, and distinctively beautiful, rhythms of Malory's prose. However, this pause or stutterstep at the brink of reading – this question of *which* Malory to read – is more broadly instructive. In choosing the Winchester manuscript we are projected back towards the irrecoverable moment of the text's composing in time of civil war: a first writing that the knight-prisoner Malory half hoped might speed his deliverance. In choosing Caxton we join the long trajectory issuing from Malory's transformation into pleasure-giving commodity: a process that *happily* coincides with the coming of the Tudor dynasty and their Arthurian and nationalist enthusiasms. Remarkably, the standard one-volume edition of Malory – the one most widely read today, and the one followed here – miscegenates: for it places "Caxton's Preface" before Vinaver's edition of Winchester. But since the Winchester manuscript lacks its opening and closing sections, all editions must, to some extent, follow Caxton. Reading Malory in a form that no pre-twentieth-century reader would have recognized is less than perfect, but not all bad: for it tacitly recognizes the Grail-like irrecoverability of "Malory" and his or its cultural endurance as a mix of manuscript and print.

The historical Sir Thomas Malory remains a shadowy figure, or series of figures. George Lyman Kittredge was the first to make a substantial case for the *Morte's* author as Sir Thomas Malory of Newbold Revel, Warwickshire (1894–97); fleshing out this suggestion has been the life's work of P. J. C. Field.[11] The historical track record of this Malory includes charges of malicious wounding, false imprisonment, slander, attempted murder, extortion, cattle rustling, deer poaching, armed robbery, jail breaking, bail jumping, and rape (twice). Some critics struggle to reconcile such a rap sheet with a text so focused on "worship": they want their Malory to be more like the *Morte's* Launcelot and less like its Gawayn. Authorship issues are not definitively settled, and some of Field's assumptions have recently been roundly challenged by Anne F. Sutton.[12] Field assumes that Malory, charged with treason, would necessarily have been held as a state prisoner at the Tower of London (and hence borrowed books from these environs). Sutton has discovered a new document in a Mercer's Hall cartulary that places Malory definitively in Newgate on 20 April 1469, witnessing a deathbed declaration; he himself was buried in the Greyfriars, Newgate Street, on 14 March 1471. Newgate, London's most important jail (reserved for the worst offenders) was run by the city and its sheriffs. Paternoster Row, heart of the London book trade, lay very close by. Malory was thus perhaps being supplied with the eight major source texts that fed his *Morte* by London merchants who, as the writing progressed, took increasing interest in its commercial potential. (These texts are the English alliterative *Morte Arthur* and the stanzaic *Le Morte Arthur*; the French *Merlin* and its *Suite de Merlin* sequel; some version of the *Prose Launcelot* and the equally massive *Prose Tristan* (first two books); and the *Queste del Saint Graal* and *La Morte le Roi Artu.*) As a prisoner of Newgate, Malory must pay for his keep; his labor of writing might usefully have doubled as show of penance and source of income. Caxton's barking of a commercial product ("herein may be seen noble chyvalrye, curtosye, humanyté ... murder, hate, vertue, and synne") might thus prove truer to the merchant-aided genesis of the text than previously thought. And Caxton, who learned his printer's art abroad, may have grasped Arthur's selling potential more quickly than his insular-bound peers: for from Danzig to Cologne, Hanseatic merchants were keeping Arthur's cultic fortunes alive while in England, following something of a post-Chaucerian slump, they dwindled.[13] At Danzig, where Margery Kempe visited her mercantile in-laws in 1433, merchants met at Arthur's Court. In Cologne, assembled in the Hansesaal, they contemplated Arthur as one of the Nine Worthies (splendid sculptures, still there today). Caxton, who moved Cologne in 1471, celebrates and promotes Arthur as part of this illustrious group of "thre Paynyms, thre Jewes, and thre Crysten men" (p. xiii).

In adapting his manuscript Malory for the press, Caxton reconfigured the work as "xxi bookes, whyche conteyne the somme of v hondred and vii chapytres."[14] The Winchester manuscript was edited by Eugène Vinaver as a work in eight sections; five of these contain subsections and three do not.[15] Vinaver has himself shaped the experience of reading Malory for some sixty years: in many ways, he has proved as forceful and idiosyncratic an editor as Caxton.[16] Vinaver resists assuming that these sections or fragments add up to a single, unified work (hence his rather dogmatic title: *The Works of Sir Thomas Malory*). The passion with which many critics argued for Malory as a single, integral entity – frequently employing Malory's own phrase, "the hool book" – says much about critical fashions of the postwar period *and* about Malory as a cultural, indeed national, icon. While we might want to champion Vinaver as commendably *avant-gardiste* in resisting suspect organicism, formal or national wholeness, one cannot help but notice how he fiddles his footnotes to obscure or deny signs of Malory's forward planning. Of course, the longer one reads any literary sequence, the more it tends to settle in the mind as a single work: such is our experience of reading the ten Ellesmere-order Fragments we call *The Canterbury Tales.* But repeated readings of the *Morte* do firm up belief in its intelligent design *as a text*; this need not commit us to the Grail-like quest of discovering (a hermeneutic impossibility) *authorial intent.*

Carol Meale has argued that, from its own internal markings, the Winchester manuscript may be read as a work "of four major sections, the subject-matter of each of which corresponds with a particular phase in the Arthurian history."[17] Helen Cooper and Stephen H. A. Shepherd, in their recent editions, stick with the eight-division structure: but certain episodes that were once seen as free-standing, such as "The Fair Maid of Astolat" in the seventh section, are now subsumed into longer runs of narrative. Although Meale's challenge to read Malory with manuscript facsimile close by may prove beyond most readers, her implicit plea that *all* editorial interventions should be noted as such commands respect. Digitization will further appreciation of the distinctive qualities of the Winchester manuscript.[18] That said, it seems useful to shape discussion, in what follows, by observing the eight-section narrative order through which most readers encounter the *Morte*. The first of these, edited by Vinaver as *The Tale of King Arthur*, sees the slow and unsteady process of Arthur's coming to power. The frailty of Arthur's claims to be a *primus* without *pares* among fellow rulers of the British Isles is striking; so too the necessarily heavy and frequent interventions of kingmaker Merlin. Yet by the end of this *Tale*, Merlin – sole architect of Arthurian power – is gone, buried under a rock from which he can never emerge. His place is taken by Nynyve, Damsel or Lady of the Lake, a female apprentice who, brilliantly exemplifying deep-seated medieval masculine fears, sucks and seduces magical knowledge from Merlin, her would-be but never-quite lover. Nynyve too fades from the scene as the Arthurian court becomes an efficiently self-regulating center from which knights set forth, and to which those seeking redress or *aventure* may make recourse. Her retirement coincides with her meeting Pelleas, her dream knight, whose love and gratitude she secures through endearingly shameless manipulation.[19] Nynyve continues, however, to make cameo, magic-making appearances throughout the text and is last seen on the ship that carries away the dead or dying Arthur (p. 717). This immediately follows the climactic battle with Mordred, in which tens of thousands die and but one man, Bedyvere, survives. But Pelleas, we are told, has been kept out of danger by Nynveh, "and so he lyved unto the uttermuste of hys dayes with her in grete reste" (p. 717). Thus in a text that is doom-laden from the start, we find one man whose personal trajectory is thoroughly (in terms that Malory would understand) *happy*: what *happens* brings him joy and pleasure. The text thus acknowledges spaces outside its own determining structure (where happiness might be found) while neatly reprising moments from its own happier first section.

The earlier part of the *Morte's* opening section lays groundwork for what follows: Arthur, Herod-like, murders children who might be Mordred (p. 37); King Pellam, Keeper of the Grail Castle, is maimed (p. 54); Arthur acquires the Round Table through marriage to Gwenyvere (the former seeming more important than the latter, pp. 59–60). The later part, however, settles into routine adventure-seeking, featuring elegant deployment of two trios of knights: Arthur, Accolon, and Uryence; then Gawayn, Yvain, and Marhalt. Reputations are built and diminished: Gawayn behaves badly in coveting a fifteen-year-old damsel (when women of thirty and sixty are available); he then promptly loses her in a forest "of stronge aventures"

(p. 97). Such cheerful and frothy tales, beginning and ending at Camelot, suggest that Arthurian authority is by now sure of itself: the second section opens with Arthur holding "a ryal feeste and Table Rounde" (p. 113). This felicitous gathering is immediately challenged, however, by a greater power: Lucius, Emperor of Rome, has sent emissaries demanding "trewage" or tribute. The mood of the court darkens, and Malory changes source: the English alliterative *Morte Arthure*, rather than French romance, now serves his needs. Malory's *Morte* is a giant anaconda of a text: it is almost always possible to detect sources read and fed into its maw, although the alliterating English *Morte* is easiest to spot (as Arthur, incensed, elects to "ryde unto Rome with my royallyst knyghtes," p. 115). Malory's willingness to maintain the local color and texture of a source, rather than reducing it to stylistic homogeneity, makes him much less like Boccaccio, the great pioneer of Italian prose narrative, and more like Chaucer. Chaucer's heterogeneity of styles and forms was less to the taste of English Renaissance writers (who turned to Italy for models), and Malory's oft-alliterating second section gave Caxton pause: modern southern and London tastes, he seems to have thought, may not have appreciated too much the "rum, ram, ruf," which Chaucer's Parson, another "southren man" so memorably parodied.

Malory's turn to the alliterative *Morte* also marks his most dramatic break from *historial* precedent: for in Geoffrey of Monmouth's *History of the Kings of Britain*, in Wace, in Laȝamon's *Brut*, and in the alliterative *Morte* itself the Roman expedition comes at the very end of the text and is aborted once Mordred grabs power back home.[20] Malory, by contrast, allows Arthur fully to achieve his imperial destiny: like Charlemagne before him, he opts "comly be Crystmas to be crowned" (p. 145). This extraordinary episode speaks at once to past and future: for Arthur's ambition to be a global "conqueror" leading "knyghtes of mery Ingelonde" (p. 125: such language is rare elsewhere in the *Morte*) evokes both Tudor ambition and past English campaigns and crusades. When Arthur scornfully dismisses a warning not to ride too close to a besieged city, lightly armed, he resembles the crusading Richard I: "shal never harlot have happe... to kylle a croned kynge that with creyme is anointed" (p. 136); when he sends Gawayn and Florens "to forrey [forage in] that forestes" (p. 136) he recalls Edward III at Calais, or Henry V at Harfleur. Perhaps most chilling for future historical precedent, however, is Arthur's righteousness in facing impure enemies, corrupted through uncleanness and miscegenation (racial and religious). This is first seen in his battle with the cannibalistic giant of Mont St. Michel (whose "genytrottis" are duly cut or *swapped* "in sondir," p. 121). It is more overtly expressed in the climactic confrontation with imperial forces, which have corrupted themselves by incorporating Saracen troops. And therefore, Arthur argues, "kill doune clene ... for they that woll accompany them with Sarezens, the man that wolde save them were lytyll to prayse. And therefore sle doune and save nother hethyn nothir Crystyn" (p. 134). One hundred thousand imperial troops are duly massacred without chance of surrender, and Rome falls. This is grim, yet the retreat from Rome is frivolous: for one day, Arthur's knights ask him "to reles us to sporte with oure wyffis." Arthur agrees: "for inowghe is as good as a feste" (p. 146).

The next two sections are dedicated first to Launcelot du Lake, and then to Gareth of Orkney. Launcelot's arrival at court was announced at the beginning of the previous section (p. 113), and he begins accumulating *worship* (perhaps *the* key Malorian value) on the Roman campaign. This process continues in the subsequent tale, although the problematics of having the best knight in the world in your midst are also flushed out. Launcelot excites feminine desire, but will not marry: what's a girl to do? One "fayre damesell," having loved him fruitlessly for seven years, plans on killing him so she can make love to his embalmed corpse (p. 168). Launcelot does come to love someone other than Gwenyvere in this part of the *Morte*: he loves Gareth, the young protagonist of the next tale. Gareth is of Orkney, and hence of Gawayn's (and Arthur's) blood: yet he will only receive "the Ordre of Knyghthod" from Launcelot (p. 181). This cross-family bond directly challenges the natural order of blood-loyalty in the Arthurian world. It flourishes as something beautiful and rare; and yet, perhaps because of this, it becomes part of the final mechanism of disaster. *Sir Gareth* is one of the *Morte's* most delightful tales: for it sees a princeling, disguised as a kitchen boy, sent on *aventure* with a young noblewoman who is thoroughly contemptuous of his (apparent) lack of pedigree. "What doste thou here?" (she asks him, in some of the most magnificent trash-talking ever): "thou stynkyst al of the kychyn, thy clothis bene bawdy of the grece and tallow ... What art thou but a luske [sluggard], and a turner of brochis [spit-turner], and a ladyll-washer?" (p. 182). The damsel, Lyonet, greets every victory and feat of arms achieved by kitchen-boy Gareth as an *unhappy* event: "for he is an unhappy knave, and unhappyly he hath done this day thorow myssehappe" (p. 184). What *happens*, in Lyonet's logic, should follow a class-based, God-given order; a greasy spit-turner's triumph over pedigreed knighthood cannot be *happy*. In fact, in Malory's world, it is impossible: no knight ever falls to a peasant. And yet Gareth *does* ultimately prove to be *unhappy*, in our diminished, modern sense of the word: for he is accidentally killed as Launcelot rushes in to rescue Gwenyvere from the stake (p. 684). This early pair of tales, then, forges bonds of cross-familial love between men that spell, ultimately, disaster. "As for Gareth," Launcelot says, "I loved no kynnesman I had more than I loved hym" (p. 695). Yet

Gareth's kinsmen, Launcelot well knows, will never forgive even an accidental killing: "I knew well that I shulde nevir aftir have youre love, my lord sir Gawayne, but everlastynge warre bitwyxt us" (p. 696).

Sir Tristram de Lyones, the fifth section of Malory's *Morte*, takes up some 40 per cent of the text; like the middle of *Piers Plowman*, it is more often skipped than read. This is a pity, since it contains illuminating parallels and counterpoints to the main narrative line: Mark and Arthur as cuckolded kings, doomed to rely on the cuckolder as chief prop and ornament of their state; Tristram and Launcelot as lovers running mad; Isode and Gwenyvere. Malory seems most often a romancer, most often creatively *dilatory*, in his *Tristram*. The most commonplace clashes of knights see him forever straining for literary variation, and he forever finds arresting or alarming turns of phrase: "I had levir [rather] kut away my hangers," says Alexander the Orphan (on learning that Morgan le Fay has him marked as a toyboy), "than I wolde do her ony such pleasure!" (p. 395). And threading through this vast narrative expanse we find one of Malory's most congenial knights, "Palomydes the Paynym." Palomydes endlessly pursues his "questynge beste" (pp. 362, 510), hopelessly competes with Tristram for the love of Isode, and precariously plays a great game of spiritual chicken: for he has sworn to defer baptism until he has "done seven trewe bataylis for Jesus sake" (p. 408). Although Palomydes is Saracen, he differs little (not at all) from the text's Christian protagonists; in Malory's world, an English peasant (such as the one casually killed by Launcelot's backhand slap, p. 654) is essentially more alien than a pagan, foreign-born knight. Palomydes delays christening until the very end of the *Tristram*; it is celebrated at the same feast that sees Galahad arriving at Camelot and the first stirrings of the Grail quest (p. 510). The Saracen convert thus easily integrates into Arthurian court structure: yet he plays no part in the *Morte's* next tale, the *Sankgreal*. Neither do women of the Arthurian court, although "laydis that loved knyghtes *wolde* have gon with hir lovis" (p. 523). The only female participant allowed on the Grail quest is Percivale's sister who, as a virgin of royal blood, bleeds to death in a good cause (p. 592). Such insistence on ritual and gendered purity, emphasized throughout the *Sankgreal* section, fuels the apotheosis of Galahad, the one pure knight. This paragon is sired by Launcelot, who, thinking to commit adultery with a queen, fornicates with a virgin (p. 480). Galahad's conception is thus as suspect as Arthur's (p. 5); these are ironies that Malory does not confront.

The Grail quest is initiated as a mass exit from the Arthurian court by Gawayn; by now he is one of its least worshipful representatives. Arthur loudly laments "the departicion of thys felyship," intuiting that it spells or prefigures the destruction of his "Table Round" (p. 522). Arthur is right, and it will be Gawayn, again, who triggers that process. Ironically, Gawayn is the first knight to give up on the Grail quest: asked to repent of his sins, he refuses on the basis that, for "we knyghtes adventures," chivalry happens (p. 535). Launcelot persists, and gets more glimpses of the Grail mystery than his sorry flesh deserves; his sanctified son, Galahad, goes all the way and is taken up into heaven (p. 607). It used to be posited that French *Queste del Sainte Graal*, Malory's immediate source, adapts chivalric texts to religious, and specifically monastic, ends; that it plays like Christian rock music. This argument might be flipped around: the *Graal* romance is borrowing trappings and bric-à-brac of religion (the Grail legend is very untidy) to forge a "messianic chivalry," "un évangile de classe."[21] The terrifying potential of this realizes itself as Malory's Grail knights, having reached a castle on the borders of Scotland, massacre the inhabitants. At first unnerved by what they have done, the knights are soon assured that these are incestuous and un-Christian people: "oure Lorde ys nat displesed with youre dedis" (p. 588). Northumbria might be classified as "the marchys of Scotlonde" (p. 587); Sir Thomas Malory actually headed for this region in October 1462 as part of a military expedition against Lancastrian castles.

The Grail, once achieved, seems soon forgotten; within one hundred words of the *Morte's* next section, Launcelot "began to resorte unto quene Gwenivere agayne" (p. 611); they soon love "more hotter" than ever, taking "many ... prevy draughtis togydir" (p. 611). This whole seventh section is dedicated to Launcelot: Malory, Pygmalion-like, falls increasingly under the spell of his own best-loved creation. The gender trouble of Launcelot's charismatic allure is most eloquently explored in the episode known as "The Fair Maid of Astolat." A brother and sister fall in love with Launcelot: what are their options? The brother, Lavayne, sees absolute parity between his dilemma and that of his sister: "she doth as I do," he tells his father, "for sythen I saw first my lord sir Launcelot I cowde never depart frome hym, nother nought I woll, and [if] I may follow hym" (p. 639). Lavayne *is* able to follow Launcelot, as a knight; his deepest desire is thus satisfied. His sister, named "Elayne le Blanke" (p. 623) but generically referred to as "the fayre mayden," has no such option: since Launcelot refuses to accept her either as wife or paramour (p. 638) she has no place in the world, and must die. Her father confessor, at her deathbed, "bade hir leve such thoughtes," but she will not:

> Why sholde I leve such thoughtes? Am I nat an erthely woman? And all the whyle the brethe ys in my body I may complayne me, for my belyve ys that I do none offence, thou[gh] I love an erthely man, unto God, for He fourmed me thereto, and all maner of good love comyth of God. (p. 639)

This magnificent speech questions, theologically, the grounding logic of courtly love. An answer comes, a little later in the text, from the heart of this ideology. It speaks of free will: "I love nat to be constrained to love," Launcelot says, "for love muste only aryse of the harte self, and nat by none constraynte" (p. 641); his heart inclines him to continue loving Gwenyvere, not Elayne or any other woman. Evidence is soon found of Gwenyvere's adultery: she has insisted on sleeping with ten wounded knights in her room (to take better care of them); her sheets are found to be bloody (p. 658). Knowing the blood to be his (he cut himself in ripping out an iron-barred window, p. 657), Launcelot truthfully defends Gwenyvere from the charge that "one of the wounded knyghtes lay wyth her" (p. 659). Through meticulous attention to specifics and verbal detail, adulterous Launcelot honestly defends an adulterous queen. Here he seems like a modern champion of justice (an attorney, *tourneying* with language); more often, however, he favors judicial combat (in which God will side with the knight in the right). Problems arise, however, if one knight can never lose; and Launcelot is routinely acknowledged as *the best knight of the world*. This appellation is underscored in the very last part of this section: for only "the beste knight of the worlde" (p. 664) can heal the incurable wounds of Sir Urry; Launcelot is again that knight (p. 668). This last episode has no known source: Malory apparently invented it to signal the full rehabilitation of Launcelot following his relative failure in the Grail quest. Malory's partiality to Launcelot thus compounds the enabling contradictions and specious wordplay that uphold his Arthurian society.

The speed and inexorability of the eighth and final section's unraveling confirms the thought that the end *might have come* much earlier: at any point, really, since the start. All will be well so long as Mordred is kept in check and word of Gwenyvere's adultery remains unspoken. Once spoken, however, that word cannot be retrieved; destruction surely follows. Arthur, we are told, "had a demyng" of Gwenyvere's infidelity, "but he wolde nat here [hear] thereof" (p. 674). Arthur needs Gwenyvere to keep Launcelot sweet and thus tied closely to the Arthurian state: "What aylith you," he asks her at the beginning of the seventh section, "that ye can nat kepe sir Launcelot upon youre side? For... who that hath sir Launcelot uppon his party hath the moste man of worship in thys worlde" (p. 615). But already Aggravayne, Gawayn's brother, is talking of the affair, "for he was ever opynne-mowthed" (p. 611); at the beginning of the final section he speaks "in kynge Arthurs chambir" (p. 673), the public domain, and *now* all is lost. Actually, the text tricks us here: for when Aggravayne first speaks "in kynge Arthurs chambir," we assume Arthur to be present. But he is not: Aggravayne first speaks to Mordred and the Orkney affinity; Arthur shows up half a page later, and Aggravayne speaks again. "*Now* is thys realme holy destroyed and myscheved," say Gawayn and Gareth, "and the noble felyshyp of the Rounde Table shall be disparbeled" (p. 674). Recurrences of *now* in the concluding section of the *Morte* play like timechecks on a doomsday machine: "alas!," exclaims Gwenyvere, as she and Launcelot are taken in adultery, "now are we myscheved both" (p. 676); "alas!" exclaims Gawayn, on learning that Gareth is slain by Launcelot, "now ys my joy gone!" (p. 686). Temporality presses harder as Arthurian society approaches zero hour (that will see "an hondred thousand leyde dede uppon the erthe," p. 713, before Arthur and Mordred kill one another). Malory compiles five independent *aventures* or episodes in his penultimate section; his last, while again comprising five episodes, develops continuous narrative momentum. So if section vii, "The Book of Sir Launcelot and Queen Guinivere," seems like an anthology of short stories, section viii rather resembles a novel. In this final, novel-like sequence of the *Morte*, speeches grow longer and drive narrative action; character analyses are performed to predict future behaviors; social signs (such as the departure of the cooks, p. 675) are assiduously read. And yet all this avails nothing: it seems cruelly ironic that such well-marked temporality, such intelligent analyses of individual traits, flowers most intensively as time runs out.

There *is* life after Arthur in the *Morte Darthur*: that of Launcelot and Gwenyvere. With an optimism that seems ebullient in the circumstances, Launcelot imagines carrying Gwenyvere off to start a new life in Benwick ("my owne royame," p. 721). But on finding her "desposed" to religion, he (always a competitor) takes up religion too and eventually priesthood (p. 722). Gwenyvere clearly fears for her eternal destiny: "I am sette in suche a plight to gete my soul hele" (p. 720), she says, and dies praying that she "may never have power to see syr Launcelot with my worldly eyen" (p. 722). Praying *not* to see someone entails, inevitably, imagining of them; Launcelot's visage threatens to obliterate, for Gwenyvere, the face of God. Launcelot, by contrast, rides to heaven in style: for as he dies the Archbishop of Canterbury, no less, sees the pearly gates swing wide as angels bear him aloft (p. 724). This is not, however, the last word on Launcelot: for his brother Ector – still equipped with shield, sword, and helmet – then arrives to lament him as a knight. Ector has missed the seven years spent by Launcelot and his companions in religious life: a time that seemed to spell the end of *chevalerie,* as "their horses wente where they wolde" (p. 722). In this last acclamation, however, Launcelot is imagined back into the saddle, sword in hand, thinking of love and women: "And thou were the truest frende to thy lovar that ever bestrade hors," brother Ector says, "and thou were the truest lover, of a sinful man, that ever loved woman, and thou were the kindest man that ever strake with swerde" (p. 725). William Empson has written of a "half-secret rival" to Christianity in Western civilization, "centering perhaps (if you made it a system) [a]round honour: one that stresses pride rather than humility, self-realization rather than self-denial, caste rather than either the communion of saints or the individual soul."[22] Empson's remark seems tailor-made for the *Morte*, this great prose epic straining towards novelistic form that ends with alternative visions, saintly and knightly, of its one true protagonist. Such visions do not merge or harmonize: they are set out sequentially by the greatest surviving authorities of, respectively, religion and blood. Such contradictoriness maps the space of the *Morte* and bespeaks its author's condition. Jailed in time of civil war, and dogged by thoughts of the religious judgment he must soon face, Malory yet succumbs to the fabulous allure of an English knightly world that, in beguiling prose, he brings to life.

NOTES

1 Sir Thomas Malory, *Complete Works*, ed. Eugène Vinaver, second edn (Oxford University Press, 1971), p. 716. All citations are to this edition. Page numbers will be given in the text.

2 See Martin Biddle, "The Painting of the Table," in Martin Biddle and Sally Badham, eds., *King Arthur's Round Table: An Archaeological Investigation* (Woodbridge: The Boydell Press, 2000), p. 427.

3 On Milton's youthful engagement with "Arthur, who carried war even into fairyland," see Roberta Florence Brinkley, *Arthurian Legend in the Seventeenth Century* (London: Frank Cass, 1967), p. 127 (the citation is from Milton's *To Manso*).

4 *General Prologue*, in *Riverside*, 1.467. Middle English and Middle Scots *thought*, especially in its adjectival form *thoughty*, can suggest anxiety and malaise: see *MED*, *thought*, 5(a).

5 Bonnie Wheeler, Robert L. Kindrick, and Michael N. Salda, eds., *The Malory Debate: Essays on the Texts of Le Morte Darthur* (Cambridge: D. S. Brewer, 2000).

6 Elizabeth Archibald and A. S. G. Edwards, eds., *A Companion to Malory* (Cambridge: D. S. Brewer, 1996), p. xii.

7 See *Caxton's Malory*, ed. James W. Spisak (Berkeley: University of California Press, 1983), 2 vols., an edition based on the copy of Caxton in the Pierpont Morgan Library, New York; and for a facsimile of this copy see *Sir Thomas Malory: Le Morte D'Arthur, Printed by William Caxton*, intr. Paul Needham (London: Scolar Press, 1976). For a complete modernized version based on Caxton, see *Le Morte D'arthur*, ed. Janet Cowan, intr. John Lawlor, 2 vols. (Harmondsworth: Penguin, 1969).

8 See *The Winchester Malory: A Facsimile*, intr. N. R. Kerr, EETS ss 4 (1976).

9 See *The Works of Sir Thomas Malory*, ed. Eugène Vinaver, rev. P. J. C. Field, third edn, 3 vols. (Oxford: Clarendon Press, 1990); Sir Thomas Malory, *Le Morte Darthur, or The Hoole Book of Kyng Arthur and of His Noble*

Knyghtes of the Rounde Table, ed. Stephen H. A. Shepherd (New York: Norton, 2004). The best (slightly) abridged and modernized version is *Le Morte Darthur – the Winchester Manuscript*, ed. Helen Cooper (Oxford University Press, 1998).

10 *Malory's Morte Darthur in the Light of a Recent Discovery* (Manchester University Press and the John Rylands Library, 1935), p. 2.

11 See *Morte Darthur*, ed. Shepherd, p. xxxiii; P. J. C. Field, *The Life and Times of Sir Thomas Malory* (Cambridge: D. S. Brewer, 1993); P. J. C. Field, "The Malory Life-Records," in *Companion to Malory*, pp. 115–30.

12 "Malory in Newgate: A New Document," *The Library*, seventh series, 1.3 (September 2000), 243–62.

13 See David Wallace, "Margery in Dansk," William Matthews Memorial Lecture, Birkbeck, University of London, 19 May 2005; available as an occasional publication. It is worth noting that Chaucer's only narrator of an Arthurian tale, the Wife of Bath, forms part of this international mercantile nexus.

14 "Caxton's Prologue," in *Caxton's Malory*, p. 4.

15 The massive *Sir Tristram* announces a division into two Books at a place in the text where division is unhelpful. This represents Malory's carrying over of a moment in his French source text where the scribe (it has been very plausible argued) comes to the second *volume* of his own source material: see *Complete Works*, second edn, ed. Vinaver, p. 343 (where none of this is explained); *Works*, third edition, ed. Vinaver, revised Field, III, 1478–80 (where it is); *Le Morte Darthur*, ed. Shepherd, pp. 228, 337.

16 "Vinaver's aim," Helen Cooper writes, "was to get as close to what he believed Malory wrote, or should have written"; to this end, he "occasionally misrepresented both the sentence division and the larger text divisions and layout of the manuscript" (*Morte Darthur*, ed. Cooper, p. xxiii; see further, and to more devastating effect, Cooper, "Opening up the Malory Manuscript," in *Malory Debate*, ed. Wheeler *et al.*, pp. 255–84).

17 Meale, "Hoole Book," p. 13.

18 These include the writing of all personal names, some place names and the word *Sankgreal* in non-current script and red ink: a tricky task for scribes, who were thus required to change pens with great frequency. See *The Winchester Malory: A Facsimile*, ed. Kerr, p. xiv; and see the variation of typefaces in Shepherd's new edition.

19 See especially p. 104: "'Thanke me therefore', seyde the Lady of the Lake."

20 The alliterative *Morte* sees Gwenyvere, abducted by Mordred, "wrought … with child"; *King Arthur's Death: The Middle English Stanzaic Morte Arthur and Alliterative Morte Arthure,* ed. Larry D. Benson (Exeter University Press, 1986), p. 216, line 3552. This poem survives in only one manuscript (not the exemplar used by Malory): see Benson, ed., p. xii.

21 These citations from Jean Frappier and Emmanuèle Baumgartner ("a class gospel") form part of Jill Mann's excellent article "Malory and the Grail Legend," in *Companion to Malory*, p. 208.

22 Cited in Alan Bennett, *Untold Stories* (London: Faber and Faber, 2005), p. 171.

18

SALLY MAPSTONE

Robert Henryson

Background

Robert Henryson lived between *c.* 1440 and the opening years of the sixteenth century. William Dunbar's poem "I that in heill was," composed by 1506, states that death "In Dunfermlyne ... has done rovne / With maister Robert Henrisoun" (81–82).[1] Dunbar's description of Henryson as "maister" is echoed in designations given to him on the title-pages of sixteenth-century printed editions of his *Fables* and *Testament of Cresseid.* Three charters of the late 1470s from Dunfermline Abbey are also witnessed by a "magister" Robert Henryson, and it is likely that they refer to the poet. The title "Maister" indicates that Henryson was university educated; this may have been at Glasgow, where there is documentary evidence of a Robert Henryson being admitted as a licentiate in arts and a bachelor in decreets (canon law) in 1462. But Henryson may alternatively or additionally have taken a degree on the continent, like so many Scots of his day.

The title-pages of the prints also describe Henryson as schoolmaster in Dunfermline. The grammar school in Dunfermline was linked to its Benedictine abbey, and a schoolmaster there would have had considerable social standing. The charters that name Robert Henryson also refer to him as a notary public. Notaries had authority to make legal deeds and instruments. Depending on their authorization, they could act as recorders at civil or ecclesiastical courts, and many notaries were also clerics, though there is no evidence that Henryson took this route. The precision of the legal references in Henryson's poetry speaks to a close acquaintance with the workings of the law. There is some later evidence for individuals combining the role of schoolmaster and notary public in Scotland.

The abbot of Dunfermline Abbey from 1444 to 1468 was Richard Bothwell, an influential figure in governmental circles during the reigns of kings James II and James III, and a man of considerable culture. Bothwell commissioned an important chronicle of the history of Scotland, the

Liber Pluscardensis. This Latin work contains two vernacular poems, one of which, "De Regimine Principum," provides an early parallel for Henryson's poetic practice in the exact referentiality of its legal allusions. Under Abbot Bothwell Dunfermline Abbey was also a base for the copying of manuscripts, including *Regiam Majestatem*, the major medieval compilation of Scottish laws. Such things suggest that Henryson would have had a responsive audience for his poetry among people associated with the abbey.

Henryson's poetry arises out of a creative fusion of Scottish, English, and European influences. As his *Testament of Cresseid* and his fable of "The Cock and the Fox" show, Henryson found much to respond to in Chaucer, especially in *Troilus and Criseyde* and the *Canterbury Tales*. Latin works were influential upon his writing, including the elegiac Romulus fable collection, which is a key source for the *Fables*, and Nicholas Trivet's commentary on Boethius's *Consolation of Philosophy*, which is the source for the *moralitas* to *Orpheus and Eurydice*. The *Fables* reveal equally Henryson's confident familiarity with French literature, such as the *Roman de Renart* cycles. It has been argued that he was acquainted with works in the tradition of Italian humanism, but this has not been proven. More recently, and more persuasively, it has been suggested that he may have had access to a Dutch version, printed in 1485, of one of the most popular of the early printed fable collections, originally published in a bilingual Latin and German edition by Heinrich Steinhöwel in 1476.[2]

Evidence indeed favors the 1470s–early 1490s as the principal period of Henryson's literary career. Nonetheless it is not possible to plot with certainty the chronology of his three great poems. *Orpheus and Eurydice*, in particular, has suffered from a pervasive critical assumption that it is an early work by a poet quite yet to hit his stride in the combination of tale and *moralitas*. It is possible, alternatively, to view this poem as an ambitious attempt to challenge the reader's sense of the relation between narrative and moral perspective, and to do so through the focus on one major protagonist. *Orpheus and Eurydice* has in these respects things to link it to both the *Fables* and the *Testament*, and it could equally well have been written after either of them.[3]

Henryson was writing mainly during the reign of King James III (1460–88), the fifth king in the Stewart dynasty initiated in 1371 by Robert II. James III was an assertive ruler, who by the end of his reign had made himself sufficiently unpopular to become the focus of a magnate rebellion, in which, to use the parlance of the first parliament after his death, he "happinnit to be slane" off the field of battle. But Scottish politics were nonetheless far less factionally chaotic and dynastically divisive than affairs south of the border, in England. The person installed to succeed James III was none other than his fifteen-year-old son.

Moreover the political problems that surfaced in James III's reign were not confined to that monarchy. The aggressive kingship that characterized the reigns of James I, II, III, and IV, was fueled by the fact that all of these kings inherited their thrones as minors and had later to assert themselves in order to establish royal superiority. Such expressions of royal power in fact could be advantageous to the country: all of the Jameses occupied themselves, particularly in the early years of their mature reigns, with improving the functioning of the judicial system. James I and James IV were keen on "justice ayres" – periods when the king himself moved round the country, accompanying the holding of the "head-courts" in regional centers. But kingly power, if exercised without discrimination, could also be disruptive to the well-being of the realm; and all of Scotland's fifteenth-century rulers showed at intervals propensities to a self-interested exercise of power which adversely affected their subjects.

This political and ideological context informs Henryson's poetry, but not in veiled allusions to contemporary political events. Rather, justice and judgment are key concerns throughout his writing, and partake in the creation of a distinctively moral hermeneutic. Legal issues interest him, but the concept of equitable justice is at the heart of his way of seeing, as is the idea of judgment, the exercise of discrimination and interpretation. Henryson's poetry directly engages the reader in the formation of the reading experience, and in the interpretive act of reading correctly as a poem unfolds. And all of his major poems involve their protagonists in acts of judgment – especially of the interpretation of their own behavior. At the heart of the *Fables* is an advice to princes fable in which the lion-king is invited to review his own judgmental and judicial decisions. In *Orpheus and Eurydice* Orpheus is brought twice to reconsider his amatory situation – but his judgments within the tale are not enough, and the poem supplies a *moralitas* in which the reader can look yet again at the story. In the *Testament of Cresseid* the judgments of the narrator, the planetary gods, and Troilus are juxtaposed with Cresseid's successive re-readings of herself. The formal complaints that the lion-king, Orpheus, and Cresseid all deliver are used by Henryson to signify stages of incomplete self-knowledge as these figures strive to conceptualize their experience; of all of them, it is Cresseid who gets furthest beyond the complaint mode.

Henryson examines the status of literary truth itself closely, asking in the *Testament*: "Quha wait gif all that Chauceir wrait was trew?" (64) His interest in the interpretive ambiguities of the written word might seem at odds with the factual precision required of the notary. Yet that interest also shows the essential need that interpretation be well informed. Thus, Henryson's legal training expresses itself not just in the depth of the legal detail apparent in fables like "The Sheep and the Dog" and "The Wolf and the Lamb," but also in deeper interpretive postures behind all his works. Similarly, Henryson's transmission of his pedagogic role as schoolmaster into his poetry is a sophisticated one. His instructive and didactic voice is well apparent, most insistently in the moralities to the *Fables*, which demand to be taken seriously. But that voice can also be a fallible, misleading, or unsuccessful one. It is fallible in the case of the narrator of the *Testament*, whose concluding moralization of the poem can hardly be taken as Henryson's own opinion. It is misleading, in the case of the pedagogic toad, in the final fable of the *Fables*, who deliberately adopts a schoolmasterly style in order to dupe the mouse. It is unsuccessful in the case of the swallow in the "Preaching of the Swallow," whose moral instruction is unheeded by the other birds. And Aesop himself, in the dream-vision prologue to "The Lion and the Mouse," memorably draws a parallel between fable-telling and preaching which casts doubt on the value of such instructive enterprises: "... quhat is it worth to tell ane fenȝeit taill, / Quhen haly preiching may na thing auaill?" (1389–90) In other words, the presence of educative material in Henryson's writing is another complex part of its interpretive working. For Henryson, right moral reading is closely connected to the idea of correct moral practice; as he sees it, reading should be a consciously moral act.

The Fables

The most complete textual witnesses of Henryson's *Fables* are two of their latest ones, printed in Edinburgh in 1570 and 1571, by Robert Lekprevick (for Henry Charteris) and Thomas Bassandyne. Despite the lateness of their date, these prints preserve the corpus more completely than earlier manuscript copies and in an order that is commonly (if not universally) accepted as representing a conception that can only be Henryson's.[4] This order can be connected both to the unfolding of the collection's meaning and to Henryson's selection of source materials. The prologue and seven of the fables (1–2, 6–9, and 12–13) are derived from the elegiac Romulus. The other six (3–5, 9–11) come either from other fable collections or nonfabular sources, such as the Reynardian tradition. Henryson thus tops and tails his collection by material based on the elegiac Romulus, which also provides the source for the three middle fables in the collection ("The Sheep and the Dog," "The Lion and the Mouse," and "The Preaching of the Swallow"). Set into each half of the corpus, at symmetrical points, is a run of three fables, from different sources, and dealing primarily with fox and wolf protagonists.

Readers might not be readily aware of this disposition of source material. But its effects are such as to suggest that Henryson set out to produce a particular kind of reading experience, which is highly dependent on arrangement. There is a striking difference in kind between the character of fables where the elegiac Romulus tradition dominates and those where other sources are used. Trickery and a rough humor are more characteristic in many of the fox and wolf fables, and those involving these protagonists often have a more marked narrative dynamic. The reader is drawn into the action of these pacey tales, with their lively dialogue and sharp narrative reversals. The tales invite identification with rascally protagonists, and then interrogate the implications of that in their moralities, which include some of the most unexpected ones in the collection. Thus in "The Trial of the Fox," the reader is determinedly taken back to the scene of blackest comedy in the tale, when the contumacious mare kicks the wolf in the head; the humor of that moment is challenged as a surprisingly moral re-reading of it is set out. The moralities can be unexpected in other ways, as when the vicious wolf of the tale of "The Wolf and the Wether" is largely ignored in the *moralitas*, which concentrates instead on the pretensions of the wether. There is no one interpretive template for reading Henryson's *Fables*, and this is part of their morally hermeneutic message.

At the center of the corpus is the fable of "The Lion and the Mouse." The narrative of this fable (that is the tale, rather than its prologue or *moralitas*) forms the middle 24 stanzas of a total of 424 for the whole collection, giving exactly 200 stanzas before it and 200 after it. That this fable has a vital centrality is also signified by its prologue, its use of dream vision, and its narration by Aesop himself. The fable that comes next, "The Preaching of the Swallow," has several elements in common with "The Lion and the Mouse," suggesting that it, also, is of a heightened status. It has a kind of prologue, a prominent narrator and it foregrounds the themes of justice and prudence. The key moral message of "The Lion and the Mouse" comes not in its *moralitas* but in a statement to the lion by the mouse in the tale itself. As the importance of this fable is signaled by its presence at the center of the corpus, so the significance of this pronouncement is indicated by its position as the central stanza of the fable, with twenty-one stanzas on either side:

> In euerie iuge mercy and reuth suld be
> As assessouris and collaterall;
> Without mercie, iustice is crueltie,
> As said is in the law is spirituall.

Quhen rigour sittis in the tribunall,
The equitie off law quha may sustene?
Richt few or nane, but mercie gang betwene.

(1468–74)

Within this single stanza mercy is presented as being inseparable from compassion, justice, and equity – the necessary emotion for judging; the actuality of judgment, and the supreme principal behind it. For a while, for obvious reasons, mercy is at the forefront of the mouse's argument, it is "The equitie off law" that is the resounding climactic phrase.

Equity was a fundamental principle in the training in Roman civil and canon law which Henryson had received. One of his contemporaries, John Ireland, defines it thus: "justice suld stand in werray richt and ressoun, and in werray equite and nocht in wourdis. And oft tymes necessite is, for werray richt to lefe the wourdis of the law, and folow the richt and gud entencioune of the lord and makare of the law."[5] Equity placed importance on the intention or spirit, rather than the letter, of the law. "Wourdis," as Ireland says, are not enough, and Henryson, too, strikingly often uses the plural noun in the context of the capacity of language to deceive (e.g. *Fables*, 315, 601, 2913). Attentive as he is to precision in the use of language, he regards the way in which language is interpreted as equally vital. The equitable judgment assesses the case on its own terms as well as against a template. These premises transfer well to the reading experience Henryson devises, where the fables inculcate morality by making the reader interrogate his own moral response to what he reads, and often do so by setting up narrative situations in which crucial acts of interpretation require to be made.

Thus, the mouse's plea in "The Lion and the Mouse" must be seen as a request for a humane appraisal of the individual details of her case. While her advisory remarks are hardly disinterested, given her perilous situation, Henryson requires his readers to read equitably, to distinguish the value of the mouse's arguments from the compromised nature of her situation. And this is the more significant, given that the nature of the figure who should symbolize equitable judgment in the fable is severely interrogated. The lion's initial response to the mouse seems authoritarian, even tyrannical, an angry, impulsive, absolute sentence of death. But her speech returns him to the recognizable responses of good kingly judgment:

Quhen this wes said, the lyoun his language
Paissit, and thocht according to ressoun,
And gart mercie his cruell ire asswage,
And to the mous grantit remissioun ... (1502–06)

This seems ideal. However, almost as soon as the mouse has gone the lion becomes again the "cruell lyoun" (1515), slaying "baith tayme and wyld, as he wes wont" (1512). When he is caught by the people his lament suggests that he has learnt little permanently from the mouse's advisory speech. With a self-centered absolutism consistent with his earlier behavior, the lion expects no succor from others. As soon as the mice release the lion he departs on his way. There is little to suggest that the experience of imprisonment has equipped him with the self-knowledge and respect of others to make him a permanently reformed king.

The *moralitas* to this fable offers a loose political reading of the reciprocal relation of kings and their subjects, which "lordis of prudence" (1594) are urged to take on board. Henryson signals his awareness that this fable speaks to a recurrent political flaw in kingship, and undoubtedly in Scottish kingship. But he is also using it to signal the contingent nature of interpretive situations, how difficult it can be to transfer a moral outlook from one circumstance to another. That is reinforced by the opening of "The Preaching of the Swallow," which emphasizes the supremely prudent viewpoint of God, at once perfect in its comprehension and inaccessible to mankind:

> The hie prudence and wirking meruelous,
> The profound wit off God omnipotent,
> Is sa perfyte and sa ingenious,
> Excellent far all mannis iugement; (1622–55)

This does not mean, however, that man should not strive to achieve his own prudent understanding. On the contrary, the swallow argues that the "inwart argument" (1757) of prudence enables man to negotiate his way in a perilous world. Yet the other birds fail to hear the swallow's counsel. Indeed, they pay even less attention to the counsel offered than did the lion. In its emphasis upon prudence and self-knowledge "The Preaching of the Swallow" marks a change of outlook in the second half of the *Fables*, a change that is thematic as well as tonal. After this fable, in which the birds suffer a violent death, there is an increasingly bleak picture of a world of harsh justice, where the weak are continually the victims of the strong. In these fables neither appeals to the law, as in "The Wolf and the Lamb," nor bonds of oath, as in "The Paddock and the Mouse," avail against forces of brutal viciousness or arbitrary power. And as the world depicted seems more unjust, less governable, so the message to which the moralities increasingly turn is that of "The Wolf and the Wether": "Thairfoir I counsell men of euerilk stait / To knaw thame self" (2609–10).

The *Fables* argue for the "inwart argument" of self-knowledge. But, through comparisons with divine prudence they also encourage a breadth of vision, a capacity to read comparatively across situations and to build a discerning wisdom from them. In the *moralitas* to the very first fable, "The Cock and the Jasp," the discarded jewel is identified with "perfite prudence and cunning" (128) and readers are urged to "Ga seik" (161) it, within, it is implied, the fable corpus itself. The reading experience that Henryson contrives invites his audience to read individual fables equitably, and the collection prudently, with a judgment informed by cross-reference and comparison. Whether readers thus view the corpus as moving increasingly toward a darker view of human judgmental capacity, or as achieving a balance in its two parts between optimistic and pessimistic ways of seeing, is finally left to them.

Orpheus and Eurydice

Orpheus and Eurydice was one of the earliest of Henryson's works to be printed, by Andrew Millar and Walter Chepman, in Edinburgh, *c.* 1508. Its contemporary popularity is another reason to challenge its present-day neglect. Like the *Fables*, *Orpheus and Eurydice* is presented in fable form. But unlike that work, a formal distinction between tale and *moralitas* is signaled. The *Orpheus* tale is in the rhyme-royal stanza that Henryson uses dominantly in both the tales and moralities of the *Fables* and in the *Testament*; the *moralitas* is in decasyllabic rhyming couplets. (*Rhyme royal* consists of a seven-line stanza with the rhyme scheme *ababbcc*; *decasyllabic* means "consisting of ten syllables.") This sense of difference between tale and *moralitas* is reinforced by the way in which Henryson draws attention at the opening of the *moralitas* to the fact that while its tale is based on Boethius's *Consolation*, its morality is indebted to Trivet's commentary.

Whereas in the *Fables* Henryson dominantly explores tensions between reason and desire by a focus on hunger and eating, in *Orpheus* and the *Testament* he explores it through the theme of love. Early on in *Orpheus* Eurydice pursues Orpheus, "With wordis sweit and blenkis amorus" (81). In the *Testament* Venus, a goddess not to be trusted, is described as "dissimulait/Prouocative with blenkis amorous" (226–27), and later in that poem when Troilus gazes upon the grotesque leper, actually Cresseid, her look brings to his mind "The sweit visage and amorous blenking / Of fair Cresseid, sumtyme his awin darling" (503–04). Henryson associates sweetness and an amorous regard with the transitory. Amorousness, even in the context of married love, does not last.

Towards the ending of the tale, it is unequivocally amorousness that leads Orpheus to lose Erudices as he leads her out of hell:

> Thus Orpheus, wyth inwart lufe replete,
> So blyndit was in grete affection,
> Pensif apon his wyfe and lady suete,
> Remembrit noucht his hard condicion.
> Quhat will ye more? (386–91)

The combined tone of judgment and sympathy is characteristic of the tale part of *Orpheus and Eurydice*. In a narrative technique comparable to the *Fables*, it invites the audience's engagement with the protagonists in a manner that they will have to reassess in the morality. In Henryson's poetry to be "blyndit with affection" is the really damaging state. The implications of this phrase encompass political, ethical and personal realms. Corrupt judges in "The Sheep and the Dog" are "so blindit with affectioun, / But dreid, for meid, thay thoill the richt go doun" (1305–06). "The Preaching of the Swallow" envisages the corruption of the soul in these terms: "Ressoun is blindit with affectioun, / And carnall lust grouis full grene and gay" (1906–07).

Within *Orpheus* Henryson produces what, for many readers, is the most troubling of all his moralizations. The tale describes Aristeus, the would-be rapist, in language that precisely draws attention to the urgency of his physical desire. The *moralitas* allegorizes him as "noucht bot gude vertewe / Quhilk besy is ay to kepe oure myndis clene" (436–37); when we flee from good virtue in the fields of pleasure the serpent of sin draws us down towards oppression. The reader's sense of tale and *moralitas* jarring against each other is, however, deliberate: for Henryson grasping good virtue in a post-lapsarian world is a difficult thing – it will often indeed go contrary to man's instincts. By contrast, no sense of tension is felt in the way that tale and allegorization treat the fated backward look, for man's reason all too naturally enables his "appetite" to go "bakwart to the syn agayn" (624).

Like the *Fables*, *Orpheus* exposes mankind's moral fragility, but something of the humane nature of the tale yet carries into the *moralitas* to enable Henryson to end the poem on a more optimistic note than we might expect. The poem finishes with a supportive image of God's "haly hand" around man. God's "manetemance" (630–31), is literally that. It means (from French), the support of his hand. As such it catches poignantly on a detail of Proserpine's instructions to Orpheus as he leaves hell with Eurydice, "Erudices than be the hand thou tak" (380). The poem encourages us to hope that for man a divine hand of love may eventually offer consoling support.

The Testament of Cresseid

The *moralitas*, however, takes mankind potentially further than the tale takes Orpheus. His last words are:

> ... I am expert, and wo is me tharfore;
> Bot for a luke my lady is forlore. (407–08)

Resonances with other passages in Henryson poetry elucidate the limits of Orpheus's comprehension of his situation. The phrasing "I am expert, and wo is me tharfore" finds echoes with the two male readers whose limitations are shown in the *Testament of Cresseid*. That poem's narrator claims early on in the poem that "*I am expert*" (35) in the business of love, but his judgments of the story are constrained by too great an investment in that kind of knowledge. Troilus's final judgment of Cresseid is "I can no moir, / Scho was vntrew and *wo is me thairfoir*" (602–03). Though Cresseid has moved to a new reading of herself, Troilus, still attached to the amatory situation, cannot see beyond her untruth, as his inscription on her tomb will also indicate. In taking Cresseid beyond that state, Henryson's *Testament* offers its readers a demanding revision of a traditional story. The poem has one named work, Chaucer's *Troilus and Criseyde*, as its major reference point.[6] However, Henryson creates for the *Testament* the idea of a mix of sources through the inclusion of the "vther quair" (61) with which his narrator supplements his reading of Chaucer's *Troilus*, and we should not presume that Chaucer's was the only version of the Troilus and Criseyde story with which Henryson was familiar. His especial focus on the role of Cressedian speech in the *Testament* suggests that he was alert to how this issue had been treated in, at the least, Guido delle Colonne's *Historia Destructionis Troiae* (1287), and the post-Chaucerian *Troy Book* of Lydgate (*c.* 1412–20). What Henryson does is the reverse of what traditionally happened to Criseyde in earlier versions of the story, including Chaucer's. Her voice and perspective traditionally recede from the narrative as the facts of her betrayal of Troilus with Diomede become known.[7]

The *Testament* establishes its narrator at its opening as a dominant figure, an aging servant of the god of love, dominant also initially in his comments on the events that befall Cresseid. But for the last third of the narrative, from the "Complaint of Cresseid" onwards, the narrator's commenting role is diminished and the voice of Cresseid and her own readings of herself assume a significant shaping role; equally strikingly, these are readings of herself that are subject to alteration and development. Early on the narrator's defensive attitude towards Cresseid recalls that of the Chaucerian narrator, particularly in Book V of *Troilus*. As soon as the new narrative begins, the narrator introduces the language of sexual indulgence and excess:

> O fair Cresseid, the flour and A per se
> Of Troy and Grece, how was thow fortunait
> To change in filth all thy feminitie,
> And be with fleschelie lust sa maculait,
> And go amang the Greikis air and lait,
> Sa giglotlike takand thy foull plesance!
> I have pietie thow suld fall sic mischance! (78–84)

The jarring tones point up the problems. What appears to be a language of moral disgust clashes with a disavowal of Cresseid's responsibility for her actions. However, that disavowal is also at this juncture close to Cresseid's view of things. Rejected by Diomede and the court, she has no recourse but to return to her father's home outside the town. In the *Testament* Calchas has become something he is not in *Troilus and Criseyde*, a keeper of the temple of Venus and Cupid. This associates Cresseid even more strongly with things amatory, and it gives an added *frisson* to the angry way in which she cries out against Venus and Cupid in the secret study to which she retreats.

The gods effectively give Cresseid the right punishment for the wrong crime. She is punished by being afflicted with leprosy, which in the Middle Ages was often deemed a form of venereal disease, and thus a fitting punishment for a promiscuous woman. But though the gods observe what Cupid terms "hir leuing vnclene and lecherous" (285) what they punish her is for the blasphemy of Cupid and Venus. The reader thus cannot trust the biased narratorial standpoints of either the narrator or the gods. After Cresseid's dream, the narrator makes one of his last direct interventions for some time, rebuking Saturn for the excessiveness of his punishment on Cresseid, "Quhilk was sa sweit, gentill and *amorous*" (326) – his last resounding epithet is revealing. It is precisely Cresseid's amorousness that has produced these difficulties for her.

However, it is also now Cresseid's judgments of herself that assume prominence. After her retreat into the leper colony outside the town, the poem moves into a major set-piece, in which the voice of Cresseid presides. For her "Complaint" Henryson switches from rhyme-royal to a stanza modeled on Chaucer's *Anelida and Arcite*, where the use of only two rhymes in nine lines tightens the claustrophobic nature of the emotions expressed. This is not straightforwardly an amatory complaint that Cresseid is delivering, but it is delivered from what is still essentially the emotionally hide-bound nature of the amatory situation. Cresseid will not blame herself, and although seeking to type, she presents herself as a "mirrour" (456) to other women as a victim of fortune. There is a telling parallel between Cresseid's state at the end of her complaint and Orpheus's state at the end of the tale part of his poem. Having lost Eurydice, Orpheus remains "chydand on with lufe" (412), fractiously chafing with the amatory state, powerfully indicative of an unresolved state of mind. Likewise, Cresseid is described as "chydand with hir drerie destenye" (470). But Cresseid can go beyond this.

The emotional epiphany of Cresseid's non-recognition scene with Troilus leads to her two last and major verbal statements in the poem. The first is another complaint, but this time one focusing on her falseness and on Troilus's truth. It concludes with the simple, powerful statement, "Nane but myself as now I will accuse" (574). Cresseid takes responsibility for her actions; she will no longer blame the gods or fortune. Her final statement is a written one, her testament.

Henryson shows here how self-knowledge transcends the amatory, and that he uses a female figure to do it is a bold step. In her final speech Cresseid castigates herself with a harshness that some readers may find hard to take – but its resonances are important. Cresseid is now employing the kind of discourse of moral revulsion at her fickle indulgence which earlier on in the poem we saw the narrator employing but failing to yoke to her own volition or responsibility. It is now Cresseid who says:

> My mynd in fleschelie foull affectioun
> Was inclynit to lustis lecherous (558–59)

These two lines pack in many of the pejorative terms that are recognizably Henrysonian, from this and his other poems. Cresseid accepts that her baser, physical desires have corrupted her mind to the degree that it "inclynes" downward rather than upward. She is thus able to analyze herself in a way that Orpheus was not, and in a way that many of the flawed protagonists in the *Fables* are incapable of achieving. This is a considerable validation of her on Henryson's part. Particularly so, as the terms in which she characterizes her failings are those commonly associated with the female. In *Orpheus* the corrupting power of the affection is represented by the female figure. Cresseid recognizes that about herself too, "Becaus I knaw the greit vnstabilnes, / Brukill as glas, into my self" (568–69). But that very act of recognition constitutes a transcendence of the stereotype through an individualized reading. Cresseid also finds within her self-castigation the value of fidelity, in a sense of love which takes it beyond the amorously physical. The last words she invokes are "trew lufe" (591). This perception forms an intense contrast with the responses at the end of the poem of the two male readers, Troilus and the narrator, whose insistence that Cresseid is only meaningful to women in a limited moral context displays the frightening blinkeredness of the still amorous male.

Henryson's three major poems have a consonance with each other that is reminiscent of the way in which in the late fourteenth-century John Gower's Latin, French, and English works all address a similar constellation of values and issues. Justice, judgment, reason, and desire, and the challenges they pose, are constants in Henryson's writing. But Henryson is always moving his readers around. The fact that in the *Testament* he avoids giving us a *moralitas* is a classic example of this. More than in any of his other poems, the *Testament* forces its final interpretation back on its audience.

NOTES

1 *The Poems of William Dunbar*, ed. Priscilla Bawcut, 2 vols. (Glasgow: Association for Scottish Literary Studies, 1998), vol. I, p. 97.
2 R. J. Lyall, "Henryson's *Morall Fabillis* and the Steinhöwel Tradition," *Forum for Modern Language Studies*, 38 (2002), 362–81.
3 Henryson's name is also associated, with varying degrees of convincingness, to twelve more minor poems, covering a wide variety of forms and subjects, from the pastoral to the pious.
4 See Denton Fox's discussion in Fox, ed., *The Poems of Robert Henryson* (Oxford: Clarendon Press, 1981), pp. lxxv–lxxxi.
5 Johannes de Irlandia, *The Meroure of Wyssdome*, ed. Charles MacPherson, vol. I, Scottish Text Society, new series 19 (Edinburgh and London: William Blackwood and Sons, 1926), pp. 113–14.
6 The earliest surviving complete witness is the anglicized version in William Thynne's 1532 edition of Chaucer's works, where the poem is presented as Chaucerian, following *Troilus* and preceding *The Legend of Good Women*.
7 Sally Mapstone, "The Origins of Criseyde," in *Medieval Women: Texts and Contexts in Late Medieval Britain*, ed. Jocelyn Wogan-Browne, Rosalynn Voaden, Arlyn Diamond, Ann Hutchison, Carol Meale, and Lesley Johnson (Turnhout: Brepols, 2000), pp. 131–47.

GUIDE TO FURTHER READING

This guide is very lightly annotated. It generally follows the organization of the volume with some exceptions. The first two subheadings concern works that apply to all or many of the topics discussed in individual chapters. Editions of primary works will all be found under the third subheading, rather than the chapter(s) where they are discussed. Finally, there are works that relate squarely to one topic but relate to another or to several others. (Thus, most of the scholarship on Malory also relates to the general topic of romance, covered in chapter 4; Anne Hudson's magisterial history of Wycliffitism *Premature Reformation* relates primarily to chapter 8, on Lollard writings, but also relates to several others.) It seemed both more logical and economical to list such works under the heading they best fit. However, these exceptions will mean that a reader following up on a particular topic will need to look not only under its chapter subheading, but also under the first three subheadings, and any other chapter subheadings that may be relevant.

Bibliographical guides and other research tools

Burke Severs, J., Albert E. Hartung, and Peter G. Beidler, eds. *A Manual of the Writings in Middle English 1050–1500*, 11 vols. Hamden, CT: Connecticut Academy of Arts and Sciences, 1967–2005.

Possibly the single most important research tool in the field.

Edwards, A. S. G., ed. *Middle English Prose: A Critical Guide to Major Authors and Genres*. New Brunswick, NJ: Rutgers University Press, 1984.

Jolliffe, Peter S. *A Check-List of Middle English Prose Writings of Spiritual Guidance*. Subsidia Mediaevalia, 2. Toronto: Pontifical Institute of Mediaeval Studies, 1974.

Lewis, Robert E., Norman F. Blake, and A. S. G. Edwards. *Index of Printed Middle English Prose*. Garland Reference Library of the Humanities, 537. New York and London: Garland, 1985.

Literary histories, overviews, and other synthetic studies

Aers, David. *Community, Gender, and Individual Identity: English Writing 1360–1430*. London and New York: Routledge, 1988.

Faith, Ethics and Church: Writing in England, 1360–1409. Cambridge: D. S. Brewer, 2000.

Aers, David and Lynn Staley. *The Powers of the Holy: Religion, Politics, and Gender in Late Medieval English Culture.* University Park, PA: Pennsylvania State University Press, 1996.

Chism, Christine. *Alliterative Revivals.* Philadelphia: University of Pennsylvania Press, 2002.

Federico, Sylvia. *New Troy: Fantasies of Empire in the Late Middle Ages.* Minneapolis: University of Minnesota Press, 2003.

Fisher, John H. *The Emergence of Standard English.* Lexington: University of Kentucky Press, 1996.

Green, Richard Firth. *A Crisis of Truth: Literature and Law in Ricardian England.* Philadelphia: University of Pennsylvania Press, 1999.

Griffiths, Jeremy and Derek Pearsall, eds. *Book Production and Publishing in Britain, 1375–1475.* Cambridge University Press, 1989.

Hanawalt, Barbara, ed. *Chaucer's England: Literature in Historical Context.* Minneapolis: University of Minnesota Press, 1992.

Hanna, Ralph. *London Literature 1300–1380.* Cambridge University Press, 2005.

Holsinger, Bruce. *Music, Body, and Desire in Medieval Culture: Hildegard of Bingen to Chaucer.* Stanford University Press, 2001.

Justice, Steven. *Writing and Rebellion: England in 1381.* Berkeley: University of California Press, 1994.

Lavezzo, Kathy. *Angels on the Edge of the World: Geography, Literature, and English Community, 1000–1534.* Ithaca and London: Cornell University Press, 2006.

Lerer, Seth. *Chaucer and His Readers: Imagining the Author in Late Medieval England.* Princeton University Press, 1993.

Matthews, David. *The Making of Middle English, 1765–1910.* Minneapolis: University of Minnesota Press, 1999.

Patterson, Lee. *Negotiating the Past: The Historical Understanding of Medieval Literature.* Madison: University of Wisconsin Press, 1987.

Rubin, Miri. *Corpus Christi: The Eucharist in Late Medieval Culture.* Cambridge University Press, 1991.

Sanok, Catherine. *Her Life Historical: Exemplarity and Female Saints' Lives in Late Medieval England.* Philadelphia, PA: University of Pennsylvania Press, 2007.

Scanlon, Larry. *Narrative, Authority, and Power: The Medieval Exemplum and the Chaucerian Tradition.* Cambridge University Press, 1994; reissued 2007.

Simpson, James. "From Reason to Affective Thought." *Medium Aevum* 55 (1986): 1–23.

Reform and Cultural Revolution 1350–1547. Oxford University Press, 2002.

Somerset, Fiona. *Clerical Discourse and Lay Audience in Late Medieval England.* Cambridge University Press, 1998.

Staley, Lynn. *Languages of Power in the Age of Richard II.* University Park, PA: Pennsylvania State Press, 2005.

Strohm, Paul. *England's Empty Throne: Usurpation and the Language of Legitimation 1399–1422.* New Haven and London: Yale University Press, 1998.

Hochon's Arrow: The Social Imagination of Fourteenth-Century Texts. With an appendix by A. J. Prescott. Princeton University Press, 1992.

Politique: Languages of Statecraft between Chaucer and Shakespeare. Notre Dame: University of Notre Dame Press, 2005.

Summit, Jennifer. *Lost Property: The Woman Writer and English Literary History, 1380–1589.* Chicago and London: University of Chicago Press, 2000.

Wallace, David. *Premodern Places: Calais to Surinam, Chaucer to Aphra Behn.* Malden: Blackwell, 2004.

gen. ed. *The Cambridge History of Medieval English Literature.* Cambridge University Press, 1999.

Watson, Nicholas. "Censorship and Cultural Change in Late-Medieval England: Vernacular Theology, the Oxford Translation Debate, and Arundel's Constitutions of 1409." *Speculum* 70 (1995): 822–64.

Winstead, Karen A. *Virgin Martyrs: Legends of Sainthood in Late Medieval England.* Ithaca NY: Cornell University Press, 1997.

Wogan-Browne, Jocelyn, Nicholas Watson, Andrew Taylor, and Ruth Evans, eds. *The Idea of the Vernacular: An Anthology of Middle English Literary Theory 1280–1520.* Exeter University Press, 1999.

Editions

Geoffrey Chaucer

The Riverside Chaucer. Third Edition. Ed. Larry Benson *et al.* Boston and London: Houghton-Mifflin, 1986.

Devotional and contemplative works

Anchoritic Spirituality: Ancrene Wisse and Associated Works. Tr. Anne Savage and Nicholas Watson. New York: Paulist Press, 1991.

The Cloud of Unknowing and Related Treatises. Ed. Phyllis Hodgson. Analecta Carthusiana, 3. Salzburg: Institut für Anglistik und Amerikanistik, Universität Salzburg; Exeter, Devon: Catholic Records Press, 1982.

Contemplations of the Dread and Love of God. Ed. Margaret Connolly. EETS os 303. Oxford University Press, 1993.

The English Text of the "Ancrene Riwle" Edited from Magdalen College, Cambridge Ms. Pepys 2498. Ed. Arne Zettersten. EETS os 274. London: Oxford University Press, 1976.

The English Text of the Ancrene Riwle Edited from ms. Corpus Christi College, Cambridge 402. Ed. J. R. R. Tolkien. EETS os 249. London: Oxford University Press, 1962.

The English Text of the Ancrene Riwle Edited from Cotton ms. Nero A XIV. Ed. Mabel Day. EETS os 225. London: Oxford University Press, 1952.

Hilton, Walter. *The Scale of Perfection.* Ed. Thomas H. Bestul. Kalamazoo: Medieval Institute Publications, 2000.

Walter Hilton's Eight Chapters on Perfection. Ed. Fumio Kuriyagawa. Studies in the Humanities and Social Relations, 9. Tokyo: Keio Institute of Cultural and Linguistic Studies, Keio University, 1967.

Richard Rolle and Þe Holy Boke Gratia Dei: An Edition with Commentary. Ed. Mary Luke Arntz. Salzburg: Institut für Anglistik und Amerikanistik, Universität Salzburg, 1981.

Rolle, Richard. *Richard Rolle: Prose and Verse.* Ed. S.J. Ogilvie-Thomson. EETS OS 293. Oxford University Press, 1988.

Þe Wohunge of Ure Lauerd and Other Pieces. Ed. W.M. Thompson. EETS OS 241. London and New York: Oxford University Press, 1958.

The Gawain-poet

The Poems of the Pearl Manuscript: Pearl, Cleanness, Patience, Sir Gawain and the Green Knight. Ed. Malcolm Andrew and Ronald A. Waldron. Rev. edn. Exeter University Press, 1987.

John Gower

The Complete Works of John Gower. Ed. G.C. Macaulay. Oxford: Clarendon Press, 1899.

Confessio Amantis. Second Edition. Ed. Russell A. Peck, with Latin translations by Andrew Galloway. Kalamazoo: Medieval Institute Publications, 2006.

Hagiography

Bokenham, Osbern. *A Legend of Holy Women.* Tr. Sheila Delany. Notre Dame: Notre Dame University Press, 1992.

Legendys of Hooly Wummen. Ed. Mary S. Serjeantson. EETS OS 206. London: Oxford University Press, 1938; reprint Millwood, NY: Kraus Reprints, 1988.

Caxton, William. *The Golden Legend or Lives of the Saints.* Ed. Frederick S. Ellis. London: J. M. Dent, 1900; reprint New York: AMS Press, 1973.

The Early South English Legendary, or, Lives of Saints: MS Laud 108. Ed. Carl Horstmann. EETS OS 87. London: N. Trübner & Co, 1887; reprint Millwood, NY: Kraus Reprints, 1987.

Þe Liflade ant te Passiun of Seinte Julienne. Ed. S.R.T.O. d'Ardenne. EETS OS 248. London and New York: Oxford University Press, 1961.

Love, Nicholas. *The Mirror of the Blessed Life of Jesus Christ.* Ed. Michael G. Sargent. Exeter University Press, 2004.

Seinte Katerine. Ed. S.R.T.O. d'Ardenne and E.J. Dobson. EETS SS 7. Oxford and New York: Oxford University Press, 1981.

Seinte Marherete þe Meiden ant Martyr. Ed. Frances M. Mack. EETS OS 193. London: Oxford University Press, 1934; reprint 1958.

The South English Legendary. Ed. Charlotte D'Evelyn and Anna J. Mill. 3 vols. EETS OS 235–6, 244. Oxford, 1956–59.

Robert Henryson

The Poems of Robert Henryson. Ed. Denton Fox. Oxford: Clarendon Press, 1981.

Thomas Hoccleve

Hoccleve's Works. Ed. Frederick J. Furnivall. 3 vols. EETS ES, 61, 72, 73. London: K. Paul, Trench, Trübner & Co., 1892–1925.

The Monk and Our Lady's Sleeves. In *The Middle English Miracles of the Virgin*. Ed. Beverly Boyd. San Marino: Huntington Library, 1964, 50–55.

"My Compleinte" and Other Poems. Ed. Roger Ellis. Exeter University Press, 2001.

The Regiment of Princes. TEAMS Middle English Texts Series. Ed. Charles R. Blyth. Kalamazoo: Medieval Institute Publications, 1999.

Julian of Norwich

A Book of Showings to the Anchoress Julian of Norwich. 2 vols. Ed. Edmund Colledge and James Walsh. Toronto: Pontifical Institute of Medieval Studies, 1978.

The Showings of Julian of Norwich. Ed. and tr. Denise N. Baker. New York: W. W. Norton & Co., 2005.

The Writings of Julian of Norwich: "A Vision showed to a Devout Woman" and "A Revelation of Love." Ed. Nicholas Watson and Jacqueline Jenkins. Brepols Medieval Women Series. University Park, PA: Pennsylvania State University Press, 2006.

Margery Kempe

The Book of Margery Kempe. Ed. Sanford Brown Meech, with prefatory note by Hope Emily Allen. EETS os 212. London and New York: Oxford University Press, 1940.

The Book of Margery Kempe. Ed. Lynn Staley. TEAMS Middle English Texts Series. Kalamazoo: Medieval Institute Publications, 1996.

The Book of Margery Kempe: A New Translation, Contexts, Criticism. Ed. and tr. Lynn Staley. Norton Critical Edition. New York: W. W. Norton, 2001.

William Langland

Piers Plowman: The Three Versions. Gen. ed. George Kane. Volume I: *Piers Plowman: The A Version*. Ed. Kane. Volume II: *Piers Plowman: The B Version*. Eds. Kane and E. Talbot Donaldson. Volume III: *Piers Plowman: The C Version*. Eds. Kane and George Russell. London and Berkeley: Athlone Press, 1960; 1975; 1997.

Now standard, but very difficult to use.

Piers Plowman: The C-text. Ed. Derek Pearsall. Corrected edition. Exeter University Press, 1994.

The Piers Plowman Tradition. Ed. Helen Barr. London: Dent, 1993.

The Vision of Piers Plowman: A Critical Edition of the B-text. Ed. A. V. C. Schmidt. Second Edition. Everyman Library. London: J. M. Dent; and Vermont: Charles E. Tuttle, 1995.

Lollard writings

English Wycliffite Sermons. Eds. Anne Hudson and Pamela Gradon. 5 vols. Oxford: Clarendon Press, 1983–96.

The Lanterne of Lizt, ed. from ms. Harl. 2324. Ed. Lilian Swinburn. EETS os 151. London: Kegan Paul, Trench, Trübner & Co., 1917. Reprinted Millwood, NY: Kraus Reprint, 1988.

Selections from English Wycliffite Writings. Ed. Anne Hudson. Medieval Academy Reprints for Teaching. University of Toronto Press, 1997.

John Lydgate

A Critical Edition of John Lydgate's Life of Our Lady. Eds. Joseph A. Lauritis, Ralph A. Klinefelter, and Vernon F. Gallagher. Duquesne Studies. Philological Series, 2. Pittsburgh: Duquesne University Press, 1961.

The Dance of Death. Ed. Florence Warren. EETS os 181. London: Oxford University Press, 1931.

Life of Saints Edmund and Fremund. In *Altenglische Legenden. Neue Folge*. Ed. C. Horstmann. Heilbronn: Gebr. Henninger, 1881, 367–445.

Lydgate and Burgh's Secrees of Old Philosoffres. Ed. Robert Steele. EETS ES 66. London: Kegan, Paul, Trench and Trübner, 1894.

Lydgate's Fall of Princes. Ed. Henry Bergen. 4 vols. EETS ES 121, 122, 123, 124. London: Oxford University Press, 1924; rpr. 1967.

Lydgate's "Siege of Thebes." Ed. Axel Erdmann and Eilert Ekwall. 2 vols. EETS ES 108, 125. London: Kegan Paul, Trench and Trübner, 1911; 1930; rpr. 1960.

Lydgate's Temple of Glas. Ed. Joseph Schick. EETS ES 60. London: Kegan, Paul, Trench, Trübner, 1891.

Lydgate's Troy Book. Ed. Henry Bergen. 4 Parts. EETS ES 97, 103, 106, and 126. London: Kegan Paul, Trench and Trübner, 1906–35.

The Minor Poems of John Lydgate. Ed. Henry Nobel MacCracken. 2 vols. EETS ES 107, OS 192. London: Kegan Paul, Trench, Trübner & Co, 1911–34; repr. London: Oxford University Press, 1961.

The Pilgrimage of the Life of Man. Eds. F. J. Furnivall, and K. B. Locock. 3 Parts. EETS ES 77, 83, 92. London: Kegan Paul, Trench and Trübner, 1911–34.

Saint Albon and Saint Amphibalus. Ed. George F. Reinecke. Garland Medieval Texts, 11. New York: Garland, 1985.

Siege of Thebes. Ed. Robert R. Edwards. TEAMS Middle English Text Series. Kalamazoo: Medieval Institute Publications, 2001.

Troy Book: Selections. Ed. Robert R. Edwards. TEAMS Middle English Text Series. Kalamazoo: Medieval Institute Publications, 1998.

Lyrics

Davies, R.T., ed. *Medieval English Lyrics: A Critical Anthology*. London: Faber & Faber, 1963.

Duncan, Thomas G., ed. *Late Medieval English Lyrics and Carols 1400–1530*. Harmondsworth: Penguin, 2000.

Dobson, E.J. and F.L. Harrison, eds. *Medieval English Songs*. Cambridge University Press, 1979.

Hirsch, John C., ed. *Medieval Lyric: Middle English Lyrics, Ballads, and Carols*. Oxford: Blackwell Publishing, 2005.

Luria, Maxwell S. and Richard L. Hoffmann, eds. *Middle English Lyrics*. New York: Norton, 1974.

Sir Thomas Malory

Caxton's Malory. Ed. James W. Spisak. Berkeley: University of California Press, 1983.

Complete Works. Ed. Eugène Vinaver. Second Edition. Oxford University Press, 1971.

King Arthur's Death: The Middle English Stanzaic Morte Arthur and Alliterative Morte Arthure. Ed. Larry D. Benson. Exeter University Press, 1986.

The Winchester Malory: A Facsimile. Intr. N.R. Kerr. EETS SS 4. London: Oxford University Press, 1976.

The Works of Sir Thomas Malory. Ed. Eugène Vinaver; rev. P. J. C. Field. Third Edition. Oxford: Clarendon Press, 1990.

Pastoralia

Book for a Simple and Devout Woman. A Late Middle English Adaptation of Peraldus's Summa de Vitiis et Virtutibus and Friar Laurent's Somme le Roi, edited from British Library Mss Harley 6571 and Additional 30944. Ed. F.N.M. Diekstra, Mediaevalia Groningana. Gröningen: Egbert Forsten, 1998.

Jacob's Well: An English Treatise on the Cleansing of Man's Conscience. Ed. Arthur Brandeis. EETS OS 115. London: Kegan Paul, Trench, Trübner & Co., 1900; repr. Millwood, NY: Kraus Reprint, 1975.

Lavynham, Richard. *A Litil Tretys on the Seven Deadly Sins*. Ed. J.P.W.M. van Zutphen. Rome: Institutum Carmelitanum, 1956.

The Lay Folks' Catechism, or the English and Latin Versions of Archbishop Thoresby's Instruction for the People. Eds. Thomas Frederick Simmons and Henry Edward Nolloth. EETS OS 118. London, 1901; repr. Millwood, NY, 1972.

Mannyng, Robert, of Brunne. *Handlyng Synne*. Ed. Idelle Sullens. Medieval & Renaissance Texts & Studies, 14. Binghamton: SUNY Press, 1983.

Robert of Brunne's "Handlyng synne," A.D. 1303, with those Parts of the Anglo-French Treaties on which it was founded, William of Wadington's "Manuel des pechiez." Ed. Frederick J. Furnivall. 2 vols. in 1. EETS OS 119, 123. London: Kegan Paul, Trench, Trübner & Co, 1901–[3].

Michel, Dan, of Northgate. *Ayenbite of Inwyt*. Ed. Richard Morris, re-edited by Pamela Gradon. 2 vols. EETS OS 23, 278. Oxford University Press, 1965–79.

Middle English Sermons, Edited from British Museum MS. Royal 18 B.xxiii. Ed. Woodburn O. Ross. EETS OS 209. London: Oxford University Press, 1940.

Mirk, John. *Mirk's Festial: A Collection of Homilies*. Ed. Theodor Erbe. EETS ES 96. London: Kegan Paul, Trench, Trübner & Co, 1905; reprint Millwood, NY: Kraus Reprint, 1987.

The Mirroure of the Worlde: A Middle English Translation of Le miroir du monde. Ed. Robert R. Raymo and Elaine E. Whitaker, with the assistance of Ruth E. Sternglantz. University of Toronto Press, 2003.

A Myrour to Lewde Men and Wymmen. Ed. Venetia Nelson. Heidelberg: C. Winter, 1981.

Re-inventing the vernacular: Middle English language and its literature (Chapter 1)

Bennett, J.A.W. and G.V. Smithers, eds. *Early Middle English Verse and Prose*. Second Edition. Oxford: Clarendon Press, 1968.

Blake, Norman. *The English Language in Medieval Literature.* London: Methuen, 1979.

ed. *The Cambridge History of the English Language: Volume II, 1066–1476.* Cambridge University Press, 1992.

Burnley, David. *The Language of Chaucer.* London: Macmillan, 1989.

Burrow, J.A. and Thorlac Turville-Petre, eds. *A Book of Middle English.* Third Edition. Oxford: Blackwell Publishing, 2005.

Fisher, John H. *The Emergence of Standard English.* Lexington: University Press of Kentucky, 1996.

Trotter, D.A., ed. *Multilingualism in Later Medieval Britain.* Woodbridge: D. S. Brewer, 2000.

Textual production and textual communities (Chapter 2)

Connolly, Margaret. *John Shirley: Book Production and the Noble Household in Fifteenth-Century England.* Aldershot: Ashgate, 1998.

Hanna, Ralph III, "Reconsidering the Auchinleck Manuscript." In *New Directions in Later Medieval Manuscript Studies: Essays from the 1998 Harvard Conference.* Ed. Derek Pearsall. Rochester NY: York Medieval Press, 2000, 91–102.

"Sir Thomas Berkeley and His Patronage," *Speculum* 64 (1989): 878–916.

"Some Norfolk Women and Their Books, *c.* 1390–1440." In *The Cultural Patronage of Medieval Women.* Ed. June Hall McCash. Athens: University of Georgia Press, 1996, 288–305.

Justice, Steven and Kathryn Kerby-Fulton. "Langlandian Reading Circles and the Civil Service in London and Dublin, 1380–1427." *NML* 1 (1997): 59–84.

Knapp, Ethan. "Bureaucratic Identity and the Construction of Self in Hoccleve's *Formulary* and *La Male Regle.*" *Speculum* 74 (1999): 357–76.

Krug, Rebecca. *Reading Families: Women's Literate Practice in Late Medieval England.* Ithaca: Cornell University Press, 2002.

Minnis, A.J., ed. *Late-Medieval Religious Texts and their Transmission: Essays in Honour of A. I. Doyle.* Woodbridge: D. S. Brewer, 1994.

Mooney, Linne. "Chaucer's Scribe." *Speculum* 81 (2006): 97–138.

Moore, Samuel. "Patrons of Letters in Norfolk and Suffolk, c. 1450, II." *PLMA* 28 (1913): 79–105.

Parkes, M.B. and Andrew G. Watson, eds. *Medieval Scribes, Manuscripts & Libraries: Essays Presented to N. R. Ker.* London: Scolar Press, 1978.

Pearsall, Derek. "The 'Troilus' Frontispiece and Chaucer's Audience." *YES* 7 (1977): 68–74.

ed. *Studies in the Vernon Manuscript.* Cambridge: D. S. Brewer, 1990.

Stock, Brian. *The Implications of Literacy: Written Language and Models of Interpretation in the Eleventh and Twelfth Centuries.* Princeton University Press, 1983.

Religious writing: hagiography, pastoralia, *devotional and contemplative works (Chapter 3)*

Blake, Norman F. "Varieties of Middle English Religious Prose." In *Chaucer and Middle English Studies in Honour of Rossell Hope Robbins.* Ed. Beryl Rowland. Kent, OH: Kent State University Press, 1974, 348–56.

Boyle, Leonard E. "The Fourth Lateran Council and Manuals of Popular Theology." In *The Popular Literature of Medieval England*. Ed. Thomas J. Heffernan, Tennessee Studies in Literature, 28. Knoxville: University of Tennessee Press, 1985, 30–43.

"The *Oculus Sacerdotis* and Some Other Works of William of Pagula." *Transactions of the Royal Historical Society*, ser. 5, vol. 5 (1955): 81–110. Reprinted as section 4 in *Pastoral Care, Clerical Education and Canon Law, 1200–1400*. London: Variorum Reprints, 1981.

Brady, M.T. "*The Pore Caitif*: An Introductory Study." *Traditio* 10 (1954): 529–48.

"Rolle's 'Form of Living' and 'The Pore Caitif'." *Traditio* 36 (1980): 426–35.

Clark, John P.H. "*The Cloud of Unknowing*, Walter Hilton and St John of the Cross: A Comparison." *Downside Review* 96 (1978): 281–98.

"Late Fourteenth-Century Cambridge Theology and the English Contemplative Tradition." In *The Medieval Mystical Tradition in England: Exeter Symposium V*. Ed. Marion Glasscoe. Cambridge and Rochester, NY: D. S. Brewer, 1992, 1–16.

Connolly, Margaret. "Books for the "helpe of euery persoone þat þenkiþ to be saued": Six Devotional Anthologies from Fifteenth-Century London." *YES* 33 (2003): 170–81.

Delany, Sheila. *Impolitic Bodies. Poetry, Saints, and Society in Fifteenth-Century England: The Work of Osbern Bokenham*. Oxford University Press, 1998.

Denley, M. "Elementary Teaching Techniques and Middle English Religious Didactic Writing." In *Langland, the Mystics and the Medieval English Religious Tradition: Essays in Honour of S. S. Hussey*. Ed. Helen Phillips. Cambridge: D.S. Brewer, 1990, 223–41.

Dillon, Janette. "Margery Kempe's Sharp Confessor/s." *Leeds Studies in English*, ns 27 (1996): 131–8.

Doyle, A.I. "Books Connected with the Vere Family and Barking Abbey." *Transactions of the Essex Archaeological Society*, NS 25:2 (1958): 222–43.

"A Survey of the Origins and Circulation of Theological Writings in English in the 14th, 15th, and Early 16th Centuries with Special Consideration of the Part of the Clergy Therein." Dissertation. Cambridge University (Downing College), 1953.

Edwards, A.S.G., ed. *A Companion to Middle English Prose*. Cambridge: D. S. Brewer, 2004.

Erler, Mary C. "Devotional Literature." In *The Cambridge History of the Book in Britain, 3: 1440–1557*. Ed. Lotte Hellinga and J.B. Trapp. Cambridge University Press, 1999, 495–525.

Gillespie, Vincent. "Doctrina and Predicacio: The Design and Function of Some Pastoral Manuals." *Leeds Studies in English*, NS 11 (1980): 36–50.

Görlach, Manfred. *Studies in Middle English Saints' Legends*. Anglistische Forschungen, 257. Heidelberg: C. Winter, 1998.

The Textual Tradition of the South English Legendary. Leeds Texts and Monographs, NS 6. Leeds: University of Leeds, School of English, 1974.

Hanna, Ralph. "Miscellaneity and Vernacularity: Conditions of Literary Production in Late Medieval England." In *The Whole Book: Cultural Perspectives on the Medieval Miscellany*. Ed. Stephen G. Nichols and Siegfried Wenzel. Ann Arbor: University of Michigan Press, 1996, 37–51.

Heffernan, Thomas J. *Sacred Biography: Saints and their Biographers in the Middle Ages*. Oxford University Press, 1988.

"Additional Evidence for a More Precise Date of *The South English Legendary*." *Traditio* 35 (1979): 345–51.

Jankowsky, Klaus P. "Entertainment, Edification, and Popular Education in *The South English Legendary*." *Journal of Popular Culture* 11 (1977): 706–17.

Keiser, George R. "*Ordinatio* in the Manuscripts of John Lydgate's *Lyf of Our Lady*: Its Value for the Reader, Its Challenge for the Modern Editor." In *Medieval Literature: Texts and Interpretation*. Ed. Tim William Machan. Medieval & Renaissance Texts & Studies, 79. Binghamton, NY: SUNY Press, 1991, 139–57.

"Þe Holy Boke Gratia Dei." *Viator* 12 (1981): 289–317.

Lewis, Robert E. and Angus McIntosh. *A Descriptive Guide to the Manuscripts of the "Prick of Conscience."* Medium Aevum Monographs, NS 12. Oxford: Society for the Study of Mediaeval Languages and Literature, 1982.

Martin, C.A. "Middle English Manuals of Religious Instruction." In *So meny people longages and tonges: Philological Essays in Scots and Mediaeval English Presented to Angus McIntosh*. Eds. M. Benskin and M. L. Samuels. N.P., 1981, 283–98, 405–8, 238–98, 405–08.

Meale, Carol. "'oft siþis with grete deuotion I þought what I miȝt do pleysyng to god': The Early Ownership and Readership of Love's *Mirror*, with Special Reference to its Female Audience." In *Nicholas Love at Waseda*. Eds. Shoichi Oguro, Richard Beadle, and Michael G. Sargent. Woodbridge: D. S. Brewer, 1997, 19–46.

Miller, Mark. "Displaced Souls, Idle Talk, Spectacular Scenes: *Handlyng Synne* and the Perspective of Agency." *Speculum* 71 (1996): 606–32.

Millett, Bella. "The Audience of the Saints' Lives of the Katherine Group." *Reading Medieval Studies* 16 (1990): 127–55.

Minnis, Alastair J., ed. *Late-Medieval Religious Texts and Their Transmission. Essays in Honour of A. I. Doyle*. York Manuscripts Conferences. Proceedings Series, 3. Woodbridge: York Medieval Press, 1994.

Newhauser, Richard. *The Treatise on Vices and Virtues in Latin and the Vernacular*. Typologie des sources du moyen âge occidental. Volume 68. Turnhout: Brepols, Belgium, 1993.

"The Parson's Tale and Its Generic Affiliations." In *Closure in The Canterbury Tales: The Role of The Parson's Tale*. Eds. David Raybin and Linda T. Holley. Studies in Medieval Culture 41. Kalamazoo, MI: Medieval Institute Publications, 2000, 45–76.

Owst, G.R. *Preaching in Medieval England*. Cambridge University Press, 1926; repr. New York: Russell and Russell, 1965.

Pantin, W.A. *The English Church in the Fourteenth Century*. Cambridge University Press, 1955.

Pfander, H.G. "Some Medieval Manuals of Religious Instruction in England and Observations on Chaucer's Parson's Tale." *JEGP* 35 (1936): 243–58.

Pickering, O.S. "*The South English Legendary*: Teaching or Preaching?" *Poetica* 45 (1996): 1–14.

Riehle, Wolfgang. "The Authorship of the *Prick of Conscience* Reconsidered." *Anglia* 111 (1993): 1–18.

Russell, George H. "Vernacular Instruction of the Laity in the Later Middle Ages in England: Some Texts and Notes." *The Journal of Religious History* 2 (1962–63): 98–119.

Samson, Annie. "The *South English Legendary*: Constructing a Context." In *Thirteenth-Century England, I: Proceedings of the Newcastle upon Tyne Conference 1985*. Ed. P.R. Cross and S.D. Lloyd. Woodbridge: Boydell Press, 1986, 185–95.

Scase, Wendy. "Reginald Pecock, John Carpenter and John Colop's 'Common-Profit' Books: Aspects of Book Ownership in Fifteenth-Century London." *Medium Aevum* 61 (1992): 261–74.

Spencer, H. Leith. *English Preaching in the Late Middle Ages*. Oxford: Clarendon Press, 1993.

Strohm, Paul. "*Passioun, Lyf, Miracle, Legende*: Some Generic Terms in Middle English Hagiographic Narrative." *The Chaucer Review* 10 (1975–76): 62–75, 154–71.

Taylor, Cheryl. "A Contemplative Community? The *Cloud* Texts and *Scale* 2 in Dialogue." *Parergon* NS 19 (2002): 81–100.

Thompson, Anne B. *Everyday Saints and the Art of Narrative in the South English Legendary*. Burlington, VT: Ashgate, 2003.

Watson, Nicholas. *Richard Rolle and the Invention of Authority*. Cambridge University Press, 1991.

Wenzel, Siegfried. *Latin Sermon Collections from Later Medieval England: Orthodox Preaching in the Age of Wyclif*. Cambridge University Press, 2005.

Macaronic Sermons: Bilingualism and Preaching in Late-Medieval England. Ann Arbor: University of Michigan Press, 1994.

"Vices, Virtues, and Popular Preaching." In *Medieval and Renaissance Studies. Proceedings of the Southeastern Institute of Medieval and Renaissance Studies, Summer, 1974*. Ed. Dale B. J. Randall. Medieval and Renaissance Series, 6. Durham: University of North Carolina Press, 1976, 28–54.

Romance (Chapter 4)

Barron, W.R.J. *English Medieval Romance*. London: Longman, 1987.

Cooper, Helen. *The English Romance in Time: Transforming Motifs from Geoffrey of Monmouth to the Death of Shakespeare*. Oxford University Press, 2004.

Crane, Susan, *Insular Romance: Politics, Faith, and Culture in Anglo-Norman and Middle English Literature*. Berkeley: University of California Press, 1986.

The Performance of Self: Ritual Clothing, and Identity During the Hundred Years War. Philadelphia: University of Pennsylvania Press, 2002.

Field, Rosalind. "The Anglo-Norman Background to Alliterative Romance." In *Middle English Alliterative Poetry, Seven Essays*. Ed. David Lawton. Cambridge: D. S. Brewer, 1982, 56–69.

Heng, Geraldine. *Empire of Magic: Medieval Romance and the Politics of Cultural Fantasy*. New York: Columbia University Press, 2003.

Ingham, Patricia Clare. *Sovereign Fantasies: Arthurian Romance and the Making of Britain.* Philadelphia: University of Pennsylvania Press, 2001.
Kay, Sarah. *The Chansons de geste in the Age of Romance: Political Fictions.* Oxford University Press, 1996.
Krueger, Roberta L., ed. *The Cambridge Companion to Medieval Romance.* Cambridge University Press, 2000.
Pearsall, Derek. "The Development of Middle English Romance." *Mediaeval Studies* 27 (1963): 91–116.
Smith, D. Vance. *Arts of Possession: The Middle English Household Imaginary.* Minneapolis: University of Minnesota Press, 2003.
Strohm, Paul. "Story, Spelle, Geste, Romaunce, Tragedie: Generic Distinctions in the Middle English Troy Narratives." *Speculum* 46 (1971): 348–59.
Warren, Michelle R. *History on the Edge: Excalibur and the Order of Britain.* Minneapolis: University of Minnesota Press, 2000.

Dialogue, debate, and dream vision (Chapter 5)

Bestul, Thomas H. *Satire and Allegory in Wynnere and Wastoure.* Lincoln: University of Nebraska Press, 1974.
Brown, Peter, ed. *Reading Dreams: The Interpretation of Dreams from Chaucer to Shakespeare.* Oxford University Press, 1999.
Cherniss, Michael. *Boethian Apocalypse: Studies in Middle English Vision Poetry.* Norman, OK: Pilgrim Books, 1987.
Conlee, John W., ed. *Middle English Debate Poetry: A Critical Anthology.* East Lansing: Colleagues Press, 1991.
Hume, Kathryn. *The Owl and the Nightingale: The Poem and Its Critics.* University of Toronto Press, 1975.
Kruger, Steven F. *Dreaming in the Middle Ages.* Cambridge University Press, 1992.
Lynch, Kathryn L. *The High Medieval Dream Vision: Poetry, Philosophy, and Literary Form.* Stanford University Press, 1988.
Means, Michael H. *The Consolatio Genre in Medieval English Literature.* Gainesville: University of Florida Press, 1972.
Reed, Thomas L. *Middle English Debate Poetry and the Aesthetics of Irresolution.* Columbia: University of Missouri Press, 1990.
Russell, J. Stephen. *The English Dream Vision: Anatomy of a Form.* Columbus: Ohio State University Press, 1988.
Spearing, A.C. *Medieval Dream-Poetry.* Cambridge University Press, 1976.

Drama (Chapter 6)

REED (Records of Early English Drama) aim to publish an astonishingly rich collection of records of dramatic activity in the British Isles from the Middle Ages until 1642. So far 27 volumes have been published by the University of Toronto Press.
Beadle, Richard, ed. *The Cambridge Companion to Medieval English Theatre.* Cambridge University Press, 1994.

Beckwith, Sarah. *Signifying God: Social Relations and Symbolic Act in the York Corpus Christi Cycle*. University of Chicago Press, 2001.
Bevington, David. *From Mankind to Marlowe: The Growth of Structure in the Popular Drama of Tudor England*. Cambridge, MA: Harvard University Press, 1962.
Clopper, Lawrence. *Drama, Play and Game: English Festive Culture in the Medieval and Early Modern Period*. University of Chicago Press, 2001.
Coletti, Theresa. *Mary Magdalene and the Drama of the Saints: Theater, Gender, and Religion in Late Medieval England*. Philadelphia, PA: University of Pennsylvania Press, 2004.
Cox, John and David Kastan, eds. *A New History of Early English Drama*. New York: Columbia University Press, 1997.
Gibson, Gail McMurray. *The Theater of Devotion: East Anglian Drama and Society in the Late Middle Ages*. University of Chicago Press, 1989.
Kolve, V. A. *The Play Called Corpus Christi*. Stanford University Press, 1966.
Mills, David. *Recycling the Cycle: The City of Chester and its Whitsun Plays*. University of Toronto Press, 1998.
Nissé, Ruth. *Defining Acts: Drama and the Politics of Interpretation in Late Medieval England*. Notre Dame, IN: University of Notre Dame Press, 2005.
Potter, Robert. *The English Morality Play: Origins, History and Influence of a Dramatic Tradition*. London and Boston: Routledge & Kegan Paul, 1975.
Stevens, Martin. *Four Middle English Mystery Cycles*. Princeton University Press, 1987.
Twycross, Meg and Pamela King. *Masks and Masking in Medieval and Early Tudor England*. Aldershot: Ashgate, 2002.

Lyric (Chapter 7)

Boffey, Julia. *Manuscripts of English Courtly Love Lyrics in the Later Middle Ages*. Woodbridge: D. S. Brewer, 1985.
"The Reputation and Circulation of Chaucer's Lyrics in the Fifteenth Century." *Chaucer Review* 28 (1993): 23–40.
Burrow, J. A. "Poems Without Contexts." *Essays in Criticism* 29 (1979): 6–32.
Dronke, Peter. *The Medieval Lyric*. Third Edition. Woodbridge: D. S. Brewer, 1968.
Duncan, Thomas G., ed. *A Companion to the Middle English Lyric*. Cambridge University Press, 2005.
Fein, Susanna, ed. *Studies in the Harley Manuscript: The Scribes, Contents, and Social Contexts of British Library MS Harley 2253*. Kalamazoo: Medieval Institute Publications, 2000.
Gray, Douglas. *Themes and Images in the Medieval English Religious Lyric*. London and Boston: Routledge & Kegan Paul, 1972.
Stevens, John, E. *Music and Poetry in the Early Tudor Court*. Reprinted with corrections. Cambridge University Press, 1979.
"Medieval Song." In *The Early Middle Ages to 1300*. Ed. Richard Crocker and David Hiley. *The New Oxford History of Music*, vol. II. Oxford University Press, 1990, 357–451.

Stevens, John, E. and Ardis Butterfield. "Troubadours, Trouvères." *The New Grove Dictionary of Music and Musicians*. Ed. Stanley Sadie. Second Edition. London: Grove, 2001.

Taylor, Andrew. *Textual Situations: Three Medieval Manuscripts and their Readers*. Philadelphia: University of Pennsylvania Press, 2002.

Wenzel, Siegfried. *Verses in Sermons: "Fasciculus Morum" and its Middle English Poems*. Cambridge: Medieval Academy, 1978.

Wilkins, Nigel. *Music in the Age of Chaucer*. Second Edition with Chaucer songs. Woodbridge: D. S. Brewer, 1995.

Woolf, Rosemary. *The English Religious Lyric in the Middle Ages*. Oxford: Clarendon Press, 1968.

Zumthor, Paul. *Toward a Medieval Poetics*. Tr. Philip Bennett. Minneapolis: University of Minnesota Press, 1992.

Lollard writings (Chapter 8)

Aston, Margaret. *Lollards and Reformers: Images and Literacy in Late Medieval Religion*. London: The Hambledon Press, 1984.

Aston, Margaret and Colin Richmond, eds. *Lollardy and the Gentry in the Later Middle Ages*. Stroud: Sutton Publishing; New York: St. Martin's Press, 1997.

Biller, Peter and Anne Hudson, eds. *Heresy and Literacy 1000–1530*. Cambridge University Press, 1995.

Copeland, Rita, ed. *Criticism and Dissent in the Middle Ages*. Cambridge University Press, 1996.

Deanesly, Margaret. *The Lollard Bible and other Medieval Biblical Versions*. Cambridge University Press, 1920; rpr. Eugene, OR: Wipf and Stock Publishers, 2002.

Havens, Jill, Derek Pittard, and Fiona Somerset, eds. *Lollards and Their Influence in Late Medieval England*. Woodbridge: Boydell Press, 2003.

Hudson, Anne. *The Premature Reformation: Wycliffite Texts and Lollard History*. Oxford: Clarendon Press, 1988.

Hudson, Anne and Michael Wilks, eds. *From Ockham to Wyclif*. Oxford: Blackwell, 1987.

Lawton, David. "Lollardy and the *Piers Plowman* Tradition." *Modern Language Review* 76 (1981): 780–93.

Leff, Gordon. *Heresy in the Later Middle Ages: The Relation of Heterodoxy to Dissent c. 1250–c. 1450*. 2 vols. Manchester University Press, 1967.

Pearsall, Derek. "Langland and Lollardy: From B to C." *YLS* 17 (2003): 7–24.

Rex, Richard. *The Lollards*. Basingstoke: Palgrave Macmillan, 2002.

Strohm, Paul. "Counterfeiters, Lollards, and Lancastrian Unease." *NML* 1 (1997): 31–58.

Thomson, John A.F. *The Later Lollards, 1414–1520*. London: Oxford University Press, 1965.

William Langland (Chapter 9)

Aers, David. *Chaucer, Langland and the Creative Imagination*. London: Routledge, 1980.

Community, Gender and Individual Identity: English Writing 1360–1430. London: Routledge, 1988.

"Reflections on the 'Allegory of the Theologians': Ideology and *Piers Plowman.*" In *Medieval Literature: Criticism, Ideology and History.* Ed. David Aers. Brighton: Harvester, 1986, 58–73.

Alford, John A., ed. *A Companion to Piers Plowman.* Berkeley: University of California Press, 1988.

Blanch, Robert J., ed. *Style and Symbolism in Piers Plowman.* Knoxville: University of Tennessee Press, 1969.

Classic older essays

Bloomfield, Morton W. *"Piers Plowman" as a Fourteenth-Century Apocalypse.* New Brunswick, NJ: Rutgers University Press, 1961.

Hanna, Ralph. *William Langland.* Authors of the Middle Ages: English Writers of the Late Middle Ages 3. Aldershot: Variorum, 1993, 1994, with corrections and supplements in *Yearbook of Langland Studies* 14 (2000): 185–98; and 16 (2002): 169–77.

Harwood, Britton J. *"Piers Plowman" and the Problem of Belief.* University of Toronto Press, 1992.

Hussey, S. S., ed. *"Piers Plowman": Critical Approaches.* London: Methuen, 1969.

Justice, Steven and Kathryn Kerby-Fulton, eds. *Written Work: Langland, Labor, and Authorship.* Philadelphia, PA: University of Pennsylvania Press, 1997.

Kane, George. *"Piers Plowman": The Evidence for Authorship.* London: Athlone, 1965.

Kirk, Elizabeth. *The Dream Thought of "Piers Plowman."* New Haven: Yale University Press, 1972.

Lawton, David A. "The Subject of Piers Plowman." *YLS* 1 (1987): 1–30.

Martin, Priscilla. *"Piers Plowman": The Field and the Tower.* London: Macmillan, 1979.

Middleton, Anne. "The Audience and Public of *Piers Plowman.*" In *Middle English Alliterative Poetry and Its Literary Background: Seven Essays.* Ed. David Lawton. Cambridge: D. S. Brewer, 1982, 101–23, 147–54.

"Narration and the Invention of Experience: Episodic Form in *Piers Plowman.*" In *The Wisdom of Poetry: Essays in Early English Literature in Honor of Morton W. Bloomfield.* Eds. Larry D. Benson and Siegfried Wenzel. Kalamazoo: Medieval Institute, 1982, 91–122.

"Two Infinites: Grammatical Metaphor in Piers Plowman." ELH 39 (1972): 169–88.

"William Langland's 'Kynde Name': Authorial Signature and Social Identity in Late Fourteenth-Century England." In *Literary Practice and Social Change in Britain, 1380–1530.* Ed. Lee Patterson. Berkeley: University of California Press, 1990, 15–82.

Salter, Elizabeth. *Piers Plowman: An Introduction.* Second Edition. Oxford: Blackwell, 1969.

Scase, Wendy. *Piers Plowman and the New Anticlericalism.* Cambridge University Press, 1989.

Simpson, James. *Piers Plowman: An Introduction to the B-Text.* London: Longman, 1990.
Smith, D. Vance. *The Book of the Incipit: Beginnings in the Fourteenth Century.* Minneapolis: University of Minnesota Press, 2001.
Stokes, Myra. *Justice and Mercy in "Piers Plowman."* London: Croom Helm, 1984.

The Gawain-*poet (Chapter 10)*

Barr, Helen. "*Pearl* – or 'the Jeweller's Tale'." *Medium Aevum* 69 (2000): 59–79.
Benson, Larry D. *Art and Tradition in Sir Gawain and the Green Knight.* New Brunswick, NJ: Rutgers University Press, 1965.
Bowers, John. *The Politics of Pearl: Court Poetry in the Age of Richard II.* Cambridge: D. S. Brewer, 2001.
Brewer, D. S. "Courtesy and the *Gawain*-Poet." In *Patterns of Love and Courtesy: Essays in Memory of C. S. Lewis.* Ed. John Lawlor. Evanston, IL: Northwestern University Press, 1966, 57–66.
Brewer, D.S. and Jonathan Gibson, eds. *A Companion to the Gawain-Poet.* Cambridge: D. S. Brewer, 1997.
Bullon-Fernandez, Maria. "Beȝonde þe Water: Courtly and Religious Desire in *Pearl.*" *SP* 91 (1994): 35–49.
Cooke, W. G. "*Sir Gawain and the Green Knight*: A Restored Dating." *Medium Aevum* 58 (1989): 34–48.
Crawford, Donna. "The Architectonics of *Cleanness.*" *SP* 90 (1993): 29–45.
Fein, Susanna G. "Twelve-Line Stanza Forms in Middle English and the Date of Pearl." *Speculum* 72 (1997): 367–97.
Frantzen, Allen. "The Disclosure of Sodomy in *Cleanness.*" *PMLA* 111 (1996): 451–64.
Ingledew, Francis. "Liturgy, Prophecy, and Belshazzar's Babylon: Discourse and Meaning in *Cleanness.*" *Viator* 23 (1992): 247–79.
Keiser, Elizabeth. *Courtly Desire and Medieval Homophobia: The Legitimation of Sexual Pleasure in Cleanness and its Contexts.* New Haven: Yale University Press, 1997.
Lecklider, Jane K. *Cleanness: Structure and Meaning.* Woodbridge and Rochester NY: D. S. Brewer, 1997.
Putter, Ad. *An Introduction to the Gawain-Poet.* Longman: New York, 1996.
Sir Gawain and the Green Knight and French Arthurian Romance. Oxford: Clarendon Press, 1995.
Spearing, A. C. *The Gawain-Poet: A Critical Study*, Cambridge University Press, 1970.
"The Subtext of *Patience*: God as Mother and the Whale's Belly." *Journal of Medieval and Early Modern Studies* 29 (1999): 293–323.
Staley, Lynn. "*Pearl* and the Contingencies of Love and Piety," in *Medieval Literature and Historical Inquiry: Essays in Honor of Derek Pearsall.* Ed. Davod Aers. Cambridge, D. S. Brewer, 2000, 83–114.
Stanbury, Sarah. *Seeing the Gawain-Poet: Description and the Act of Perception.* Philadelphia: University of Pennsylvania Press, 1991.
Tomasch, Sylvia. "A *Pearl* Punnology." *JEGP* 88 (1989): 1–20.

John Gower (Chapter 11)

Astell, Ann W. *Political Allegory in Late Medieval England*. Ithaca: Cornell University Press, 1999.

Bullón-Fernández, María. *Fathers and Daughters in Gower's "Confessio Amantis": Authority, Family, State and Writing*. Cambridge: D. S. Brewer, 2000.

Craun, Edwin D. *Lies, Slander and Obscenity in Medieval English Literature: Pastoral Rhetoric and the Deviant Speaker*. Cambridge University Press, 1997.

Echard, Siân, ed. *A Gower Companion*. Cambridge: D. S. Brewer, 2004.

Lochrie, Karma. *Covert Operations: The Medieval Uses of Secrecy*. Philadelphia: University of Pennsylvania Press, 1999.

Scala, Elizabeth. *Absent Narratives, Manuscript Textuality and Literary Structure in Late Medieval England*. Basingstoke: Palgrave Macmillan, 2002.

Geoffrey Chaucer (Chapter 12)

Blamires, Alcuin. *Chaucer, Ethics, and Gender*. Oxford University Press, 2006.

Burger, Glenn. *Chaucer's Queer Nation*. Minneapolis: University of Minnesota Press, 1998.

Cannon, Christopher. *The Making of Chaucer's English*. Cambridge University Press, 1998.

Correale, Robert M. and Mary Hamel. *Sources and Analogues of "The Canterbury Tales."* Volume I. Cambridge: D. S. Brewer, 2002.

Crane, Susan. *Gender and Romance in Chaucer's "Canterbury Tales."* Princeton University Press, 1994.

Dinshaw, Carolyn. *Chaucer's Sexual Poetics*. Madison: University of Wisconsin Press, 1989.

Donaldson, E. Talbot. *Speaking of Chaucer*. New York: W. W. Norton and Co., 1970.

Ellis, Steve. *Chaucer at Large: The Poet in the Modern Imagination*. Minneapolis: University of Minnesota Press, 2000.

Fradenburg, L. O. Aranye. *Sacrifice Your Love: Psychoanalysis, Historicism, Chaucer*. Minneapolis and London: University of Minnesota Press, 2002.

Hansen, Elaine Tuttle. *Chaucer and the Fictions of Gender*. Berkeley: University of California Press, 1992.

Horobin, Simon. *The Language of the Chaucer Tradition*. Cambridge: D. S. Brewer, 2003.

Kittredge, George Lyman. *Chaucer and His Poetry*. Cambridge, MA: Harvard University Press, 1915.

Knapp, Peggy. *Chaucer and the Social Contest*. New York and London: Routledge, 1990.

Knight, Stephen. *Geoffrey Chaucer*. Oxford: Basil Blackwell, 1986.

Leicester, H. Marshall, Jr. *The Disenchanted Self: Representing the Subject in the "Canterbury Tales."* Berkeley: University of California Press, 1990.

Lynch, Kathryn L. *Chaucer's Philosophical Visions*. Cambridge: D. S. Brewer, 2000.

Mann, Jill. *Chaucer and Medieval Estates Satire*. Cambridge University Press, 1973.
Miller, Mark. *Philosophical Chaucer: Love, Sex, and Agency in the "Canterbury Tales."* Cambridge and New York: Cambridge University Press, 2004.
Muscatine, Charles. *Chaucer and the French Tradition*. Berkeley: University of California Press, 1957.
Patterson, Lee. *Chaucer and the Subject of History*. Madison: University of Wisconsin Press, 1991.
"The *Parson's Tale* and the Quitting of the *Canterbury Tales*." *Traditio* 34 (1978): 331–80.
Pearsall, Derek. *The Canterbury Tales*. London and New York: Routledge, 1985, rpr. 1993.
Strohm, Paul. *Social Chaucer*. Cambridge, MA: Harvard University Press, 1989.
Trigg, Stephanie. *Congenial Souls: Reading Chaucer from Medieval to Postmodern*. Minneapolis: University of Minnesota Press, 2001.
Wallace, David. *Chaucerian Polity: Absolutist Lineages and Associational Forms in England and Italy*. Stanford University Press, 1997.

Julian of Norwich (Chapter 13)

Aers, David. *Salvation and Sin in the Fourteenth Century*. Notre Dame: University of Notre Dame Press, 2008.
Aers, David and Lynn Staley. *The Powers of the Holy: Religion, Politics, and Gender in Late Medieval English Culture*. University Park, PA: Pennsylvania State University Press, 1996.
Baker, Denise Nowakowski. *Julian of Norwich's Showings*. Princeton University Press, 1994.
Oliva, Marilyn. *The Convent and the Community in Late Medieval England: Female Monasteries in the Diocese of Norwich, 1350–1540*. Woodbridge: Boydell Press, 1998.
Staley, Lynn. "The Man in Foul Clothes and a Late Fourteenth-Century Conversation About Sin." *SAC* 24 (2002): 1–48.
Tanner, Norman P., *The Church in Late Medieval Norwich, 1370–1532*. Toronto: Pontifical Institute of Medieval Studies, 1984.
Watson, Nicholas. "Visions of Inclusion: Universal Salvation and Vernacular Theology in Pre-Reformation England." *JMEMS* 27 (1997): 145–87.
Windeatt, Barry. "Julian of Norwich and Her Audience." *Review of English Studies* 28 (1977): 1–17.

Thomas Hoccleve (Chapter 14)

Batt, Catherine, ed. *Essays on Thomas Hoccleve*. Westfield Publications in Medieval Studies. London: Centre for Medieval and Renaissance Studies, Queen Mary and Westfield College, University of London, 1996.
Bryan, Jennifer E. "Hoccleve, the Virgin, and the Politics of Complaint." *PMLA* 117 (2002): 1172–87.
Burrow, John. *Thomas Hoccleve*. Authors of the Middle Ages. Aldershot: Variorum, 1994.

"Autobiographical Poetry in the Middle Ages: The Case of Thomas Hoccleve." *Proceedings of the British Academy* 68 (1982): 389–412.

"Hoccleve's Series: Experience and Books." In *Fifteenth Century Studies: Recent Essays*. Ed. Robert Yeager. Hamden: Archon Books, 1984, 259–74.

Knapp, Ethan. *The Bureaucratic Muse: Thomas Hoccleve and the Literature of Late Medieval England*. University Park, PA: Pennsylvania State University Press, 2001.

Patterson, Lee. "'What Is Me?': Self and Society in the Poetry of Thomas Hoccleve." *Studies in the Age of Chaucer* 23 (2001): 437–70.

Pearsall, Derek. "Hoccleve's *Regement of Princes*: The Poetics of Royal Self-Representation." *Speculum* 69 (1994): 386–410.

Perkins, Nicholas. *Hoccleve's Regiment of Princes: Counsel and Constraint*. Cambridge: D. S. Brewer, 2001.

Simpson, James. "Madness and Texts: Hoccleve's *Series*." In *Chaucer and Fifteenth Century Poetry*. Ed. Julia Boffey and Janet Cowen. London: King's College London Centre for Late Antique and Medieval Studies, 1991, 15–29.

"Nobody's Man: Thomas Hoccleve's *Regement of Princes*." In *London and Europe in the Late Middle Ages*. Ed. Julia Boffey and Pamela King. London: Centre for Medieval and Renaissance Studies, Queen Mary and Westfield College, University of London, 1995, 149–80.

Thompson, John J. "Thomas Hoccleve and Manuscript Culture." *Nation, Court and Culture: New Essays on Fifteenth-Century English Poetry*. Ed. Helen Cooney. Dublin: Four Courts Press, 2001, 81–94.

Tolmie, Sarah. "The Prive Scilence of Thomas Hoccleve." *SAC* 22 (2000): 281–309.

John Lydgate (Chapter 15)

Benson, C. David. *The History of Troy in Middle English Literature: Guido delle Colonne's "Historia Destructionis Troiae" in Medieval England*. Woodbridge, Suffolk: D. S. Brewer, 1980.

Boffey, Julia. "Lydgate's Lyrics and Women Readers." In *Women, the Book and the World*. Ed. Lesley Smith and Jane H. Taylor. 2 vols. Cambridge: D. S. Brewer, 1995. Vol. I, 139–49.

Ebin, Lois. *John Lydgate*. Twayne's English Authors, 407. Boston: G. K. Hall, 1985.

Edwards, A. S. G. "Lydgate Scholarship: Progress and Prospects." In *Fifteenth Century Studies: Recent Essays*. Ed. R. F. Yeager. Hamden, CT: Archon, 1984, 29–47

Mortimer, Nigel. *John Lydgate's "Fall of Princes": Narrative Tragedy in its Literary and Political Contexts*. Oxford University Press, 2005.

Nolan, Maura. *John Lydgate and the Forms of Public Culture*. Cambridge University Press, 2005.

Patterson, Lee. "Making Identities in Fifteenth Century England: Henry V and John Lydgate." In *New Historical Literary Study: Essays on Reproducing Texts, Representing History*. Eds. Jeffrey N. Cox and Larry J. Reynolds. Princeton University Press, 1993, 69–107

Pearsall, Derek. *John Lydgate*. London: Routledge & Kegan Paul, 1970.

John Lydgate (1371–1449): A Bio-Bibliography. English Literary Studies, 71. University of Victoria Press, 1997.

Scanlon, Larry and James Simpson, eds. *John Lydgate: Poetry, Culture, and Lancastrian England*. Notre Dame: University of Notre Dame Press, 2006.

Margery Kempe (Chapter 16)

Arnold, John H. and Katherine J. Lewis, eds. *A Companion to the Book of Margery Kempe*. Woodbridge: D. S. Brewer, 2004.

Atkinson, Clarissa W. *Mystic and Pilgrim: The Book and World of Margery Kempe*. Ithaca: Cornell University Press, 1983.

Bartlett, Anne Clark. "Reading it Personally: Robert Glück, Margery Kempe, and Language in Crisis." *Exemplaria* 16 (2004): 437–57.

Beckwith, Sarah. "Problems of Authority in Late Medieval English Mysticism: Agency and Authority in *The Book of Margery Kempe*." *Exemplaria* 4 (1992): 171–200.

Benson, C. David. "Public Writing: *Mandeville's Travels* and the *Book of Margery Kempe*." In *Public Piers Plowman: Modern Scholarship and Late Medieval English Culture*. University Park, PA: Pennsylvania State University Press, 2004, 113–57.

Craun, Edwin. "Fama and Pastoral Constraints on Rebuking Sinners: *The Book of Margery Kempe*." In *Fama: The Politics of Talk and Reputation in Medieval Europe*. Ed. Thelma Fenster and Daniel Lord Smail. Ithaca: Cornell University Press, 2003, 187–209.

Despres, Denise. "Re-visioning in *The Book of Margery Kempe*." In *Ghostly Sights: Visual Meditation in Late Medieval Literature*. Norman, OK: Pilgrim Books, 1989, 57–86.

Erler, Mary C. "Margery Kempe's White Clothes." *Medium Aevum* 62 (1993): 78–83.

Holbrook, Sue Ellen. "Order and Coherence in *The Book of Margery Kempe*." In *The Worlds of Medieval Women: Creativity, Influence, and Imagination*. Eds. Constance Berman, Charles W. Connell, and Judith Rice Rothschild. Morgantown: West Virgina University Press, 1985, 97–110.

Lavezzo, Kathy. "Sobs and Sighs Between Women: The Homoerotics of Compassion in the *Book of Margery Kempe*." In *Premodern Sexualities*. Eds. Louise Fradenburg, Carla Freccero, and Kathy Lavezzo. New York: Routledge, 1996, 175–98.

Lochrie, Karma. *Margery Kempe and Translations of the Flesh*. Philadelphia: University of Pennsylvania Press, 1991.

McEntire, Sandra, ed. *Margery Kempe: A Book of Essays*. New York: Garland Press, 1992.

Mueller, Janel M. "Autobiography of a New 'Creatur': Female Spirituality, Selfhood, and Authorship in *The Book of Margery Kempe*." *New York Literary Forum* 12–13 (1984): 63–75.

Newman, Barbara. "What Did It Mean to Say 'I Saw'? The Clash between Theory and Practice in Medieval Visionary Culture." *Speculum* 80 (2005): 1–43.

Riddy, Felicity. "Text and Self in *The Book of Margery Kempe*." In *Voices in Dialogue: Reading Women in the Middle Ages*. Eds. Linda Olson and Kathryn Kerby-Fulton. Notre Dame: University of Notre Dame Press, 2005, 435–53.

Salih, Sarah. "Like a Virgin? The *Book of Margery Kempe*." In *Versions of Virginity in Late Medieval England*. Rochester, NY: D. S. Brewer, 2001, 166–241.

Schirmer, Elizabeth. "Orthodoxy, Textuality, and the 'Tretys' of Margery Kempe." *Journal X: A Journal of Criticism and Culture* 1 (1996): 31–55.

Staley, Lynn. *Margery Kempe's Dissenting Fictions*. University Park, PA: Pennsylvania State University Press, 1994.

Voaden, Rosalynn. *God's Words, Women's Voices: The Discernment of Spirits in the Writing of Late-Medieval Women Visionaries*. Suffolk: York Medieval Press, 1999.

Watson, Nicholas. "The Making of *The Book of Margery Kempe*." In *Voices in Dialogue: Reading Women in the Middle Ages*. Eds. Linda Olson and Kathryn Kerby-Fulton. Notre Dame: University of Notre Dame Press, 2005, 395–434.

Sir Thomas Malory (Chapter 17)

Archibald, Elizabeth and A. S. G. Edwards, eds. *A Companion to Malory*. Cambridge: D. S. Brewer, 1996.

Barber, Richard. *The Holy Grail: The History of a Legend*. London: Penguin, 2005.

Batt, Catherine, *Malory's Morte Darthur: Remaking Arthurian Tradition*. The New Middle Ages. New York and Basingstoke: Palgrave Macmillan, 2002.

Cannon, Christopher. "Malory's Crime: Chivalric Identity and the Evil Will." In *Medieval Literature and Historical Inquiry: Essays in Honor of Derek Pearsall*. Ed. David Aers. Cambridge: D. S. Brewer, 2000, 159–83.

Edwards, Elizabeth. *The Genesis of Narrative in Malory's "Morte Darthur."* Cambridge: D. S. Brewer, 2001.

Field, P. J. C. *Life and Times of Sir Thomas Malory*. Cambridge: D. S. Brewer, 1993.

Hodges, Kenneth. *Forging Chivalric Communities in Malory's "Le Morte Darthur."* New York: Palgrave Macmillan, 2005.

Lynch, Andrew. *Malory's Book of Arms: The Narrative of Combat in "Le Morte Darthur."* Cambridge: D. S. Brewer, 1997.

Parins, Marylyn Jackson, ed. *Malory: The Critical Heritage*. London: Routledge, 1988.

Riddy, Felicity. *Sir Thomas Malory*. Leiden: E. J. Brill, 1987.

Sutton, Anne F. "Malory in Newgate: A New Document." *The Library*, 7th series, 1.3 (September 2000): 243–62.

Takamiya, Tosiyuki and Derek Brewer, eds. *Aspects of Malory*. Woodbridge: D. S. Brewer, 1986.

Wallace, David, "*Imperium*, Commerce, and National Crusade: the Romance of Malory's *Morte*." *NML* 8 (2006): 45–66.

Wheeler, Bonnie, Robert L. Kindrick, and Michael N. Salda, eds. *The Malory Debate: Essays on the Texts of "Le Morte Darthur."* Cambridge: D. S. Brewer, 2000.

Robert Henryson (Chapter 18)

Aronstein, Susan. "Cresseid Reading Cresseid: Redemption and Translation in Henryson's *Testament*." *Scottish Literary Journal* 21 (1994): 5–22.

Fradenburg, Louise. "Henryson Scholarship: The Recent Decades." In *Fifteenth-Century Studies: Recent Essays*. Ed. Robert F. Yeager. Hamden, CT: Archon Books, 65–92

Gopen, George D. "The Essential Seriousness of Robert Henryson's *Moral Fables*: A Study in Structure." *SP* 82 (1985): 42–59.

Gray, Douglas. *Robert Henryson*. Leiden: E. J. Brill, 1979.

Greentree, Rosemary. *Reader, Teller and Teacher: The Narrator in Robert Henryson's Moral Fables*. Frankfurt am Main: Peter Lang, 1993.

Kratzmann, G.C. *Anglo-Scottish Literary Relations 1430–1550*. Cambridge University Press, 1980.

Lyall, R.J. "Henryson's *Morall Fabillis* and the Steinhöwel Tradition." *Forum for Modern Language Studies* 38 (2002): 362–81.

MacQueen, John. *Robert Henryson: A Study of the Major Narrative Poems*. Oxford: Clarendon Press, 1967.

McDiarmid, Matthew P. *Robert Henryson*. Edinburgh: Scottish Academic Press, 1981.

McDonald, Craig. "The Perversion of Law in Robert Henryson's Fable of 'The Fox, the Wolf, and the Husbandman'." *Medium Aevum* 49 (1980): 244–53.

McKenna, Steven R. *Robert Henryson's Tragic Vision*. New York: Peter Lang, 1994.

"Legends of James III and the Problem of Henryson's Topicality." *Scottish Literary Journal* 17 (1990): 5–20.

McNamara, John. "Language as Action in Henryson's *Testament of Cresseid*." In *Bards and Makars, Scottish Language and Literature: Medieval and Renaissance*. Eds. A. J. Aitken, M. P. McDiarmid, and D. S. Thomson. University of Glasgow Press, 1977, 41–51.

Patterson, Lee. "Christian and Pagan in the *Testament of Cresseid*." *Philological Quarterly* 52 (1973): 696–714.

Powell, Marianne. *Fabula Docet: Studies in the Background and Interpretation of Henryson's Fables*. Odense University Press, 1983.

Riddy, Felicity. "'Abject odious' : Feminine and Masculine in Henryson's *Testament of Cresseid*." In *The Long Fifteenth Century*. Eds. Helen Cooper and Sally Mapstone. Oxford: Clarendon Press, 1997, 229–48.

Rutledge, Thomas. "Robert Henryson's *Orpheus and Eurydice*: a Northern Humanism?" *Forum for Modern Language Studies* 38 (2002): 396–411.

Wheatley, Edward. *Mastering Aesop: Medieval Education, Chaucer and his Followers*. Gainesville: University of Florida Press, 2000.

INDEX

Cambridge Companions To...

AUTHORS

Edward Albee *edited by Stephen J. Bottoms*

Margaret Atwood *edited by Coral Ann Howells*

W. H. Auden *edited by Stan Smith*

Jane Austen *edited by Edward Copeland and Juliet McMaster*

Beckett *edited by John Pilling*

Aphra Behn *edited by Derek Hughes and Janet Todd*

Walter Benjamin *edited by David S. Ferris*

William Blake *edited by Morris Eaves*

Brecht *edited by Peter Thomson and Glendyr Sacks* (second edition)

The Brontës *edited by Heather Glen*

Frances Burney *edited by Peter Sabor*

Byron *edited by Drummond Bone*

Albert Camus *edited by Edward J. Hughes*

Willa Cather *edited by Marilee Lindemann*

Cervantes *edited by Anthony J. Cascardi*

Chaucer, *second edition edited by Piero Boitani and Jill Mann*

Chekhov *edited by Vera Gottlieb and Paul Allain*

Kate Chopin *edited by Janet Beer*

Coleridge *edited by Lucy Newlyn*

Wilkie Collins *edited by Jenny Bourne Taylor*

Joseph Conrad *edited by J. H. Stape*

Dante *edited by Rachel Jacoff* (second edition)

Daniel Defoe *edited by John Richetti*

Don DeLillo *edited by John N. Duvall*

Charles Dickens *edited by John O. Jordan*

Emily Dickinson *edited by Wendy Martin*

John Donne *edited by Achsah Guibbory*

Dostoevskii *edited by W. J. Leatherbarrow*

Theodore Dreiser *edited by Leonard Cassuto and Claire Virginia Eby*

John Dryden *edited by Steven N. Zwicker*

W. E. B. Du Bois *edited by Shamoon Zamir*

George Eliot *edited by George Levine*

T. S. Eliot *edited by A. David Moody*

Ralph Ellison *edited by Ross Posnock*

Ralph Waldo Emerson *edited by Joel Porte and Saundra Morris*

William Faulkner *edited by Philip M. Weinstein*

Henry Fielding *edited by Claude Rawson*

F. Scott Fitzgerald *edited by Ruth Prigozy*

Flaubert *edited by Timothy Unwin*

E. M. Forster *edited by David Bradshaw*

Benjamin Franklin *edited by Carla Mulford*

Brian Friel *edited by Anthony Roche*

Robert Frost *edited by Robert Faggen*

Elizabeth Gaskell *edited by Jill L. Matus*

Goethe *edited by Lesley Sharpe*

Thomas Hardy *edited by Dale Kramer*

David Hare *edited by Richard Boon*

Nathaniel Hawthorne *edited by Richard Millington*

Seamus Heaney *edited by Bernard O'Donoghue*

Ernest Hemingway *edited by Scott Donaldson*

Homer *edited by Robert Fowler*

Ibsen *edited by James McFarlane*

Henry James *edited by Jonathan Freedman*

Samuel Johnson *edited by Greg Clingham*

Ben Jonson *edited by Richard Harp and Stanley Stewart*

James Joyce *edited by Derek Attridge* (second edition)

Kafka *edited by Julian Preece*

Keats *edited by Susan J. Wolfson*

Lacan *edited by Jean-Michel Rabaté*

D. H. Lawrence *edited by Anne Fernihough*

Primo Levi *edited by Robert Gordon*

Lucretius *edited by Stuart Gillespie and Philip Hardie*

David Mamet *edited by Christopher Bigsby*

Thomas Mann *edited by Ritchie Robertson*

Christopher Marlowe *edited by Patrick Cheney*

Herman Melville *edited by Robert S. Levine*

Arthur Miller *edited by Christopher Bigsby*

Milton *edited by Dennis Danielson* (second edition)

Molière *edited by David Bradby and Andrew Calder*

Toni Morrison *edited by Justine Tally*

Nabokov *edited by Julian W. Connolly*

Eugene O'Neill *edited by Michael Manheim*

George Orwell *edited by John Rodden*

Ovid *edited by Philip Hardie*

Harold Pinter *edited by Peter Raby* (second edition)

Sylvia Plath *edited by Jo Gill*

Edgar Allan Poe *edited by Kevin J. Hayes*

Alexander Pope *edited by Pat Rogers*

Ezra Pound *edited by Ira B. Nadel*

Proust *edited by Richard Bales*

Pushkin *edited by Andrew Kahn*

Philip Roth *edited by Timothy Parrish*

Salman Rushdie *edited by Abdulrazak Gurnah*

Shakespeare *edited by Margareta de Grazia and Stanley Wells*

Shakespeare on Film *edited by Russell Jackson* (second edition)

Shakespearean Comedy *edited by Alexander Leggatt*

Shakespeare on Stage *edited by Stanley Wells and Sarah Stanton*

Shakespeare's History Plays *edited by Michael Hattaway*

Shakespearean Tragedy *edited by Claire McEachern*

Shakespeare's Poetry *edited by Patrick Cheney*

Shakespeare and Popular Culture *edited by Robert Shaughnessy*

George Bernard Shaw *edited by Christopher Innes*

Shelley *edited by Timothy Morton*

Mary Shelley *edited by Esther Schor*

Sam Shepard *edited by Matthew C. Roudané*

Spenser *edited by Andrew Hadfield*

Wallace Stevens *edited by John N. Serio*

Tom Stoppard *edited by Katherine E. Kelly*

Harriet Beecher Stowe *edited by Cindy Weinstein*

Jonathan Swift *edited by Christopher Fox*

Henry David Thoreau *edited by Joel Myerson*

Tolstoy *edited by Donna Tussing Orwin*

Mark Twain *edited by Forrest G. Robinson*

Virgil *edited by Charles Martindale*

Voltaire *edited by Nicholas Cronk*

Edith Wharton *edited by Millicent Bell*

Walt Whitman *edited by Ezra Greenspan*

Oscar Wilde *edited by Peter Raby*

Tennessee Williams *edited by Matthew C. Roudané*

August Wilson *edited by Christopher Bigsby*

Mary Wollstonecraft *edited by Claudia L. Johnson*

Virginia Woolf *edited by Sue Roe and Susan Sellers*

Zola *edited by Brian Nelson*

Wordsworth *edited by Stephen Gill*

W. B. Yeats *edited by Marjorie Howes and John Kelly*

TOPICS

The Actress *edited by Maggie B. Gale and John Stokes*

The African American Novel *edited by Maryemma Graham*

The African American Slave Narrative *edited by Audrey A. Fisch*

American Modernism *edited by Walter Kalaidjian*

American Realism and Naturalism *edited by Donald Pizer*

American Travel Writing *edited by Alfred Bendixen and Judith Hamera*

American Women Playwrights *edited by Brenda Murphy*

Australian Literature *edited by Elizabeth Webby*

British Romanticism *edited by Stuart Curran*

British Romantic Poetry *edited by James Chandler and Maureen N. McLane*

British Theatre, 1730–1830, *edited by Jane Moody and Daniel O'Quinn*

Canadian Literature *edited by Eva-Marie Kröller*

The Classic Russian Novel *edited by Malcolm V. Jones and Robin Feuer Miller*

Contemporary Irish Poetry *edited by Matthew Campbell*

Crime Fiction *edited by Martin Priestman*

The Eighteenth-Century Novel *edited by John Richetti*

Eighteenth-Century Poetry *edited by John Sitter*

English Literature, 1500–1600 *edited by Arthur F. Kinney*

English Literature, 1650–1740 *edited by Steven N. Zwicker*

English Literature, 1740–1830 *edited by Thomas Keymer and Jon Mee*

English Poetry, Donne to Marvell *edited by Thomas N. Corns*

English Renaissance Drama, second edition *edited by A. R. Braunmuller and Michael Hattaway*

English Restoration Theatre *edited by Deborah C. Payne* Fisk

Feminist Literary Theory *edited by Ellen Rooney*

Fiction in the Romantic Period *edited by Richard Maxwell and Katie Trumpener*

The Fin de Siècle *edited by Gail Marshall*

The French Novel: from 1800 to the Present *edited by Timothy Unwin*

Gothic Fiction *edited by Jerrold E. Hogle*

The Greek and Roman Novel *edited by Tim Whitmarsh*

Greek and Roman Theatre *edited by Marianne McDonald and J. Michael Walton*

Greek Tragedy *edited by P. E. Easterling*

The Harlem Renaissance *edited by George Hutchinson*

The Irish Novel *edited by John Wilson Foster*

The Italian Novel *edited by Peter Bondanella and Andrea Ciccarelli*

Jewish American Literature *edited by Hana Wirth-Nesher and Michael P. Kramer*

The Latin American Novel *edited by Efraín Kristal*

The Literature of the First World War *edited by Vincent Sherry*

The Literature of World War II *edited by Marina MacKay*

Literature on Screen *edited by Deborah Cartmell and Imelda Whelehan*

Medieval English Literature 1100–1500 *edited by Larry Scanlon*

Medieval English Theatre *edited by Richard Beadle and Alan J. Fletcher* (second edition)

Medieval French Literature *edited by Simon Gaunt and Sarah Kay*

Medieval Romance *edited by Roberta L. Krueger*

Medieval Women's Writing *edited by Carolyn Dinshaw and David Wallace*

Modern American Culture *edited by Christopher Bigsby*

Modern British Women Playwrights *edited by Elaine Aston and Janelle Reinelt*

Modern French Culture *edited by Nicholas Hewitt*

Modern German Culture *edited by Eva Kolinsky and Wilfried van der Will*

The Modern German Novel *edited by Graham Bartram*

Modern Irish Culture *edited by Joe Cleary and Claire Connolly*

Modernism *edited by Michael Levenson*

The Modernist Novel *edited by Morag Shiach*

Modernist Poetry *edited by Alex Davis and Lee M. Jenkins*

Modern Italian Culture *edited by Zygmunt G. Baranski and Rebecca J. West*

Modern Latin American Culture *edited by John King*

Modern Russian Culture *edited by Nicholas Rzhevsky*

Modern Spanish Culture *edited by David T. Gies*

Narrative *edited by David Herman*

Native American Literature *edited by Joy Porter and Kenneth M. Roemer*

Nineteenth-Century American Women's Writing *edited by Dale M. Bauer and Philip Gould*

Old English Literature *edited by Malcolm Godden and Michael Lapidge*

Performance Studies *edited by Tracy C. Davis*

Postcolonial Literary Studies *edited by Neil Lazarus*

Postmodernism *edited by Steven Connor*

Renaissance Humanism *edited by Jill Kraye*

Roman Satire *edited by Kirk Freudenburg*

The Spanish Novel: from 1600 to the Present *edited by Harriet Turner and Adelaida López de Martínez*

Travel Writing *edited by Peter Hulme and Tim Youngs*

Twentieth-Century Irish Drama *edited by Shaun Richards*

For EU product safety concerns, contact us at Calle de José Abascal, 56–1°, 28003 Madrid, Spain or eugpsr@cambridge.org.

www.ingramcontent.com/pod-product-compliance
Ingram Content Group UK Ltd.
Pitfield, Milton Keynes, MK11 3LW, UK
UKHW020338140625
459647UK00018B/2212

* 9 7 8 0 5 2 1 6 0 2 5 8 7 *